6

STRANGERS ON FAMILIAR SOIL

The Agrarian Studies Series at Yale University Press seeks to publish outstanding and original interdisciplinary work on agriculture and rural society—for any period, in any location. Works of daring that question existing paradigms and fill abstract categories with the lived experience of rural people are especially encouraged.
—James C. Scott, *Series Editor*

For a complete list of titles in the Yale Agrarian Studies Series, visit yalebooks.com/agrarian

STRANGERS ON
FAMILIAR SOIL

Rediscovering the Chile-California Connection

Edward Dallam Melillo

Yale
UNIVERSITY
PRESS
New Haven & London

Published with assistance from the income of the Frederick John Kingsbury
Memorial Fund and from the foundation established in memory of
Amasa Stone Mather of the Class of 1907, Yale College.

Yale University Press books may be purchased in quantity for educational, business, or
promotional use. For information, please e-mail sales.press@yale.edu (US office) or
sales@yaleup.co.uk (UK office).

Set in PostScript Electra and Trajan types by IDS Infotech, Ltd.
Printed in the United States of America.

Library of Congress Control Number: 2015941173
ISBN 978-0-300-20662-3 (clothbound: alk. paper)

A catalogue record for this book is available from the British Library.

This paper meets the requirements of ANSI/NISO Z39.48–1992
(Permanence of Paper).

10 9 8 7 6 5 4 3 2 1

CONTENTS

v

Contents

Epilogue: Worlds Not Realized   196

PREFACE

Strangers on Familiar Soil explores the long-term environmental and social connections between Chile and California. In the following chapters, I investigate these linkages, starting in 1786 when a French expedition brought the potato from Chile to California and ending in 2008 when Chilean President Michelle Bachelet visited the Golden State. During the 222 years between these two episodes, new crops, foods, fertilizers, mining technologies, laborers, and ideas from Chile radically altered California. Likewise, California's systems of servitude, exotic species, and capitalist development schemes dramatically shaped Chile. Drawing on unpublished archival materials, historic newspapers, letters, journals, promotional pamphlets, maritime logbooks, and long-forgotten trade and scientific publications, I examine the emergence of these transnational connections. I also trace how an awareness of these interactions disappeared from official records, historical accounts, and collective memories.

To pursue these relationships and vanishings, I approach the history of the Americas from three unique vantage points. First, the early chapters begin on the Pacific coast and follow eastward-moving trends in United States history. As a result, this account offers an alternative perspective to US historical narratives that start on Atlantic shores and describe westering processes. Second, much of this book examines the influences that Latin Americans exerted on North America's development. Although the effects of US foreign policies on the countries and regions to the south have attracted much attention, Latin American historians rarely discuss trends that flowed northward. Third, I depart from Atlantic-centered histories of the Americas. Instead, I adopt the Pacific World—the interconnected cultures and environments in and around the earth's largest body of water—as my analytical framework. The Pacific Ocean provided a vast aquatic highway, linking the people, commodities, and ideas that circulated between the Mediterranean-type ecosystems and former Spanish colonies of Chile and California.

From eighteenth-century botanical transfers to the most recent cooperative agreements, Chile and California have been deeply connected with each other and with a wider Pacific World for centuries. Despite such comprehensive and enduring interdependencies, Chileans and Californians have each asserted their exceptionalism, the notion that their histories and destinies are distinct from those of other nations or regions in the Americas. In the pages that follow, I argue that these declarations of singularity hide the countless shared external influences that have shaped the histories of Chile and California.

ACKNOWLEDGMENTS

This book represents a decade of research in two countries and twenty archives throughout the Americas. It also embodies an imagined community that spans nations and hemispheres. Although I am the only person who has met everyone mentioned here, these mutual strangers came together in shaping the pages that follow.

At Swarthmore College, Mark Wallace and Lillian Li cultivated my budding environmentalism and my passion for history. At Yale University, Beatrice Bartlett skillfully advised my studies in Chinese history, and Bob Harms helped me navigate the transoceanic transition toward Chile and California, "the other Pacific World places that begin with the letter C." Jim Scott and many scholars in the Yale Agrarian Studies Program provided constant inspiration. Gil Joseph could not have been a stronger advocate for this project or a more encouraging adviser during my moments of doubt. I owe a tremendous debt of gratitude to my dissertation supervisor, Jean-Christophe Agnew, whose capacious intellect and generous spirit pushed me to think along new trajectories. Likewise, Robert Johnston shared his friendship and wisdom as I explored the history of the Americas. I feel honored to have met Michael Jo, Bethany Moreton, Michael Mullins, Rebecca Rix, and Owen Williams in Robert's US history graduate seminar. In similar fashion, my fellow graduate students—Carlos Aramayo, Tom Barton, J. Celso Castro Alves, Rachel Chrastil, Gretchen Heefner, Arash Khazeni, Shafali Lal (1971–2003), Jana Lipman, Kieko Matteson, Bob Morrissey, Barry Muchnick, David Sanders, Anita Seth, Ashley Sousa, Kristie Starr, George Trumbull, Stephen Vella (1975–2010), and J. T. Way—taught me how to integrate the study of the past with the transformation of the present. During the five years that I spent in New Haven, my colleagues and fellow organizers in the Graduate Employees and Students Organization demonstrated that they are among the finest teachers and leaders anywhere.

Throughout California, many institutions and individuals supported my work. At the Huntington Library, Peter Blodgett and other staff members provided invaluable research assistance. During my summer in San Marino, Bill Deverell, Lori Flores, Eric Hayot, Gregory Jackson, Ben Johnson, Alexandra Kindell, and Coya Paz Brownrigg shared their insightful views on history and life. Thanks, also, to Linda Johnson at the California State Archives, Daryl Morrison at the UC-Davis Special Collections, Jeff Rankin at UCLA's Young Research Library, Marva Felchlin and Manola Madrid at the Autry Museum/Braun Research Library, Marion E. Oster at the Atherton Heritage Association, Patricia Keats at the Society of California Pioneers, Mary Morganti and Alison Moore at the California Historical Society, and Bill Kooiman (1927–2011) at the San Francisco Maritime Museum.

During countless visits to the Bancroft Library, I benefited from the advice and friendship of the following staff members: Anthony Bliss, Walter Brem, Iris Donovan, Peter Hanff, Amy Hellam, David Kessler, Jessica Lemieux, Crystal Miles, Erica Nordmeier, Theresa Salazar, Dean Smith, Susan Snyder, Baiba Strads, Kat Weber, and Tracy Wong. While researching at the Bancroft, I had the tremendous fortune of meeting Jim Gatewood. Over the years that have followed, his kindness, humor, and resiliency have been uplifting. In a similarly auspicious archival encounter, I met Ben Madley. At every phase of this book's development, Ben contributed his historian's wisdom, his editorial acumen, and his extraordinary camaraderie.

While I was living in Berkeley, Kent, Cherise, Sophia, and Ella Udell welcomed me into their family. Several years later, Dan Robbin and Wendy Oser kindly hosted me at their North Berkeley home. My neighbors Bruce and Lily Mordecai taught me much about Bay Area botany, and the comrades I met at La Peña Cultural Center's Café Valparaíso in Berkeley—including Marci and Ricardo Valdivieso, Félix Hernández, and Marisol González—inspired me in countless ways.

In the southern hemisphere, my Chilean friends could not have been more generous or welcoming. Professor Cristián Guerrero Yoacham, Claudia Videla, and Cecelia Riveros assisted me with my research. Fernando Marchant and the musically talented staff of Santiago's Café Mosqueto became my instant circle of friends. Sofia Sepúlveda introduced me to *pastel de choclo* and shared her poignant reminiscences about life along the Chile-California Cordillera. Johanna Bergström showed me around Lota and Concepción, and Miguel Salas guided me through the Atacama Desert. In Santiago, my terrific colleague and friend Alison Bruey helped me find an apartment, assisted me with bureaucratic details, and took me to my first *asado Chileno*.

On my return from Chile, a Kiriyama Visiting Fellowship at the University of San Francisco's Center for the Pacific Rim introduced me to the many possibilities of Pacific World history. Barbara Bundy, Ken Kopp, Chiho Sawada, and Tom Wilkins shared countless new perspectives on the past.

During the following year at Oberlin College, Ruma Chopra, Andrea Estepa, Michael Fisher, Jessica Green, John Harwood, Jenny Kaminer, Gary Kornblith, Carol Lasser, Jill Massino, Tom Newlin, John Petersen, Jordan Suter, and Steve Volk offered a vibrant community of scholars and friends. The following year, a visiting position at Franklin and Marshall College was made all the more pleasurable because of friendships with Doug Anthony, Michael Juarbe, Dorothy Merritts, Roger Thomas, Bob Walter, and Xiangyu Zhao. Since 2009, I have benefited tremendously from the intelligence and camaraderie of my colleagues in the Environmental Studies and History Departments at Amherst College. I extend a special thanks to the staff members who have so expertly supported my teaching and research: Lisa Ballou, Rhea Cabin, Karen Graves, Mary Ramsay, and Lisa Stoffer.

Many other friends and colleagues contributed to this project. Chris Boyer, Ray Craib, Steven Gray, Hannah Greenwald, Juan E. Ibañez, Barbara Krauthamer, Rick López, Dana Mock-Muñoz de Luna, Dawn Peterson, Khary Polk, Liz Pryor, Joshua Rosenthal, John Soluri, Madeline Weeks, Joel Wolfe, and Ben Wurgaft offered their astute observations and editorial suggestions at various stages in the book's development. Nick Springer created the extraordinary maps featured here. Tucker Clark and Laura Jones Dooley offered perceptive and meticulous copyedits. Kara Pekar crafted the excellent index. Yale University Press senior executive editor Jean Thomson Black did an outstanding job of guiding the manuscript through review, revision, and production stages. Thanks also to Jean's dexterous assistant, Samantha Ostrowski.

While researching and writing this book, I received generous financial support from a John Haskell Kemble Fellowship at the Huntington Library, a Miner D. Crary Junior Sabbatical Fellowship from Amherst College, and a Fellowship for Scholars of the West at Stanford University's Bill Lane Center for the American West. In addition, awards from the Yale Graduate School of Arts and Sciences, the Yale Agrarian Studies Program, the Yale Center for International Area Studies, the Historical Society of Southern California, the Amherst College Dean's Fund, and the Frederick John Kingsbury Trust helped bring this project to fruition.

Throughout my life, my parents—Lalise and Jerry Melillo—have been my role models and my best friends. I thank them for supporting me at every stage in this process. I dedicate this book to the two people who make my world possible, *mi media naranja* Nina Gordon and *mi hijo* Simon Zev Melillo.

NOTES ON TERMINOLOGY

When referring Chile and its citizens, many eighteenth- and nineteenth-century English speakers used the alternate spellings, *Chili* and *Chilians*. Other common variants included: *Chileanoes*, *Chillians*, and *Chilianians*. Nineteenth-century writers also employed a variety of terms to describe white North Americans of non-Hispanic or non-French descent. Throughout the book, I use *Anglo* or *Yankee* when referring to people from this group, and I follow the convention of calling the first wave of North American gold-seekers who traveled to California *forty-niners*. I describe those who come from and identify with the countries of present-day Latin America, along with those living in North America who are descended from such groups, as *Latinos*. I use the term *Californios* for the Spanish-speaking residents of Alta California. This group included the descendants of Spanish and mestizo settlers from Mexico, as well as California Indians who adopted Hispanic culture and converted to Christianity.

As a historical notion, *Hispanoamérica* [Hispanic America] designates the geographic and linguistic region of Spanish colonial control in the Americas. I use the term *Pacific World* to signify the people, ecosystems, cultures, territories, and countries located in and around the Pacific Ocean. California has long been called the *Golden State* by its residents and outsiders alike. California counties to which I refer throughout the book appear on the two state maps in map 3, detailing the boundaries of these administrative regions in 1850 and 1907.

In most cultures where Spanish colonial customs predominated, women and men carry a given name (*nombre*) and two surnames (*apellidos*). Traditionally, the first surname is the father's first surname (*apellido paterno*) and the second is the mother's first surname (*apellido materno*). In the chapters that follow, I abide by the custom of dropping the maternal surname from subsequent references. For example, I refer to Chilean president Salvador Allende Gossens as Salvador Allende. In a few cases, however, I comply with nineteenth-century precedents and use both surnames for well-known individuals. As many of his contemporaries did, I write "Pérez Rosales" when discussing Chilean gold rush chronicler Vicente Pérez Rosales.

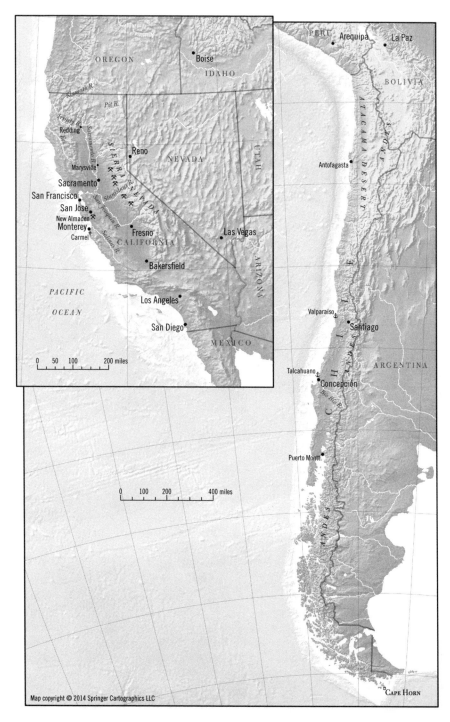

Map 1. California and Chile, featuring major sites discussed in this book. *Produced by Springer Cartographics LLC for Edward D. Melillo.*

Map 2. The nineteenth-century "Cape Horn Route" from the northeastern United
States to California via Chile. *Produced by Springer Cartographics LLC for
Edward D. Melillo.*

Map 3. California Counties in 1850 and 1907. By 1907, most of California's county boundaries matched those of today. *Produced by Springer Cartographics LLC for Edward D. Melillo.*

STRANGERS ON FAMILIAR SOIL

INTRODUCTION

Fueron las cordilleras—"There were cordilleras . . . ." So begins the third line of Pablo Neruda's *Canto general,* an epic poem written by a Chilean exile in Mexico City, an ode to Chile's history by the country's future poet laureate, an elegy of transcontinental proportions, and a cycle of verses that invites movement across hemispheres. The word *cordillera,* derived from the old Castilian term for rope, *cordilla,* describes the nearly continuous geological spine that stretches from the northernmost Sierra Nevada of California to the tip of the Andes in southern Chile. For far too long, historians have treated the Cordillera as an obstacle to connection and an impediment to contact. Rather, this intercontinental backbone and the Pacific Ocean that washes its shores have served as figurative and literal connective tissue, linking Chile and California along a vast longitudinal axis.[1]

A profound array of transequatorial exchanges between the southern and northern reaches of the Americas began in 1786, when the French navigator Jean-François de Galaup de La Pérouse brought the potato by ship from central Chile to the Franciscan mission at San Carlos Borromeo in Carmel, California. The northward passage of the humble spud exemplified the role of ships as "dispersal agents" in world history and inaugurated more than two centuries of environmental and cultural interactions between Chile and California.

The dimensions of this transpacific exchange expanded exponentially during the California gold rush (1848–53), when reports of James W. Marshall's discovery of gold on the American River in January 1848 triggered an unprecedented convergence of prospectors on the foothills of the Sierra Nevada. Chile's opportune location along the predominant sea route to San Francisco meant that its citizens were among the first people in the world to catch *la fiebre del oro* (gold fever). By the mid-1850s, eight thousand Chileans had arrived in San Francisco with hopes of finding their fortunes in California.

Although they could not know it, these South American Argonauts inaugurated a century of profound Chilean influences on California's environmental and cultural development. During California's gold rush, scores of abandoned Chilean ships provided much of the wooden scaffolding on which San Francisco's developers expanded the city's waterfront real estate. Chilean grain merchants exported more than seventy thousand metric tons of wheat flour to California's growing markets; prospectors from around the world adopted Chilean mining techniques and gold-extraction technologies; planters introduced a Chilean nitrogen-fixing crop called alfalfa to the western United States and cultivated wheat from Chilean seed stock; and California's citrus farmers fueled their bonanza harvests with millions of metric tons of Chilean sodium nitrate fertilizer. In addition, Chileans helped build the commercial world of nineteenth-century California. Some of these women and men labored as bricklayers, shopkeepers, and sex workers in San Francisco, while others taught Yankees how to mine gold in the Sierra Nevada or extracted precious mercury ore in the Santa Clara Valley.

Taken together, the ships, people, plants, commodities, and ideas that traveled from Chile during the nineteenth and early twentieth centuries altered the character of the US West in far-reaching ways. California's phenomenal economic and demographic growth from 1848 onward stretched the limits of its own natural wealth, and newcomers began reconstituting regional landscapes with resources drawn from beyond California's borders. Chile furnished a vast share of the inputs that propelled California's economic expansion from the gold rush to World War II. Chilean natural resources landed alongside Chilean women and men, whose labor and ideas rearranged California's physical geography and dramatically shaped its cultural terrain.

Likewise, people, species, and ideas moving in the opposite direction reorganized Chilean ecosystems and social spaces. To ensure a reliable labor force for his South American railroad-construction enterprises, a fugitive Californian entrepreneur named Henry Meiggs instituted the *enganche* system of debt peonage in Chile during the 1860s. Many of the thirty thousand Chilean workers who accompanied him to Peru to build the first trans-Andean railways eventually mined the fertilizer for California's citrus boom.

California's coastal forests also contributed key elements to Chile's landscapes. In the late 1800s, German botanist Arturo Junge began growing one of California's most emblematic species, the Monterey pine (*Pinus radiata*), in his botanical garden at Concepción, Chile. This nonnative tree later became the basis of the Chilean forestry sector, initiating an era in which exotic sylvan monocultures replaced Chile's native forests and displaced indigenous Mapuche communities from their traditional homelands.

California's influence on Chile expanded during the twentieth century. After World War II, Californian agronomists collaborated with their Chilean counterparts to build a fruit export sector that many economists have hailed as miraculous, despite its contributions to social inequality and environmental degradation. In addition, California's government conducted a pair of technical and educational exchanges with Chilean administrators in which the Golden State served as the executor of US foreign policy initiatives. As the *Economist* magazine commented in 2001, "Much of the Chilean countryside could nowadays pass for part of California, covered with artificially irrigated vineyards, trim orchards and modern packing plants." This "Californianization" of Chile remade the geography and social structures of Latin America's Pacific coast, much as the "Chileanization" of California's ecological and cultural landscapes reshaped North America's western shores.[2]

Although Chile and California exhibit striking similarities on both cultural and ecological fronts, the enduring connections that emerged between their human populations and their nonhuman environments were hardly inevitable. As Latin American historian Emilia Viotti da Costa framed the precarious balance of autonomy and structure that underwrites the past, "History is not the result of some transcendental 'human agency,' but neither are men and women the puppets of historical 'forces.' Their actions constitute the point at which the constant tension between freedom and necessity is momentarily resolved." The search for these fleeting resolutions is a continuous struggle against factors that would ensure their erasure. Despite the depth and breadth of the relations between Chile and California, these connections remain elusive, if not imperceptible, today.[3]

This book is an account of origins. Throughout its chapters, I follow the dialectical approach of German philosopher Walter Benjamin, who contended, "Origin [*Ursprung*], although an entirely historical category, has, nevertheless, nothing to do with genesis [*Einstehung*]. The term origin is not intended to describe the process by which the existent came into being, but rather to describe that which emerges from the process of becoming and disappearance. Origin is an eddy in the stream of becoming, and in its current it swallows the material involved in the process of genesis." Benjamin's assertion prioritizes the pursuit of kinetic routes over the excavation of static roots. Applying his insights to the writing of history requires more than just rendering visible the processes of production. It demands attentiveness to the production of invisibility.[4]

The taxi driver who picked me up at the Santiago Airport during my first research trip to Chile in 2005 listened to my rationale for making such a long journey from the Northern Hemisphere. Then he shared a haunting observation: "Chileans have a funny way of changing the world and then vanishing." His comment was, undoubtedly, a reflection on Chile's recent past. In a military coup on September 11, 1973, General Augusto Pinochet and his cadres overthrew the democratically elected socialist government of Salvador Allende. Through the systematic torture, incarceration, and murder of tens of thousands of political dissidents at home and abroad, the Pinochet regime produced a generation of *desaparecidos*, literally "the disappeared." At a further remove, the cab driver's remark serves as the epigraph for this project. In the pages that follow, I focus on the emergence and vanishing of landscapes on the Pacific shores of the Americas. The transnational aspects of this shifting geography have, for too long, existed outside the pages of written history. Chileans and Chile are conspicuously absent from nearly all of the major encyclopedias of the western United States, and historians have paid scant attention to Chileans in the voluminous literature on California's history.[5]

In part, the omission of the Chile-California connection from popular consciousness is the product of persistent historiographical trends. Over the past four decades, a group of scholars known as the New Western Historians has succeeded in recovering the voices of previously ignored minorities in North American history. These historians have also asserted the importance of human interactions with nonhuman nature as a central dynamic in the development of the western United States. Despite such noteworthy advances, the customary depiction of the North American West as the product of a westward-moving frontier zone has remained entrenched. Reliance on this seemingly unshakable trajectory has diverted attention from eastward-trending environmental and cultural transformations. In addition, it has led historians to neglect land-use patterns, species introductions, cultural contributions, and landscape aesthetics that originated on the Pacific coast during the 1800s.[6]

Occasionally, scholars hint at an alternative approach, such as the following suggestion from a photograph caption in the 1991 collection *Trails: Toward a New Western History*: "In spite of the old habit of calling the migration into the western United States 'westering,' many of the immigrants were in fact 'eastering.' People in the Pacific Basin . . . provided essential labor for western industries, supplied miners and were miners themselves, and added considerably to the diversity of languages and customs in western America." As the authors propose, attentiveness to the peoples and processes of "eastering" may offer the most promising new route into the study of North America's western borderlands.[7]

Unfortunately, the terrestrial imagery of "trails" toward a new western history obscures the many maritime linkages between the world and North America's western shores. As marine archaeologist James P. Delgado pointed out, "The general impression [of immigration to California] depicts a nation's trend westward by the Oregon Trail. It is important, however, to remember that the California Gold Rush was first and foremost a maritime event." In 1849, eighty-five thousand North Americans journeyed to California. Of this total, more than half came by ship, while the rest took trails from the East. Such data suggest that zones of historical migration and arenas of intercultural contact are not always borderlands. They may just as well be littoral spaces, such as beaches, wharves, or harbors, where land and water converge.[8]

Problems of scale have also masked innumerable connections along the Cordillera. The durability, depth, and diversity of flows between Chile and California are perceptible only if we examine them at various timescales and across official boundaries. By tracing these linkages from the end of the eighteenth century to the beginning of the twenty-first century, I follow the *longue durée*—or long duration—approach to history, which members of the French Annales school pioneered during the twentieth century. Chapters move among the three timescales that historian Fernand Braudel defined as the temporal dimensions of his magnum opus, *The Mediterranean and the Mediterranean World in the Age of Philip II*: (1) "a history whose passage is almost imperceptible, that of man in his relationship to the environment, a history in which all change is slow, a history of constant repetition, ever-recurring cycles"; (2) "another history, this time with slow but perceptible rhythms . . . the history of groups and groupings"; and (3) "traditional history—history, one might say, on the scale not of man, but of individual men [and women]." I approach Chile, California, and the Pacific World from these three frames in order to transcend the conceptual limitations that have characterized the humanities and social sciences since the late nineteenth century.[9]

Environmental and social linkages often stem from commercial relations, but trade does not imply equal exchange. Throughout history, flows of labor and capital across gradients of political and economic power have produced divergent outcomes for the people and places involved. Likewise, the trans-hemispheric interactions described in this book are not functionally interchangeable processes. Building wharves on abandoned ships' hulls and promoting coup d'états are by no means morally or materially equivalent acts. Similarly, the arrival of Chilean potatoes at California's Mission Carmel in 1786 is not connected to President Michelle Bachelet's trip to California in 2008 by an ineffable historical necessity. Despite their contribution to a much larger narrative of connections, such events exemplify diverse processes that had distinct effects.[10]

In the chapters that follow, I distinguish among *displacements, exchanges,* and *influences. Displacements* are instances in which an organism, an object, or a person moves from one place to another in a single trip or a few journeys. These relocations can happen suddenly and may have little effect on their zones of origin. The transfer of Chilean alfalfa to California, the importation of Californian Monterey pines to Chile, and the transmission of Chilean mining techniques and technologies to prospectors in the Sierra Nevada epitomize such shifts. In contrast, *exchanges* are far more extensive processes whereby the long-term flows of commodities, biota, or people have profound transformative effects for both sides of the interaction. The Chilean nitrate trade exemplified such a trend. Although it impoverished the Atacama Desert and the Chilean debt peons who mined there, it enriched the soils of California's Inland Empire and ensured enduring fortunes for large-scale agriculturalists. *Influences*, in contrast, constitute intentional efforts by one or more parties to transform an environ-ment or society in a particular way. The attempts of Chilean travelers to instill elements of their culture in California, the efforts of the US government to limit Salvador Allende's economic policies, or the agendas of Chilean students who returned to their home country to Californianize the nation's economy and its countryside display such patterns.[11]

These displacements, exchanges, and influences between Chile and California connected similar ecosystems. Chile and California possess analogous climates, biotas, and topographies. When Chilean and Californian travelers reached the end of their transequatorial journey along the Cordillera, they encountered envi-ronments strikingly similar to the ones they had left in their own hemispheres. As a result, they were well adapted to their new surroundings. I propose that trans-equatorial links between peoples from similar environments have led to crucial developments in world history. Chile and California exemplify the characteristics of what I call complementary zones, two ecosystems, including their human inhabitants, with a wide variety of basic environmental conditions in common. These underlying geographical similarities dramatically increase the likelihood that flora, fauna, microorganisms, technologies, and land-use patterns will transfer successfully from one zone to the other. In other words, links between comple-mentary zones are likely to produce profound ecological effects because these sites offer elevated potential for long-term integration.

Chile and California share a Mediterranean-type environment with the coun-tries ringing the Mediterranean Sea, the southwestern Cape region of South Africa, and Australia's southern and western zones (fig. 1). All five ecosystems

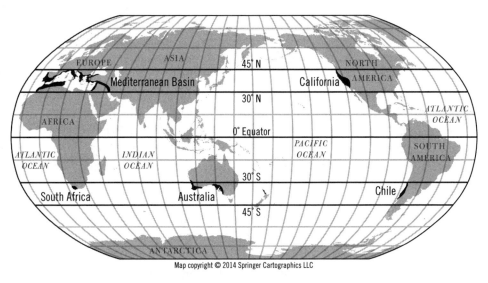

Map copyright © 2014 Springer Cartographics LLC

Figure 1. The world's Mediterranean-type ecosystems. *Produced by Springer Cartographics LLC for Edward D. Melillo.*

feature coastal plains with mountainous backdrops. Their climates exhibit cool, wet winters and hot, dry summers with temperatures often exceeding 89° Fahrenheit (32° Celsius). As much as three quarters of the annual rainfall in these zones occurs from October to March in the Northern Hemisphere and from April to September in the Southern Hemisphere, and the growing season tends to conclude with a late-summer drought. Mediterranean-type ecosystems display recurring patterns of tough, woody, and evergreen vegetation, such as chaparral, coastal sage, evergreen forest, and foothill woodlands, which make these zones especially fire-prone during dry summer months. In addition, these environments exhibit astounding levels of biodiversity. As plant ecologist Richard M. Cowling and his colleagues noted, "The five Mediterranean climate regions of the world occupy less than 5 percent of the Earth's surface yet harbour about 48,250 known vascular plant species, almost 20 percent of the world total."[12]

Here, a caveat is in order. Despite their enormous comparative potential, Mediterranean-type complementary zones—without the connections that humans provide—offer nothing more than ecological analogs separated by immense stretches of land or water. When people bridge the spatial gaps between such complementary zones, the consequences are as much about culture as they are about nature. Mutually constituted through environmental and cultural processes, settlement landscapes often come to resemble colonists' home environments.[13]

Historical outcomes in California and Chile were never simply the inexorable workings of nature. Theories of environmental determinism, the view that
culture is a direct function of the physical environment, rather than a product
of social conditions, are inadequate explanatory tools. They offer nothing but
demonstrations of how misdirected invocations of natural phenomena erase
historical actions. Instead, developments along the Chile-California axis reflect
an ongoing interplay among social and environmental factors. In the making of
the two places, Mediterranean ecosystems, vast Pacific coastlines, and mineral-
rich tectonic zones on the western edge of the Americas offered possibilities
and limits to routes traveled and pathways forged.[14]

For many millennia, the movement of people, organisms, and commodities
across vast oceanic expanses has had tremendous consequences. Since the 1972
publication of historian Alfred Crosby's groundbreaking book, *The Columbian
Exchange*, scholars have explored links between cross-cultural conquest and
environmental change. Particularly important among these transformations
was the conversion of vast regions of Chile and California into landscapes
that bore the environmental and cultural markings of the Iberian Peninsula.
In *Ecological Imperialism*, published fourteen years after *The Columbian
Exchange*, Crosby used the concept of "Neo-Europes" to refer to the array of
temperate regions with similar latitudes and climates analogous to the home
environments of colonizers. The conquistadors who first arrived in Chile during
the sixteenth century were delighted to find a physical environment that bore
remarkable similarities to Spain. The Mediterranean crops and livestock that
accompanied the conquest of the Americas thrived in the familiar conditions of
Chile's coastal valleys. Presented with surprisingly recognizable topographic
and environmental circumstances, Spaniards could manufacture the olive oil,
wine, and wheat bread that comprised the cornerstones of their culinary and
religious traditions.[15]

A similar pattern emerged in California. In the late 1800s, a Yankee emigrant
reflected on the changes that came with the arrival of Franciscan missionaries
along the eighteenth-century California coastline: "Olive orchards, vineyards,
and wheat fields after a while yielded their increase. Rude manufactures were
started. America was being gradually changed into Europe." Thus, over many
decades, Spaniards remade both Chile and California in the image of their
southern European homeland. I evaluate the implications of this transequatorial Spanish conveyor belt of linkages, which helped transfer Mediterranean
land-use patterns to the western shores of the Americas.[16]

Today, it is likely that US consumers experience the fruits of these
connections unconsciously. Most of the apples, grapes, peaches, pears, berries,

avocados, and table wines that fill shelves and shopping carts in supermarkets throughout the United States began their journey in one of two places, Chile or California. The Chilean agro-export sector, which expanded rapidly under General Augusto Pinochet's laissez-faire policies of the 1970s and 1980s, was an ideal source for meeting US demand for off-season produce. Influenced by Californian agricultural models, Chile has become the world's largest fresh fruit and vegetable exporter during the Northern Hemisphere's winter season, when California's crop production plummets. Counterseasonal production cycles allow North American consumers to select from a bountiful array of fruits and vegetables that bear little correspondence to the season, regional climate, and local geography beyond their grocery store walls. Yet the alternating phases of intense and moderate demand for agricultural labor dramatically affect the lives of the workers who plant, pick, and pack the produce in these two agricultural zones. Socially stigmatized and politically marginalized, these women and men comprise vast reserve armies of migrant laborers whose legions exist in the shadows of national citizenship.[17]

In contrast to the treaty-bound perimeters of modern nation-states, the contours of ecosystems and the edges of cultural zones are porous and constantly shifting. Consequently, a transnational perspective offers the most viable framework for studying such systems. Where it has thrived, transnational history has often highlighted the restrictions and opportunities that vast bodies of water have afforded civilizations. Braudel's *Mediterranean*, historians Kirti N. Chaudhuri's and Ashin Das Gupta's innovative writings on the Indian Ocean, and the vast field of Atlantic World studies exemplify this tendency. In *The Black Atlantic* (1992), sociologist Paul Gilroy reframed black identity in Europe and the Americas as a transatlantic process of cultural circulation, driven by the dialectic of diaspora and emancipation.[18]

Unlike Atlantic World studies, to which scholars like Gilroy have made such crucial contributions, historians have just begun to appreciate the Pacific Ocean as its own "coherent unit of analysis," a starting point for inquiry and a basis for rediscovering historical undercurrents. The Pacific Ocean region—"the enormous water world covering one-third of the Earth's surface, framed by continents, joined by islands"—has had few champions. This dearth of scholarship may derive from the linguistic heterogeneity and cultural diversity of the region, characteristics that pose practical and methodological obstacles. In addition, Oceania offers no convenient diasporic analog to the "black Atlantic." The Pacific has seen many Middle Passages, each with radically different trajectories and destinations.[19]

In recent years, historian David Igler's *The Great Ocean* (2013), historian Matt Matusda's *Pacific Worlds* (2012), and historian Gregory Cushman's *Guano and the Opening of the Pacific World* (2013) have illuminated the experiences of Pacific peoples and their environments. Igler's account of the "eastern Pacific" moves dexterously among different spatial and temporal scales without losing focus on the forces that created an interdependence of places. Likewise, Matsuda's book revolves around "multiple sites of trans-localism," rather than relying on a linear sequence of eras or civilizations, to show how interconnected enclaves created multiple Pacific worlds. Even so, Chile's presence is negligible in both Igler's and Matsuda's depictions of the Pacific Ocean region. Cushman goes much further than his colleagues in situating Latin America within a dense matrix of historical linkages with this wider transoceanic contact zone. Nonetheless, Chile, California, and north-south connections in the Americas are not the primary concerns of *Guano and the Opening of the Pacific World*. In contrast, I suggest that the aquatic corridor between Chile and California was both a real and imagined space of connections, flows, and aspirations for those living along the Cordillera.[20]

For thousands of years, people and ecosystems in geographically distinct regions of the world have interacted in far-reaching ways. The challenge now facing practitioners in the emerging field of global environmental history is to transcend approaches based solely on local, regional, or national comparisons and to move toward models that emphasize transnational displacements, exchanges, and influences. Such expansions of scope and scale are necessary for comprehending processes as diverse as imperial conquest, changing land-use patterns, capital accumulation, species migrations, and strategies of political resistance. Although this book pursues comparisons between Chile and California, the emphasis is on connections—including the antagonisms that these encounters generated—among the peoples and ecosystems in both places.[21]

A few historians have called attention to the long-distance maritime contacts that shaped the histories of California and the wider Pacific World. In his account of Australian-Californian environmental connections, *True Gardens of the Gods* (1999), historian Ian Tyrell argued that the shared peripheral positions and semicolonial status of Australia and California during the nineteenth century encouraged the development of similar techniques of ecological control and comparable anthropogenic landscapes in both zones. Despite the strengths of his account, Tyrell did not engage with environmental history scholarship or the emerging field of Pacific World history, and he had few things to say about nonelite migrants who moved between the two places. Even so, his descriptions of long-distance exchanges, which included pest-control techniques and nonnative tree species, along with irrigation strategies and acclimatization theories, provide an effective model for constructing transpacific environmental and social histories.[22]

One of the greatest challenges when following such heterogeneous leads is to avoid producing "contributionist" history. Writing about well-known events, such as California's gold rush or Chile's coup d'état, and then simply cataloging the involvement of Chileans and Californians in these developments, does not generate a whole that is greater than the sum of the parts. It produces studies that are empirically rich but bereft of major theoretical contributions. To avoid such pitfalls, I focus on major aspects of social and environmental change in each place that would not have been possible, or would have occurred in dramatically different ways, without such transnational linkages.[23]

Successful histories of such biological and cultural flows uproot notions of our environments that we take for granted. Reframing givens as contingencies calls into question the historical inevitability of so-called natural landscapes. Landscapes are also vantage points that fluctuate with shifts in perspective. The task of recovering marginalized viewpoints poses challenges at every turn. Nonelites rarely leave durable accounts of their everyday experiences. As Haitian anthropologist Michel-Rolph Trouillot remarked, "Production of historical narratives involves the uneven contribution of competing groups and individuals who have unequal access to the means of such production." In pursuit of these overlooked viewpoints, I have explored a diverse array of sources on both sides of the equator, which range from maritime bills of lading and notarized debt peonage contracts to transcripts of university committee meetings and gold prospectors' correspondence with faraway loved ones.[24]

This book explores the environmental and social displacements, exchanges, and influences that connected Chile and California during 222 years. It focuses on both the emergence and the disappearance of these linkages at multiple timescales, thereby offering a new framework for further studies of the Americas and the Pacific World.

Part One

CHILE AND THE MAKING OF CALIFORNIA

———————————◆————————————

CORDILLERAS IN MIND

Long before the Rio Grande became the watery margin that transformed travelers into immigrants, California and Chile constituted the northern and southern frontiers of a single, ambitious imperial project. Spain's American empire, which occupied most of the Pacific Ocean's eastern edge, became an integrated zone of transoceanic contact during the late 1700s. In 1786, French explorer Jean-François de Galaup de La Pérouse introduced the common potato (*Solanum tuberosum*) from Chile to California. This botanical transfer, what I call a displacement for its one-way effects on the receiving environments and cultures, demonstrates the enduring function of ships as dispersal agents, which rapidly transferred species across vast distances. During the century after the Frenchman's intrepid voyage, vessels that sailed and steamed from Chilean ports to California harbors continued to create maritime conduits for the exchange of flora and fauna between these two Mediterranean ecosystems.

The Pacific World also provided Yankee whalers, sealers, and sea otter hunters with access to bountiful new hunting zones and lucrative commercial outlets. During the eighteenth and nineteenth centuries, the commodification of marine mammals was crucial to the integration of Pacific islands and continental coastlines, which became key stopovers for recruiting crew members and resupplying ships. The incursions of US trading vessels into foreign ports and uncharted waters opened the Pacific to North American imperial expansion and prefaced the annexation of California at the end of the Mexican War (1846–48). In the wake of California's 1848 gold strike, well-established connections between the port cities of San Francisco and Valparaíso facilitated a large-scale Chilean migration to the *El Dorado* of the Northern Hemisphere.[1]

From the sixteenth century onward, the Pacific Ocean functioned as both the medium of separation and the causeway of connection between the colonial extremities of Spain's massive American empire. In the tales imperialists tell, the sea often marks the terminus of continents, the end of frontiers, the boundary of national territories, and the limits of terra firma. To take the Pacific as a starting point challenges traditional conceptualizations of the Americas. Essayist Richard Rodriguez offered one such relocation of the horizon when he invited readers to "imagine how California must have appeared to the first Europeans— the Spaniards, the English, the Russians—who saw the writing of the continent in reverse, from the perspective of Asia, adjusting the view of California through a glass." This inversion repositions the western edge of North America as a starting point for United States history. It also relegates the agents of empire— the conquistador, the cartographer, the fur trader—to the margins of familiar terrain.[2]

The establishment of Spain's American colonies was an unrivalled projection of arrogance. On May 4, 1493, Pope Alexander VI issued the *Inter Caetera Bull*, partitioning the territories on either side of the Atlantic Ocean between Spain and Portugal. With the signing of the Treaty of Tordesillas on June 7, 1494, these rival naval powers formalized the division. They agreed to respect a north-south demarcation line, which passed through a point 370 leagues west of the Cape Verde Islands. This agreement granted to the Spanish all non-Christian islands and continents to the west of the meridian, while the Portuguese acquired control over the lands to its east.[3]

Equipped with guns, horses, oceangoing ships, and Eurasian diseases, the Spanish rapidly dominated several highly developed indigenous societies west of the papal division. Between 1519 and 1521, Hernán Cortés subjugated the sophisticated Aztec civilization of central Mexico, while from 1530 to 1534, Francisco Pizarro conquered the immense Inca Empire, defeating a people who had successfully expanded across the mountainous territory now bounded by Peru, Ecuador, Bolivia, and northern Chile. This vast domain, which the conquistadors dubbed *Las Indias*, was a wellspring of two indispensable resources for the expansion of Spain's mercantile empire, bullion and Indian labor power.[4]

During the sixteenth, seventeenth, and eighteenth centuries, Spain aggressively expanded its holdings on the eastern edge of the Pacific and established military outposts and settlements from the fertile plains of central Chile north to the San Francisco Bay Area. Both Alta California (Upper California) and Baja California (Lower California) were part of the Virreinato de Nueva España (Viceroyalty of New Spain), the formal name of Spanish colonial Mexico until Mexican independence in 1821. The margins of Alta California were those of the present-day state of California, from San Diego northward. To the south, Baja California remained in Mexican possession after the Treaty of Guadalupe

Hidalgo (1848) and is today Mexico's northernmost state. In 1804, the Spanish divided the two Californias between the Dominican mission territories in the south and the Franciscan religious colonies in the north. Thus, Alta California and Chile were the geographical ballast at either end of a vast longitudinal Cordillera.[5]

In the minds of Spanish colonial officials, colonists, and soldiers, these isolated territories topped the list of dreaded hinterland postings. Known predominantly for their inaccessibility, slow communications with regional capitals, uncooperative Indian populations, and scarcity of precious minerals, these endpoints of the Spanish domain closely resembled a pair of imperial penal colonies. Manuel de Salas (1754–1841), one of Chile's foremost promoters of independence, wrote in 1796, "The kingdom of Chile, without contradiction the most fertile in America and the most adequate for human happiness, is the most wretched of the Spanish dominions." Deportation to colonial Chile was a devastating legal punishment. In 1678, a Spanish court tried a group of maritime smugglers for engaging in illegal trade between the Viceroyalty of Peru and Mexico (then known to the Spanish as La Nueva España, or New Spain). The tribunal doled out the sentence of "four years of exile from Callao [Peru] at a distance of not less than fifty leagues on pain of being sent to Chile." In the Spanish imagination, the prospect of exile to Chile was a frightening fate.[6]

Alta California was Chile's colonial twin in the Northern Hemisphere. Franciscan padre Junípero Serra wrote to the forty-sixth viceroy of New Spain in 1773 in an attempt to convince him "not to look upon Monterey [California] and its missions as the China or Cueta [Morocco] of exile for the soldier. . . . Being sent to our missions should not be a form of banishment, nor should our missions be filled with worthless people who serve no purpose but to commit evil deeds." Serra's entreaties failed to alter this perception.[7]

Indeed, southern Chile and Northern California were also comparable for the fierce resistance that native residents carried out against imperial expansion. The Mapuche—whom the Spanish called Araucanians—contested encroachment on their homelands in south-central Chile for three centuries, from the mid-1500s until the 1880s. The Spanish military and their Chilean successors faced enormous difficulties wresting the territory south of the Bío Bío River from indigenous control, in large part because the Mapuche were skilled horsemen and accomplished mountain fighters.[8]

Likewise, the Modoc War (1872–73) in Northern California and southern Oregon demonstrated the durability of native resistance to colonial incursion. The conflict, one of the so-called Indian Wars between the US Army and various Native American tribes, stemmed from government attempts to forcibly relocate the Modoc to the Klamath Reservation. The Modoc people took refuge on the south shores of Tule Lake, where ancient basaltic lava formations provided a stronghold of natural caves and tunnels. Kintpuash, also known as Captain Jack, led a band of fifty-five warriors against one thousand federal troops, causing major casualties among federal forces—including the only death of a US general during the Indian Wars—and delaying the relocation of the tribe by more than half a year.[9]

By the conclusion of the nineteenth century, state-sponsored campaigns against the Modocs and the Mapuche had finally succeeded in expropriating the traditional homelands of these peoples and opening the northern and southern reaches of the Cordillera to Euro-American settlement. Historian Charles Edward Chapman, one of the founders of the *Hispanic American Historical Review*, was simply assenting to commonly held beliefs when he wrote in 1937, "The climate of central Chile, where the bulk of the people live, is one of the best in the world for the white race, vigorous, but with no great extremes of either heat or cold—much like that of the somewhat famous California."[10]

Nearly half a century before white colonists flooded into "somewhat famous California," North American commercial vessels began plying Pacific trade routes. The earliest ship to enter the South Seas under the Stars and Stripes, the *Empress of China*, departed from New York on February 22, 1784. The 360-ton vessel sailed from its East Coast port laden with 57,687 pounds of ginseng, thirty-eight barrels of tar and turpentine, twenty thousand dollars in silver, and eleven pipes of wine and brandy, bound for Canton, China. The ship carried all the diplomatic accoutrements that the newly convened Congress of the Confederation (1781–89) could muster. Unhampered by British blockades, which had previously stifled commercial connections between the colonies and the outside world during the War of Independence, Yankee traders began their aggressive expansion into the Pacific. A year after the *Empress of China* returned home, five ships left North American ports for Canton.[11]

From 1784 to the end of the Civil War, crews out of New England or mid-Atlantic harbors steered their vessels into the most remote regions of the Pacific. Captains' logbooks from this period tell of stops at a dizzying array of ports. Between 1815 and 1819, Captain C. Reynolds and his Boston-based ship the *Sultan* traded for sea otter pelts along the California coast, picked up cargoes of sandalwood in Hawai'i, and exchanged wares and currency at the Marquesas Islands, Coquimbo (northern Chile), and the Chinese treaty ports of Canton and Macao. Historian Jean Heffer called this North American expansion into the Pacific World a "great frontier," where "Yankees were active throughout the entire expanse of the ocean. They could just as easily be found off New Zealand or Chile as whaling in the Bering Sea, or in China—a magnet for traders eager to profit and for Protestant missionaries in search of souls to save." Capitalist ambition and religious zealotry were contented shipmates during this era of transoceanic exchanges.[12]

Yet opportunities for profits and proselytizing were not the only incentives for Pacific exploration. Historian Mary Louise Pratt has argued that the mid-1700s witnessed a shift toward voyages aimed at expanding the geographic scope of natural history and promoting the development of European-type landscapes elsewhere on earth. In 1769, British explorer Captain James Cook anchored his ship *Endeavor* in Tahiti and began to realize his aspirations of transferring Europe's "portmanteau biota" to the Pacific World. As one of the two professional botanists in Cook's company wrote on May 10, 1769, "Captn Cooke planted divers seeds which he had brought with him in a spot of ground turned up for the purpose. They were all bought of Gordon of Mile End and sent in bottles seald up, whether or no that method will succeed the event of this plantation will show." This transplantation marked a crucial turning point in global environmental history. Even though at least 450 ships from Spain, Holland, France, and Britain had engaged in trade and piracy in the Pacific between 1520 and 1769, there was no significant ecological exchange between the Atlantic World and the Pacific World until the Cook expedition.[13]

As the first navigator equipped with the chronometer and a comprehensive knowledge of longitude and latitude, Cook benefited from precise temporal and spatial measurements. Applying this synoptic knowledge to his accounts of the expedition's discoveries, he offered a legible description of the Pacific World to his European contemporaries. During three voyages between 1768 and 1779, Cook and his crew visited such wide-ranging Pacific destinations as New Zealand, Australia, the Dutch East Indies, Antarctica, Hawai'i, Tahiti, and the coast of North America from California to the Bering Strait. Acts of mapping and claiming territory for the Crown proved vital to Cook's expedition. Secretly, the Admiralty had instructed its representative to "observe with accuracy the Situation of such Islands as you may discover in the Course of your Voyage that have not hitherto been discover'd by any Europeans, and take possession for His Majesty and make Surveys and Draughts of such of them as may appear to be of Consequence." As soon as Cook's journals reached a public audience in the 1770s, Europeans began to envision, with tantalizing fixity, the places that they had so recently imagined as mysterious ocean isles and elusive shorelines. By 1800, cartographers had charted nearly all of the world's continental contours, allowing for the integration of coastal peoples and ecosystems into capitalist circuits of labor and commerce.[14]

The passage of "divers seeds" in bottles from Gordon of Mile End to a Tahitian garden illustrated the boldness of British claims about their expanding presence in the Pacific World. Before long, other European powers sought a stake in this game. During the 1780s, French navigator La Pérouse followed in the wake of Cook's expedition when he sailed his two aptly named frigates, *La Boussole* (the magnetic compass) and *L'Astrolabe* (the astrolabe), into the Pacific. While investigating scientific and commercial dimensions of this aquatic realm, La Pérouse established the first major biological connection between Spain's hinterland provinces of California and Chile. The common potato journeyed from the Andes to the shores of California in the dark holds of the two French vessels, enabling the expedition's gardener to present the humble tubers as a gift to a gathering of Franciscan friars and their California Indian laborers at Mission Carmel.

La Pérouse, a great admirer of Captain Cook, spent most of his life at sea. An experienced French naval officer, he had fought the British during the Seven Years' War, also known as the French and Indian War (1754–63). La Pérouse had nimbly commanded vessels in the West Indies and the Indian Ocean and had led a fleet against the British during the US War of Independence. In 1782, at the age of forty-one, he distinguished himself in Hudson's Bay by capturing a pair of British fortifications and receiving the surrender of Samuel Hearne, the commander of Fort Prince of Wales at the mouth of the Churchill River. These actions temporarily paralyzed the fur-trading operations of the Hudson's Bay Company and severely hampered Britain's strategic interests in the North Atlantic. Likewise, La Pérouse's daring expedition into the Pacific Ocean originated as a challenge to British imperial dominance on the high seas.[15]

Captain Cook's exploits earned the British unparalleled prestige throughout Enlightenment-era Europe. Jealous of their neighbor's accomplishments, King Louis XVI (1754–93) and the Académie Royale des Sciences strove to match their anglophone rivals in global scientific exploration. They selected La Pérouse to seek out "all the lands which had escaped the vigilance of Cook." The king and a group of French scholars engrossed themselves in preparations for the expedition, compiling an exhaustive list of all that was then known of New World geography, scouring dozens of extant maps to chart the most efficient route for the ships, and selecting eminent scientists in fields as diverse as botany, zoology, and astronomy to accompany the expedition.[16]

French diplomacy also lent a hand. The Pacte de Famille of 1761, signed during the French and Indian War by the Bourbon kings Charles III of Spain and Louis XV of France, still applied to Franco-Hispanic relations when La Pérouse embarked on his journey. This declaration of mutual protection between the two Continental powers smoothed the way for the French explorers as they stopped at Spanish ports in the Americas.[17]

Before the ships departed, stevedores loaded a veritable arboretum onto the decks of *La Boussole* and *L'Astrolabe*. The frigate *La Boussole* featured a root cellar, a storage room crammed with gardening tools, and "some fifty living trees and vines—Montmorency cherry trees, black heart cherry trees, white heart cherry trees, olive trees, quince trees, grape vines, fig trees, chestnut trees, lilac bushes, the 'hundred-leaved rose-tree.'" *La Boussole* was nothing short of a floating garden.[18]

Although the La Pérouse expedition was motivated by scientific intentions, commercial objectives loomed large among its goals. The king and his ministers anxiously sought news of Pacific whaling opportunities, and they hoped to learn more of the lucrative trade in seal and otter furs between the Americas and China. Experienced navigator Paul-Antoine-Marie Fleuriot de Langle captained *L'Astrolabe*, while La Pérouse took charge of *La Boussole*. With a combined crew of 225 men, the expedition sailed from Brest on August 1, 1785. From the tip of the Brittany peninsula, the frigates forged westward across the Atlantic. After several stopovers to take on food, wood, and water, the expedition rounded Cape Horn and entered the Pacific Ocean.[19]

The passage was surprisingly uneventful. On February 23, 1786, the ships reached the Bay of Concepción, Chile. Although La Pérouse scrutinized the charts drawn by Amédée-François Frézier—an engineer and cartographer who had visited Chile and Peru from 1712 to 1714—he was unable to locate the town of Concepción. Eventually, Spanish pilots arrived to welcome the visitors, informing the French that an earthquake and the ensuing tidal wave had destroyed the old city some thirty-five years earlier. The governor at that time, Don Ortiz de Rosas, had supervised the rebuilding of the settlement approximately eight miles from the Pacific shoreline on the banks of the Bío Bío River. French ignorance of both the natural disaster and the resulting urban relocation demonstrates Chile's geopolitical isolation and the mystery that continued to enshroud Pacific geography throughout the eighteenth century.[20]

Intercontinental communications between Spain and Chile served the French explorer well, however. Diplomatic dispatches sent aboard Spanish ships before the departure of *L'Astrolabe* and *La Boussole* had reached the distant South American colony ahead of the French arrival. When La Pérouse and his men stepped onshore at the village of Talcahuano, they received warm greetings from Don Quexada, the settlement's temporary commander. Captain General Ambrosio O'Higgins sent a formal apology for his absence. He was fighting a tenacious army of Mapuche Indians along the Bío Bío River. Toward the end of the French visit, O'Higgins returned from his military expedition and held a sumptuous banquet for his guests. This event capped off three weeks of extravagant receptions, lavish balls, and bountiful feasts in their honor. Rested and well fed, the French prepared to sail north with a large quantity of potatoes from their hosts.[21]

The potato is endemic to the Andes. Cultivation of this tuber began more than six thousand years ago in the region now encompassed by high-altitude zones in Chile, Argentina, Bolivia, and Peru. Grown "8,000 feet above the maize or Indian corn line," potatoes served as the staple food for early inhabitants of the Andean *Altiplano* (High Plain) for four main reasons. Potatoes can withstand frosts and so are able to survive at high altitudes where other plants cannot, their caloric yield per acre is far higher than that of other anchor starches such as rice or wheat, they require minimal labor to cultivate, and they store well over long periods. The diversity of the common potato is tremendous. Scientists have identified upward of five thousand varieties grown worldwide.[22]

Despite the potato's culinary appeal to indigenous Andean consumers, the Spanish conquistadors who invaded Chile in the sixteenth century initially rejected potatoes as food. Pedro de Valdivia (c. 1500–1554), the founder of Santiago de Chile (1541), Concepción (1550), and Valdivia (1552), wrote to Holy Roman Emperor Charles V in 1551 about the potatoes grown by the natives whom he had encountered on his travels. Yet, when Valdivia and his troops experienced a dire food shortage during one of their campaigns, surviving on one daily handful of grains per man, they refused to consume the odd-looking tuber. Eventually, the Spaniards warmed to the potato's culinary virtues.[23]

On March 17, the La Pérouse expedition departed from Concepción. Tracing a northward arc across the Pacific, the two ships stopped at Rapa Nui (Easter Island), Hawai'i, and Alaska before turning south toward California. On September 14, 1786, the pair of frigates emerged from a dense blanket of fog off the Monterey coast. The padres, soldiers, California Indians, and colonial officials at the Mission San Carlos Borromeo in Carmel—located 123 miles along the coast south of San Francisco—eagerly anticipated the arrival of these ocean-borne visitors (see map 1). Colonial authorities in Chile had sent word to the military governor of Alta California, Pedro Fages, that a pair of ships would soon visit the remote province. Before the La Pérouse expedition, the friars of Spanish-controlled Alta California had never hosted foreign visitors. Their northern frontier communities were, like the Chilean settlements to their south, worlds apart from the bustling metropolises of Madrid, Mexico City, and Lima. The padres who founded and maintained California's Catholic communities lived hardscrabble lives on the fringes of Hispanoamérica (fig. 2).[24]

Figure 2. José Cardero, "The reception of Jean-Francois de la Perouse at Mission Carmel in 1786, California." Note California Indian converts in line on left and La Pérouse shaking hands with Pedro Fages at center. *Courtesy of the Bancroft Library, University of California, Berkeley*

La Pérouse and his ships arrived only seventeen years after the Franciscans had settled in the region. In 1769, José de Gálvez, the visitor-general of Mexico, had directed the governor of Baja California, Gaspar de Portolá, to found a series of missions along the coast of Alta California, a colossal Spanish territory that extended from the northern regions of the Baja California peninsula all the way to present-day Oregon. These frontier outposts played three roles: they served as bulwarks against the incursions of Russian fur traders from the north, they protected the silver mines in the northern reaches of New Spain from British privateers, and they functioned as outposts for Christianizing California's diverse Indian population.[25]

Following in Cook's wake, La Pérouse and his colleagues acted as global cultivators, diffusing seeds and plants at each new stopover. In California, the

Frenchman related, "We enriched the gardens of the Governor and the mission with differents [*sic*] seeds . . . which had kept perfectly and will provide them with added benefits." The most important of these biological contributions was the potato. La Pérouse recognized the significance of this interhemispheric transfer: "Our gardener gave the missionaries some potatoes from Chile, in perfect condition; I think this is not the least important of our gifts, and that this tuber will take perfectly in the light and rich soil of the Monterey district." This biotic relocation exemplifies a displacement, a sudden transfer that had few consequences for one party—in this case, Chile—but produced major changes for the other, namely California.[26]

Botanical migrations rarely occur as one-time, isolated events. Often, species require multiple introductions to take root in new ecosystems. With cultivars, successful transfer from a home environment to a new landscape is shaped as much by cultural practices as it is by geographical factors. We know, however, that the potato was one of the few plant introductions during Spanish California's mission era that was not the work of priests or overland settlers from New Spain. As California historian Rockwell D. Hunt remarked, "[Father Francisco] Palóu, in his classic biography of Padre Serra, tells of many kinds of seeds of garden vegetables and flowers brought by the first party [from Baja California] to San Diego, in 1769; but the impressive list does not include the potato." Unbeknown to the members of the French expedition, the Franciscan friars, or the California Indians present at this biological exchange, the event marked the beginning of a long and illustrious career for the potato in California.[27]

California's twenty-one Franciscan missions, as well as its *presidios* (forts) and *pueblos* (towns), served as way stations for the northward and southward diffusion of the Chilean potato from Mission Carmel. The physiological similarities between the Andean potato and varieties of camas (*Camassia quamash*), a starchy native bulb regularly consumed by California Indians, made the potato highly adaptable to local indigenous foodways. As they had long done with camas bulbs, Ohlone Indians of the greater San Francisco Bay Area roasted potatoes over coal-filled fire pits. They then peeled the tubers and dipped them in oil to enhance the flavors.[28]

Potatoes also became a key cultivar in California's nineteenth-century agricultural boom. More than a century after the French brought the potato to Monterey and Franciscan missionaries and Ohlone communities added it to their culinary repertoires, British businessman Charles Dowsett published a promotional pamphlet in London, describing the prospects for farmers who wanted to emigrate to California: "A settler might make a really good return out of potatoes while his Fruit trees are maturing, which is a food more in use in America than in England. Potatoes are not only served at luncheon and dinner, but also at breakfast everywhere, and, if every settler planted his land with potatoes, there would be no fear of overstocking the market." The potato was only the first in a series of Chilean plants to arrive by ship and take root in California's fertile soil.[29]

Despite his commitment to the botanical mission at hand, La Pérouse did not forget his commercial obligations to the king. While in Monterey, the French commander met a Spanish merchant named Vicente Vasadre y Vega, who, two years earlier, had traded beads, metal objects, and abalone shells to California Indians in exchange for a load of sea otter (*Enhydra lutris*) pelts. In 1785, Vasadre y Vega expanded his operations, sending the furs to Acapulco for tanning before exporting them to China onboard several Manila-bound galleons. Sea otter fur, prized for its dense, velvety-soft texture, had become the fashion rage among elite women in eighteenth-century Qing dynasty China. La Pérouse attempted to profit from this trend by selling several thousand furs to the Chinese, but rumors of a market glut of pelts concurrent with the French expedition's arrival at Macao gave him a disappointing return on his product.[30]

Far more successful at such commercial ventures were *promyshlenniki*, Russian fur traders who employed, or violently coerced, skilled native Aleut and Alutiiq hunters to supply coveted pelts for sale in China. Sea otters in the vicinity of the Kamchatka Peninsula and the Komandorski (Commander) Islands of the northern Pacific were so abundant in the mid-1700s that Russian merchants dubbed the area the "Otter Sea." It was not long before North Americans staked their fortunes on the profitable trade. John Ledyard, a Connecticut Yankee who had traveled with Captain Cook on the British navigator's third and final journey in the Pacific (1776–79), found that the fifteen hundred otter pelts the expedition acquired, "which did not cost the purchaser sixpence sterling, sold in China for 100 dollars."[31]

Such colossal sums convinced Yankee merchants to pursue the furry mollusk-eaters with reckless abandon. In 1801, fifteen ships out of US ports traded for pelts along the Northwest coast. When these vessels reached China, their cargoes brought astounding returns. During 1805 and 1806, Yankees sold one million dollars' worth of sea otter pelts, seal fur, and sandalwood in Canton. That same year, these North American merchants returned to the United States with more than ten million pounds of Chinese tea. Yet this bonanza had finite potential. By the late 1800s, the aggressive, market-driven hunt had devastated the sea otter populations that had once inhabited the entire northern edge of the Pacific Rim.[32]

Before this rapacious animal harvest reached its tipping point, the commercial sea otter trade inspired the first published account of California by a North American writer. In 1808, Philadelphia's *American Register* printed William Shaler's "Journal of a Voyage between China and the Northwestern Coast of America, Made in 1804." Shaler, a Connecticut sea captain with a penchant for risky commercial schemes, illegally collected sea otter pelts along California's Spanish coast from 1803 to 1805. At the time, Spanish maritime law forbade foreign vessels from anchoring in imperial harbors without special permission from the crown.[33]

In the decade before Shaler's arrival on California's coast, about a dozen other North American captains had attempted fur-smuggling voyages to California's harbors, including Captain Ebenezer Dorr of the aptly named *Otter*, which docked at Monterey in 1796. Complaining of the arrogance of British and North American mariners, a Spanish governor wrote to his superiors that these foreigners "not only frequent the waters surrounding our possessions in quest of fish, pearls, and furs, but confident that there is nobody to restrain them, they come with arrogant boldness to anchor in our harbors, and to act with the same liberties as if they were Spaniards."[34]

Shaler followed the lead of his predecessors, effortlessly evading the paltry bureaucracy along California's shores. The ease with which he violated Spain's imperial dictates heightened Shaler's awareness of the empire's fragile control over Alta California: "The Spaniards have complete possession of the peninsula of [Baja] California; but that is not the case above: there their domination is bounded by the Sierra Madre, which in no part is far removed from the coast; so that in reality they are masters of the maritime part of the country only." These words resonated with North American expansionists who favored the conquest of Alta California. For many years, the US Navy had coveted the strategically positioned bay of San Francisco. On November 11, 1818, naval officer John B. Prevost wrote to the State Department about the desirability of annexing the bay and California: "The port of St. Francis is one of the most convenient, extensive, and safe in the world, wholly without defence, and in the neighbourhood of a feeble, diffused, and disaffected population. Under all these circumstances, may we not infer views as to the early possession of this harbour, and ultimately to the sovereignty of all California?" So began the official justifications for US expansion to Pacific shores.[35]

Throughout the 1830s and 1840s, US political opinion increasingly favored the conquest of California. In 1835, President Andrew Jackson made an unsuccessful bid to purchase San Francisco Bay from Mexico for half a million dollars. A number of Yankees encouraged their government to continue its acquisition efforts. Faxon D. Atherton (1815–77), a Massachusetts businessman who had spent several years in Chile and Hawai'i, enthusiastically supported annexation. Writing from Tahiti in 1893, Atherton told his North American commercial associates that California's occupation made strategic sense for the United States: "I have hopes that the U.S. will acquire California by purchase or otherwise, as it is a most beautiful country very similar to Chile. The Bay of San Francisco is one of the most beautiful harbours in the world. It would make a famous naval station for the U.S. There is no such harbour in the Pacific." Before Atherton's vision was realized, he became one of many Yankees to cement an alliance with a prominent Chilean lineage. On July 7, 1843, he married Dominga de Goñi, the daughter of one of Chile's elite families. After the gold rush, Atherton emerged as a well-known California merchant. In 1860, he purchased 640 acres of land in San Mateo County—in the San Francisco Bay Area—and built a home for his wife and seven children. Venerating his Chilean connections, Atherton called the estate Valparaíso Park.[36]

Long before Atherton built his Northern California homestead, his hopes for US colonial expansion came to fruition under decidedly hostile circumstances. In 1845, President James K. Polk tried to buy the New Mexican and California territories, to no avail. In Polk's view, military conquest was the only remaining option; all he required was a casus belli. In April 1846, a skirmish between a US army patrol and a Mexican cavalry detachment in contested territory south of the Nueces River and north of the Rio Grande provided the president and his congressional supporters with the requisite premise. A declaration of war ensued. On July 7, 1846, Commodore John Sloat and his troops occupied California's Mexican capital of Monterey, claiming it for the United States.[37]

During the Mexican War (1846–48), the United States forced its southern neighbor to relinquish 525,000 square miles of national territory. In Mexico, the war remains known as La intervención norteamericana en México (the North American intervention in Mexico). The Treaty of Guadalupe Hidalgo, signed on February 2, 1848, established the new international border between the United States and Mexico.[38]

The following month, news emerged that altered world history. As Faxon Atherton's friend and business partner, Thomas O. Larkin, put it, "A complete revolution in the ordinary state of affairs is taking place." The first announcement of a gold sighting in California appeared, rather unobtrusively, on the back page of San Francisco's *Californian* newspaper. On March 15, 1848, *Californian* editor B. R. Buckelew publicized the discovery of precious metal in a tailrace at John Sutter's Mill on the American River. John Augustus Sutter, a Swiss-German settler who came to California in 1839, had received a land grant

Mexican government on which he founded a 48,827-acre colony ew Helvetia, located near present-day Sacramento. Buckelew's succinct ent read, "Gold Mine Found—In the newly made raceway of the Saw ecently erected by Captain Sutter, on the American Fork, gold has been found in considerable quantities. One person brought thirty dollars worth to New Helvetia, gathered there in a short time. California, no doubt, is rich in mineral wealth; great chances here for scientific capitalists."[39]

Ultimately, miners from around the world unearthed gold throughout a four-hundred-mile territory, extending from the Klamath River in the north to the Kern River in the south. This vast mineral region—called the Mother Lode—is among the richest gold deposits ever discovered. One estimate suggests that California's gold exports between 1848 and 1860 totaled $650 million, an astounding sum in nineteenth-century terms.[40]

Two months after Buckelew's brief description of the discovery appeared in print, Edward C. Kemble—editor of the *Californian's* rival, the *California Star*—reported his hopes and apprehensions for the new mines: "There is an area explored, within which a body of 50,000 men can advantageously labor. Without maliciously interfering with each other, then, there need be no cause for contention and discord, where as yet, we are gratified to know, there is harmony and good feeling existing." Kemble continued, "We really hope no unpleasant occurrences will grow out of this enthusiasm, and that our apprehensions may be quieted by continued patience and good will among the washers." As many immigrants to California later found out, Kemble's unease had ample justification.[41]

Faxon Atherton was among those who were incredulous at the news. He wrote to Thomas Larkin, "It is reported here that California is *all gold*, probably a little *glitter* has blinded them . . . a good copper or coal mine is worth more than any gold mine ever discovered." Like the skepticism of many Chileans and North Americans, Atherton's doubts proved ephemeral. On August 19, 1848, the *New York Herald* became the first East Coast newspaper to report the gold discovery. That same day, a cargo of California gold arrived in Chile aboard the brig *J.R.S.*, owned by affluent Valparaíso merchant José Ramón Sánchez. Ten days later, the schooner *Adelaida* docked at the port laden with $2,500 in Californian gold dust.[42]

Further confirmation for aspiring prospectors came on December 5, 1848, when President Polk announced, "The accounts of the abundance of gold in that territory are of such an extraordinary character as would scarcely command belief were they not corroborated by the authentic reports of officers in the public service." As more vessels arrived from California, Chileans witnessed incontrovertible evidence that the gold strike was, indeed, something more than "a little glitter." The *Huntress* sailed into Valparaíso harbor on February 5, 1849, sixty days out of San Francisco, with a ballast of one hundred thousand pesos' worth of gold. There could no longer be any doubt that immense wealth existed in the Sierra Nevada foothills.[43]

The promise of extraordinary treasure inspired thousands of Chileans to seek their fortunes in the icy mountain streams of the Sierra Nevada, but no extant documents reveal exactly when the first Chilean Argonauts arrived in California. As Anglo forty-niner William Perkins observed, "The immigration of Chile is much more of a mixed character. Men of all classes have come from there; for Chile is not only a seaboard country, but its people are infinitely more enterprising than any other of the Spanish Republics of South America; and they have a very respectable marine." This was to be the final voyage for many of the ships in Chile's merchant fleet. Gold-smitten crews and passengers abandoned most of these vessels after arriving at San Francisco.[44]

Frequently, North American ships bound for California called at the Chilean ports of Talcahuano or Valparaíso to replenish their stocks of fruits and vegetables, take on freshwater, and allow passengers to stretch their sea legs or receive medical treatment. Between December 7, 1848, and December 31, 1849, 762 ships from Canada and the United States sailed around Cape Horn at the southern tip of South America, bound for California. Of this total, 430—or 56 percent—stopped at a Chilean port after they had entered the Pacific Ocean (map 2).[45]

Yankees who sojourned in Chile during the early years of the gold rush commented on the fervor with which the South American nation responded to California's news. Henry David Cooke visited California in 1848 and then returned to Valparaíso, where he stayed with his sister, Sara, and her husband, US consul William G. Moorhead. Cooke wrote home to his family in Newport, Rhode Island, on November 29, 1848, "Every body here and all along this Coast, as far as Panama, are in a great state of excitement on account of the news of the discovery of the gold Mines in California." Cooke quipped, "I have been asked so many questions since I arrived here that I have learned to hate the sound of the word 'gold-mine.'"[46]

By August 1849, gold fever had saturated Chile's port cities. San Francisco resident Howard C. Gardiner spoke to a ship's captain just back from Chile: "He told me that he had put in at Talcuhana [*sic*] for supplies, and on his arrival found the whole country in a state of wildest excitement over the news recently received of the discovery of gold in California." Having sailed from New York in eighty-eight days, George Bruce Jr. arrived in Valparaíso on April 6, 1852. As he wrote to his father, "Great quantities of Chilians have gone to [California] within the last months and complaints are made on [account] of the great loss of population." Such grievances emerged in a variety of venues.[47]

More than a few Chileans fretted about the ramifications of a mass exodus to California. On December 28, 1848, Chile's leading paper, *El Mercurio*, warned of devastating labor shortages and debilitating financial losses that would result from the departure of thousands of Chileans. As residents of Valparaíso boarded ships for San Francisco, Rafael Minvielle, the director of the city's drama school, hastily penned a play titled *Ya no voy a California* (I'm not going to California). The theatrical production, a hollow satire aimed at dissuading potential emigrants, opened at Santiago's Teatro de La República on the same day that *El Mercurio*'s cautionary editorial appeared in print. Neither the playhouse performance nor a subsequent Valparaíso show received favorable reviews. Critics agreed that *Ya no voy a California* was the worst production of Minvielle's career. In fact, on the play's opening night in Santiago, two hecklers tossed a turkey onto the stage. Even so, the drama played to thousands of Chileans and contributed to the ensuing debate over the detrimental effects of gold fever on the country's well-being.[48]

During the months following the play's disastrous debut, Chilean vessels sailed for California in droves. Writing from Valparaíso, a correspondent for Connecticut's *Hartford Daily Courant* described the emigration from Chile: "Our Consul informed me that more than two thousand of the inhabitants of this port had taken passports and gone up to California, and that they were continually going from every part of the western coast." Likewise, when New Yorker Elias P. Overton's ship stopped at Valparaíso in June 1849, Overton heard that "the news from California is very flattering and the Chilians are selling out by hundreds, and paying very high prices for a passage." Advertisements in Chilean newspapers announced available berths aboard departing vessels. One such notice read: "*For San Francisco, California:* The very beautiful and swift-sailing national frigate, the 'California Dorado,' of 500-tons, accepting cargo and passengers, favoring those who have the means."[49]

Although quite a few scholars have estimated the number of Chileans who came to California during the gold rush, most have failed to supply adequate supporting evidence for their figures. These headcounts range from as low as "thousands" to as high as fifty thousand. In 1850, the seventh decennial US census contained the first attempt to calculate California's post-annexation population. However, the omission of three crucial California counties—San Francisco, Contra Costa, and Santa Clara—from that survey has made accurate counts difficult. These three regions, among California's twenty-seven organized counties at the time, were territories where many Chileans resided during the early years of the gold rush (see map 3). In one of a litany of vanishings discussed in this book, the results for these critical counties never made it to Washington, DC. A fire destroyed the San Francisco census documents, while couriers lost the folios for Contra Costa and Santa Clara counties. The remaining twenty-four counties had a combined recorded population of 92,597.[50]

The surviving California census data are notoriously inaccurate. Many Chileans harbored a strong suspicion of government surveyors. In Chile, noncompliance among the poor was especially widespread because landless peasants tended to suffer the most from the taxes and episodes of military conscription that followed national head counts. During the Chilean census of 1875, British consul Horace Rumbold reported that in many regions "nearly all the 'peones' or labourers . . . took to the hills for refuge." As Rumbold noted, "The pervading fear seems to have been either that war was declared and a forced 'levée en masse' intended, or that the heads of the population were to be counted, preparatory to the imposition of a poll-tax." Chileans brought this mistrust to California. When interrogated by California's census takers, they often contrived ridiculous names for themselves, such as *el cabrón* (the bastard), *mamacita* (hot mama), and *greaser* (a derogatory term for Latinos). A surfeit of awkward transliterations of Spanish surnames among the California census records suggests that few of the data collectors spoke Spanish.[51]

Despite the patchwork quality of extant demographic data, there is ample evidence for calculating the number of Chileans who resided in California during the gold rush. Studies of nineteenth-century Chilean emigration data, examinations of the California and US censuses, and indexes of passports issued to Chileans departing for San Francisco strongly suggest that at least eight thousand Chileans came to California between 1848 and 1853.[52]

The influx of Chileans received widespread commentary in California's popular press. As San Francisco's major English-language paper, the *Daily Alta California*, reported in the spring of 1851: "The city appears full of Chilenos who have lately arrived, and who present a singular appearance, parading the street with their short ponchos and turned up straw hats. They are an unoffending and industrious race, and are about proceeding to the mines." Along the backbone of the Cordillera, the Americas were being remade once again.[53]

Spanish imperial expansion along the eastern Pacific Rim, British and French exploration beyond the aquatic boundaries of the Atlantic World, an unrelenting global hunt for marine mammals, and expanding US commercial and strategic interests on North America's western shores created new maritime circuits of trade and migration throughout the eighteenth- and nineteenth-century Pacific

World. Between 1786 and the mid-nineteenth-century gold rush, ships served as the dispersal agents that brought the biotas and people of Chile and California into sustained contact.

Like so many other vectors connecting Chile and California, La Pérouse and his expedition eventually disappeared. After *L'Astrolabe* and *La Boussole* departed from Botany Bay, Australia, in March 1788, they ran aground on a coral reef and sank near Vanikoro, one of the Solomon Islands. Although curious mariners and teams of determined archaeologists spent years searching for clues about the lost expedition, it was not until 2005 that divers discovered the sunken ships and confirmed their identities as La Pérouse's frigates. Fortunately, the explorer had sent his journals back to France in installments from Kamchatka Peninsula and Botany Bay. Without this precaution, his valuable observations—and our knowledge of the botanical connection he forged between Chile and California—would have been lost to posterity.[54]

A Venice of Pine

The poet W. H. Auden once wrote, "Every port has its name for the sea." Before the Mexican War, the Spanish-speaking residents of Alta California called the entrance to San Francisco Bay La Boca del Puerto de San Francisco, or "the mouth of the Port of San Francisco." John C. Frémont, who served as the US military governor of California during the early months of 1847, renamed it the Golden Gate. Despite this nominal shift, the underlying metaphor of consumption remained fitting for the Pacific port city. It was through the Golden Gate that immigrants and commodities from around the world fueled California's insatiable appetite. Because of San Francisco's rapid transformation from peripheral port to global commercial hub, this "instant city" demonstrates how flows of migrants and matter combine to reshape urban space.[1]

Chile made indispensable contributions to California's spectacular growth. Chilean ships and wheat provided the literal foundations for San Francisco's swift territorial and demographic expansions during the mid-1800s. Beginning in 1848, the city's developers incorporated nearly all of Chile's merchant fleet into an expanding network of wharves and landfill, initiating a process known as *landmaking*. Such extensions of solid ground have received little scholarly attention, despite being among the most important human modifications of the world's coastal zones. San Francisco's waterfront history aptly demonstrates the contingency of nineteenth-century shoreline development on displacements of materials from faraway regions.

Just as Chilean ships provided key anchor points for the extension of San Francisco's piers and landfill, wheat from Chile fed the city's burgeoning population. During the mid-1800s, merchants sold 72,575 metric tons of Chilean wheat flour to the city's newcomers. Because of Chile's unique position as a wheat-producing nation relatively close to California, the South American nation furnished most of the flour consumed by California's gold rush population. As the distinguished Chilean poet and diplomat Juan Guzmán Cruchaga reminisced a century after the gold rush, "The early settlers in California supplied themselves with Chilean merchandise and without this assistance they would have probably perished."[2]

In turn, this boom in wheat exports triggered profound agrarian changes in Chile. Among the most important of these was the clearing of hundreds of thousands of acres of native forest in Chile's south-central provinces to open land for wheat cultivation. This alteration of traditional land-use patterns exposed these regions to swift colonization by Monterey pines during the twentieth century. The Chilean wheat trade with California was therefore an exchange because of its profound effects on both places. Chilean biota also altered California's agricultural practices. By the late 1850s, California began producing large volumes of its own grain, and Chile Club wheat (*Triticum compactum*) was among the most successful varieties for the Golden State's farmers.[3]

For the eight thousand Chileans who disembarked at California's docks during the mid-1800s, the San Francisco waterfront was the aperture through which a strangely familiar world came into focus. A quintessential image of the California gold rush is William Shew's five-plate daguerreotype, "San Francisco from Rincon Point" (fig. 3).

Figure 3. William Shew, "Panorama of the waterfront" (1853). Roy D. Graves Pictorial Collection. *Courtesy of the Bancroft Library, University of California, Berkeley.*

This sepia-toned panorama offers a striking view of the so-called forest of masts jutting skyward from the hundreds of ships that crammed San Francisco's Yerba Buena Cove at the start of the gold rush. "The ships in the harbour [look] like a cedar swamp," wrote a Bostonian who sailed through the Golden Gate in September 1849. "Ships are arriving here every day," continued Thomas Reid. "I went up the mast head and tried to count them but they were so thick I found it impossible." No wonder Reid had trouble calculating the number of boats anchored in the bay: the San Francisco Harbormaster's Records show that 39,888 people arrived aboard 805 ships between April 1849 and January 1850.[4]

Many of these vessels never returned to their home ports. By July 1850, five hundred ships lay abandoned in San Francisco Harbor, their crews having hurried off to pan for gold in the Sierra. A Chilean immigrant wrote home from San Francisco that the captain of his vessel had permitted most of the ship's sailors to head for the mines, "so there were only four men to unload approximately one thousand two hundred tons of cargo."[5]

Some of the abandoned ships fell victim to entrepreneurial scavengers who salvaged leftover cargoes, brass and copper fittings, and rare hardwoods, all of which fetched high prices in the city. In the 1850s, pioneer businessman Charles Hare employed Chinese laborers from a nearby fishing village to disassemble ships moored off the Market Street Wharf. Hare reclaimed and sold everything from the iron bolts to the cordage of the waterlogged wooden carcasses. Other vessels succumbed to the flames of the eight separate fires that blazed throughout the city between December 1849 and June 1851.[6]

The ships that survived often ended up as anchor points in an intricate network of wharves, earthen fill, foundation piles, and gangplanks. Hundreds of hulking wooden structures, which had once cruised the world's oceans, became makeshift storehouses, hotels, hospitals, prisons, and saloons. Connecticut pioneer Linville Hall lamented the degradation of his ship into one of these landlocked stockrooms: "Many buildings have been erected for business purposes, on piles over the waters of the bay, and many hulls of ships that rounded the Horn have been driven as far as possible toward the shores, to serve as storerooms for the rapid increase of merchandise." In fact, the demand to send all seaworthy vessels to California helped purge aging fleets from East Coast harbors and stimulated a shipbuilding bonanza in the Northeast.[7]

Likewise, ships crowded with anxious passengers departed en masse from Valparaíso and Talcahuano, clearing out a generation of timeworn seacraft from Chile's ports. Most of these vessels spent their last days beached along the mudflats of San Francisco Bay. In 1850, British miner William Kelly described the Chilean merchant ship *Niantic*, landlocked at the foot of Clay Street, as "a fine vessel of 1,000 tons, no longer a buoyant ship, surmounted by lofty spars and streamers in the wind, but a tenement anchored in the mud, covered with a shingle roof, subdivided into stores and offices and painted over with signs and showboards of the various occupants." The *Niantic* had sailed from Liverpool to Valparaíso in the 1820s. The Chilean company Morehead, Whitehead and Waddington eventually purchased it and sent it to haul cargo and passengers from Panama to San Francisco.[8]

James J. Ayers, a recent arrival from Missouri, met a group of sailors who had recently beached the *Niantic*: "The hulk was snugly in place, at the northeast corner of Clay and Sansome streets. My friends told me all about how they had floated the *Niantic* over the shallow flat. They lashed the empty oil casks, with which she was abundantly supplied, to her bottom, and thus floated her by slow stages when the tide was high into the berth she was destined to occupy." Thus, the *Niantic* began its landlocked life as one of at least 140 ships turned into working structures by the beginning of 1850. A notice in the January 28, 1850, issue of the *Daily Alta California* advertised, "STORAGE—in the *Niantic* Warehouses, foot of Clay Street." The ship's owners also profited from their marooned vessel by supplying potable water to passersby from an artesian well bored under the *Niantic*'s stern. After the fires of that year, workers converted the scorched hull of the *Niantic* into the edifice of a guesthouse, which locals considered to be San Francisco's top hotel at the time. The Niantic Hotel housed boarders until its demolition in 1872 (fig. 4).[9]

The profitability of converting ships into waterfront structures was driven by astronomically high lumber prices from 1849 onward. As the captain of the ship *Suliot* discovered, spruce boards from Belfast, Maine, fetched thirty times their purchasing price when sold in California. Likewise, in August 1849, Chilean merchant José Ignacio Palma heard news of the demand for construction materials and packed his vessel *Balance* with eight hundred tons of wooden planks before his ship departed Talcahuano for California.[10]

Prices for imported lumber were amplified by shortages of local timber. After loggers quickly depleted woodlots around the city, developers extended their search for wood into Oakland's five-square-mile coast redwood (*Sequoia sempervirens*) forest. Lumberjacks cut every one of the trees, some over three hundred feet tall, by 1860. Two of the tallest redwood trees that sawyers felled from this stand had once guided captains toward the Golden Gate from sixteen miles offshore. By 1872, one-third of California's forests had been cut down.[11]

The transformation of vessels into impromptu buildings thus made sound financial sense. When forty-niner George Payson returned to San Francisco in early 1851, he found that "the most striking feature was the old hulks lying in the

Figure 4. Francis S. Marryat, "High and Dry." Lithograph, 1855. The Niantic Hotel is depicted as the second building from the right. *Courtesy of the Bancroft Library, University of California, Berkeley.*

very heart of the city, with streets and houses all about them, and suggesting vague and puzzling analogies to the ark on Mount Ararat." Surrounded by earthen fill and connected by wooden planks, these ships became part of a dense matrix of waterfront property. By 1852, the harbormaster concluded that 164 vessels served as permanent structures along the city's shoreline.[12]

The sight of so many landlocked ships made a lasting impression on immigrants to the city. After disembarking from his own brig onto this city of condemned boats, Chilean diplomat Benjamín Vicuña Mackenna aptly nicknamed San Francisco's waterfront "a Venice of pine in place of marble." The *Niantic* was just one of many Chilean vessels immobilized in this wooden district. By December 1849, 92 of Chile's 119 registered ships were moored in San Francisco Bay: their passengers and crews were trekking to the mines or testing their entrepreneurial skills in California's emerging frontier towns.[13]

Chilean shipowner Wenceslao Urbistondo found an opportune use for his vessel on arrival in San Francisco: "Taking advantage of the high tide, he beached his ship in San Francisco and transformed it into a comfortable boarding house." Urbistondo toppled his masts and employed them as an impromptu bridge between the ship's stern and Vallejo Street, thereby connecting his hostel to a thriving commercial stretch of shoreline real estate.[14]

San Francisco was not the first North American metropolis to experience large-scale landmaking along its tidal margin. Many decades before North America's colonies achieved independence from Britain, tenacious developers in New York and Boston extended wharves outward from their shores, creating new terra firma by filling the spaces between these man-made extensions of the landscape. Bostonians commenced landmaking in the mid-1600s and more than doubled the acreage of the city's peninsula by 1900.[15]

Although the process of landmaking in San Francisco bore similarities to the ways East Coast cities had developed their waterfronts, hundreds of abandoned ships in Northern California's principal harbor added a new element to the list of ingredients in the typical "fill" of earth, boulders, and wood pilings. In 1916, the journalist Walter J. Thompson dubbed these landlocked vessels "the Argonauts' Armada of golden dreams . . . sepulchered in the clammy ooze beneath the tread of scurrying thousands and uproar of a great city's industry." The burial of ships beneath the city was a quite literal production of invisibility. To this day, archaeologists, construction crews, and landowners have unearthed forty-two partially intact ships from under the city's streets and have marked some of their locations with small brass plaques set into San Francisco's sidewalks. Scores more, many of them Chilean, lie submerged below nearly two centuries of accumulated waterfront development.[16]

Landmaking on such a vast scale dramatically reoriented the city's commercial life. The beached fleet of vessels among the waterfront fill served as storehouses for many Chilean products. The *John Brewer*, moored near Pacific Wharf, and the *Eleanor* and the *York*, both wedged along the California Street Wharf, became convenient depots for the Chilean *harina* (flour) and *trigo* (wheat) imported by the firms of W. Meyer and Co., Cramer, Rambach and Co., and Isaac Friedlander. It was from waterfront repositories such as these that wheat grown almost six thousand miles away in Chile fed California's hungry population.[17]

Between 1848 and 1854, nearly everyone who set foot in California tasted bread, flapjacks, pies, cakes, or biscuits baked with Chilean flour. As forty-niner Lorena Hays wrote in 1853: "We eat flour, sugar and dried fruit from Chile which seems very strange to a resident of the United States." During the gold rush, Chile exported eight hundred thousand barrels (72,575 metric tons) of its principal agricultural commodity to California. As a result, Chilean flour became a ubiquitous ingredient in the meals served at mining camps, restaurants, and home kitchens across the state. This flour was, in the words of Lieutenant Isaac

Strain, "of a fine quality, and of a flavour unsurpassed in any part of the world which I have visited." One forty-niner recalled a rest stop along an overland trail to the gold mines where he and his companions dined on bread "baked for us by a lady at the ranch, and was very good indeed and made from flour imported from Chile." Likewise, the first commercial bakers in San Joaquin County— Louis Mersfelder, Charles Potter, and John Inglis—baked bread exclusively with Chilean flour.[18]

In the mid-1800s, milled Chilean wheat was often the only flour available in California. New Yorker Daniel Knower recollected that in Stockton during 1850, "About all the grain and flour came from Valparaiso and Chili, put up very nicely in fifty and one hundred pound sacks, so it was easy to handle." The packaging in which Chilean flour reached California gave the product marked advantages over the milled wheat shipped from North America's eastern ports. East Coast flour came in cumbersome wooden barrels; their contents had to be unloaded and repacked in bags before supply caravans could carry the flour to the mining districts. Not only was the journey from the Atlantic Seaboard to California six months or more—compared to just four or five weeks from Chile—but the flour shipped from the Northeast suffered from double exposure to the humidity and increased temperatures of two equatorial crossings (see map 2). North Carolina writer Hinton Helper explained, "As these provisions are sent around by Cape Horn, they must pass through the tropics before they arrive in San Francisco; consequently, most of them become more or less sour, musty, or rancid, which, as we all know, renders them not only repugnant to the palate, but also injurious to health." In contrast, Chilean flour could be shipped aboard swift clipper ships in burlap sacks without risk of perishing. Stevedores unloaded these bags in San Francisco or the inland port cities of Stockton, Marysville, and Sacramento. There, workers immediately packed the flour sacks onto donkey trains bound for the scores of camps and outposts scattered throughout the Sierra Nevada. As the Chilean diplomat Benjamín Vicuña Mackenna noted, in the mid-1850s, bags of milled Chilean wheat sold for an average of thirty pesos in San Francisco, while the price of identical sacks of flour in Valparaíso was only eight pesos.[19]

The hallmark of an exchange, as I have defined it, is that the connection affects both of the places involved. This was most certainly the case with the Chile-California flour trade. Chilean *hacendados* (estate owners) responded to California's burgeoning food demands by expanding their wheat farms. This single-crop regime spread into new areas of the fertile Aconcagua Valley and the regions around Talcahuano and the Maule River. Captain George Coffin, who anchored his ship *Alhambra* at Valparaíso on August 16, 1849, remarked,

"In the staple article of flour California has opened a new and extensive demand, and hundreds of acres are now in wheat where last year was nothing but weeds and thistles."[20]

In its early years, the Chilean flour trade with California implied the emergence of a vibrant, long-term economic relationship. As forty-niner James Morrison contended, "Chile and the United States have never been so intimately connected in interest as at present. For some years to come California will probably be dependent on this country as she is in a great measure at present for her breadstuffs. This will operate as a strong bond to bind the two countries more closely." Indeed, commercial relations with Chile in the mid-1800s were significant enough to merit mention in the State of the Union addresses of three presidents: James K. Polk (December 5, 1848); Zachary Taylor (December 4, 1849), who died just sixteen months into his term; and Millard Fillmore (December 2, 1850).[21]

The Chilean economy experienced a five-year boom after the emergence of the export trade with California. Diplomatic historian Henry Clay Evans argued that the flour business had such a resounding effect on Chile that "money was borrowed on the strength of future exports; with it palatial homes were built and speculative enterprises of all kinds were started." Balie Peyton, the US minister to Chile during the gold rush, sent a dispatch to Washington on March 24, 1850, in which he discussed the profound consequences that the opening of the California market generated for Chile's farmers: "Before [the gold rush] the agricultural interests of Chile were in a deplorable state of depression ... whereas Chile has sent to California within the last year more than a million [dollars'] worth of her agricultural products." California's soaring fortunes had—at least momentarily—resuscitated the Chilean economy.[22]

The development and maintenance of Chile's wheat trade with California depended on the shipping capacities of an international merchant fleet. The US Customs House officer for San Francisco listed 143 cargo ships that arrived from Valparaíso or Talcahuano between 1849 and 1853. Almost all of the commercial officers aboard these vessels declared Chilean flour their principal freight. The ships involved in the wheat trade carried enormous quantities, transporting as much as 750,000 pounds of flour per voyage. The brigantine *Castor*, like many of its fellow grain transports, sailed from Talcahuano to San Francisco in 1850 loaded with 3,750 bags of flour, each weighing 200 pounds. Given the success of this transnational transportation network and the explosive demand for foodstuffs generated by California's rapidly expanding population, it is hardly surprising that Chile's wheat exports to California grew by nearly 1,000 percent between 1848 and 1850.[23]

In the early years of the gold rush, the system of exchange for a wide range of imported products—including flour—amounted to little more than a water-borne circus. As ships approached San Francisco Bay, tenacious businessmen vied with each other to clamor aboard, survey the contents of cargo holds, and purchase valuable goods to sell onshore. Charles Ross, a trader from New Jersey, recounted that in 1849, "Merchants would board vessels at the Heads [on either side of the entrance to San Francisco Bay], and offer in some cases a hundred percent advance, without looking at the invoice, for the entire cargo, no matter what it consisted of." The Golden Gate served as a literal "threshold of exchange" in which the market consisted more of a bounded physical space than an omnipresent organizational principle.[24]

The theatrics of this nautical commerce featured the visible hands of market players. "We had our boats, and men on the lookout for us, and when a vessel came in, there was quite a rush of boats to board her, and the merchant who got to the vessel first was generally the luckiest fellow," wrote businessman James R. Garniss. "There were no regular prices and we made what we could." Prussian merchant Harris Newmark found that the unanticipated entrance of a cargo ship through the Golden Gate could easily ruin the fortunes of traders who depended on shortages to drive up prices. In the 1850s, when "red beans then commanded a price of twelve and a half cents per pound . . . a sailing vessel from Chile unexpectedly landed a cargo in San Francisco and sent the price dropping to a cent and a quarter; when commission men, among them myself, suffered heavy losses." At other times, however, this unpredictable price variability generated splendid yields for lucky vendors.[25]

The prices of flour from Chile astounded San Francisco resident William Redmond Ryan. In the winter of 1848–49 he found that in the city, "Chili flour sold lately as high as $45 per sack of 200 [pounds], on shore. . . . A vessel came in from Chili when the rage was at its height. She cleared $50,000 gain to the shipper, and made $10,000 commissions to the consignee." Another miner recalled that his party paid exorbitant prices for Chilean flour "in anticipation of a scarcity." Meanwhile, in the northern mines, where food was in short supply, sacks of Chilean flour fetched $100 apiece during the spring of 1849.[26]

On occasion, a surfeit of flour portended disaster for San Francisco's grain traders. A general oversupply of goods—punctuated by shortages resulting from devastating fires, torrential downpours, and unanticipated influxes of immigrants—perpetuated the city's boom-and-bust cycle. Wheat was no exception. In October 1849, the grain market reached saturation. Thomas Reid lamented the flour wasted in the market glut: "I saw four or five thousand dollars worth of flour on the beach / it was Chillian flour put up in bags / the bags were rotting off the flour on account of being exposed to the air." The adventurers who stepped off boats onto the city's ramshackle walkways did not find the streets of their El Dorado paved in gold. A French journalist captured the bizarre scene: "There was the famous sidewalk in San Francisco on the west side of Montgomery Street composed of 100 pound bags of Chilean flour, a long line of cooking stoves, a damaged piano which bridged a gully, and ending in a double row of boxes of shoes."[27]

By the 1850s, a single commission house, the Chile and California Flour Company, dominated the wheat trade with Chile. The US Customs House Records for 1850 are replete with invoices for flour shipped by this prominent firm. Although this concentration of purchasing power diminished the chaotic aspects of grain buying, it did not stabilize commodity prices. Englishman J. G. Player-Frowd contended that hundred-pound bags of flour, which would have sold for five or six dollars in Chile, went for fifteen to twenty dollars in the mines because merchants withheld supply to stimulate demand. A pioneer merchandiser from New Jersey recalled that the monopoly on grain trading caused prices to skyrocket throughout 1850, driving shipments up. Toward the end of the year, such an enormous surplus of Chilean flour filled San Francisco's storehouses that prices collapsed, "scarcely paying costs and charges."[28]

The reasons for this crash were straightforward. In 1850, Morehead, Whitehead and Waddington, the representative agents of the Chile and California Flour Company and the owners of the beached storeship *Niantic*, made a $120,000 contract with the leading mills in Chile and four major San Francisco grain merchants. The company promised to deliver no fewer than 100,000 barrels of flour over the coming months. At the time, California faced a drastic grain shortage and prices were climbing to new highs. The deal seemed like a lucrative proposition to all parties involved, but in a concerted effort to time their shipments strategically, Morehead, Whitehead and Waddington became overzealous. When dozens of ships arrived at San Francisco harbor carrying more than 175,000 barrels of flour, the city's grain merchants recognized the impending market saturation. They bought only 50,000 barrels, paid a modest severance fine, and forfeited their remaining contractual obligations to the Chile and California Flour Company.[29]

Before 1855, the first year when the state's farmers produced a consistent and substantial supply of their own wheat, the irregular peaks and slumps in California's grain market had severe ramifications for the merchants involved. Without the ability to rapidly exchange information on prices, stockpiles, shipping details, and farming conditions, traders had to improvise ways to bridge the vast chasm between demand and supply. Like miners, who often squandered the fruits of their labors at gambling tables, the shareholders of the Chile and California Flour Company learned the hard way that high-stakes betting could leave the loser saddled with massive debts.

Meanwhile, Chilean wheat farmers and millers remained temporarily insulated from California's fluctuating markets. In addition to well-established customers in Peru and their newfound export outlet in California, Chile's grain merchants benefited from a new wave of Australian demand in 1851. That year, a series of gold strikes in New South Wales and Victoria drew an immense influx of miners. Eager to feed the waves of newcomers, Australian merchants turned to Chilean wheat. At their peak in 1855, annual exports of Chilean flour to Australia totaled 32,361 metric tons (2.7 million pesos/dollars), surpassing even the vast quantities exported to California.[30]

North American millers also profited from Chile's pivotal position in the transpacific wheat trade. During the decades following the end of British colonial rule, Yankees led the world in the development of grain-milling technologies. Delaware native Oliver Evans developed an automated flour-making mechanism during the 1780s. In *The Young Mill-Wright and Miller's Guide* (1795), Evans described his innovative system, which linked conveyor belts, elevators, and a "hopper boy," a device to spread the flour as it cooled. This integrated process, which predated Ford's assembly line by more than 130 years, revolutionized the volumes of flour and rates of grinding that a miller could achieve.[31]

As millwrights mastered these new production techniques, they found their skills in high demand. During the mid-nineteenth century, a number of them boarded vessels for Valparaíso or Talcahuano to run mills in central Chile's wheat-producing regions. New Yorker David W. Cunningham stopped in Valparaíso in 1853, writing, "I have now been ten days acquainted with Mr. Allen who has been a year passed engaged in putting up flour mills in Talca [near the Maule River] and is now going home to send out some machinery." Likewise, Levi Floyd Walker, who visited Talcahuano on his way from Maine to San Francisco, visited a highly profitable steam flourmill, which had been built "and is owned by a Yankee formerly from Bangor [Maine]." Another Yankee, Silas Smith, supplied his technical expertise to the nearby Corinto Mill. By the early 1870s, Chile boasted 130 modern mills.[32]

While North Americans were helping to develop the Chilean milling business, other Yankees began cultivating wheat in California. On November 3, 1851, the *New York Daily Times* announced somewhat prematurely that in California "a home agriculture has been introduced, which promises, in another year, to supply the entire population with flour." California still required massive imports of flour, but by the early 1850s, kiln-drying techniques made it possible for the state's food merchants to import cheaper wheat from the Atlantic coast. Once East Coast exporters began to use swift-sailing clipper ships to transport their agricultural cargo, they mounted a significant challenge to Chile's dominance of the transpacific flour market.[33]

By 1854, California was still importing a majority of its wheat, but the editor of the *California Farmer* suggested that his state might soon reach self-sufficiency in grain production. That goal became reality the following year. In an ironic reversal of fortunes, California shipped its first cargoes of homegrown wheat to Chile during the winter of 1855–56. Looking back on California's midcentury agricultural revolution, the Reverend Albert Williams—founder and pastor of San Francisco's First Presbyterian Church—reflected, "By degrees, home production has arisen. The fact began to be palpable and make its impression when the soil yielded to the husbandman its teeming product of golden wheat. Chilean and Richmond [Virginia] breadstuffs long since disappeared from our markets." By 1856, California's farmers had planted more than two hundred thousand acres of wheat. One year later, San Francisco land speculator and financier Alexander B. Grogan wrote to his friend Faxon D. Atherton in Valparaíso, "There will be ample supply of [California] wheat and barley for home consumption and a surplus for exports."[34]

During California's emergence as a self-sufficient grain producer, a key Chilean ingredient fueled the young state's expanding productive capacities. The stout and hard-grained Chile Club wheat (*Triticum compactum*), introduced to California in 1853, became one of California's most popular export crops. In the 1860s, historian John S. Hittell remarked that Californians cultivated many varieties of wheat, but "the Chili gives general satisfaction, and is more cultivated than the others." Millers valued Chilean wheat for its firm texture. Hittell continued, "In flintiness or dryness, Californian wheat has no superior, and no equal save in the Chilian."[35]

The success of Chilean wheat varieties on California's farms surprised many Yankee agriculturalists. After President James Monroe sent Theodorick Bland on a special diplomatic mission to South America in 1817–18, the Virginia physician and statesman brought back seeds of Chilean Club wheat. Attempts at cultivation in the Northeast fared poorly because of disparities in soil conditions and climatological differences between central Chile and New England. Yet Chilean wheat thrived in the familiar terrain and Mediterranean climate of California's Central Valley. This successful botanical transfer mirrored similar botanical displacements of the potato, alfalfa, and the Monterey pine.[36]

During the late nineteenth century, farmers in California's Central Valley grew four varieties of Chilean wheat: White Chile, Red Chile, Bearded Chile, and Chilean Club. Of these, Chilean Club wheat was the most successful. In the 1850s, Judge Benjamin Hayes—who served as the first judge of the Southern District of California from 1852 to 1864—met one "Captain Bogart," a mariner-turned-farmer who had achieved tremendous yields from the wheat sown on his coastal ranch. "The wheat was raised in California from seed brought last year from Chili," remarked Hayes. Testimonials about the successes of Chilean wheat varieties abounded at midcentury. In 1871, a correspondent wrote to the *Banner* (Sutter County), "Tuesday morning we were shown some fine samples of bearded Chili wheat by Wm. Bush. . . . The yield will be immense. This grain will not shell out in the hot dry wind, like many other varieties."[37]

Domestic wheat production on this scale could hardly have been envisioned twenty years earlier. On November 20, 1852, Sonora (Tuolumne County) resident Elizabeth Le Breton Gunn wrote to family members in Philadelphia, complaining, "In consequence of the fires at San Francisco, Sacramento, and Marysville, and of the speculators holding back the flour, it has risen to the enormous price of sixty dollars a barrel, and it is said by those who know that it is likely to rise to one hundred dollars. We bought a barrel tonight and paid sixty dollars for it; three weeks ago it was only forty dollars. Don't you want to live in California?" As Gunn's acerbic comments suggested, both flour prices and the state's wood-framed boomtowns were liable to implode with little warning.[38]

Although San Francisco's "Venice of pine" provided a network of storage spaces, dwellings, and commercial establishments, this timber labyrinth turned out to be a volatile arrangement. Six major fires ravaged the city between 1849 and 1851, shaking residents' faith in the suitability of wooden buildings. As the Reverend Albert Williams pointed out, the fires stimulated commerce by creating demand for construction materials and labor. The conflagrations rid the city of outmoded wooden structures and made room for new brick-and-mortar edifices, which required the skills of thousands of construction workers. In the summer of 1853 alone, San Franciscans erected more than six hundred such structures.[39]

Although gold was California's economic cornerstone, bricks constituted its more durable foundation. As historian Bill Deverell argued in his account of the Mexicans who made Los Angeles, "The color of brickwork is brown." Latino labor was fundamental to San Francisco's brickmaking business as well. Chileans and Mexicans filled the ranks of the reserve army of workers who built the city in the mid-nineteenth century. Chileans brought their brick manufacturing and masonry skills north, applying these abilities to the structural transformation of San Francisco's urban landscape.[40]

"There was a novel method of brick making going on," forty-niner William McCollum observed. In the early years of the gold rush, "a large number of Mexicans and Chillians, were molding them from clay, 8 by 18 inches, and drying them in the sun. When laid in housewalls they were plastered on the inside with sand and clay, and made a tolerable good substitute for the ordinary burnt brick." Higher-quality kiln-fired bricks, prepared by Chilean and Mexican laborers at brickyards around San Francisco Bay, commanded extraordinary prices. At the beginning of 1849, Garnkirk and Stourbridge charged forty-five dollars per thousand bricks, but at other times, prices rose as high as a dollar each.[41]

Premium brickwork buttressed the elaborate commercial structures of post-1851 San Francisco. At least a dozen Chilean bricklayers worked on William C. Ralston's Palace Hotel at the corner of Market and New Montgomery Streets. The eight-floor luxury structure cost five million dollars to build, occupied an entire city block, and required "24,660,596 hard bricks." Ironically, the walls that Chileans built formed the contours of an increasingly segregated city. When the hotel opened in 1875, it divided Nob Hill's mansions from the working-class neighborhood south of Market Street.[42]

In many instances, San Francisco's foundations were—quite literally—Chilean ships and buildings that relied on Chilean brickwork. San Franciscans and prospectors throughout the state ate imported Chilean flour, much of which had been milled by Yankee expatriates who resided along South America's western shores. Chilean farmers responded to this new transpacific demand by expanding their estates, often in regions that would later be converted into plantations of a tree native to California, the Monterey pine. The emergence of California's highly speculative wheat trade contrasted starkly with the development of far more reliable harvests of its own Chilean Club wheat, a displacement that anchored the Golden State's midcentury agricultural boom. Fortunes in Chile and California had become inextricably entangled.

3

CHILECITO AND SPANISHTOWN

On April 10, 1866, journalist Bret Harte mailed his weekly installment from California to the Boston-based Unitarian paper the *Christian Register*. In evocative prose, Harte depicted his visit to San Francisco's oldest graveyard, the Mission Dolores Cemetery, contrasting "the strife and turmoil of the ocean" with the serene burial ground, tucked behind the mission's well-worn adobe walls. "The Mission hills lovingly embrace the little graveyard, and break the summer gales," he wrote, adding, "The foreign flavor is strong."[1]

The granite headstones of three Chileans contributed to this "foreign flavor." Louis de Cross, Marie Ruiz, and Carmelita Besa each died young and received a Catholic burial from the Mission Dolores padres in the mid-1850s (fig. 5). Before their untimely death, these three individuals had been part of a much larger diaspora from Chile. On arriving at California's "Venice of pine," many Chilean women, men, and children settled in a thriving barrio at the foot of Telegraph Hill, which they proudly called Chilecito (Little Chile). Others traveled south to the Santa Clara Valley, where they worked in the New Almaden mercury mines and established a community called Spanishtown. Along with their fellow Latin American immigrants, Chileans in San Francisco and New Almaden formed *juntas patrióticas* (patriotic associations), which connected them to California's burgeoning Latino communities and linked them to political and cultural developments in their home countries.

Today, a shoebox-sized brass plaque embedded in the concrete sidewalk of San Francisco's Columbus Avenue and a weathered cemetery in the New Almaden woods are the only remaining physical markers of Chilecito and Spanishtown, yet these sites were once focal points of the extensive Chilean presence in Northern California. Little Chile was also a crucible of interethnic

Figure 5. Gravestone of Louis de Cross "late of Chili." Mission Dolores Cemetery, San Francisco. *Photograph by author.*

conflict during the summer of 1849 when a Yankee mob known as the Hounds ransacked the neighborhood, robbing, raping, and killing many of its residents. Writing in 1886, philosopher Josiah Royce defined nativism as "a hearty American contempt for things and institutions and people that are stubbornly foreign and that would not conform themselves to American customs and wishes." The attack on Chilecito exemplified nativist aggression and presaged the violent reception that Chileans encountered in California's mining regions.[2]

Chilecito and neighboring Chinatown also became the heart of San Francisco's sex-work district, forecasting later trends in the city's sexual geography. Writing about San Francisco's complex erotic landscape, gender studies scholar Nan Boyd highlighted the racialized layout of its prostitution: "At the start of the gold rush, a colony of Mexican and South American prostitutes settled on the southeastern slopes of Telegraph Hill, forming the nucleus of what would become the city's North Beach district." In the smoky saloons and bordello backrooms of San Francisco, prostitutes from Talcahuano, Coquimbo, and Valparaíso appealed to the erotic desires of lonely miners. Sex work in nineteenth-century San Francisco relied heavily on Latina laborers. Despite this, few historians have remarked on the working lives of these women, focusing instead on the city's Anglo and Chinese sex workers.[3]

During the early years of the gold rush, female companionship was in short supply. For some men, this gender imbalance presented novel opportunities to break with heterosexual conventions. As scholars such as sociologist Clare Sears have shown, the city's unusual mid-nineteenth-century demographics generated "spaces of possibility" in which cross-dressing, transgender explorations, and gay relationships flourished. Likewise, Nan Boyd has demonstrated that nineteenth-century San Francisco was a "wide-open town" where men frequently passed as women and homosexual sex was common.[4]

The prevailing social theorists of the day denied the possibility of any such alternatives and suggested that women furnished the moral bedrock of North America's frontier cities. "Woman, to society, is like a cement to the building of stone," declared one California immigrant. In letters, diaries, and published accounts of California life, San Francisco's first wave of male residents frequently mentioned the glaring shortage of females. According to such testimonials, this city of men desperately needed the social stability that women provided. Merchant and longtime Tahiti resident Edward Lucett wrote of gold rush San Francisco, "*Men* of all nations, and countries, and tongues, are assembled together at a spot, which two years ago was only known by name to the rest of the world: when I say men, I mean literally the masculine gender, as there is not one woman present to 500 men; consequently, the bull-like-herding of society may be imagined." Decrying the city's skewed sex ratio, Sacramento's *Placer Times* reported that during the month of July 1849, 3,565 men and only 49 women came to San Francisco by sea.[5]

This disparity made the Golden Gate a gendered entry point, as well as a doorway to potential riches. The merging of a bachelor frontier with a society founded on speculative capitalism bothered Victorian era propagandists and proselytizers. In general, the exodus of young men from rural towns to newly industrialized cities during the mid-1800s caused tremendous anxiety for middle-class moralists. Antebellum advice manuals warned of a new era of the confidence man. This most devious member of his species swindled and corrupted unsuspecting youth with a repertoire of wily mechanisms, from political deceits to investment scams. In these cautionary tales, the confidence man's female counterpart was the prostitute, an archetype embodying immorality and sexual lewdness. The more zealous midcentury moral primers contended that traffic with such women brought bodily disaster upon the individuals who partook of such sinful exchanges. In his *Lectures on the Formation of Character, Temptations and Mission of Young Men* (1853), the Reverend Rufus W. Clark maintained that visitation with prostitutes "palsies the limbs, shatters the frame, and makes every bone, muscle and nerve, an avenue of pain." Clark's diatribe was just one of many Victorian attempts to cleanse the body politic through aggressive new corporeal doctrines.[6]

San Francisco's Anglo press categorized most Chilean women as iniquitous harlots. To be sure, a few of California's courtesans from Valparaíso—such as the redoubtable club owner Felice Álvarez and Faxon D. Atherton's wife, Dominga de Goñi—earned reputations as ladies of high society in the City by the Bay. These women emphasized their whiteness and their European descent. Yet they were exceptions to the norm. Terms such as "virtuous lady" and "respectable female" offered convenient code words for "White, Anglo-Saxon, and Protestant." The editors of the *Daily Alta California* made no attempt to disguise their racial preferences and ethnic prejudices when they asserted in 1851, "We want an emigration of respectable females to California; of rosy-cheeked, 'down east' Yankee girls—of stout 'hoosier' and 'badger' lasses, who shall be wives to our farmers and mechanics, and mothers to a generation of native Yankee Californians." Chilean officials also espoused such views. In 1851, the Chilean consul in San Francisco, Samuel Price, claimed that the vast majority of Chilenos who had come to California were members of "the inferior class of the Chilean population."[7]

San Francisco's social commentators often used poor and dark-skinned Hispanic women as foils against which to imagine their ideal civilizing female. The editors of the *Annals of San Francisco* (1855) referred to the city's Latina residents with derision and contempt: "The Mexicans and Chileans, like the people of negro descent, were only of the commonest description. The women of all these various races were nearly all of the vilest character, and openly practiced the most shameful commerce. The lewdness of fallen white females is shocking enough to witness, but is far exceeded by the disgusting practices of these tawny visaged creatures." Remarks such as these fashioned a lasting equivalency between "brown-skinned" and "harlot."[8]

Chilean immigrants came to California from a culture that stigmatized women's work outside the home. Indeed, many nineteenth-century Chilean men considered female domestic work to be among the few *labores propias de su sexo* (labors appropriate to their sex). Once they arrived in California, it was not rare for Chilean women to deviate from these strictures of propriety. According to the state's 1852 census, twenty-six-year-old Mercedes Miranda of Mariposa County earned a living "catching wild horses." Her countrywoman, Marina Barjas, told the census taker that she was an independent farmer in Contra Costa County. In 1860, Francisca Muñoz ran a saloon in Calaveras County, while another Chilena, Josefa Rojas, owned a Tuolomne County bar. That same year, Petronila Ruiz turned out candies for sale in Fresno County, and Magdalena Lopez owned a Del Norte County dressmaking business near the Oregon border. Among the more fascinating Chilenas who transgressed social norms was Beatrice Peña Guadillo. After arriving in California, she traveled with Lee and Ryland's Cosmopolitan Circus and eventually gained notoriety for shooting her deceitful lover, Juan Morales, with "a small Sharp's four-shooter" on San Francisco's Jackson Street in 1867.[9]

The data collectors for the 1850, 1852, and 1860 California censuses listed some Chilenas as "housewives." Other women from Chile used their housekeeping skills outside of their own homes. Cleaning and cooking for wealthier California families offered opportunities for steady wages. In 1849, Margaret DeWitt complained to her mother about the cost of domestic laborers: "A number of families who came this spring and who commenced keeping house have been obliged to break up, and—the ladies return home as it was so expensive and difficult to get along without several servants and that besides the high wages cost a great deal—the Canacca [Native Hawaiian] and Chillians—are most the only kind here—and they are poor enough—and never know how to do more than one thing and then they are very clannish and have a great deal of company which costs more than family expenses." What these Hawaiian and Chilean housekeepers demanded in payment was probably on par with the going rate for gold rush era laborers. In the spring of 1849, J. D. Stevenson wrote to his son-in-law in New York City that "a woman servant, Indian or Chilian" cost "from $40 to $60" per month.[10]

Chilenas could frequently earn more if they sold their sexual labor in San Francisco. The most common employment designation for Chilean women in the 1852 and 1860 censuses was "prostitute." Such descriptions may well have been the products of census takers' racism, but they also likely reflected the fact that a substantial number of Chilenas in San Francisco worked in the sex trade.[11]

Infamous San Francisco madam Nell Kimball recalled meeting a retired prostitute called Old Sugar Mary who had known many Latina sex workers during the gold rush. In Kimball's words, "Old Sugar Mary said she remembered back to the first days of prostitution on an impressive scale; it was in the tents and shacks of the Mexican and South American whores called *Chilenos*. They worked the waterfront and the long climb up Telegraph Hill. The demand was steady and the work rewarding as the competition was only nigrahs and squaws." Once again, such accounts conflated race, class, and gender to suggest that Latinas, blacks, and California Indians made up the demographic profile of San Franciscan sex workers.[12]

This labor might have offered occasional financial rewards, but it followed the prevailing trends in the mines: a few struck it rich, while most barely kept up with their daily expenses in the overpriced world of gold rush California. As historian Patricia Nelson Limerick has pointed out, throughout the West, "most prostitutes did well to keep revenue a fraction ahead of overhead costs—rent, clothing, food, payoffs to law officers."[13]

Anglos tended to refer to these women with the same crude economic vocabulary they used when discussing other commodities. In an 1850 journal entry, twenty-two-year-old Timothy Coffin Osborn from Martha's Vineyard wrote, "Had a long and interesting chat with Gurney upon the 'sights' he saw in the little city of Stockton. He informed us of the steady importation of *'Ladies'* from the Atlantic side, and an increased immigration of *females* from Australia and China! Of the latter class he informs us the market is well supplied and 'trade' is light, with market quotations ranging from $50 to $100 *tout la nuit!"* Sex with prostitutes embodied the same speculative nature as transactions on the grain market. In a letter to "Our loved ones at home" from San Francisco on May 30, 1852, pioneer Mary Jane Megquier wrote, "Captain Mann arrived to day with a *cargo* of Chile women." "I got a crack at a very hansom girl last Sunday," miner Simon Stevens bragged to his Maine cousin in 1853. "It only cos mee a 20." Such comments exposed the bodily commerce at work in California's cities, towns, and mining camps.[14]

Although "hats were removed and bows executed" when the wealthier madams and the Anglo women in their charge sauntered along downtown streets, San Francisco men rarely extended the same courtesies to California Indian, Chilean, Mexican, and Chinese sex workers. Forty-niner Enos Christman complained in 1851, "The women of other nations, what few there are, are nearly all lewd harlots, who are drunk half the time, or sitting behind the gambling table dealing monte." Another Anglo writer grumbled, "Excepting saloons and gambling houses there were no other places of amusement, unless one went among the Chilean encampment where the lowest of women, owned by men lower than themselves, aided in the robbery, often the murder, of those who came to them; or among the cribs and taverns of the waterfront."[15]

Greaserita became the disparaging term of choice for Anglo journalists when describing Latina sex workers. The *Daily Alta California* wrote of the "Bacchanalian resorts on Pacific street, where Chilian maids and drinkers of bad liquor most do congregate," and women who sold their services in saloons with "walls covered in dingy paper" and "ornamented with Chilian and Mexican flags, and a low bench [which] encircles the room seated on which are some twelve or fifteen women, Mexicans and negresses of different ages from ten to forty. Here may be seen the parent and her offspring practicing the same life of infamy." The *Daily Alta's* editors, known for their thinly veiled racism, published stories that displayed the seamy side of San Francisco life. These sensationalist reports titillated readers while also appealing to their moral indignation and fueling their deep-seated prejudices.[16]

Although the popular press portrayed prostitution as an unfortunate by-product of San Francisco's explosive growth, the buying and selling of sex was hardly a new phenomenon in California. Pimping became commonplace after the eighteenth-century arrival of Spanish soldiers and colonists. As historian Albert Hurtado has noted, "In 1780 Father Serra complained about Nicolas, a neophyte who procured women for the soldiers at San Gabriel. A few years later a Spanish naturalist observed that the Chumash men had 'become pimps, even for their own wives, for any miserable profit.'" The young Boston Brahmin Richard Henry Dana may have been speaking from personal experience when he recounted that during the 1830s, "I have frequently known an Indian to bring his wife, to whom he was lawfully married in the church, down to the beach, and carry her back again, dividing with her the money which she had got from the sailors. If any of the girls were discovered by the alcalde to be open evil livers, they were whipped, and kept at work sweeping the square of the presidio, and carrying mud and bricks for the buildings; yet a few *reals* would generally buy them off." Official tolerance, and even endorsement, of prostitution continued throughout the first few decades of statehood.[17]

During the 1850s, the availability of a sexual encounter to match one's social status became a regular feature of San Francisco's urban landscape. In his recollections of the city during its early years, Captain George Coffin quipped, "The most genteel house in San Francisco was a brothel." Herbert Asbury waxed eloquent in *The Barbary Coast*, about "one popular French courtesan [who] is said to have banked five thousand dollars clear profit during her first year of professional activity in [San Francisco]." Likewise, a few Chinese women ascended San Francisco's social ladder by selling their services to wealthy customers. "The first Chinese courtesan who came to San Francisco was Ah Toy," wrote Elisha Oscar Crosby. The former New York lawyer continued, "She arrived I think in 1850 and was a very handsome Chinese girl. She was quite select in her associates, was liberally patronized by the white men and made a great amount of money." The parlors and dance floors of downtown establishments afforded a socially acceptable meeting place for men to interact with extravagantly dressed prostitutes.[18]

The opulence of these social settings was merely a veneer. San Francisco's clubs and bordellos could suddenly become arenas of bloody confrontation. "Hither I was called one night to attend a Creole girl from New Orleans, who had just been stabbed, at a masked ball in the saloon, by a jealous Chilena," recalled San Francisco physician John W. Palmer. After arriving at the

Washington Hall Club, "I found the beautiful fury—Camille La Reine, they called her—blaspheming over a gashed shoulder, and devoting the quick-striking vixen of Valparaiso to a hundred fates." La Reine soon took revenge. "Six weeks after that, the *Pacific News* announced that the notorious Mariquita, the beautiful Chilian spitfire, had had her throat cut with a bowie-knife, in the hands of the splendid Creole Camille, in a 'difficulty' at one of those mad masked balls at La Señorita saloon." Likewise, in 1854, the California papers reported the case of a man named Dick Marble who severely beat a Chilean prostitute and then shot her pimp, a Chileno named Baleris. As was so often the case, the unnamed party in the media's portrayal of this violent encounter was the sex worker herself.[19]

Obscurity and evanescence were defining features of San Francisco's sex trade. During his passage to California, Vicente Pérez Rosales penned a vivid description of one of the three women on board, a prostitute named Rosario Améstica. She "had been born as Izquierdo in Quilicura, lived in Talcahuano as Villaseca, in Talca as Toro, and in Valparaíso, till the day before, as Rosa Montalva." Although the Valparaíso harbormaster questioned her for using a passport under an assumed name, the male passengers protested his inquiries, and he allowed her to remain aboard. On arrival in San Francisco, "Rosarito [*sic*], dressed to kill in a magnificent silk gown, cape, and parasol, fawned and fluttered over by everyone who came on board, soon went ashore and, surrounded by a crowd of admirers, disappeared into the low fog or semi-drizzle that obscured everything." The "Venice of pine" had performed another vanishing act. Even so, Rosario's disappearance from the historical record should not obscure the fact that Chileans played key roles in shaping San Francisco's nineteenth-century sex trade and the sexual geography of the city.[20]

For new arrivals, gold rush San Francisco was a disorienting mixture of the familiar and the strange. The transient nature of the city's occupants—miners and merchants captivated by hearsay—left indelible marks on San Francisco's metropolitan geography. The city's 1864 directory listed 172 lodgings, 135 hotels, and 106 boardinghouses. In addition to noticing its ephemeral character, travelers must have sensed a certain odd intimacy to the budding municipality. San Francisco at midcentury was a "walking city," dominated by pedestrian traffic and face-to-face interactions. Elite visitors from foreign nations often encountered friends and acquaintances from their transplanted social groups. Along the wharves, Pérez Rosales and his brothers saw many familiar faces from Chile, "but we had to look at them long and hard to recognize, under the rags and threadbare trousers and a heavy seaman's jacket, the refined Santiago dandy or the Valparaíso merchant." For those who had eked out an existence in Chile as farmhands, prostitutes, bricklayers, or washerwomen, the spontaneous appearance of a relative or friend was far less probable. Only eight thousand Chileans—of a total national population of nearly one and a half million by the 1850s—followed their gold rush dreams and sailed north. A proletarian exodus from Chile to the mines of California did not occur as officials of President Manuel Bulnes's government (1841–51) had so stubbornly predicted.[21]

San Francisco's demographic development from the mid-1800s to the turn of the century was typical in some ways and unusual in others. Historian Peter Decker has demonstrated that the city's expansion between 1850 and 1860 was similar to, or below, population growth rates in other comparable US cities of the period. What was atypical, however, was San Francisco's inordinately high proportion of residents born outside the United States. Between 1870 and 1890, the city had a greater percentage of immigrants from abroad than any other major North American metropolis, including the Atlantic seaports of New York and Boston and the midwestern industrial hubs of Chicago and Detroit.[22]

As early as the 1850s, a socially segregated urban geography, driven by increasing class and racial stratification, began to stifle interaction between the wealthy white residents of the city and their less fortunate nonwhite counterparts. By 1851, many of the poorer Chileans dwelled in "the space bounded by Montgomery, Pacific, Jackson, and Kearney streets." Chilecito was, according to Hubert Howe Bancroft, California's first professional historian, "filled with little wooden huts planted promiscuously, with numberless recesses and fastnesses filled with Chilians—men, women, and children." In his less-than-flattering portrait of Chilecito, Bancroft wrote, "The women appeared to be always washing, but the vocation of the men was a puzzle to the passers-by. Neither the scenery of the place nor its surroundings were very pleasant, particularly in hot weather. One side was a slimy bog, and on the other rubbish heaps and sinks of offal." Bancroft conceded, "Notwithstanding, it was home to them, and from their filthy quarters they might be seen emerging on Sundays, the men washed and clean-shirted, and the women arrayed in smiling faces and bright-colored apparel." He continued, "Round the chief hut or *tienda* lounged dirty men in parti-colored serapes and round-crowned straw hats, smoking, drinking, and betting at monte. Most of these were either on their way to, or had lately returned from the mines."[23]

A more charitable, albeit romanticized, description of Chilecito flowed from the pen of Charles Warren Stoddard. A teenager in the mid-1850s, Stoddard grew up in San Francisco and eventually became a celebrated travel writer. Referring to Chilecito as "the Spanish Quarter," Stoddard recalled "the delicious odors that were wafted to us from the tables where Mexicans, Spaniards, Chilians, Peruvians, and Hispano-Americans were discussing the steaming *tamal*, the fragrant *frijol*, and other fiery dishes that might put to the blush the ineffectual pepper-pot." Likewise, a Lithuanian observer wrote of Chilecito during 1851, "It is South American in its morals, its costumes and its gaiety. Although the populace has not received a careful education, the people are distinguished by their exquisite politeness." He noted that the men wore ponchos and smoked cigarettes, while the women donned flowing dresses and puffed liberally on cigars.[24]

Chilecito offered a space for ethnic and racial intermixing, similar to the lower Manhattan port culture that emerged during the same period. Poor whites, blacks, and Latinos lived near one another, often mingling in the crowded eateries, dance halls, gambling houses, and open-air markets at the base of Telegraph Hill. The authors of *The Annals of San Francisco* made no attempt to hide their disdain for this racially mixed, working-class district: "The Hispano-Americans dwell chiefly about Dupont, Kearny and Pacific streets—long the blackguard quarters of the city. In these streets, and generally in the northern parts of the city, are many dens of gross vice, which are patronized largely by Mexicans and Chilians. Their dance, drink and gambling houses are also the haunts of Negroes and the vilest order of white men." At times, cross-cultural events in this neighborhood assumed a more organized character, such as the elaborate masquerade balls occasionally organized by African Americans and Latinos.[25]

In 1849, Chilecito came under attack from a band of racist marauders known as Los Galgos (the Hounds). Many of these men had traveled to California to impose the dictates of manifest destiny on the long-established population of Spanish-speaking Californians. At the conclusion of the Mexican War, the US military discharged one thousand soldiers from Colonel Jonathan D. Stevenson's New York Volunteer Regiment. These "New York Volunteers," called on to fight for the occupation and annexation of Mexican California, had originally landed at San Francisco between March 6 and April 17, 1847, aboard four transport ships. Subsequently, Stevenson had divided them into various companies whose members served the war effort in Sonoma, San Francisco, Monterey, Santa Barbara, and Los Angeles. By the end of September 1848, with hostilities over, ten of Stevenson's dragoons deserted for the gold mines. Others hastily followed suit, hoping to unearth their fortunes in the Sierra Nevada.[26]

Many of these men returned to San Francisco during the winter of 1848–49 to take refuge from the frigid mountain winter. They gathered at the Old Shades Tavern on the northeast corner of Pacific Street between Kearney and Dupont to commiserate, drink, and gamble. The Shades, as locals called it, was an infamous boardinghouse and grog shop, known for its clientele of "the wildest characters in San Francisco." Before long, a band of men from Stevenson's regiment, along with a gang of ruffians from the city's underworld, began to act in concert. Using the Shades as their headquarters, they called themselves the Hounds. According to observer Charles F. Winslow, "They took this name from their custom of going throughout the place every night at eleven o'clock and barking like hounds as a sort of impudent serenade to the quiet and respectable people of San Francisco." The Hounds roamed San Francisco's streets, perpetrating wanton acts of harassment and extortion in the city's immigrant neighborhoods and nonwhite establishments.[27]

Among their favorite targets were Chilean merchants and miners, who drew resentment from some Anglos because of their aptitude for gold prospecting and their shrewd business practices. Popular stereotypes of Latinos played into the Hounds' hands. In many accounts of life along the Barbary Coast, Chileans received the bit part of the greasy criminal. A white correspondent for the *New York Tribune* and *Chicago Tribune* wandered into the back room of a store near San Francisco's waterfront district and found "a promiscuous crowd of Chileños, Peruvians, and other Spanish-American cut-throats, playing 'pool,' with any amount of small change changing hands at every game." Such unflattering portraits encouraged an atmosphere of hostility toward Chileans and other Latino residents of San Francisco.[28]

One of the most detailed accounts of the Hounds' predatory practices came from a former officer of Stevenson's regiment, William Redmond Ryan. As Ryan explained,

> In illustration of their lawless practices, and of the manner in which [the Hounds] harassed the poor Chilians, three of them one day entered the store of a native of that country, and demanded goods on credit to the amount of seventy-five dollars, saying they resided at the 'Shades,' and were well known. So they were; but not in the sense they wished to imply. The poor fellow, who was totally unacquainted with them, declined their patronage, being by no means prepossessed in their favour, nor at all reassured by their manner. Upon his refusal, they assumed a threatening attitude, and so effectually terrified him by their menaces, that he supplied them with what they wanted; and even offered no resistance, when, on their taking their departure, they helped themselves to several articles to which they had, apparently, taken a sudden fancy.

Throughout the summer of 1849, such incidents became increasingly frequent and overt. The Hounds would march into eating establishments, demand to be served fine food and drink, devour the meal with great relish, and refuse to pay. If rebuked, they wrecked the furniture and destroyed the interiors of the restaurant or saloon whose owner dared refuse their orders.[29]

No organized authority checked the Hounds' crimes. San Francisco had neither a municipal police force nor a stable metropolitan government. "On one occasion a Negro accidentally touched the august person of a Hound in passing, and his ears were promptly shorn from his head," wrote *Barbary Coast* author Herbert Asbury. The author added, "A few days later a Mexican's tongue was torn out by the roots because he had replied in kind to an insult hurled at him by one of the thugs." One San Franciscan explained the complacency of the city's more peaceable residents in the face of such brutality: "Though we were every day getting more and more afraid of this volunteer police, as they pretended to be, no one made a movement against them. First, because we did not know our own strength at that time, and, secondly, because every one had too much of his own private business on hand to make it at all prudent or safe for him to meddle in any business of a public nature." In addition, a number of accounts suggest that San Francisco's mayor at the time, Judge Thaddeus K. Leavenworth, was both an ally and an employer of these criminals. Leavenworth had formerly served as chaplain to the New York volunteers and "was openly charged with being in sympathy with the regulators [aka Hounds] and of using them to further his political aspirations." This air of impunity encouraged the Hounds' audacious behavior.[30]

Eventually, the gang established a new public headquarters in a tent on Kearney Street, between Clay and Sacramento Streets. This canvas lodge soon acquired the name Tammany Hall, after the infamous headquarters of New York City's Democratic political machine. Membership required a ten-dollar fee, collected by Jack Patterson, the proprietor of the Shades. Sam Roberts, an ex-member of the Stevenson regiment, adopted the title of lieutenant, donned regimental dress, and directed the escapades of the loosely organized band of outlaws. Among the other elected officers were prominent New York volunteers: "C.R.V. Lee as president; W. Anderson, vice-president; J.T. Downey, secretary; . . . and J.C. Pullis as steward."[31]

These criminals cultivated a reputation for fanciful attire and reckless behavior. According to one San Francisco merchant, "The worthless members of Col. Stevenson's regiment of New York volunteers . . . lived by gambling, and they dressed in a flashy, ridiculous style, white vests embroidered beautifully, showy silk neckties, fine cloth coats and pants, the coats often lined with red silk." A shotgun wedding had taken place in San Francisco between two nineteenth-century archetypes, the thug and the dandy.[32]

The Hounds developed close ties with certain San Francisco businessmen and frequently hired themselves out as a brute squad. Attempting to lend further legitimacy to their ad hoc organization, they drew up a constitution at Portsmouth Square on July 13. The document stated their purpose as a society for mutual aid and renamed the group "the San Francisco Society of Regulators." Just two days later, the Hounds mounted a full-scale assault on Chilecito. Missouri pioneer James Findla recalled, "They commenced by committing outrages on the Chilenos, assaulted them, robbed them, broke into their tents, and killed some of them." The dark hollow "filled with little wooden huts" was suddenly thrust into the spotlight as San Franciscans watched the onslaught transpire in their midst.[33]

Although the Hounds had shown overt hostility toward Chileans for months, several incidents precipitated the frontal assault on Chilecito during the night of July 15, 1849. Less than a month before the attack, a Chilean shopkeeper had shot Benjamin B. Beatty, a thirty-year-old native of Albany, New York, and a former New York volunteer. On June 21, 1849, Beatty had quarreled with the South American merchant, "who became frightened and produced a pistol." According to the *Daily Alta California*, "[The weapon] was instantly wrested from him by Beatty's companion, between whom and the shop-keeper a scuffle ensued; during which Beatty retired toward the entrance of the tent and was in the act of passing out when a pistol was discharged." William Redmond Ryan, who witnessed the ensuing events, wrote: "On one occasion, I saw a crowd of persons ransacking a tent and store, situated near the 'City Hotel,' and kept by a Spaniard, who, as it appeared, had, on the preceding evening, murdered a volunteer named Beattie, and then taken refuge in the woods, in the interior of the country. In less than half an hour the entire contents of the store had disappeared, their value being probably not less than a thousand dollars." The Hounds assembled that afternoon, confiscated the Chilean shopkeeper's possessions, and auctioned them—along with his tent—to the highest bidder.[34]

On July 4, 1849, the Hounds perpetrated two more abuses on San Francisco's Chileans. Sam Roberts, the gang's lieutenant, allegedly stole ten ounces of gold from his sometime mistress, Chilean madam and club owner Felice Álvarez. In addition, Roberts and several other men attempted to extort money from a Chilean merchant named Pedro Cueto. Cueto, who would later serve as Chile's first consul in California, stubbornly refused to yield to Roberts's ultimatum, despite the fact that the lieutenant threatened to return with a posse of forty men to enforce his demands.[35]

Things came to a head on Sunday, July 15, when Sam Roberts and the Hounds swaggered into San Francisco after a drunken episode of pillaging and parading in Contra Costa County. Roberts burst into Felice Álvarez's room and found a German, Leopold Bleckschmidt, sitting on her bed. In a fit of rage, Roberts beat Bleckschmidt senseless with a stick before storming off to a bar where he and a dozen Hounds "had four bottles of champagne, and went away without paying; broke some glasses." Later that evening, the Hounds gathered at Tammany Hall, where one witness heard them remark, "They were going to run the Chilenos out that night." Shortly thereafter, the gang gathered at the Parker House, and "a party of the association was seen parading the streets, with drums beating and colours flying. That same night, the store of a Chilian was broken into by them, and the unfortunate proprietor nearly murdered; he being so severely beaten, as to have been left for dead. His neighbour and fellow-country-man, apprehending a similar fate, fled to an adjacent house, and, creeping underneath the floor of it, lay there trembling until the noise had subsided, and the deed of blood was perpetrated." Rumors of an impending massacre spread though the city. That night, twenty-nine-year-old carpenter Levi Stowell wrote in his journal, "The Hounds are out after some Chileanoes; a hard gang, some one has to suffer tonight." Stowell's predictions were correct.[36]

Dr. Charles Frederick Winslow wrote from San Francisco on July 19, 1849, "The Chileans in large numbers are living in tents on the outskirts of town. About 10 o'clock at night the Hounds made an assault upon them, tore down more than a dozen of their tents, broke open their chests, stole their money, tore their clothing and scattered their property, and fired upon them with pistols intending to kill as many as they could." Among the dwellings they attacked was the tent of Chilean Domingo Alegría. In the wake of the incident, his son Reinaldo reported that the Hounds "commenced pulling down the tent. I ran out, was struck, caught and held by five or six and shot by another." Reinaldo later died from the gunshot wounds.[37]

Leading San Francisco merchant William Heath Davis described the commotion on July 15: "One night in the early hours of the morning my slumber was disturbed by screams of women and children from the hamlet of canvas. While I was reflecting, in a half awake and half asleep condition, as if emerging from a dream or a nightmare, I heard a sharp knock at the door of my dwelling. In opening it, there stood before me several women, trembling with fright. They had escaped from their temporary homes; the poor creatures came to my house for protection, which I gave them." Davis continued, "One of the number, who proved to be a cultivated Chilean lady, Doña Rosa Gaskell, asked my wife to permit them to remain for the rest of the night. Mrs. Gaskell was terribly alarmed for her life. Her husband had gone to the mines. During the melee at the scene of the disturbance, the tents and their fixtures were destroyed, and many persons were injured bodily by the hands of a band of ruffians who styled themselves the 'Hounds.' " Other Chilenas did not manage to find sanctuary from their would-be predators. Moses Pearson Cogswell of New Hampshire wrote that the Hounds invaded Chileno dwellings, "ravished their women, and committed other shameful outrages."[38]

Pérez Rosales, who did not witness the attack, recounted the episode as though he had been present. Giving his compatriots the benefit of the doubt, he wrote, "Once the Chileans had recovered from their surprise they began to rain stones on their attackers. A respectable Chilean gentleman, unable to flee through the door of his tent because it was blocked by several Hounds who were assailing him, laid the first comer low with a pistol shot and, slashing the canvas of his tent with his knife, managed to escape through that improvised door and rejoin his companions unharmed." Surely, other residents of Chilecito took up arms that evening, but surviving accounts of the Hounds' assault provide limited evidence about the extent of Chilean resistance.[39]

The next morning, San Franciscans emerged from their tents, shacks, and boardinghouses to inspect the results of the previous night's savagery. Charles Frederick Winslow told his wife, "I went the next morning to see the devastation. It was painful to look upon. Men, women and children were crouched around their miserable little store of property, looking forlorn and wretched." While the Hounds slept off the fatigue from their nocturnal thuggery, Mormon leader and millionaire merchant Sam Brannan stepped atop a barrel at the corner of Clay and Montgomery Streets to address the residents of San Francisco. As the crowd swelled, the meeting migrated to Portsmouth Square. Brannan, always hungry for an impulsive audience, clambered onto the roof of the mayor's office on Clay Street from where the throngs could better hear him. Before long, he had secured a relief fund for the Chileans and had gathered a volunteer police force of 230 citizens to pursue and apprehend those responsible for assaulting Chilecito. By nightfall, seventeen Hounds had been put in custody aboard the warship USS *Warren*.[40]

On July 17, a grand jury indicted the prisoners on a variety of charges, including "conspiracy, riot, robbery, and assault with intent to kill." Mayor Leavenworth and two other magistrates presided over the trial. Issuing their verdict in prompt frontier-court fashion, a jury found Sam Roberts and eight of his companions guilty. Roberts and another man received a ten-year sentence of hard labor, while the jury gave the other offenders prison terms in a location to be determined by the governor.[41]

None of these men actually served his sentence, but several met with swift and terminal punishment in the mines. On the fate of the Hounds, Sacramento journalist Samuel Upham commented, "It is universally conceded in this country, that hanging *is not* one of the 'Lost Arts,' and, so long as Judge Lynch shall continue to occupy the bench, justice will be meted out with an impartial hand." In this case, the harsh retribution "meted out" to the Hounds favored the Latino denizens of San Francisco. Nevertheless, as so many Chilean miners would find out, the lynching rope of the miner's impromptu court was rarely on their side.[42]

Economic justice proved as elusive as legal impartiality. Like their compatriots who worked as bricklayers and prostitutes in San Francisco, Chileans who found wage work outside California's cities often ended up on the bottom rung of the employment hierarchy. In the quicksilver mines of the Santa Clara Valley, Chilean men hauled two-hundred-pound leather sacks of mercury ore up steep wooden ladders from dank and cavernous mineshafts. The low-paying, arduous labors of Chilean and Mexican porters and miners contrasted starkly with the higher wages and supervisory roles reserved for the white engineers who worked above ground. As such arrangements demonstrated, the privileges of whiteness in California were not merely superficial. Yet, both below and above ground, Chileans created spaces that were conspicuously their own.

Because mercury was essential to the amalgamation process used by miners when removing precious metals from ores, it was a much-sought-after commodity throughout the Americas. From the 1550s until the late 1700s the Spanish had shipped large quantities of *azogue*—known to English speakers as mercury or quicksilver—from Almadén, Spain, across the Atlantic to imperial silver mines in Zacatecas (Mexico) and Potosí (in the region now called Bolivia). Once a miner added quicksilver to a solution that contained mineral compounds, the fine silver or gold particles bound with the mercury to the exclusion of other materials, such as quartz or sand. The resulting amalgam sank to the bottom of the miner's pan, trough, or basin in lumps. The prospector then recovered the precious metals and removed the mercury by heating the amalgam. Mercury changes to a gas at a lower temperature than gold or silver, so the vapors from this process can be collected in a distilling vessel, while the desired metal remains behind in solid form.[43]

Deposits of cinnabar, the major ore from which mercury is extracted, were located close to California's gold regions. Long before the Spanish arrived in Alta California, Ohlone Indians had adorned their faces and bodies with vermilion cinnabar pigments taken from a place they called Pooyi. The hills of Pooyi were just twelve miles from where Juan Bautista de Anza founded the pueblo of San José in 1777. Only one year before the US Army invaded

Alta California, a Mexican cavalry officer knowledgeable in mineralogy located the cinnabar deposits and immediately recognized their economic value. As Monterey's French consul Jacques-Antoine Moerenhout explained in his diplomatic correspondence, "It was in November, 1845, that Captain [Andres] Castillero, up from Mexico on a secret mission, became interested in the vermillion earth that was being used to paint the Mission church at Santa Clara." In November 1846, the British company Barron, Forbes and Co. of Tepic, Mexico, assisted Castillero in the mine's development. The firm leased the mine, changed its name to New Almaden, and eventually bought majority shares in the operation.[44]

Initially, Santa Clara Mission Indians excavated mercury ore from the caves under Mexican supervision, but the company expanded in the 1850s and needed to enlarge its workforce. To meet this demand for experienced miners, Barron, Forbes and Co. recruited laborers from Mexico, Chile, Britain, and Ireland. The New Almaden Quicksilver Mine in Santa Clara County operated thirteen brick furnaces near Los Alamitos Creek. This smelting facility, called the Hacienda de Beneficio, enabled operators to burn off the sulfur compounds to which the precious mercury was bound.[45]

Miners and administrators lived separately. On the hills overlooking the furnaces, California Indians, Mexicans, and Chileans formed a settlement known as Spanishtown. This hodge-podge cluster of dwellings contrasted sharply with "a row of neat cottages, some six or eight in number, forming quite a little hamlet," nestled in the lush meadow below. As a correspondent for the San Francisco magazine the *Pioneer* put it, "Some of these [houses] are of large size, and are handsomely finished; each inclosed with a paling fence, containing a small flower-garden with shrubbery, while a vegetable garden in the rear bespeaks usefulness combined with taste and beauty. These cottages are occupied by the families of the superintendents of the works." New Almaden's configuration positioned poor Chileans on the hillsides above the domain of the wealthy. In the nearby Hacienda Cemetery on the east bank of the Arroyo de Los Alamitos Creek, Latino miners buried their dead (fig. 6).[46]

According to one estimate, two hundred men worked at New Almaden in 1851. By 1866, the workforce had expanded to thirteen hundred. Most of these employees toiled for eleven-hour stretches underground. As an *Overland Monthly* correspondent noted: "There are two classes of miners in these subterraneous caverns: laborers and ore-carriers. The former use the pick and shovel; while the latter, being men of superior muscular power, pack the heavy bags of ore on their shoulders, up the perpendicular steps—over deep pits on a single plank, where a misstep would precipitate them to fearful depths below—and

Figure 6. Grave marker of Maria A. Lopetegui, a Chilean resident of "Spanishtown." Hacienda Cemetery, New Almaden, California. *Photograph by author.*

through the various winding passages of the mine to the level, from which it is hoisted to the outer world."[47]

The ore-carriers, known as *tenateros*, were invariably Latinos. In 1851, a visitor to New Almaden commented, "The mine is worked by Mexicans and Chilians, who carry the ore in raw hide sacks upon their shoulders from the bottom of the vein to the opening above, a distance of between three and four hundred feet." These sacks weighed more than two hundred pounds and required tremendous exertion from their porters. "It is impossible to witness the straining nerves and quivering muscles of the carriers, as they pass slowly up from the depths below, without feeling that the heavy breathing and painful expression of face is produced by such labor as human beings cannot long endure," wrote William Wells in *Harper's Monthly*. Despite enduring such physical stress, tenateros received only two or three dollars per day, less than half the daily wage of the Anglo mechanics who supervised the smelting machinery above ground.[48]

Notwithstanding such pay discrepancies, Mexicans and Chileans exerted complete cultural control over their subterranean workplace. The mines were spaces governed by Roman Catholic tradition and bathed in the unremitting echoes of Spanish. On the day of dedication of the Enriqueta quicksilver mine neighboring the New Almaden property, Mexican and Chilean families donned their finest attire and turned out for the blessing of the mine. James Mason Hutchings, the editor of California's earliest pictorial monthly, witnessed the festive scene and wrote, "On the morning of the day set apart for this ceremony, at the Enriquita [*sic*] or San Antonio quicksilver mine, the Mexican and Chilian señors and señoras began to flock into the little village at the foot of the cañon, from all the surrounding country, in anticipation of a general holiday, at an early hour." Hutchings continued, "Arriving in procession at the entrance to the mine, Father Goetz, the Catholic curate of San Jose, performed mass, and formally blessed the mine, and all persons present, and all those who might work in it; during which service, a band of musicians was playing a number of airs." At the conclusion of the dedication, two hundred guests gathered for a picnic in the nearby Sycamore grove.[49]

In addition to public assertions of their cultural traditions, Chilean laborers in California's Santa Clara Valley expressed their national pride through patriotic associations. Between 1862 and 1867, Mexicans, Chileans, and other Latinos organized at least 123 *juntas patrióticas* across the state. These organizations claimed an impressive total of nearly fourteen thousand members. During a naval standoff between Spain and Chile that lasted from September 1865 to March 1866, Chilean miners at New Almaden expressed solidarity with their compatriots through their local junta patriótica, a group that listed 456 men and women on its roster. As San Francisco's *El Nuevo Mundo* newspaper reported, members from New Almaden's junta patriótica collected donations throughout the Santa Clara Valley and sent the money to a defense fund in Chile. During their campaign, they consciously appealed to a sense of Latin American fraternity—*raza española*—that united them with their fellow Mexican community members.[50]

Multiethnic mining crews were equally organized and tenacious when demanding control over the conditions of their own labor. During the late 1860s, strikes occurred almost every year over such issues as the miners' rights to gamble, the presence of noncompany peddlers selling wares in the community, and the contract bidding system on which workers' wages were based. On numerous occasions, such labor actions produced substantial gains for the strikers.[51]

The fruits of their labors also yielded durable transequatorial commercial connections, comprising what I refer to as exchanges for their effects on both sides of the linkages. During 1853, a total of 1,350,000 pounds of quicksilver left San Francisco aboard ships bound for foreign ports. Valparaíso was among the primary destinations for these exports. That year alone, Chile purchased 148,275 pounds of mercury from the New Almaden mines. During the 1850s and 1860s, Chile continued to be a leading consumer of California's quicksilver.[52]

Mercury was far from an innocuous commodity, however. Health concerns profoundly affected Latinos in mercury mining communities. William H. Brewer, a Yale chemistry professor who worked on California's first geological survey, visited the New Idria Quicksilver Mines in 1861. Deep in the El Diablo Range of southern San Benito County, Brewer found that "the miners are mostly Chileans, a hard set, and their quarters are in shanties covered with bushes, in huts, and even in deserted workings." He was appalled by conditions in the smelter facilities, where "sulphurous acids, arsenic, vapors of mercury, etc., make a horrible atmosphere, which tells fearfully on the health of the workmen. . . . The ore is roasted in furnaces and the vapors are condensed in great brick chambers, or 'condensers.'" Working conditions were horrendous: "[Condensers] have to be cleaned every year by workmen going into them, and many have their health ruined forever by the three or four days' labor, and all are injured; but the wages, twenty dollars a day, always bring victims. There are but few Americans, only the superintendent and one or two other officials; the rest are Mexicans, Chileans, Irish (a few), and Cornish miners."[53]

During the nineteenth century, the drastic consequences of mercury exposure for environmental and human health were barely understood. Miners blithely handled the toxic substance, not knowing that mercury exposure causes brain damage, cardiovascular disease, and skin poisoning. Prospector Prentice Mulford and his comrades worked the waters of Swett's Bar (Tuolumne County) through a four-hundred-foot-long wooden flume, applying copious quantities of quicksilver to their man-made stream. Mulford later recalled, "We used quicksilver plentifully in the sluices; and the amalgam was taken to my cabin in a gold-pan and put on the hot coals to drive off the mercury, which it did, and salivated the four of us besides. The sublimated mineral covered walls, tables and chairs with a fine, frost-like coating, and on rubbing one's finger over any surface a little globule of quicksilver would roll up before it." Mulford, who eventually became a well-respected journalist and a friend to authors Mark Twain and Bret Harte, died in 1891, at the age of fifty-seven.[54]

Although Mulford never displayed overt symptoms of mercury poisoning, California's environment exhibited obvious signs of distress from exposure to this toxic element. Writing in *Harper's Monthly*, William Wells remarked, "One of the most curious circumstances connected with the New Almaden mine is the effect produced by mercurial vapors upon the surrounding vegetation." Wells noticed that "every tree on the mountain-side above the works is dead, and some of the more sensitive natures farther removed exhibit the influence of the poison in their shrunken and blanched foliage." In addition, "Cattle feeding within half a mile of the hacienda sicken and become salivated; and the use of the waters of a spring rising near the works is guarded against." The precipitous degradation of California's mining landscapes was just one of the many consequences of the transition to a new, more aggressive era in the state's economic expansion. Another was soil exhaustion, which farmers began addressing with two Chilean imports, nitrogen-fixing alfalfa and nutrient-rich sodium nitrate fertilizer.[55]

For Chilean women and men living in San Francisco's Chilecito, New Almaden's Spanishtown, and other regions of California, such long-term concerns about landscape degradation were generally eclipsed by the daily grind of quicksilver mining, sex work, domestic labor, and a vast array of other menial jobs. As the 1849 attack on Little Chile so vividly demonstrated, navigating the treacherous landscape of California's race relations could be among the most basic hazards to one's health. Throughout the gold-mining regions of the state, similar relations of risk prevailed.

MANIFEST DESTINY AT THE END OF A ROPE

California has long been a site of struggle between xenophobic tendencies and cosmopolitan impulses. In the 1848 Treaty of Guadalupe Hidalgo, Mexico ceded a vast swath of occupied territory to the United States. Concurrently, prospectors from across the globe streamed through the Golden Gate. These events generated starkly contrasting visions of the North American West. In 1872, General Joseph Warren Revere enlisted Newtonian logic in the service of conquest when reminiscing about the Yankee uprising against Mexican rule in California: "The 14th of June, 1846, must be regarded as a memorable day in the history of California; for then her 'manifest destiny' became apparent, impelling her to 'gravitate' towards the Union."[1]

To Chileans joining the gold rush, matters looked quite different. "As I said, then, today's California does not owe her population and her progress to any one race but, with a few exceptions, to the cream of the enterprising spirit of all nations," wrote the diplomat and adventurer Vicente Pérez Rosales. Episodes of anti-Chilean violence in San Francisco—such as the 1849 attack on Little Chile—heightened tensions between Latinos and Anglos. Yet inter-ethnic conflict during the gold rush was not confined to the City by the Bay. Contradictory claims of nativism and internationalism also collided in the foothills of the Sierra Nevada.[2]

Exemplifying a type of connection that I call a displacement for its profound one-way effects on the receiving region, many Chileans arrived in California with time-tested mining techniques, geological knowledge, and advanced mineral-processing technologies, such as an ore-crushing apparatus called the Chile Mill. As a result, Chileans were among California's most successful miners. Although their accomplishments earned them the respect, and even the apprenticeship, of some Yankees, their efficient handiwork bred resentment among other North American prospectors. In addition, many Anglos were offended by the practice of Chilean debt peonage. At a time when US debates over slavery were reaching the Pacific coast, the practice of indenture challenged California's status as a domain of "free labor." During the nineteenth century, free labor connoted contractual wage work with the freedom to quit. Despite Yankee objections to Chilean employment hierarchies, many North Americans were unapologetic about their own use of indentured California Indian and unfree African American laborers for their own mining operations. This is one of many cases where the perspective of transnational history reveals ideological debates and contradictory practices that remain imperceptible from national, regional, or local vantage points.[3]

Conflicting customs, jealousy, and rising nationalist sentiment drove anti-Latino violence in the mining regions. From 1848 onward, California became what theater studies scholar Coya Paz Brownrigg has called a "Linchocracia," a space dominated by aggressive performances of manifest destiny and nativist ideology. Lynching—or public retributive acts of murder in which the perpetrators claim to be acting in the name of popular justice or some higher moral authority—has never fit conventional historical categories. Even so, historians and social scientists have rarely studied lynching outside the context of the South, a region where white gangs committed extralegal murders of blacks. As a result, countless lynchings targeting American Indians, Chinese, and Latinos have gone unnoticed in official records and the public imagination. Throughout California, however, the gruesome rope work of Anglo mobs left hundreds of Chileans and Mexicans dangling from "the old Hangtown Oak."[4]

Interethnic violence was a crucial component of the racialized class structures that prevailed throughout the region. The massacre of twenty-eight unarmed Chinese laborers by an Anglo mob at Rock Springs, Wyoming, in 1885 is just one of myriad examples that demonstrate the deep connections among violent acts, claims of racial privilege, and assertions of class status in the late 1800s. Yet even the most meticulous scholars have mistakenly claimed that lynching in the nineteenth-century US West consisted primarily of white-on-white mob hostility. Historian Gail Bederman—in her otherwise powerful treatment of "remaking manhood" in the late 1800s—concluded, "Prior to 1889, most American lynchings occurred in the West, under frontier conditions, and mostly white men were lynched." Here, Bederman misses the mark. Anglo mobs were responsible for the lynching of at least 597 people of Mexican origin or descent in the United States from 1848 to 1928. In California alone, mobs lynched no fewer than 64 individuals of Chilean or Mexican heritage between

1850 and 1855. Hundreds of California Indians and Chinese immigrants suffered similar fates.[5]

The multiethnic character of lynching in California complicates our understanding of how this gruesome practice varied among regions. An array of abrupt cross-cultural encounters that accompanied the gold rush, paired with an unrelenting drive by whites to assert supremacy in complex and highly racialized labor hierarchies, ensured that public acts of mob violence acquired dimensions that they did not exhibit elsewhere. Yet California's lynching landscape should be treated less as a regional exception to national trends and more as a particular example of larger patterns. Writing about lynching in the United States, American studies scholar Jacqueline Goldsby made passing mentioned of the need to include "the lynching murders of Mexicans and Chinese in the West" in our comprehension of how racialized violence was a key component of North American modernity. Goldsby's entreaty has yet to be fully answered.[6]

A prominent feature of California's lynching landscape was the dispassionate coverage the English-language press gave to such spectacles of mob violence. The following news item, printed unobtrusively on page 2 of the January 27, 1855, *Sacramento Daily Union*, typifies the mainstream media's treatment of the public murders of nonwhites: "Three men were hung to-day by the populace in Contra Costa county for cattle stealing. Two of them were Chileans, the other a Mexican." Such unremarkable reporting reinforced the notion that lynching—especially when the victims were not white—was a socially acceptable act.[7]

Before their murder by an enraged mob, these three Latinos were like many prospectors who joined the steady stream of miners heading up the San Joaquin and Sacramento Rivers to California's interior port cities of Stockton, Sacramento, and Marysville. Vicente Pérez Rosales, his brothers, and their mining crew secured passage to Sacramento aboard the *Dicey My Nana*. The Mexican sloop had once been called *Dice Mi Ñaña*—or "my honey says"—before Yankees purchased the ship and butchered its name. Pérez Rosales described the motley assortment of miners who rode upriver with his party: "Our vessel was under the command of the memorable Captain Robinson, an irascible old Yankee, short, lisping, and habitually drunk. His crew was composed of a Scotsman with a nose like an overripe tomato and two Yankees who, lacking money for their passage, had just signed on as sailors. Trying to describe the bandit-like appearance of my other traveling companions would be to bite off more than I could chew." As Pérez Rosales noted, "What they had in common was the indispensable equipment of the time: enormous boots studded with nails, knives at their waist, and rifles and pistols, which even on board they did not stop fingering for a moment." The Chilean's description of his ship-mates aptly foreshadowed the prevalence of violence in the mining regions.[8]

Once these men arrived at their fabled destination, they began the monoto-nous, frustrating affair of gold prospecting. Miners' midcentury journals and letters convey the sense of despair that dampened even the most enthusiastic spirits. Forty-niner Warren Sadler wrote of his losses: "This is hard; to come all the way to California to get a fortune, then be obliged to beg for something to eat, is hard. It makes me almost discouraged or disgusted with this wild specula-tion, to see so many come short of their anticipations and become discouraged, give up all hopes of getting means to go back to the states with and be obliged to remain in this country without friends or money to help themselves with when sick." Hard luck was a collective enterprise in the Sierra Nevada.[9]

Unlike many Yankee miners, Latino prospectors often displayed tremendous proficiency at extracting California's gold. South American newspapers extolled Mexican and Chilean successes in California's goldfields. In somewhat exag-gerated terms, the editor of Lima's *El Commercio* wrote, "The Yankees, totally ignorant of this work, ridiculed this digging of pits in the ground. The Chilean, wearing his short poncho and his dagger in his belt, proceeded step by step, gave a few scoops, gathered the earth in his pan, returned it to the bank of the stream, pocketed his ounce of gold and went off to eat his beef jerky and his porridge." Chileans and Mexicans referred to the Yankees as *gringos envidiosos* (envious gringos) because of their resentment toward Latino miners' successes.[10]

These were, indeed, familiar soils to many prospectors from south of the Rio Grande. As Joseph Warren Revere commented, "All nations were repre-sented in the Sacramento dry diggings; but the luckiest miners were always the Mexicans and South Americans. They possessed all the qualities which insure success—skill in prospecting, quick eyes for gold-bearing formations, rapidity in extracting or washing the auriferous earth, and great industry and patience— although lazy, and indeed useless in other employments." Mexican and Chilean miners, who had often spent years prospecting in their home countries, perceived elements of the landscape that eluded Anglo comprehension.[11]

Customs also differed between Anglo and Latino miners. At times, entire Chilean families assisted with prospecting tasks and campsite maintenance. In the winter of 1850, Philadelphia clergyman Daniel Bates Woods met "a large settlement of Chilinos, who have come from their own gold mines to try their fortunes here." As Woods was surprised to find: "I saw one family, the father of which, assisted by the older children, was 'panning out' gold on a stream near his rude home made of hides. . . . An interesting girl of five years, with a tiny pick and spade, was digging in a hole, already sunk two feet, and putting the dirt in a pan, which she would take to the stream and wash, putting the scale or two of gold into a dipper a little larger than a thimble." The presence of children in the Chilean camps must have seemed strangely comforting and yet resolutely alien to the many Anglo men who left families behind in order to seek their fortunes in California.[12]

Unsurprisingly, most Yankees proved incapable of communicating with their Chilean and Mexican counterparts. Louise Clappe, who signed her letters "Dame Shirley," caricatured the feeble attempts of her male compatriots to converse with California's Spanish-speakers, writing, "Nothing is more amusing, than to observe the different styles, in which the generality of the Americans talk *at* the unfortunate Spaniard. In the first place, many of them really believe, that when they have learned *sabe* and *vamos* (two words which they seldom use in the right place), *poco tiempo, si,* and *bueno* (the last they will persist in pronouncing *whayno*) they have the whole of the glorious Castillian at their tongue's end." Dame Shirley's joking aside, linguistic differences presented formidable obstacles to interethnic relations.[13]

Even some native Spanish-speakers found themselves disoriented by California's mixture of dialects. Pedro Ruiz Aldea, a Chilean revolutionary who left his country in 1859 for exile in California, recalled, "In spite of being among Chileans, a good part of the talk was over my head because they used Mexican words whose meaning I did not know." Chileans called a farm *fundo,* while Mexicans used the term *rancho. Choclos* meant young corn to a Chilean, while a Mexican would use the word *elotes.* Making tamales was *hacer humitas* in Chile, as opposed to *envolver tamales* in Mexico.[14]

Ethnic and national differences among Spanish-speaking miners also emerged in displays of fashion. William Perkins, a merchant and official in the California town of Sonora, vividly described the clothing of various miners: "The dress of the South Americans was something similar to the Mexican; but instead of the long *zarape* of the latter, they have a short one, which is called a *poncho,* put over the shoulders in the same way, by means of the slit through which the head is passed. The Peruvian *poncho* is generally of thick white cotton, with colored bands along the edge; the Chilian is black, or some dark color, of thick woolen material, with red, blue, and yellow bands." As with all attempts at ethnic taxonomies, Perkins's scheme glossed over many real-life complexities. Even so, it stressed the diversity of people who had been pigeon-holed as "greasers" by indifferent Anglo observers.[15]

Much like California's heterogeneous population, mining parties could be remarkably diverse affairs. Englishman William Shaw traveled to the diggings with a band as varied as the crew aboard Captain Ahab's *Pequod:* "The company was composed mostly of Americans of different grades, two Chilians, a Frenchman, two Germans, and two Cornish miners. Our followers, the two Chinese and the Malay boy, stuck pertinaciously to us."[16]

Within these parties, apprenticeship arrangements were common, often demonstrating how Chileans brought their mineral extraction expertise north, imparted it to non-Chileans, and thus shaped the nineteenth century's largest gold rush. British miner William Kelly arrived in the Pleasant Valley (El Dorado County) diggings on July 26, 1849. Kelly was a greenhorn, so he and the members of his group "spent a novitiate of three days amongst the Chileans and Mexicans, looking on at their operations, and getting odd lessons in the art of imparting the rotary motion to the contents of the wash-basin," after which a Chilean found them a choice spot for prospecting. Grateful for this free guidance, Kelly stressed his disapproval of the Yankees who benefited from the same goodwill, only to double-cross Latino miners down the road. "Nine-tenths of the new arrivals were Americans, who resorted, as we did in the first instance, to the Chilians and Mexicans for instruction and information, which they gave them with cheerful alacrity; but as soon as Jonathan got an inkling of the system, with peculiar bad taste and ungenerous feeling he organised a crusade against those obliging strangers, and ran them off the creek at the pistol mouth," wrote Kelly.[17]

Kelly was, by no means, alone in his scorn for Yankee belligerence toward Latino miners. Other prospectors also gratefully took instruction from Chileans. In 1849, Stephen L. Fowler of Long Island, New York, recounted that he and his brother James had "been diggin with a Chillanian, they understand mining very well." Prospectors with more capital hired Chileans to survey deposits for signs that they would "prove out" as worthwhile investments. New York banker Samuel Ward and six fellow shareholders hired "an old Chilean miner who had once been a *capataz* [foreman] of similar works in his native country" to examine a mine near the aptly named town of Quartzburg in Mariposa County. After Don Gregorio "formed a highly favorable opinion of our vein," Ward expended fourteen thousand dollars for half of the mine. Miners even named rich veins of gold "Chileans," in reference to the recurring successes of their Latino counterparts.[18]

Yankee prospectors also depended on Latin American mining technologies. Experienced Mexican miners crushed ores with a device known as the *arrastre* (often spelled *arastra* or *arrastra* by Anglos). Once gold-laden quartz had been pulverized beneath the heavy stone wheel of an arrastre, miners used mercury to extract the gold in amalgamated form. As Rodman Paul noted, "A mule, plodding in a perpetual circle, provided the power to put the stones in motion, so that gold-bearing material would be ground between them and the flat-surfaced bed." The average ten-foot-diameter, mule-operated arrastre could crush four hundred pounds of quartz in four or five hours.[19]

Chileans introduced to California a more sophisticated and efficient, two-wheeled version of the Mexican arrastre, known as the Chile Mill or Chilean Mill. The Chile Mill was much heavier and more efficient than the arrastre. As forty-niner Alonzo Delano explained, mercury expanded in the hot water of the Chile Mill's trough, markedly improving the amalgamation process. This Chilean import, a displacement in my conceptual schema, profoundly altered the California gold rush by extending the period of small-scale prospecting for longer than it would have otherwise continued. When US Special Commissioner Henry Willis Baxley visited California in the 1860s, he discovered that miners in Grass Valley (Nevada County) were using Chile mills to crush clumps of quartz that remained after an initial round of pulverization from the hammerlike blows of a stamp mill. The Chile Mill also exemplified the eastward movement of a Pacific coast technology. As the Tennessee-based *Athens Post* reported in 1854, gold miners in North Carolina experienced great success after copying their California counterparts in applying this South American ore-crushing technology.[20]

Although many California Yankees emulated Latin American mining techniques and depended on Mexican and Chilean technologies, they often distrusted Latino miners. New Hampshire forty-niner Kimball Webster concluded, "There were also many Mexicans and Chilians at work in the mines, packing mule trains with provisions, mining tools, etc. Many of them were very treacherous, being mixed breeds, and if possible, worse than the Sidney Ducks [Australians from Sydney], as they were called, and I believe more treacherous than the North American Indian." Byron Nathan McKinstry of Illinois was more open to partnering with Chilean miners. On April 4, 1852, McKinstry wrote, "I worked my Chili claim with a Chilian by the name of Domingo Floris for a partner. We got $10.50." Two weeks later, however, McKinstry complained, "I saw my Chilian bucking at Monte in the evening. He came to the cabin in the night, dead broke. Sunday morning he went off and borrowed $7.25, promising to pay the rest tomorrow. So we have got rid of him." A number of jingoistic prospectors thought that getting rid of *all* foreign miners sounded prudent.[21]

The first to suggest such a drastic undertaking was General Persifor F. Smith, commander of the US Army's Pacific Division. On the way to his new post in California, Smith traveled to Panama with his wife and his military staff. After arriving in the winter of 1849, they awaited passage to San Francisco on the western shore of the isthmus. Smith soon learned that several hundred South

Americans from Valparaíso and the Peruvian port of Callao had secured berths on the crowded US steamer *California* ahead of the US citizens who were waiting to board in Panama. The general became irate. In a vitriolic letter to William Nelson, the US consul in Panama, Smith wrote, "As nothing can be more unreasonable or unjust, than the conduct pursued by persons not citizens of the United States, who are flocking from all parts to search for and carry off gold belonging to the United States in California; and as such conduct is in direct violation of law, it will become my duty, immediately on my arrival there, to put these laws into force, to prevent their infraction in the future, by punishing with the penalties prescribed by law, on those who offend." Smith insisted that Nelson translate this statement and forward it to various Chilean, Peruvian, and Californian newspapers for publication.[22]

Smith's letter received widespread exposure and heightened California's ethnic tensions. During the spring of 1849, anti-immigrant sentiments in the northern mines reached a fever pitch. New York lawyer William Wheaton met Yankees in Amador County who had assembled to voice their discontent with the Latinos digging nearby. Wheaton recalled, "After a while we were approached by what seemed to be a Committee from these people, and in coming up, they said it was a meeting to consider the advisability of banishing the Chilenos and other Latinos from the mines. They wanted to borrow our rifles, but we refused them. They gave notice to that effect, and the Chilenos were subsequently banished from the camp, or rather they left when requested." Benigno Gutiérrez, a Chilean who sailed from Talcahuano to San Francisco at age nineteen, recalled the success he had experienced as a prospector but also lamented the intimidating warnings his party had received from Anglo miners. "We many times washed as much as 16 oz. to the pan and in about six weeks took out over a thousand ounces of gold," wrote Gutiérrez. "Then our troubles began. Once more we were told that as we were foreigners, we had no right there, and threats were used against us. We appealed to the local justice, but to no purpose, and we decided to go." As the *Placer Times* noted in July 1849, "The Peruvians and Chileans have been pretty thoroughly routed in every section of the Middle and North Forks [of the American River], and the disposition to expel them seems to be extending throughout the whole mining community." Chileans were a numerical minority in a hostile environment; as a result, they had little recourse other than departure from the diggings.[23]

The constant threat of Yankee aggression kept Chileans on edge whenever they encountered a new mining party. Dr. James Tyson, a physician from Baltimore, recounted meeting a group of Chileans while prospecting in 1849. Tyson was sympathetic to their plight and remarked, "Most of these people, together with Mexicans, Peruvians and other foreigners on the Pacific coast, had been driven from the mines in every direction, hardly sufficient time in some instances being allowed them to remove their mining tools." The party of Chileans was clearly uneasy: "Not knowing but our intentions hostile, they seized their arms, quickly arose, and looked in defiance at our approach. Finding we were not enemies, but wayworn travelers like themselves, they bade us '*Buenos dios señors;*' while we regaled ourselves with *agua friá* in deep and potent draughts from the brook."[24]

During the spring of 1850, circumstances in the mining regions deteriorated for nonwhites when California legislators passed An Act for the Better Regulation of the Mines and the Government of Foreign Miners. Commonly known as the Foreign Miner's Tax, the law took effect on April 13, 1850. It decreed that "no person who is not a native, or natural-born citizen of the United States, or who may not have become a citizen under the Treaty of Guadalupe Hidalgo" could mine gold in California without a license. So-called foreign miners— a euphemism for non-Anglo prospectors—had to purchase a permit, which cost twenty dollars per month, an exorbitant rate for Mexican, South American, and Chinese prospectors who were already facing expulsion from the most productive claims by the spring of 1850.[25]

Enforcement of the Foreign Miner's Tax amounted to government-sanctioned harassment. William Hutton, a former member of the US military forces that occupied California during the Mexican War, insisted, "The people in the lower part of the country say that they will not pay their taxes, but I expect they don't think that they can easily be made to do so. There is a great ignorance of law and government among the lower classes, and they have been accustomed to have everything their own way—but times are changing with them." The "lower classes" were not so keen on giving up hard-earned gold to meet the requirements of a law that seemed prejudiced to its core. On May 19, 1850, George Jewett remarked that he "found the people of Sonoria in a state of great excitement on account of the law imposing a tax of $20.00 per month on foreigners. They rose in a mass on being called on by the collectors declaring that they will not pay it & threaten to drive the Americans out of the country if they attempt to enforce it. The Americans are laying low to-day but they must look out tomorrow." Among non-US citizens, a spirit of rebellion flourished in the mining regions.[26]

New York Tribune correspondent Bayard Taylor supported the tax. As he argued, "During the mining season of 1849, more than 15,000 foreigners, mostly Mexicans and Chilenos, came in armed bands into the mining district, bidding defiance to all opposition, and finally carrying out some $20,000,000 worth of gold dust which belonged by purchase to the people of the United States. If not excluded by law, they will return and recommence the work of plunder." Taylor's comments typified the xenophobic thinking of US citizens who sought to exclude Latinos from the mining regions.[27]

Others Yankees attacked the tax, however. The Reverend Walter Colton, a Yale graduate who served as mayor of Monterey from 1846 to 1848, disagreed with its premises. In the spring of 1849, he wrote, "Much has been said of the amounts of gold taken from the mines by Sonoranians, Chilians, and Peruvians, and carried out of the country. As a general fact, this apprehension and alarm is without any sound basis. Not one pound of gold in ten, gathered by these foreigners, is shipped off to their credit: it is spent in the country for provisions, clothing, and in the hazards of the gaming-table. It falls in the hands of those who command the avenues of commerce, and ultimately reaches our own mints." Some US citizens were displeased with the law because it sanctioned a government intrusion on a space previously controlled by prospectors themselves. Virginia-born miner James H. Carson commented, "I am one who holds that the courts of California, or of any other State in the Union, have no more right to portion out or make bounds to the claims of miners in the mineral lands of the United States, than they have to portion out the flower gardens for the Emperor of China." Like many prospectors, Carson favored self-governance and resented interference from government officials. Numerous merchants and lawyers also voiced their opposition to the tax, fearing a decline in business if the tariff drove nonwhite miners from California.[28]

The state legislature agreed with such views and dropped the twenty-dollar license fee on March 14, 1851. Anticipating the repeal, the *Stockton Times* printed: "We shall long remember how fatal were its universal results—how it ruined the trader, and was made a fearful instrument of oppression—how it turned one man against his neighbor—how it sharpened the assassin's knife and primed the barrel of his pistol—how it depopulated the hitherto flourishing settlements amidst the hills—how it made the air heavy with fear, as though a plague swept over the land and had scattered destruction with its wings." This was a premature obituary for the Foreign Miner's Tax, however. A new version of the tariff, designed to intimidate Chinese prospectors, passed legislative muster in 1852, further aggravating ethnic tensions in the diggings.[29]

One of the fundamental contradictions of California history, from the Mexican War to the present, crystallized with the arrival of thousands of newcomers during the first years of the gold rush. On the one hand, California's newly arrived Yankee occupiers relied on nonwhite labor, imported commodities, foreign ideas, introduced technologies, and exotic plants. At the same time, most of these white colonists refused to acknowledge their multifaceted dependency on resources drawn from beyond US shores. Instead, they rejected the presence of so-called foreigners in their midst. A cluster of popular ideas, collectively termed *manifest destiny*, provided a timely—if provisional—rhetorical outlet for the frustrations of California's white residents. To US expansionists, manifest destiny represented a unique, providential mission to colonize the North American continent and convert the Indian and Hispanic populations of the trans-Mississippi West to capitalist values and Protestant morality.[30]

John L. O'Sullivan coined the phrase "manifest destiny" while editor of the *United States Magazine and Democratic Review*. This New York–based periodical had won widespread repute for publishing works by such nineteenth-century literary luminaries as Nathaniel Hawthorne, Walt Whitman, Henry David Thoreau, and Ralph Waldo Emerson. O'Sullivan introduced his readers to the new concept in the July–August 1845 issue when he referred to the annexation of Texas as a part of the United States's "manifest destiny to overspread the continent." He reiterated the phrase in the *New York Morning News* of December 27, 1845. Writing about the United States' dispute with Great Britain over the status of Oregon, O'Sullivan maintained that the United States should lay claim to the Pacific Northwest, "by the right of our manifest destiny to overspread and to possess the whole of the continent which Providence has given us for the development of the great experiment of liberty and federated self-government entrusted to us." In O'Sullivan's narrative of preordained progress, God was literally in-country.[31]

Other public figures quickly adopted the catchphrase and supplemented it with their own aggressive nativism. Addressing the US Senate on May 28, 1846, Democrat Thomas Hart Benton of Missouri spoke in terms that exposed the racism underlying the national mission to colonize the continent: "Since the dispersion of man upon earth, I know of no human event, past or present, which promises a greater, and more beneficent change upon earth than the arrival of the van of the Caucasian race (the Celtic-Anglo-Saxon division) upon the border of the sea which washes the shore of eastern Asia." Reaching his rhetorical crescendo, Benton declared, "It would seem that the White race alone received the divine command, to subdue and replenish the earth!" Two years later, after the signing of the Treaty of Guadalupe Hidalgo, Benton suggested that the United States should build a colossal statue of Christopher Columbus atop the Rocky Mountains that would have one of its arms outstretched toward Asia and the Pacific Ocean.[32]

Assertions of US commercial and military dominance in the Pacific World were the ultimate goals of this ideological contention. Instead of the mestizo hybridity that emerged from the Spanish-Indian encounter, the racial narrative of manifest destiny was one of substitution. This concept was not an abstract formulation reserved for intellectual circles. It was an everyday notion embraced by many. William Francis White, a New Yorker who started an importing business in San Francisco during 1849, contended with great certitude "that the manifest destiny of this nation of ours is to gather under the protection of its wise and benign government every foot of territory of this great continent, no reflecting person can question. That all the inferior and weak races now found on it are destined to pass away and disappear, there is not a shadow of doubt." Another of San Francisco's Yankee merchants, Franklin Buck, wrote to his sister in Maine, "It is strange that wherever the American people settle, the natives, be they Indians, Kanakas or Spaniards, gradually melt away; and I firmly believe in the doctrine of *manifest destiny*, that we shall yet overrun the whole continent and spread out on the Islands and into Asia."[33]

Indeed, Asia was in Commodore Matthew Perry's sights when his squadron of gunboats steamed into Japan's Uraga Harbor on July 8, 1853. According to imperialist dictates, the United States would facilitate the "opening" of previously closed civilizations throughout the Pacific. "And if the regions of South America, of the Pacific Isles, and of that vast continent of Asia, are destined to become the seats of a civilization higher than any now enjoyed," asserted Methodist minister and future Auburn University president William J. Sasnett in 1852, "the relative position of the United States to these vast regions designates her as the instrument by which these conditions of this advancing civilization are to be fulfilled." For Yankee expansionists such as Sasnett, the westward course of empire did not end at California's shores.[34]

Once the mass migration to San Francisco and the Sierra Nevada began, the remaking of the Americas entered a new phase. California, once a dreaded hinterland outpost for Spanish colonial officials, became a bottomless storehouse of wealth, underwriting a revolution in transpacific commerce. In the 1850s and 1860s, California's landscape underwent a comprehensive industrial transformation. San Francisco's financial investors and powerful business conglomerates from eastern states provided the capital, while public land agencies supplied the property rights for expansion as industrialists attempted to maximize the efficient extraction of the state's resources. The advent of hydraulic mining (expensive operations that blasted mountainsides with high-pressure streams of water to expose gold veins), the consolidation of wheat farming operations, the mechanization of the dairy and meat businesses, the expansion of the timber industry, and the capital-intensive extraction of silver and mercury produced dramatic shifts in land-use patterns and labor regimes.[35]

During this transition, the labor markets in San Francisco and inland cities became more competitive. Former miners and new waves of immigrants began looking for steady wage work instead of rushing to the Sierra Nevada when the winter snow had melted. Working-class whites from eastern states often felt threatened by Chileans, Mexicans, Chinese, African Americans, and other nonwhite laborers who brought distinctive skills and more modest salary demands. A number of these Anglos joined anti-immigrant political groups, such as Dennis Kearney's Workingman's Party, which adopted as its slogan, "The Chinese must go!"[36]

Throughout the early years of the gold rush, however, nativist sentiments in California were focused on the roles that the territory would play in the national slavery debate. California's 1849 state constitution prohibited slavery. The following year, Congress admitted California to the Union as a free state. Also in 1850, however, the California state legislature passed An Act for the Government and Protection of Indians, which established a legal framework for the indenture of loitering or orphaned Indians. Whites could have these Indians arrested, pay their bail, and then use this fee as a debt bond to press Indians into service on ranchos or mines. As historian Richard White explained, "If the Indians then attempted to leave, they were unemployed under the law and were once more liable to arrest. When the Americans coupled these indentures with other laws providing for Indian apprenticeship, they could legally compel unpaid labor from Indians." The act thus gave Anglos state sanction to secure the forced labor of California's Indian population. As it had in so many other regions of the United States, racism found expression in California's duplicitous "free state" bargain.[37]

California Indians were one of several groups of nonwhite laborers at work under the state's deceitful blend of nominal freedom and practical indenture. Many African Americans soon became ensnared in similar arrangements. Congress passed the Fugitive Slave Act on September 18, 1850, which made it a federal offense to assist or shelter runaway slaves and levied a fine of up to one thousand dollars on any officer of the law who did not arrest the alleged escapees he encountered. The act essentially held residents of free states responsible for the enforcement of southern slaveholders' laws. This decree provoked bitterness among northerners and undermined its sponsors' purposes by stimulating abolitionist sympathies in state legislatures and civil society. By 1851, thousands of fugitive slaves had crossed the Rio Grande to take refuge in Mexico.[38]

Some entered California as well. In the 1850s, Bostonian Edwin F. Morse hired a runaway slave named Isidor to prospect with him. Morse recollected, "The old darkey had been a slave, but as California was a free State he was now free and was saving most of the eight dollars per day wages I paid him to buy his wife's liberty." Isidor's situation was not atypical. As Morse explained, "Many slaves were brought out from the South by their masters and some of them remained with their former owners for some time even after they reached this State." Other blacks were self-employed. William Lloyd Garrison's Boston-based abolitionist paper, the *Liberator*, published a letter from San Francisco in early 1850 in which thirty-seven black men announced the formation of a society for mutual aid. The group advertised that it welcomed "new-comers."[39]

Yet many blacks who arrived in California entered at the behest of their masters under the oppressive strictures of bondage. Extant primary sources indicate the presence of enslaved African Americans from Los Angeles to Redding and from San Francisco to the mining regions of the Sierra Nevada. In 1849, a California correspondent for the *Liberator* described "a negro woman and child . . . bought a month since by a merchant in this town for $1900." Likewise, in 1850, the *Alta California* mentioned "a Mississippi planter" who arrived "in California with *five slaves*, from whose labor in the [mines] he expected to obtain broad and beneficial results." The *Alta*'s editors provocatively asked, "Why is the arm of the law powerless to expose and punish this invasion of our constitutional rights?" and "How can the evil of slave labor be tolerated in the mines?"[40]

As historian Eric Foner demonstrated in *Free Soil, Free Labor, Free Men* (1970), the Republican Party built its mid-nineteenth-century ideological agenda on a robust defense of free labor, equality of opportunity, freedom of mobility, the harmony of interests among capitalists and laborers, and the bourgeois paradigm of success through individual effort. The party fused these factors into a potent critique of slavery and its attendant social institutions. To northern Republicans, the South—with its seemingly immobile class structure and idle aristocracy—appeared antithetical to a fast-paced capitalist economic order. After visiting Virginia, Republican Party stalwart William H. Seward wrote in 1857, "An exhausted soil, old and decaying towns, wretchedly-neglected roads, and, in every respect, an absence of enterprise and improvement, distinguish the region through which we have come, in contrast to that in which we live. Such has been the effect of slavery."[41]

In stark contrast to such visions of social stagnation, Chile had been the first nation in the Americas to officially abolish slavery. The Chilean congress did so in 1823, more than four decades before the passage of the Thirteenth Amendment produced the same result in the United States. Mexico followed suit in 1829. Bolivia abolished slavery in 1830, and Argentina did so in 1843. As a result, Chileans who visited California during the gold rush found the presence of enslaved African Americans unconscionable. Ramón Gil Navarro wrote in his diary, "My God! What an impression it makes on me to see slaves in California, slaves chained by Americans, who, more than any other nation in the world, stand for freedom!!" Gil Navarro's disdain for slavery in California posited a powerful critique of US institutions from a South American vantage point. Yet—like a number of his well-heeled compatriots—Gil Navarro had no qualms about bringing thirty Chilean debt peons to California. The thousands of Chilean indentured laborers who came to California in the late 1840s and early 1850s would play a major role in the gold rush and the making of modern California.[42]

Tickets for the 5,100-nautical-mile journey from Valparaíso to San Francisco were prohibitively expensive for most of Chile's *peones*. As these itinerant laborers learned of California's glittering possibilities, many signed with Chilean companies, agreeing to repay their travel expenses by working for *patrones* (bosses). Such indenture arrangements built on centuries of seasonal, migratory debt peonage. It is difficult to quantify precisely how many Chilean peons made the voyage to California because contracts were often unwritten. On January 8, 1849, a writer for *El Mercurio de Valparaíso* noted that some were simply *contratos de palabra*, verbal contracts between illiterate Chileans and labor recruiters.[43]

When the 290-ton *Virjinia* set sail on September 12, 1848, it became the first vessel to bring Chilean prospectors and their debt peons to California. Many ships loaded with laborers followed. Forty-niner William M. Case was not exaggerating when he recalled, "Contract labor from Chili was also obtained, and it was estimated that by the mid-summer of 1849 as many as five thousand such laborers were at work on the California placers." While stopped in Chile on his way to San Francisco, Dr. John Lacourt wrote to California's governor Bennett C. Riley, "A great many expeditions are fitting out from Chili to California. Yesterday sailed the 'Carmen' with a number of wild Indians (peones) who are sent to California by a Company whose manager is a Scotchman of the name of Mackay. The company is to last three years and the peons are to have a share in the gold they will pick up." Of the approximately eight thousand Chileans who came to California between 1848 and 1853, more than half were debt peons.[44]

The vast majority of these bonded laborers were male. In their home country, peones faced derisive stereotyping. As a nineteenth-century guidebook to Chile noted: "Peons do not know any source of pleasure other than playing cards and alcohol. Everything they earn they shamelessly spend in their horrible orgies, after which they are absolutely drunk. Their disposition is gentle and humble when they are in full control of all their senses, but when alcohol perturbs their minds, they easily look for trouble and often grab the daggers they carry with them in their belts." Although California offered the prospect of relief from cyclical debt and chronic violence, the Chilean peons who labored in the central and southern mines of the Sierra Nevada rarely escaped the scornful characterizations that had plagued them in their homeland.[45]

As early as 1848, many Anglos begrudged the upper-class Chilenos who arrived with hundreds of peons. Republican free labor ideology became the banner under which Anglos rhetorically, legally, and physically attacked Chilean debt peonage. At a time when debates over slavery suffused national politics, widespread evidence of South American indentured workers contradicted California's free labor status. As *Californian* editor B. R. Buckelew wrote on November 4, 1848, "We left the slave states because we did not like to bring up a family in a miserable, can't-help-one's self condition." The notion that workers and employers could enter into agreements at will was, in the words of labor historian David Brody, "the core legality underpinning a conception of free labor that imagined American labor relations as a universe of independent and equal individuals." The archetype of the self-made man was at odds with the reality of foreign debt laborers toiling for their bosses in the mining regions.[46]

Affluent Chileans were some of the most egregious violators of the free labor creed that characterized California's mining districts. José Ramirez and his business partner Juan Sampson—the two of whom eventually founded Marysville (Yuba County)—used at least ten, but perhaps as many as thirty, Chilean peons to work their Yuba River claims in 1849. Pérez Rosales also reported the presence of indentured workers in his group. When departing from Valparaíso, he related, "Four brothers, a brother-in-law, and two trusted servants made up our expedition to California." Other wealthy Chilean prospectors, such as José Antonio Alemparte and Pablo Zorrilla, formed large mining companies, which each included as many as fifty-one peons. In his diary, the Argentine Chilean Ramón Gil Navarro referred to eleven separate Chilean mining companies—all using debt peons—in California. On the South Fork of the Feather River during May 1849, one Yankee reported seeing a sizable company of peons "at a Chilean camp" laboring for their boss: "They were a half naked and servile class, who labored under the eye of masters and performed the greatest drudgery with unshaken confidence in their employers. It was a rare sight for us to see a hundred men busily engaged in gold digging!"[47]

Careful investigation of Santiago and Valparaíso legal registries reveals substantial evidence that legions of unfree laborers left Chile for California. Examples of peonage arrangements abound. On September 12, 1848, eight men—José Bustamante, Felipe Carabajal, Cruz Dias, Juan Ferreira, Bernabé Morales, José Tomás Garrido, Santos Vergara, and José Videla—met with Valparaíso notary public José Felipe Gandara to have their labor contracts validated. According to Chilean state records, these men became the debt peons of their fancifully named Yankee *patrón*, Don Santiago "James" King of William (fig. 7). They agreed "to work [in California] for the space of one year . . . obliging themselves to faithfully respect the orders that they will be given." King arranged to pay their passage, house them, and provide them with twelve to thirteen pesos per month. After completing these formalities, the party boarded

Figure 7. James King of William brought eight Chilean debt peons from Valparaíso to San Francisco in 1848. On arrival, six ran away. King's mining fortunes did not pan out, and he became a banker and later the editor of the widely circulated *San Francisco Bulletin*. Political rival and city supervisor James P. Casey murdered King on May 14, 1856, after King's *Bulletin* exposed Casey's criminal past. *Courtesy of the Bancroft Library, Berkeley, California.*

the *Virjinia*, joining dozens of other Chilean women, men, and children bound for San Francisco. Thousands of other workers signed similar notarized contracts of *peonaje* before sailing for California.[48]

Chilean peonage in California provoked Yankee ire. On April 28, 1849, the editors of Sacramento's *Placer Times* opined "strongly against Chilian gangs employed by masters." Four days later, a second such editorial described the Chileans in the southern mines as "of servile cast" and subject to the demands of their masters. Interethnic tensions in the mines were already high when the first major conflict over peonage occurred in December 1849.[49]

On the North Fork of the Calaveras River near San Andreas a wealthy Valparaísan was mining a lucrative claim with a large group of peons. As James J. Ayers, one of the Yankees who participated in the ensuing confrontation, recounted, "Situated on an elevated flat, about two miles from our camp, was a settlement of Chilean miners. One Dr. Concha was the chief and moving spirit in this settlement, supported by some eight or ten lieutenants. The rest of the people consisted of peons whom they had brought from Chile, and who stood in relation to the headmen as dependents, in fact as slaves." According to Ayers and other nearby Anglos, Dr. Concha routinely staked out choice mining claims under the name of each peon in his service.[50]

Aggrieved by Dr. Concha's attempts to control a large swath of North Fork territory, Calaveras County Yankees organized a mass meeting, elected a leader named Collier, and drew up restrictions limiting the size of a claim that an individual could occupy. After the Chileans repulsed an initial attempt by several of these miners to work among their diggings, Collier and his men drafted a resolution ordering all "foreigners" to leave the county within fifteen days. Soon thereafter, Anglos ransacked the Chilean camp and seized several men at gunpoint.[51]

In response, a few Chileans packed their mules and left. The feisty Dr. Concha was not so easily frightened. He appealed to a regional judge in Stockton named Reynolds who provided a warrant for the arrest of the offending Anglos. When the Chileans returned to their camp to serve the warrant, the Yankees attacked. After several days of skirmishes, during which both sides took prisoners, at least two Anglos and two Chileans lay dead. In the end, several hundred Yankees got the upper hand. An impromptu vigilante court hurriedly condemned three Latino miners. On January 12, 1850, a band of Anglos lynched two Chileans and a Mexican. In his journal, Gil Navarro transcribed the last words of his countryman Terán, who cried out, "'I only regret not being able to kill two or three more of these bandits before dying.'" The conflict ended with seven men dead and no resolution in sight.[52]

During the drafting of California's founding documents as a US state, Chilean debt peonage and anti-Chilean violence became topics of heated political debate. Between September 1 and October 13, 1849, forty-eight elected delegates attended the Constitutional Convention in the territory's administrative capital, Monterey. Delegate Morton McCarver of Sacramento used anti-Chilean violence in the mines as a cautionary tale in support of his proposition that *free* African Americans be banned from entering California. As he told fellow delegates, "Sir, you will see the most fearful collisions that have ever been presented in any country. You will see the same feeling, only to a much greater extent, that has already been manifested against the foreigners of Chili. It is the duty of the Legislature to provide against these collisions." Many Chilean debt peons thought otherwise. Instead of waiting for long-overdue government protection, they began eroding the Chilean peonaje system by running away. Others served the duration of their contracts and transitioned to entrepreneurial mining or other occupations.[53]

Interracial violence involving Chileans and Anglos fed the ethnic stereotyping that flourished in gold rush California. Edward Gilbert, who served as the editor of the *Alta California* and one of San Francisco's delegates to the California Constitutional Convention, blamed immigrants from the Pacific region for California's woes: "Look at the miserable natives that come from the Sandwich Islands and other Islands of the Pacific; look at the degraded wretches that come from Sydney, New South Wales—the refuse of population from Chili, Peru, Mexico, and other parts of the world. Why do you not insert a provision preventing them from polluting the soil of California?" Although Gilbert's suggestion failed to become enshrined in the state constitution, California's "soil" had already acquired a vast array of Chilean contributions.[54]

Little did Gilbert know that in a few years the very ground outside of the hall from which he made his lofty pronouncements would be covered in a thick layer of Chilean alfalfa. A Chilean field hand might have cut this hay to feed the cows for Monterey's profitable dairy industry. It is not a stretch to imagine that Gilbert ate bread baked with Chilean flour that afternoon and returned several weeks later to his San Francisco office in a building constructed from bricks fashioned by Chilean workers. The extant records are too vague to confirm whether Gilbert ever laced a sluice with mercury that had been carried by a Chilean tenatero or obtained gold from a quartz vein using a Chile Mill or visited a Chilean prostitute. Yet we know for certain that Gilbert had been a member of Stevenson's New York Volunteer Regiment. He had surely befriended many of the Hounds who attacked Little Chile on the night of July 15, 1849.[55]

In the same way that Chilean influences on California's development became invisible during the late nineteenth century, violence against Latino immigrants in the US West has remained hidden from view in contemporary scholarship. The work of legal scholars Richard O. Zerbe Jr. and C. Leigh Anderson has perpetuated this problem. In 2001 they contended, "The prediction that the mines would be the scene of chaotic violence was wrong. Rather than anarchy or violent gang rule, what quickly emerged in the California gold fields were social institutions and rules for gold mining that relied upon a system of norms without unusual violence." Few statements about California's history could be further from the truth. At least 380 lynchings occurred in California between 1849 and 1902. Approximately half of these incidents happened in the five years from 1849 to 1853. Gold rush California was a staggeringly violent place.[56]

Nobody felt safe, and miners often resorted to extreme measures for protection. Prospectors spent more than six million dollars arming themselves with guns and knives during the five years following Sutter's discovery of gold. In the summer of 1850, a young British miner in California recorded in his journal, "I felt no fear; but I always kept my double barrel pistol and revolver under my pillow; and my double barrel fouling piece and a good rifle well loaded standing at the head of my bed; to say nothing about a small quantity of sharp steel." Albert Bernard de Russailh, a Frenchman who visited San Francisco in the 1850s, wrote that the men of the city "have all the characteristics of savages and think only of death and slaughter. They always carry revolvers and they draw them at the least provocation, and threaten to blow your head off. I often wonder if this great people will revert altogether to barbarism." As if to excuse such deplorable conditions, writer Charles H. Shinn argued that Latinos and Anglos constituted California's most irreconcilable dichotomy. As Shinn put it, "The foreign invasion (for it can be termed little else) was held in check and finally turned back, only by the energy and inborn capacity for creating order displayed by some of the Americans." This innate tendency toward social structure must have skipped a few generations, for it was markedly absent during the era of manifest destiny.[57]

It was Francisco P. Ramírez, the editor of *El Clamor Público*—California's earliest Spanish-language newspaper following the Mexican War—who first demonstrated how the widely accepted lynching of Latinos contradicted Anglo assertions of racial and moral superiority in the former Mexican territory. Referring to two recent lynchings of Mexicans in November 1857, Ramírez lambasted the English-language media for their casual portrayal of the horrifying events: "By saying that both victims of these scoundrels were Spanish, everything is explained. What one has to admire is the cynicism and hypocrisy with which they decant their *liberty*, their *equality*, and their *justice*." Such comments struck at the heart of Yankee duplicity in this era of westward expansion.[58]

References to hangings and mob killings of Latinos recur like well-rehearsed scenes in the diaries, newspapers, and published firsthand accounts of California's post-Mexican period. Connecticut miner Alfred T. Jackson wrote in his journal, "Only three weeks ago the mob hung a Chilean at Rose's Bar for horse stealing and the next day the horse he was accused of stealing was found in the hills above French Corral." At Stockton in 1849, Anglos charged a dozen Chileans with the murder of three Yankees. An anonymous miner described the incident, "Twelve were taken to the murder spot and nine were shot and three were hung without trial." Likewise, an article in the July 29, 1853, *Sacramento Daily Union* reported, "The prisoner . . . is now swinging from the old oak tree. He is a Chilean." After the murder of Sheriff James A. Barton and three of his deputies near San Juan Capistrano in 1857, vigilantes lynched the accused murderer, Juan Flores, and another Mexican, Pancho Daniel, without ever suggesting the need for a trial. The hangings continued, and as a Los Angeles judge noted, "In the interval there were eleven other lynchings of suspected persons." California lynch mobs operated in broad daylight within full view of a judicial system that condoned the practice of Anglo vigilantism.[59]

This would have been impossible without the complicity of many men who defended lynching as crucial to establishing social stability. As a *San Joaquín Republican* writer argued in 1852, "The civilized world may cry down the short but concise code of Judge Lynch, but I feel confident that every honest man in California has hailed it as a God-blessed evil to them." Lynchings were so common in California that a Calaveras County sheriff's deputy jokingly called them "extra-legal necktie parties." Some foreign observers were shocked and dismayed to find that North American miners considered such grisly spectacles entertaining. A British naval officer wrote from a rain-soaked gold mine in March 1852, "This weather 'riles' our Yankee friends here very much; they want the excitement of work, hunting a deer, hanging an Indian, or lynching a Sydney convict."[60]

Other Anglo portrayals of California lynching suggest a more purposeful practice of culling dark-skinned outcasts who threatened to disrupt class hierarchies. "While upon the subject of lynching," wrote wealthy Los Angeles merchant Harris Newmark, "I wish to observe that I have witnessed many such distressing affairs in Los Angeles; and that, though the penalty of hanging was sometimes too severe for the crime . . . the safety of the better classes in those troublous times often demanded quick and determined action." John Borthwick, who lived in California from 1851 to 1854, explained, "In the mines, where Lynch law had full swing, the amount of crime actually committed by the large criminally disposed portion of the community, consisting of lazy Mexican *ladrones* and cutthroats, well-trained professional burglars from populous countries, and outcast desperadoes from all the corners of the earth, was not so great as would have resulted from the presence of the same men in any old country, where the law, clothed in all its majesty, is more mysterious and slow, however irresistible, in its action."[61]

In reality, the "outcast desperadoes" were Anglo mobs whose members rarely assessed the evidence before exacting devastating punishment for alleged crimes. In February 1854, "forty armed volunteers, who arrived in a couple of hours and gave the preponderance to the lynch party," hung a Chilean at Bear Valley in Mariposa County on the suspicion that he was an accomplice to the murder of "an old man named Nathan Pratt." A year later an *Alta* correspondent reported, "sixteen Mexicans and Chilenos were known to have been hung" in retribution for the suspected murder of five Amador County Anglos. "Judge Lynch's Court" unswervingly imposed the tenets of manifest destiny throughout frontier California.[62]

Ideology is always as contested as the terrain it purports to dominate. During the gold rush, Chileans, Mexicans, and a minority of courageous US citizens refused to accept the dictates of nativism and the hollow claims of Anglo racial superiority. On May 1, 1850, a group of Yankee miners appealed to California governor Peter H. Burnett from their Calaveras County camp:

> We, the undersigned, Citizens of the U.S. respectfully beg leave to submit to the consideration of your Excellency the following facts. First: That there are present in this camp about two hundred men mostly foreigners from the different states of Mexico and Chili labouring in the mines. Many of them intelligent and respectable men and all quiet and peaceable in their habits. Second: That a great many men are now collecting at this place for the avowed purpose of driving them by force and arms from these mines. We therefore most earnestly request that your Excellency will speedily take such steps as will prevent any acts of violence or outrage which there is abundant reason to fear. [Signed] S. P. Hyde, Thos. E. Wiggins, John F. Stewart, Addison Beson Leurs Odell.

The camaraderie these Yankees expressed with their fellow Chilean and Mexican miners exemplified a Pan-American fellowship alien to men like Thomas Hart Benton, Commodore Perry, or General Persifor Smith. Instead, it prefigured Walt Whitman's cautionary vision in *Democratic Vistas* (1871): "The great word Solidarity has arisen. Of all dangers to a nation, as things exist in our day, there can be no greater one than having certain portions of the people set off from the rest by a line drawn—they not privileged as others, but degraded, humiliated, made of no account."[63]

Whitman's prophetic idealism did not fill the sails of the Chilean boats that carried refugee miners back to Valparaíso and Talcahuano. Hearing reports of assaults against its citizens in California, the Chilean congress appropriated forty thousand pesos to contract ships for their safe passage home. "Kip," a young Albany lawyer who spent six months mining in Northern California's Mokelumne region, remarked in 1850, "The Chilians also have been gradually disappearing, being taken back free in vessels chartered by their own government." Kip's comments captured a poignant moment in the production of invisibility (fig. 8).[64]

As Vicente Pérez Rosales sailed homeward during the waning days of 1849, he felt that his golden hopes had been fleeced by *Yanqui* nativism. Even so, the intrepid adventurer was satisfied with the impression that he and his countrymen had made on California's residents: "We went for wool and, like

Figure 8. A Chilean couple in James Mason Hutchings, "The World in California,"
Hutchings' Illustrated California Magazine 1, no. 9 (1857): 387. Published after years
of anti-Chilean violence, the article noted, "The number of Chilians in California are
less numerous than they were three or four years ago, and are annually decreasing."

so many others, we came back shorn, but satisfied because we had steadfastly stood our ground till we had fired our last shot." What Pérez Rosales did not mention was that the encounter between his compatriots and the newly arrived white residents of California had acutely altered the development of the US West. Anglo settlers were poorly prepared to engage with the cosmopolitan populations of San Francisco and the mining districts, the uncanny expertise of foreign miners, the unfamiliarity of a Mediterranean-type environment, and the radically divergent views on labor and freedom that they found when they arrived in California.[65]

Manifest destiny blinded many Yankees to the recognition that immigrants from the Pacific World were remaking North America in ways that were equally as profound and durable as those of westward-moving Anglos. The comments of California lawyer Willard Farwell in 1897 exemplify such myopia: "The years since the great influx of population began in California in 1849, had been fraught with exciting events and remarkable accomplishments. American energy and intelligence had established a new civilization, had founded good government, had brought order out of careless disorder, promoted public morality and educational and religious culture, and converted a solitude into a land of bustling activity, brimming with plenty and filled with promise." Looking west from California's shores, men like Farwell were oblivious to the longitudinal Cordillera behind them, that sinewy geological rope, which extended through the Americas and all the way south to the wheat fields, gold mines, and bustling port cities of Chile. Indeed, it was from the Cordillera itself that debt peons in Chile's Atacama Desert mined millions of tons of sodium nitrate, a substance crucial to another transformation of California.[66]

5

Supplementing the Soil

Edward Berwick came to California in 1865. Four years after his arrival, the British-born banker began raising pears, walnuts, apples, strawberries, and market vegetables in Monterey County. Like many of his fellow farmers, Berwick worried about fertilizing his crops and amending his exhausted soils. He outlined his apprehensions and sketched possible remedies in the June 1890 San Francisco *Overland Monthly*. His article, "Farming in the Year 2000, A.D.," featured a dialogue between the two main characters from socialist author Edward Bellamy's widely read utopian novel, *Looking Backward: 2000–1887* (1888). The conversation explored what agriculture might look like a century on. At one point in Berwick's imaginary exchange, the young Julian West—awakened after a 113-year slumber—asks his twenty-first-century guide, Dr. Leete, how the farmers of the future fertilize their soils. Leete answers, "These, by the aid of our slave of the lamp, electricity, we obtain in any quantity from that omnipresent and inexhaustible nitrogen mine, the atmosphere." The fictional dialogue showcased Berwick's prediction of industrial fixation of atmospheric nitrogen two decades before this process became commercially viable in Germany.[1]

Nitrogen depletion in California's soils was a major concern for late nine-teenth- and early twentieth-century farmers. Before World War I, Berwick's high-tech vision of industrial nitrogen fixation was mere speculation. Instead, farmers relied on two imports from Chile—nitrogen-rich Chilean alfalfa (*Medicago sativa*) and Chilean sodium nitrate ($NaNO_3$)—to meet the nutrient demands of a continuously expanding agricultural system. In particular, Chilean alfalfa was indispensable to the emergence of Northern California's profitable dairy businesses, which made California into the nation's top milk, butter, ice cream, and yogurt-producing state by the end of the twentieth century. Likewise, Chilean sodium nitrate was essential to Southern California's prosperous citrus-fruit industry, which served as that region's primary engine of economic growth from the 1880s through World War II.[2]

The arrival of Chilean alfalfa was a momentous event in California's history. This nitrogen-rich crop not only allowed Californian farmers to feed their expanding herds of cattle; it also helped to restore fertility to fields denuded by other nutrient-depleting plantings. Its appearance punctuated a longer sequence of botanical displacements from the Southern Hemisphere. Similarities between the soil profiles and Mediterranean-type climates of central Chile and central California facilitated alfalfa's successful transplantation during the gold rush. The latitudinal range of an herbaceous plant species in its native habitat is among the surest predictors of its invasiveness potential, or its probable success in a new environment. As biologist John Gerlach has noted, "Until 1898 almost all alfalfa growing in the western United States originated from seed which had been either imported directly from Chile or harvested locally from plants that were descendants of Chilean seed." During the late 1800s, the eastward movement of this nitrogen-fixing crop into North America's heartland changed western hydrology and land-use patterns in profound and enduring ways.[3]

Other plants also stowed aboard northbound vessels and arrived in mid-nineteenth-century California to find familiar environmental conditions in the Mediterranean-type ecosystem north of the equator. The Mediterranean grass red brome (*Bromus madritensis* ssp. *rubens*) reached gold rush California in contaminated shipments of Chilean wheat. Likewise, yellow starthistle (*Centaurea solstitialis*), an annual rangeland weed of Mediterranean origin, which crowds out native species and is toxic to horses, arrived in California among cargoes of Chilean alfalfa before spreading north and east.[4]

Of the flora that humans transported from Chile to California, Chilean alfalfa had the most dramatic impact. Plant growth is limited by the availability of macronutrients such as nitrogen. Because alfalfa is a legume, it can absorb nitrogen from the atmosphere. Nitrogen is an essential component of DNA, RNA, proteins, and enzymes, making it an indispensable building block of life. The earth's atmosphere consists of about 80 percent triple-bonded nitrogen gas (N_2), while the remaining 20 percent is oxygen, along with trace amounts of argon and other gases. Despite the omnipresence of gaseous nitrogen, only a small percentage of this atmospheric supply is readily available to earth's terrestrial organisms. Atmospheric N_2 is highly unreactive, and biological systems can use this nitrogen only after it is chemically transformed into reactive (Nr) forms, which include nitrogen oxides (NO_x), nitrate (NO_3^-), and ammonia (NH_3).

Lightning, volcanic activity, and forest fires can produce the extreme temperatures necessary for the fixation of nitrogen, while the recycling of crop residues,
manures, or human waste can help to preserve the pool of labile nitrogen within
an ecosystem.[5]

One of the few pathways through which nitrogen becomes usable by
plants is biofixation, a process involving the conversion of inert atmospheric
nitrogen into organic compounds, such as amino acids. Biofixation can be
carried out by *Rhizobium* bacteria affixed to the roots of leguminous plants,
including alfalfa and soybeans, or by microscopic cyanobacteria. On average,
alfalfa can fix from 200 to 250 pounds of nitrogen per acre. The amount of
nitrogen fixed—or converted from atmospheric molecular form to a compound
such as ammonia, nitrate, or nitrogen dioxide—alters the protein content of
the plant.[6]

Before its arrival in California, alfalfa had already traveled widely. Native to
Mesopotamia, Persia, and Siberia, where nomads began feeding it to horses
some time before 1300 BCE, its name may have derived from the Persian *aspo-
asti* (horse fodder), the Arabic *al-fasfasa* (horsepower), or the Kashmiri *ashwa-
bal* (horsepower). Farmers in Iran's Parthian Empire (247 BCE–227 CE) grew
protein-rich alfalfa as food for the horses of the imperial cavalry. Alfalfa then
spread to Greece in 480 BCE during the Persian invasion and arrived in Spain
with the Moorish incursion of the early eighth century CE. Eight hundred
years later, the Cortés and Pizarro expeditions brought alfalfa to Mexico and
Peru, where it thrived. By 1775, it had spread to Chile, Argentina, and Uruguay.
Beginning in 1736, North American colonists also began sowing alfalfa—known
to Western Europeans as lucerne—wherever they went. However, overly acidic
soils, harsh winters, and pests endemic to the Atlantic Seaboard impeded these
attempts.[7]

In contrast, the legume prospered in California from the early 1850s onward.
The dry, calcareous soils of North America's Pacific coast provided optimal
pH and soil density for this botanical immigrant. As the editors of the *California
Farmer* wrote in 1875, "Alfalfa, or Chili clover, is especially adapted for a dry, hot
climate. No matter how hot the weather may be, so long as the soil has been
cultivated deep enough for the roots to go down in search of moisture—some
twenty inches—Alfalfa will flourish." Between 1850 and 1875, at least eighteen
San Francisco–bound ships added "hay" or "threshes of hay," common euphe-
misms for alfalfa, to their holds during Chilean stopovers. Vessels traveling this
route frequently listed "clover seed" among their cargoes. The arrival of these
shipments became displacements, transfers that had little effect on their home
environments while dramatically altering their new landscapes.[8]

Just who introduced Chilean alfalfa to California is not known, but Chilean coal miner Manuel Oyarzo is a prominent candidate for this distinction. He sailed to San Francisco in 1849 "with a large collection of valuable seeds of trees and shrubs from the Andes for propagation and introduction here." During his youth, Oyarzo worked as a *huaso* (cowboy) on the southern Chilean island of Chiloé, where he fed alfalfa to his cattle. Subsequently, he took a job as a coal miner near Concepción, a region known for its sprawling alfalfa fields. Hearing tales of California gold, Oyarzo joined the northward exodus in 1849. After arriving, he abandoned mining, opting instead to work as a cowboy at Sonoma County's Rancho Arroyo de San Antonio. It is extremely likely that he sowed Chilean *Medicago sativa* seeds there. Speculation aside, W. E. Cameron made California's first recorded attempt to grow Chilean alfalfa in large quantities, planting it along the Yuba River near Marysville in 1851. Regardless of where credit is due, alfalfa thrived in California. By 1870, the state's farmers harvested around 550,000 tons of this nitrogen-fixing plant.[9]

Chilean alfalfa triumphed as livestock fodder for the California dairies that emerged in the 1850s, and it soon became indispensable for the state's milk, butter, and cheese production. In 1869, Monterey's county assessor wrote, "Cows taken from the native grasses, and pastured on fields of Chile Clover, will increase in the product of milk and butter, or cheese, from sixty to seventy per cent. Also, that one acre of land, well seeded with [Chilean alfalfa], will produce more pasturage in a year than ten acres of the same quality of land will in the native grasses." In his 1873 guide for California settlers, Charles Nordhoff recommended, "Of alfalfa, the Chilian clover, a quarter of an acre will keep a cow in hay, by successive cuttings, for nine months in the year." During the twentieth century, California's dairy industry became the largest in the nation. By the year 2000, California produced 19.2 percent of the US total, surpassing Wisconsin in aggregate annual volume. Chilean alfalfa facilitated this transformation. Because it can play these two key roles— fertilizer and cattle fodder—alfalfa became a focal point of California's irrigated landscape.[10]

By the late 1800s, Chilean alfalfa was a prominent component of California's agrarian landscapes. William Ellsworth Smythe—whom the author Wallace Stegner called "the John the Baptist of irrigation"—wrote of Kern County, "In this locality one knows of the existence of winter only by the dispatches in his morning newspaper, and those seem like fairy tales in the land where alfalfa fields are putting forth their leaves, and roses and violets are blooming in the dooryards." Similarly, when the Austrian archduke Ludwig Salvator visited Los Angeles in 1876, he found "Chilean clover" to be among the most conspicuous environmental features. Indeed, the plant was a vegetable sponge; its successful irrigation required water diversion projects on a scale unprecedented in US history.[11]

The vast hydraulic engineering projects of central Chile's grain and alfalfa belt may well have inspired some of California's first major agricultural irrigation projects. In 1849, John Bensley stopped in Valparaíso while sailing from New York to San Francisco. According to the historian Hubert Howe Bancroft, "The idea of irrigating the barren deserts of California was suggested to Mr. Bensley by having seen fields of grain and alfalfa successfully irrigated in Chile." Beyond Bancroft's tantalizing hint, little evidence remains to confirm the entrepreneur's inspiration. What is certain is that Bensley founded the San Joaquin and Kings River Canal Company in 1870. This ambitious scheme used a 160-mile canal to irrigate the San Joaquin Valley and was among the first such large-scale agricultural irrigation ventures in California's history.[12]

We know far more about "James Moore's Ditch" and "the Adams' Canal," two alfalfa irrigation projects in Northern California's Yolo County. In 1854, Moore and his workers dug a channel on the Gordon Ranch in the central Sacramento Valley to water his alfalfa crops. Ten years later, they lengthened it to irrigate 15,000 acres of alfalfa. In 1870, David Quincy Adams completed his dam of nearby Cache Creek to water his 4,500-acre parcel of pastureland, which was covered in "Chili clover." These were massive operations that presaged the vast water diversion and dam projects that eventually epitomized the twentieth-century "hydraulic West."[13]

By the early 1900s, Chilean alfalfa had become increasingly important throughout California's agricultural regions. As of 1904, alfalfa covered 98 percent of the irrigated farmland in the Turlock district of central California (Stanislaus County). In 1913, writer Tom Gregory called alfalfa "the Busiest Plant on Earth" and remarked that Chilean clover constituted nearly 85 percent of the hay crop in Yolo County. Alfalfa was winning hearts and minds while reshaping California's hydrology in the process.[14]

This successful botanical transfer also had wide-ranging implications for the development of farming and cattle ranching throughout the western United States. Because of its prodigious nitrogen-fixing capabilities, Chilean alfalfa improved the soil for subsequent crops. A 1908 wheat-growing manual suggested, "No crop, nor even any one class of crops, such as the cereals, should be continuously grown on a soil that will produce a variety of crops. On ordinary soils, cereal crops should be rotated every two to four years with a leguminous crop such as clover or alfalfa." Time and again, alfalfa renewed its reputation as a trustworthy rotation crop.[15]

Chilean alfalfa's national success depended heavily on US government promotion. In 1853, the US Patent Office mailed thousands of alfalfa seed packets to farmers across the country. In the *Southern Planter*, Commissioner of Patents Charles Mason wrote that the seed "was procured at considerable cost direct from the mountain valleys of Chili, and has been sent in small parcels to every State in the Union for experiment." Mason encouraged US farmers to give the new crop "a fair trial, and, if successful, to save the seed they raise, and report to this office the result." With the federal government's sponsorship, Chilean alfalfa quickly moved eastward. Californians successfully field-tested it, the US government facilitated its migration into the country's heartland, and farmers from California to Utah, Colorado, Kansas, and Nebraska planted it enthusiastically. By 1927, California and Nebraska alone had cultivated over a million acres with Chilean alfalfa.[16]

Planters throughout the western United States agreed that Chilean alfalfa offered a sound financial investment. As a Los Angeles dairyman put it, "The accession of alfalfa is as sure and as steady as the accretion of interest, and the investment in alfalfa-producing land is as regular in its returns as that in United States bonds." A midwestern farmer added, "Alfalfa is the best mortgage-lifter ever known." Ironically, a crop known for its financial reliability had arrived in California during the gold rush, a time of unparalleled speculation in which fortunes emerged and vanished in an instant.[17]

At the end of the nineteenth century, Chile provided California's farmers with another means of addressing soil degradation and nitrogen deficiency. Chilean sodium nitrate became an expensive, but widely used, alternative to domestically produced organic fertilizers. During the mid-1800s, many farmers on the Eastern Seaboard substituted imported sources of nitrogen and phosphates for human and animal manures. Starting in the 1840s, agriculturalists on the Atlantic coast and in the southern states adopted imported bird guano from Peru's Chincha Islands as their fertilizer of choice. By the 1870s, however, supplies of this nutrient-rich substance began dwindling owing to its rapid extraction to meet worldwide demand for guano.[18]

During the 1890s, California citrus farmers turned their attention toward Chilean sodium nitrate ($NaNO_3$), or *salitre* in Spanish. This inorganic fertilizer provided California agriculturalists with an unmatched infusion of nitrogen to support their ambitious venture into commercial orange cultivation. Riverside and San Bernardino Counties, known as the Inland Empire, became the center of California orange cultivation by 1900. Chilean sodium nitrate fueled the Inland Empire's citrus boom through the 1930s. To supply global markets with their valuable fertilizer, Chileans and the British entrepreneurs financing their operations recruited miners from throughout the Andean nations. Chileans, Bolivians, and Peruvians mined salitre under the enganche system, a debt-peonage regime introduced to Chile by a California entrepreneur named Henry Meiggs.[19]

The desire to acquire nutrient-rich resources also stimulated Chilean military conquest. By the end of the War of the Pacific (1879–83), Chile had defeated the allied forces of Peru and Bolivia, thereby attaining dominance over South America's Pacific coast. In the 1883 Treaty of Ancón, Chile obtained the provinces of Tarapacá, Tacna, and Arica. The following year, Bolivia forfeited its access to the Pacific when it ceded the seaport of Antofagasta to Chile. Chile's victory gave it exclusive control over the valuable nitrate mines in the northern Atacama Desert (fig. 9).[20]

Beneath the parched sands of the world's driest desert, a crucial element of life abounded. Profits from the nitrogen-rich white salts of Chile's newly acquired provinces filled the bank accounts of stockbrokers and Chilean bureaucrats, while the powdery substance fueled the valuable cash crops of distant cultivators in Europe and North America. At the end of the nineteenth century, California's citrus growers became some of the most significant beneficiaries of Chile's sodium nitrate industry. As their fellow citizens had done in previous decades, California horticulturalists depended on resources from their Pacific neighbors to meet their emergent economic needs and reinvent their agricultural practices.[21]

During the 1870s, farmers throughout the United States grew increasingly excited about South American sodium nitrate's potential as a reliable nutrient supplement. One reason for its popularity as a fertilizer was that sodium nitrate dissolved easily in water, making its nitrogen readily available to plant roots shortly after application. The *Saturday Evening Post* published a story in 1877 titled, "Immense Nitre Deposits, Which Will Prove of More Value Than Guano." That same year, the editors of the Atlanta-based *Southern Cultivator* wrote of sodium nitrate, "Few fertilizers act so rapidly when judiciously applied." Agriculturalist M. G. Ellzey wrote to Baltimore's *American Farmer* to recommend that farmers use nitrate of soda: "Wheat following corn, or even tobacco, must have artificial supplies of nitrogen, or a maximum crop cannot be made. The feeding of stock on the field for a few months before the corn is planted, gives the land some nitrogen, but certainly much less than is provided in 100 lbs. per acre of nitrate of soda and less than is removed by the corn."[22]

This was hardly new information to many farmers. United States planters were aware of sodium nitrate as early as the 1830s. An item titled "On the Saltpetre of Chile, (Nitrate of Soda)," appeared in the June 1833 *Journal of the*

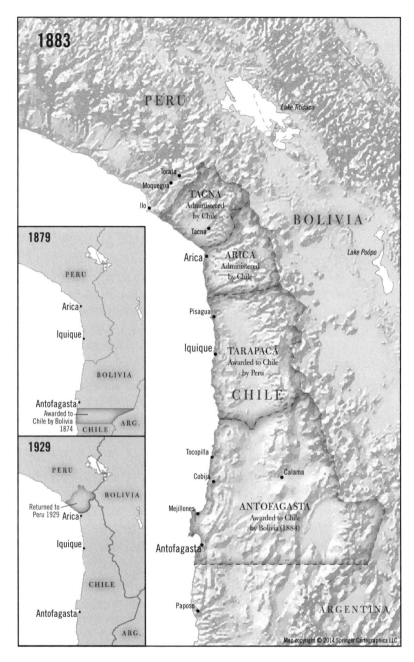

Figure 9. Map showing territorial changes resulting from the War of the Pacific (1879–83) and the 1929 Tacna-Arica Compromise, which allowed Peru to reacquire Tacna Province while leaving Arica Province under Chilean control. *Produced by Springer Cartographics LLC for Edward D. Melillo.*

Franklin Institute. "A question of some importance to a class of manufacturers, is now pending," wrote the editors, "[relating] to the substitution of nitrate of soda (saltpetre of Chili) for nitrate of potash." While exploring South America in the mid-1830s, Charles Darwin visited active nitrate mines near the Peruvian port of Iquique. As he recorded in his journal, "This salt was first exported in 1830: In one year an amount in value of one hundred thousand pounds sterling, was sent to France and England. It is principally used as a manure." By 1861, Alfredo Leubel—a Frenchman traveling in Peru—predicted, "Nitrate of soda, is one day going to be called to replace guano in the markets of Europe when these become exhausted; salitre is going to last for centuries and Europe is going to be obligated to buy it to feed its impoverished soils." United States farmers soon began purchasing substantial amounts of salitre. In 1873, Chile exported $155,332 worth of "Nitrate of Soda" to the United States.[23]

That year, a global economic depression devastated the Chilean economy. A decade later, just when it looked as if the governing administration of Aníbal Pinto was about to embark on a program of economic restructuring to avert further financial collapses, Chile's victory in the War of the Pacific allowed it to abandon these reforms and revert to a dependence on taxes from raw material exports as the country's main source of revenue. Until 1879, transnational companies and their agents in Bolivia, Peru, and Chile competed for shares of the lucrative nitrate trade. By the war's end, Chile had attained exclusive control over all of South America's nitrate mines, which covered four hundred miles from north to south.[24]

Before they could build an economic foundation based on sodium nitrate exports, Chileans and their foreign backers had to find effective ways to extract this valuable resource from the harsh and remote landscape of the Atacama Desert. Sodium nitrate is a type of salt, which contains approximately 16 percent nitrogen and 27 percent sodium. Nearly all of the world's mined sodium nitrate has come from the arid regions of northwestern South America, where it occurs in a mixture with other salts, such as potassium nitrate, and assorted trace metals, iodine, and insoluble compounds. The richest form of extractable nitrate is known as *caliche*, often found beneath two to sixty-five feet of gravel and powdered composites. The laborers who dug the caliche, or *calicheros*, worked for the nitrate refineries (*oficinas*), which were owned by wealthy Chilean *salitreros* and financed by British, and later, US capital.[25]

In the 1880s, recruiters for the nitrate companies convinced poor peones from Chile, Bolivia, and Peru to sign contracts for transportation to the mining zones (fig. 10). The *enganchadores*, operating on their own or as employees of the Asociación Salitrera (Nitrate Producers Association), "hooked" laborers

Figure 10. Nitrate miner, ca. 1945, at the Oficina Salitrera Victoria nitrate mines,
72 miles southeast of the city of Iquique in northern Chile. Photographer unknown.
Courtesy of the University of Chile, Santiago.

at carnivals with promises of the astounding wealth to be made in the mineral
districts of El Norte Grande, the Great North. Once these laborers signed on,
they were at the mercy of the nitrate bosses, who routinely ignored contractual
obligations and paid the workers far below a minimum wage or in scrip that was
valid only at overpriced, company-run stores. A worker's debt for his passage to
the mines became the bond that kept him toiling for his contractor. Nitrate
workers, who earned their meager pay for twelve-hour days of backbreaking
labor in the parched desert landscape, had every reason to feel bitter toward
their employers. Under these conditions, it is not surprising that the nitrate
regions became a hotbed of labor militancy early in the 1900s.[26]

Resentment also arose from the lavish lifestyles of the foreigners who ran the nitrate mining operations. In turn-of-the-century Iquique, a principal nitrate port and the terminus of the railroads that served the nitrate industry, explorer and travel writer Marie Robinson Wright found "clubs for gentlemen, the English Club having on its roll of membership names distinguished in the financial circles of Europe as well as America. A broad driveway along the beach connects the city with its suburb, Cavancha, a delightful resort with a dancing pavilion and promenade." She continued, "This place is always filled with people in the evening. About halfway along the beach between the city of Cavancha is the race track, and near it the clubhouse, a popular resort at all times of the year for the club members, their families and friends."[27]

Exhibitions of upper-class opulence amid a seemingly barren wasteland were just some of the many incongruities that characterized the nitrate regions. A visitor from the United States pointed out another blatant contradiction: "Foodstuffs for man and beast must be imported to the nitrate region. This food problem, therefore, develops into an enormous business and might be called one of the ironies of commerce—*foodstuffs* on a large scale entering a country in order that *food-growing materials* may be sent out of a country."[28]

During the late 1800s, a number of agronomists and agricultural commentators began to contend that nitrogen shortages posed a drastic threat to the world's food supply. In 1898, Sir William Crookes, president of the British Association for the Advancement of Science, stated that the exhaustion of soil nitrogen had the potential to cause a large-scale wheat shortage, in which "all England and all civilized nations stand in deadly peril of not having enough to eat." After spending two years in Chile, Marie Robinson Wright explained,

> In suggesting a remedy, Professor Crookes recommended the use of nitrate of soda, this product forming, according to his judgment, the cheapest and most important natural source from which to derive the supplies of nitrogen necessary for the restoration of the soil. Other scientists have expressed the same opinion; and agriculturalists, especially of the United States, have generally endorsed this view by increasing the demand for nitrate of soda annually, giving it preference over all other fertilizing products.

In other words, the transatlantic scientific establishment had validated Chile's sodium nitrate as the most appropriate antidote to the depletions of soil fertility that plagued the fields, orchards, and croplands of industrialized nations.[29]

Concurrently, California's farmers were shifting their attention to citrus cultivation, which demanded markedly higher amounts of nitrogen than grains

or other crops. Although Californians grew Eureka lemons and Marsh grape-
fruits, oranges rapidly became the focus of their citriculture efforts. California's
first oranges had come north from Mexico with Junípero Serra and his
Franciscan followers, who planted the fruit trees near the San Gabriel Mission
in 1804. Their six-acre orchard was home to four hundred seedlings and became
the basis for the trees and cuttings used in later California citriculture during
the Mexican period (1821–46). In 1841, pioneering agronomist William Wolfskill
established a two-acre orchard in the Los Angeles area using trees from San
Gabriel. By 1862, there were still no more than twenty-five thousand trees in the
state, with two-thirds of those growing under Wolfskill's care. The pioneer
planter died in 1866, but his son Joseph took charge of the family business and
eventually shipped a railroad car full of oranges to Saint Louis in 1877.[30]

Train tracks linked California's orange groves with fruit markets throughout
the country. The completion of the Central Pacific Railroad in 1869 established
the first transcontinental connection between California and eastern markets,
and by 1876, railroads extended southward from Oakland to Los Angeles.
Five years later, with the completion of the Southern Pacific, Southern
California had a direct link to the port of New Orleans. Business historian
Alfred Chandler Jr. has described the way nineteenth-century railroads rearranged geographical relations throughout the United States: "In 1830, 23 miles
of railroad track were being operated in the United States; by 1890 that figure
had grown to 166,703 miles as cities and villages were linked across the land."[31]

In Southern California, the dry, perpetually sun-drenched Inland Empire
became a hub of railroad-driven commerce by the late 1800s. According to journalist Charles Dudley Warner, "Riverside may without prejudice be regarded as
the centre of the orange growth and trade. The railway shipments of oranges
from Southern California in the season of 1890 aggregated about 2400 car-loads,
or about 800,000 boxes, of oranges . . . valued at about $1,500,000." The two
major varieties that filled these crates were Valencia oranges and Washington
navels, the so-called King of Oranges. London nurseryman Thomas Rivers
brought Valencias from the Azores to his greenhouses in the mid-1860s. From
Rivers's stock, lawyer Alfred B. Chapman took cuttings for cultivation on his
estate near Los Angeles. In 1870, US Department of Agriculture (USDA) botanist William Saunders brought the Washington navels to Washington, DC,
from Bahia, Brazil. He sent several trees to pioneer horticulturalist Eliza Tibbets
for cultivation at her new home in Riverside, California, in 1873.[32]

Owners of private orange gardens and small groves soon found themselves in
the company of sizable citriculture estates. The Austrian archduke Salvator
visited some of these large operations when he traveled to Los Angeles in 1876.

After touring the San Gabriel Valley by carriage, he described the 1,300-acre estate of Lake Vineyard and the 500-acre estate of Mount Vineyard: "Both groves produced this year more than 1,000,000 oranges and 75,000 lemons, as well as limes, olives, and walnuts." This was only the beginning. Between 1880 and 1890, the number of orange trees in California increased from 1,250,000 to 3,378,000.[33]

Nitrogen deficiencies plagued the dry regions where farmers cultivated their irrigated orange groves. In these production zones, a dearth of cover crops and grazing animals made leguminous matter and manures scarce. Thus, when a prominent fruit merchant from London visited Southern California in 1895, he "'noticed that our orange-growers used vast amounts of fertilizer and water upon their groves for the purpose of forcing the growth and producing large crops of fruit.'"[34]

Such practices did not emerge spontaneously; they had to be learned and adapted to local conditions. In 1900, the California State Board of Horticulture published a manual entitled *The Culture of the Citrus in California*, which drew on testimonies from agricultural experts and accomplished growers. The booklet included an eighteen-page section on how to fertilize orange trees. These pages featured accounts by cultivators who had used various nutrient-enhancing blends on their orchards. One such agriculturalist, N. W. Blanchard, recalled, "I bought and applied in the fall Chile saltpetre, a small amount per tree, with the evident result that I had more puffy fruit than I ever had before up to that date. I say evident result, as the orange-growers who used it in Los Angeles County had the same experience."[35]

Balfour, Gutherie and Company, a principal importer of Chilean sodium nitrate at the turn of the century, encouraged farmers to use its product by publishing marketing materials featuring testimonials from horticultural pioneer Luther Burbank. In one such testimonial, Burbank wrote, "After testing a great variety of Fertilizers on my Orchard and Experimental Grounds, I find that [Chilean] Nitrate of Soda and Thomas Slag Phosphate have given the best results at the least expense, and I shall not look further at present, as my trees, bulbs, plants, flowers and fruit have been, by the use of about 150 lbs. each per acre, nearly doubled in size and beauty in almost every instance."[36]

Shipments of Chilean sodium nitrate reached California sporadically until 1907, when regularly scheduled consignments began arriving at the Port of Los Angeles. This shift marked the development of a lucrative business for transpacific shipping companies. Travel writer Marie Robinson Wright noted, "Nearly three-fourths of the commerce between the United States and Chile is represented by Chile's export of nitrate of soda."[37]

Between 1913 and 1923, California farmers nearly doubled their annual consumption of imported fertilizer, increasing it from 36,000 tons to 71,364 tons. Nitrogen was the key ingredient in these nutrient supplements. In 1924, agronomist Sidney B. Haskell surveyed the data on fertilizer usage throughout the United States and found that farmers on the Pacific coast used soil amendments with far higher percentages of nitrogen than their counterparts in eight other regions of the United States. The heavy nitrogen demands of fruit production drove this discrepancy.[38]

Fertilizer suppliers advertised Chilean sodium nitrate in many venues. Some promotions used a "doubters, go and see for yourself" approach. A 1925 issue of the *California Citrograph* featured an advertisement for "Chilean Nitrate of Soda" that read, "If you would see what the proper use of these fertilizers will do, go and see those beautiful and highly profitable orange groves of Highland and many other places where the growers use all of these freely." Four years later, another ad in the *Citrograph* claimed that the profits of Fontana Farms—a large, successful Stanislaus County orange grower—had risen by $89.76 per acre after the application of Chilean sodium nitrate.[39]

As beneficiaries of this rapidly expanding market, fertilizer companies were anxious to assert that their product transcended the limits of nature. Their advertising pamphlets showcased rigorous chemical analyses, highlighted scientific breakthroughs, and distinguished between nature's unreliable organic manures and precise, laboratory-manufactured preparations of inorganic nitrate of soda. Their product was—as they never hesitated to point out—a measurable white powder that came packaged, labeled, and ready for application. As advertisers contended, animal dung was full of vague, unquantifiable elements; therefore, it posed risks. A scientist for the New York–based "Nitrate Propaganda" firm warned citrus growers, "Where large amounts of organic fertilizers are used, *die-back* will almost surely affect the trees, and fruit containing a large amount of *rag* and of poor shipping and keeping quality is the result." In contrast, chemically precise supplements—such as nitrate of soda—offered a scientifically testable set of ratios and results that nature could never supply on its own.[40]

This logic characterized a new relation between cash-crop cultivation and the inputs on which it depended. It also brought fruit production into the realm of commodification. In 1902, the *Los Angeles Times* quoted a professor who had determined the amount of sodium nitrate entering and leaving California's farms in each individual orange: "Figuring the percentage of nitre in each orange grown in California, Prof. Bailey estimated that there was shipped from this State last year 50,000 tons of nitre in the form of oranges." Despite the usefulness of his innovative calculations, Bailey did not calculate the number of broken backs, stolen years, and lives of hardship, on both sides of the equator, which made California's juicy pulp possible.[41]

In Carey McWilliams's 1939 exposé of the appalling working conditions on California's corporate farms, *Factories in the Field*, the journalist contended that the Golden State's cornucopia amounted to the nation's largest food factory. Its operations were predicated on a bevy of imported inputs, an unprecedented level of concentrated land ownership, and the wholesale exploitation of Chinese, Japanese, South Asian, Armenian, Filipino, and Mexican migrant farmworkers. McWilliams's dystopian portrait provided an unprecedented account of the labor and the land-use changes that underwrote California's expanding agricultural system.[42]

For the state's citrus growers, labor from around the Pacific World and nutrient supplements from South America built an economy of surplus, producing far more food than the state's residents could ever consume. Simultaneously, these supplements became necessary to California fruit and vegetable production. Fears of supply shortages and price hikes caused many US bureaucrats to frame questions of dependence on Chilean nitrates as "Our Nitrogen Problem." In an article with this title, Harry A. Curtis of the US Department of Commerce wrote in 1924, "The Chilean nitrate industry is a striking example of the control of a raw material by the producers thereof" (fig. 11).[43]

Before World War I, commercial geologists had searched in vain for viable nitrate deposits in California's deserts. The authors of the report from one such expedition asked, "Can the California Nitrates be produced so as to compete with the Chilean, which are handicapped with an export duty of $0.555 gold per hundred pounds?" An article in a 1916 issue of *Science* posited an answer:

> Nitrates are found in unusually large quantities in some soils and in some clay hills, particularly in southern California. These deposits have been examined by many persons and the general conclusion reached has been unfavorable to the idea of their practical utilization. The nitrate content, although unusually large as compared with the content of ordinary soils, probably does not average over 1 or 2 per cent of the soil or clay, and it is very doubtful whether the material could be worked commercially.

The same year, the editors of the *Washington Post* argued that the US government should abandon the hope of finding viable sodium nitrate sources in California and instead build nitrogen synthesis factories. The editors concluded with a plea for independence from Chilean nitrogen: "This country should wait no longer. It should not be compelled to depend upon Chile for its nitrates."[44]

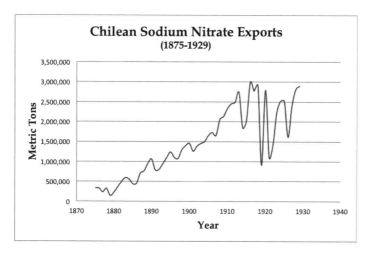

Figure 11. Several of the steep declines in nitrate exports from 1919 through the 1920s were due to widespread mining strikes among Chile's increasingly organized coal miners and stevedores. These labor actions disrupted coal-powered coastal rail and steamship transportation and thus dramatically affected the nitrate trade. Data derived from Carmen Cariol Sutter and Osvaldo Sunkel, *La historia económica de Chile, 1830 y 1930: Dos ensayos y una bibliografía* (Madrid, 1982), 126–27. Graph created by author.

In fact, industrially synthesized nitrogen was no longer a mirage. Edward Berwick's 1890 prediction had come true: humans had figured out how to "obtain in any quantity from that omnipresent and inexhaustible nitrogen mine, the atmosphere." On July 3, 1909, chemist Fritz Haber sent a letter to the directors of the chemical firm Badische Anilin- und Soda-Fabrik (BASF) in Ludwigshafen, Germany. In his communication, Haber described test results that he had shown to several colleagues the day before: "Yesterday we began operating the large ammonia apparatus with gas circulation . . . and were able to run it for about five hours without interruption. During this whole time it functioned correctly and produced liquid ammonia continuously." The process used high temperatures between 842° and 1,112° F (450° and 600° C) and very high pressures (200 to 400 atmospheres) to produce a reaction of nitrogen and hydrogen, which generated ammonia (NH_3). German chemist and engineer Carl Bosch soon overcame the practical engineering obstacles that had hindered the process and commercialized nitrogen synthesis two years later, at which time it became known as the Haber-Bosch process. On September 9, 1913, BASF began commercial ammonia production. Scientist and policy analyst Vaclav Smil has called the Haber-Bosch process the "detonator of the population explosion," because it provided unprecedented quantities of nitrogen to enhance crop yields around the world and feed a growing population.[45]

What neither Berwick nor any of California's gentleman farmers could have imagined was that the world would be engulfed by war in 1914. Nitrogen supplies became a central concern, not only as fertilizer to feed domestic populations, but also as a key weapons ingredient. Manufacturers produced blasting powders with a mixture of saltpeter (either potassium nitrate or sodium nitrate), charcoal, and sulfur. As of 1900, half of the sodium nitrate imported by the United States supplied explosives manufacturers. A British blockade of the Chilean coast looked as if it might shorten World War I, but German chemical plants at Oppau and Leuna synthesized enough ammonia (converting it to nitric acids and nitrates) to keep the German war machine running until its defeat in November 1918.[46]

Once industrialized countries adopted the Haber-Bosch process, economic proselytizers and political pundits sounded the death knell for the Chilean nitrate industry. In 1931, an economic geographer assured readers, "The phenomenal increase in the output of manufactured nitrogen compounds, which actively compete with Chilean nitrate, has not only destroyed the Chilean monopoly but threatens the very life of the great industry." Two years later, the chief of the USDA Bureau of Chemistry and Soils claimed that because of the construction of industrial nitrogen fixation factories, "Chile can no longer dictate what we shall pay for nitrates. Nitrogen prices have dropped consistently since 1925." By 1937, approximately 850 firms operated a thousand fertilizer factories throughout the United States and sold 8.2 million tons of fertilizer to farmers at just over $217 million. Little did either author know that World War II would renew US demand for Chilean sodium nitrate.[47]

As a 1944 *New York Times* article noted, "In the years of this war the imports of Chilean nitrate have been limited only by the amount of shipping available. Chilean nitrate is of strategic importance, not for munitions but for food and feed." As late as 1955, the *Times* pointed out that Chile's nitrate business, "even in its present crippled state[,] is bringing more than $40,000,000 in foreign exchange to the inflation-ridden coffers of the Chilean Government." World War II had offered Chile's nitrate industry a stay of execution, but by the mid-twentieth century, the Haber-Bosch process had replaced the Atacama Desert as the world's main nitrogen source. Fertilizer exports from industrialized countries to the developing world soon became a major component of the so-called Green Revolution in world agriculture.[48]

Despite its profound transformation of California's soil fertility, the Chilean nitrate trade has received almost no attention from historians. Richard Wines relegated Chile's nitrate era to the margins of *Fertilizer in America* (1985), writing only that "a few farmers experimented with Chilean nitrates . . . but until changed political conditions and the introduction of the 'Shanks process' in the 1880s, these were too expensive for use in fertilizers." Among California historians, sodium nitrate has fared even worse. Major studies of California's agricultural history barely mention Chilean fertilizer and its essential role in subsidizing the state's citriculture boom.[49]

Such omissions point—once again—to the production of invisibility. Eastward-moving trends that began on North America's Pacific coast have eluded most US historians. Together, the displacement of Chilean alfalfa and the exchange of sodium nitrate gave California indispensable ingredients for the growth of its nationally dominant dairy industry and its extraordinary orange bonanza. In 1911, *Chicago Tribune* publisher William D. Boyce was onto something when he wrote, "We Americans point with becoming pride to our great western prairies of rolling wheat lands and luxurious tracts of alfalfa and orchard country, but I think that but few of us know how much we are indebted to the nitrate workings of northern Chile." For most Chileans, however, salitre took more life than it gave. As an Atacama resident told a visiting *Washington Post* journalist in 2005, "Chile's history is intimately linked to the nitrate story. We lived off nitrate for many years. . . . It was a glorious past but it was also covered in blood."[50]

Part Two

CALIFORNIA AND THE MAKING OF CHILE

6

A Railroad in the Clouds

In 1877, the literary periodical *Scribner's Monthly* published a story by erstwhile diplomat James Eglinton Montgomery titled "A Railroad in the Clouds." Describing the triumphs of Yankee engineer Henry Meiggs, Montgomery declared, "It will be seen that a railway over the Andes is virtually an accomplished fact. There must be a force inherent in this portion of the American continent, which compels to Herculean labours. The Cordilleras themselves were not produced from the bosom of the ocean but by mighty throes." The man responsible for these prodigious achievements profited from the California gold rush before becoming the Golden State's most notorious debtor. After his high-stakes financial gambles collapsed in 1854, Meiggs fled San Francisco for South America, where he temporarily reversed his misfortunes.[1]

After building an extravagant new life in Santiago—replete with a million-dollar mansion and an entourage of devoted followers—Meiggs traveled north to Peru, where he pioneered the *enganche* debt peonage system and coordinated an unprecedented geographical rearrangement of Latin American commerce, demography, and mobility. As the so-called Yankee Pizarro of Latin America, Meiggs reshaped Chile's working class by recruiting and relocating thirty thousand Chilean workers to build the first railroad lines across the Andean Cordillera. A majority of the debt peons who toiled on these high-altitude engineering projects eventually migrated to Chile's Atacama Desert, where they mined the sodium nitrate that fertilized California's turn-of-the-century citrus bonanza. Meiggs was thus a human vector, precipitating both exchanges and influences between California and Chile.

Meiggs never returned to San Francisco, but his South American exploits captivated the Golden State's popular imagination. Between his hasty 1854 departure from the state and his death in 1877, California newspapers featured more than 250 stories about Meiggs. Unfortunately, the one full-length biography of Meiggs, historian Watt Stewart's 1940 *Henry Meiggs: Yankee Pizarro*, neglected these crucial sources and is incomplete in many areas. Stewart did not address Meiggs's involvement in the enganche labor system, nor did he consult any of California's rich archival materials. Because of these and other factors, his biography of Meiggs is filled with mistakes. Wherever possible, I have endeavored to correct these omissions, inaccuracies, and inconsistencies.[2]

I also suggest a framework for developing an environmental history of the Western Hemisphere's railroads, a project that scholars have yet to undertake but one that promises to disclose countless unexamined transnational linkages. Despite national and regional differences, the extensive railroad networks that emerged in the Americas during the late nineteenth century had four pronounced environmental effects: they encouraged deforestation, stimulated the expansion of mining frontiers, promoted plantation monocultures, and created new corridors for biotic transfers. Meiggs's Chilean and Peruvian railways contributed to all four of these outcomes.[3]

During his short life, Meiggs acquired a reputation for histrionics. The New York–based *Phrenological Journal*—displaying a nineteenth-century fixation with correlating cranial capacity and intellectual aptitude—described Meiggs as "a man of imposing appearance, about 5 feet 8 inches in height, broad-shouldered, muscular, and weighing in health about 225 pounds. He had what was called the largest head in South America; was a great mathematician, and so remarkably quick at figures that the Chilians and Peruvians are fond of telling about his wonderful arithmetical performances." Born in Catskill, New York, on July 7, 1811, Henry spent his youth building boats in his father's shipyard. At age twenty-four, Meiggs struck out on his own and traveled to New York City, where he opened a Manhattan lumberyard in 1837. Within the year, one of the most severe banking crises in US history triggered a stock market crash, launched a five-year depression, and produced record-high unemployment rates. Meiggs found himself, for the first of many times, bankrupt and bereft of the financial success and fame he so desperately sought (fig. 12).[4]

In 1849, Meiggs joined the rush to California, sailing around Cape Horn on the *Albany* with his second wife, Caroline, and their three sons. After arriving in San Francisco, Meiggs promptly sold the ship's cargo of lumber for twenty times what he had paid for it back east, netting a handsome fifty-thousand-dollar profit. Finding himself in a wood-scarce city where every abandoned vessel or nearby patch of forest was its own golden opportunity, Meiggs wasted no time becoming the timber baron of this "Venice of pine." He hired a team

Figure 12. Portrait of Henry Meiggs, "Hon. John B. Felton with compliments of H. Meiggs, Lima, Peru," February 27, 1872. Retratos Album, Courret Hermanos, Lima, Peru. *Courtesy of the Bancroft Library, University of California, Berkeley.*

of lumberjacks to fell trees in Contra Costa and Alameda Counties and floated immense rafts of logs across San Francisco Bay to his steam-powered mill in the city's waterfront district. During the summer of 1852, Meiggs borrowed one hundred thousand dollars from San Francisco bankers and incorporated the California Lumber Manufacturing Company, later known as the Mendocino Lumber Company. He shipped a complete sawmill to Mendocino aboard the abandoned gold rush schooner *Ontario* and began logging the coast redwoods (*Sequoia sempervirens*) with a crew of five hundred men, many of them Australians and Hawaiians. This was not the last time in his career that Meiggs would recruit a multicultural workforce from around the Pacific World to reap the natural wealth of its eastern rim. These operations were also part of the larger transformation of Northern California's forests during the mid-1800s. By 1872, one-third of the state's available timber supply had been depleted.[5]

While establishing a dominant presence in California's lumber trade, Meiggs also enhanced his civic credentials, serving three terms on the Board of Aldermen of the San Francisco City Council. Using the clout of elected office, he focused on developing the city's North Beach district, the same neighborhood where Little Chile's turbulent fortunes had risen and fallen. A devoted patron of the arts, Meiggs cofounded the Philharmonic Society of San Francisco with concert pianist Rudolph Herold and built the Music Hall at Bush and Montgomery Streets, where "quiet folk are entertained with concerts, oratorios, lectures, fairs, and the like." Meiggs also played a crucial role in the city's "land-making" efforts with the construction of Meiggs' Wharf in 1853. This wooden pier projected two thousand feet into San Francisco Bay from the base of Powell Street at Clarke's Point and reached depths that could accommodate his lumber schooners (fig. 13). By the end of 1853, Meiggs's company was shipping more than two million board feet of lumber per month from the Mendocino Coast southward to the city. Meiggs secured a contract to plank the city streets with wood from his sawmills and then used his extensive commercial contacts to obtain five hundred thousand dollars in illicit bonds, a massive sum in the mid-1850s. To accomplish this ruse, he forged signatures in a book of city warrants obtained from San Francisco's mayor and comptroller, thereby securing the bank loans to finance his extravagant paving project. When California suffered a financial crash in 1854, Meiggs's dishonest transactions threatened to permanently derail his fortunes.[6]

Before his widespread deceptions came to light, Meiggs gathered his family, servants, and close business associates at his Montgomery Street mansion and informed them of his plans for a clandestine departure from San Francisco. He chartered the brig *American*, loaded its hold with canned meats, wines, and provisions, and told acquaintances that he was heading out for a leisurely sail around the bay. At three o'clock in the morning on October 6, 1854, Captain Jacob Cousins piloted the *American* through the thick fog and away from California's coast. In his hasty departure, Meiggs left behind his possessions, "including his wharf, his city lots, and even his beautiful home on Telegraph Hill 'with fire burning in the hearth and the birds singing in their cages.'"[7]

Figure 13. "North Beach and Meiggs' Wharf, from Russian Hill, San Francisco."
Lawrence and Houseworth, Publisher, ca. 1870. *Courtesy of the Society
of California Pioneers.*

On the morning of Sunday, October 8, the *Daily Alta California* greeted
readers with the headline: "Astounding Developments!" The story began, "The
city was thrown into a tremendous state of excitement yesterday afternoon,
by the discovery that stupendous forgeries had been committed in City
Comptroller's Warrants, all the circumstances tending to fix the guilt upon
a man who, until within a day or two past, has stood high in the estimation of
the community." By then, "Honest Harry"—as San Franciscans formerly knew
him—was already far across the Pacific. After stopping in Tahiti, his ship
followed a southeasterly course toward Chile.[8]

After arriving in Talcahuano, Meiggs dodged California governor John
Bigler's attempts to secure his extradition. The prominent California fugitive
spent his first few years lying low in Chillán, a small city 249 miles southwest of

Santiago, before reinventing himself as a financier of ambitious engineering projects. His early endeavors included the completion of the Maipó Bridge on the railway then being built southward from Santiago.[9]

In 1861, Meiggs undertook the construction of El Ferrocarril de Santiago a Valparaíso (the Santiago-Valparaíso Railroad, or FCSV), which he compelled his sixty engineers and ten thousand workers to finish more than a year ahead of schedule. Meiggs made $1,326,000 on the project. As William Delano, one of Faxon D. Atherton's associates, wrote from Concepción on July 9, 1863, "We have just heard that Mr. Meiggs' splendid American locomotive the 'Contratista' was run through from Valparaiso to Santiago on the 1st inst. The grand opening I believe is to be on the 18th September." Delano continued, "The successful termination of this undertaking (the road from Valparaiso to Santiago) is a matter in which we Americans all take great pride, and Mr. Meiggs' antecedents are in a measure forgotten in the admiration caused by his energy and ability in carrying out this great work. You would be surprised to perceive how the Yankees have risen in the estimation of the Chileans since you left Chile."[10]

Little more than a decade before this festive occasion, the completion of such a bold project had seemed implausible to many observers. Samuel Brown, who stopped in Chile on his way to California in 1849, wrote to his wife in Connecticut: "There is a tolerable road through this country to St. Iago and near it the route which Mr. [Seth] Barton imagined for a Rail Road. The government have not commenced it however and it is doubted whether they ever will." In 1852, prominent businessman William Wheelwright of Newburyport, Massachusetts, had attempted to build a rail link between Santiago and Valparaíso. His crews hit many snags, including the death of two engineers, inadequate funding, unforeseen topographical challenges, and chronic government incompetence. As the Santiago newspaper *El Ferrocarril* (The railroad) remarked in 1858, "In Chile it is the current practice (without blaming anyone in particular) to quit undertakings without giving them the last touch; before finishing them we are seized with discouragement or our enthusiasm is exhausted." Indeed, this combination of unfortunate circumstances compelled Wheelwright to abandon the project altogether.[11]

By succeeding where Wheelwright had failed, Meiggs established an indisputable reputation as Chile's railroad impresario. The year after he completed the Santiago-Valparaíso line, he commissioned Jesse L. Wetmore—the architect of Meiggs' Wharf and the San Francisco Music Hall—to build him a million-dollar mansion in the suburbs of Santiago. Meiggs's opulence knew no bounds. As one commentator noted, "His wines were the best money could buy, and his cigars, made especially for him in Cuba, were of the same brand used by the Emperor Napoleon III."[12]

Meiggs was neither the first nor the last California resident to depart for Chile during the mid-nineteenth century. In 1861, James Churchman of the US consulate in Valparaíso responded to a flood of inquiries about "whether the Chilean Government encourages immigration to Chile." The *Daily Alta California*'s editors printed Churchman's reply, which read, "If you are a sober, industrious, well meaning man, who come[s] to the country to pursue any calling for which you are duly qualified, they will, if they become satisfied that you are worthy of full confidence, do all in their power to aid and encourage you." Churchman concluded his letter by noting, "P.S.—Sell your revolver and derringer, and invest in a plough and harness, or a few mining tools."[13]

Meiggs's ambitions transcended those of the farmer and the prospector. In 1868, the restive entrepreneur extended his energies northward when Juan Manuel Polar, the former Peruvian ambassador to Chile, invited him to Lima. At the behest of the Peruvian government, Meiggs supervised the demolition of the capital city's crumbling colonial era walls and oversaw their replacement with a pair of modern boulevards evocative of Baron Haussmann's renovated Paris. That same year, Meiggs donated fifty thousand dollars to assist the victims of a devastating earthquake that had destroyed the Peruvian towns of Arica, Arequipa, Moquegua, Mollendo, and Ilo.[14]

These demonstrations of architectural acumen and financial largesse led to a string of railroad-building agreements with the Peruvian government. Between 1868 and 1871, Meiggs signed contracts with President José Balta's administration to build eight lines, or more than 1,076 miles of railroads, in Peru. The Peruvian state's fixation with railroad construction proved extremely expensive. One estimate put the total cost of these eight projects at $118,959,000, while another suggested that it surpassed $133,000,000.[15]

President Balta justified such colossal expenditures on both commercial and military grounds. In the words of historian Fredrick Pike, "Balta in particular came to believe that by crisscrossing Peru with railroads, the full economic potentialities of so richly-endowed a country could be readily realized, while at the same time anarchy and revolutionary activity would be stamped out." Throughout the nineteenth century, the lingering memory of two anticolonial Indian uprisings against Spanish rule—Túpac Amaru II's revolt (1780–81) and Mateo García Pumacahua's Cuzco Rebellion (1814–15)—haunted Balta and his fellow Peruvian *criollos* (people of Spanish descent born in South America). Because railroads facilitated rapid troop deployment from military bases to remote locations, they provided the state with a "force multiplier." Troops could be swiftly concentrated and quickly moved from point to point, thus augmenting the military effectiveness of each soldier. Trains and breech-loading rifles, which reloaded faster than their muzzle-loaded predecessors, forged a powerful combination. The mid-nineteenth-century pairing of "Remington rifles and railroads" provided a lethal toolkit for state-sponsored campaigns of Indian extermination throughout the Americas.[16]

In Chile, Meiggs immersed himself in plans to use these innovations in a genocidal campaign against the country's Mapuche population. As the *Sacramento Daily Union* reported in 1871, "Meiggs offered to take the contract of the Chilean Government to subdue the Araucanians [the Mapuche], who have for over two hundred years rendered southern portions of Chile uninhabitable except by their own wild hordes, and whom it was impossible for the Spaniards, and has also ever been impossible for the Chileans to conquer." The editors continued, "It is alleged that Meiggs proposed to organize a force of Americans, imported from the Pacific coast, and wipe out the freebooting Araucanians altogether, but that the Chilean Government, not being able to see their way clear to getting rid of the proposed exterminators of the Araucanians, and fearing that they might take a notion to hold the country they should conquer, preferred to bear the evils they already had, rather than fly to others that they knew not of."[17]

Such sensational media accounts may appear exaggerated, but Meiggs's private correspondence bears the markings of a ruthless pragmatist with few scruples when enforcing his own vision of progress. As a widely read businessman, Meiggs was certainly aware of California's vigilante, state militia, and US Army Indian hunting campaigns and their mass killings, which state newspapers routinely covered during the 1850s.[18]

Like so many of history's demagogues, Meiggs projected an amiable, charismatic, and persuasive public persona. He also found dozens of ways to display his penchant for spectacle. Meiggs inaugurated his Peruvian railroad projects with grandiose festivities that "approached hyperbolic absurdities," according to historian Paul Gootenberg. During the opening ceremonies for the construction of the Ferrocarril Central Transandio (Trans-Andean Central Railroad), which would eventually connect the port city of Callao with Lima, Oroya, and stations beyond, Meiggs proclaimed that his Peruvian sponsors had launched "a great social revolution whose triumph and whose benefits are entrusted to the locomotive, that irresistible battering ram of modern civilization. . . . Its whistle will awaken the native race from [its] lethargy" (fig. 14). Subsequent portrayals of Meiggs's feats were generally effusive. After traveling on the Trans-Andean Central Railroad in 1935, US journalist and novelist Christopher Morley wrote,

Figure 14. "In the heart of the mighty Andes-Oroya Railroad Bridge in the sublime Infurnillo Gorge, Peru." H. C. White Co., ca. 1908. Photographic print on stereograph card. *Courtesy of the Library of Congress.*

"Up the hill, they call it; the most effective understatement I know. That's Lima's phrase for crossing the spine of the Andes on the Central Railway of Peru; the highest standard-gauge railroad in the world. I daresay the phrase originated with Henry Meiggs, the New York engineer who planned the road as early as 1868. They tell me he was eccentric, whatever that means. At any rate he was one of the world's great poets and built a rhyme loftier than [Milton's] Lycidas."[19]

Such praise was gratuitous, if not baseless. Although Meiggs was a talented financier and a nimble orator, he possessed only rudimentary engineering skills.

He therefore depended on the specialized skills of many associates from his California days. "The Americans were the civil engineers and skilled mechanics of the lines," wrote Major Alfred F. Sears. "If a man from California could assure Don Enrique that he had smoked a cigar on Meiggs's Wharf, he found a way at once to the good will of that most benevolent of men." One such individual, Richard Gird, met Meiggs in San Francisco and served as the surveyor on the Santiago-Valparaíso line before returning to the United States and making millions on Arizona's Tombstone silver mine. Another, New Yorker John L. Thorndike, accompanied Meiggs from California to South America and eventually carried out most of his former employer's projects, which included a million dollars' worth of railroads and mines in Peru and Chile. Engineers from California thus became profound influences on the economies and environments of Chile and Peru.[20]

Not all of Meiggs's employees were his San Francisco cronies, however. Among the most gifted men to work for him was the Polish émigré Ernest Malinowski (1808–99), who designed the Trans-Andean Central Railroad. Until the 2006 opening of China's Qingzang Railway, which connects Xining, Qinghai Province, and Lhasa, Tibet, the Trans-Andean Central Railroad was the world's highest railway, reaching a vertigo-inducing elevation of 15,700 feet above sea level and featuring an astounding twenty-six switchbacks, sixty-one bridges, and sixty-five tunnels.[21]

The economic rationale for such a gargantuan undertaking was the connection of Peru's Andean hinterlands with its coastal ports. Malinowski claimed that once Peru possessed reliable rail transport, it "should be able to compete with analogous goods from other countries. And not just in foreign markets, but even in this country, as wheat, coffee, cacao, and so on prove, which for the coastal consumer now come largely from abroad—even when interior growers can supply them in sufficient quantity, even superior quality." When agreeing to construct the Trans-Andean Central Railroad, Meiggs planned to control a sizable share of Peru's inland resources. Astoundingly, he obtained rights to all of the government-controlled silver-, copper-, lead-, and gold-mining regions in the Cerro de Pasco District, which would be serviced by his railway. Anyone working the deposits there was legally bound to pay Meiggs 30 percent of their take or relinquish their claims and receive 20 percent of the value of the extracted ore. Although Meiggs never lived to see these aspirations realized, his investment strategies demonstrated a long-term commitment to railroads as avenues of wealth extraction.[22]

During the late nineteenth century, railroads became yardsticks of modernity throughout the Americas. William Tecumseh Sherman, who achieved fame as a Union Amy general during the Civil War, was an avid supporter of the civilizing effects of the "iron horse." As Sherman told Congress in 1883, "Immigration and the occupation by industrious farmers and miners of lands vacated by the aborigines have been largely instrumental to that end, but the railroad which used to follow in the rear now goes forward with the picket-line in the great battle of civilization with barbarism, and has become the greater cause." Ironically, Sherman was among Meiggs's many San Francisco creditors. During Sherman's service as the manager of the West Coast branch of Lucas, Turner and Co., a Saint Louis–based bank, he lost eighteen thousand dollars from Meiggs's unpaid California debts. Although Sherman and Balta might have disagreed about whether Meiggs was a crook or a savior, they would have concurred that railroads afforded novel means of imposing economic and racial transformations of frontier landscapes and their indigenous populations.[23]

In similar fashion, Manuel Pardo—Balta's successor and Peru's first civilian president (1872–76)—called railroads "the missionaries of civilization" and was determined to convert dwindling guano profits into iron rails. Pardo's railway construction schemes received ample endorsement from foreigners. United States citizen Charles Rand, who later mediated the negotiations that ended the War of the Pacific, wrote in 1873, "The Railroads of Peru cost less per mile, than those of many other countries having more favorable conditions for obtaining labor and material; that their building is a wise measure of public policy; that they are urgently needed for the development of the immense resources of the country . . . aside from the great indirect advantages bestowed upon the people, which cannot be disputed."[24]

French chemist Héctor Davelouis, the director of La Casa de Moneda de Lima, the Lima Mint, bolstered such arguments for unhindered Peruvian railroad expansion. In 1863, he claimed that a railroad from the high-altitude mercury mines at Huancavelica would help Peru replace costly imports of quicksilver from California's New Almaden mines with cinnabar ore from its own mountains. At the time the Frenchman penned this argument for import substitution, California was the Pacific World's dominant quicksilver supplier. Davelouis did not know that Chilean workers were already mining mercury in New Almaden and would soon be building the very railroads in Peru that he hoped would free his adopted country from dependence on California's quicksilver supplies.[25]

Other encouragement for railroad expansion took a more decidedly racial tone. To Anglo proponents of manifest destiny, the Meiggs contracts exemplified the transformation of Spanish colonial backwaters into manifestations of Yankee advancement. On February 9, 1873, former Republican presidential candidate and former California senator John C. Frémont wrote to New York capitalist Simon Stevens: "I knew of [Meiggs] in California and since have followed his successful course in grappling with the crude civilization of the South American coast and forcing our Progress into it. His railroads there were in every sense up-hill work. He certainly has Americanized Chili and Peru and is a striking instance of how the energy and force of one man can impress itself upon a State." In Frémont's view, Anglo ingenuity was an inexorable tide that would eventually engulf the entire hemisphere.[26]

Yet the entrepreneurial exertions of Yankees such as Meiggs did not delight everyone. In the words of the eminent Peruvian historian Jorge Basadre, "The iron rails which Meiggs extended 'to the clouds' ruined Peru and were the precursors, not of regeneration and progress as so many trumpeted, but of bankruptcy and international catastrophe." Built during the waning years of Peru's guano era, Meiggs's railroads consumed far more capital than the state's coffers could supply. The South American nation became, like Meiggs, an infamous debtor to a legion of financiers. As a result, Peru defaulted on its national debt in 1876. Unperturbed by this development, Honest Harry simply printed his own currency—the "billete de Meiggs," Peruvians called it—to finance his projects until he secured his final construction contract with the government in 1877 (fig. 15).[27]

Even before Meiggs arrived in Peru, the country had faced a far-reaching fiscal crisis. In 1863 the national budget deficit reached $3.5 million, an astounding sum in nineteenth-century terms. The costs of a civil war in 1865, an armed conflict with Spain over the guano islands in 1866, the suppression of

Figure 15. The "billete de Meiggs," a five soles note printed by "The Company of Public Works and Development of Peru," July 4, 1876. Note Meiggs's signature (*Enrique Meiggs*) in the lower right-hand corner of the bill.

several internal rebellions, and advances on debts to foreign shipping companies only compounded Peru's fiscal woes. The most notorious of these financial follies was the 1869 "Dreyfus contract," in which Peru's government canceled all other consignment agreements and granted a quasi-monopoly on guano sales to the French merchant house Dreyfus Frères. The state borrowed its way into economic disarray with only its dwindling fertilizer supplies as collateral, funneling the Dreyfus loans directly into Meiggs's ambitious railway schemes. Vocal opposition to such hollow bargains emerged on Peru's streets and in its boardrooms, helping to ensure the collapse of Balta's government in 1872 and the termination of the Dreyfus contract in 1875.[28]

Despite draining the Peruvian economy, the trans-Andean railroads generated widespread fame for Meiggs. He was familiarly known as "Don Enrique," but that was just one of his many nicknames. Others included the "American Aladdin" and the "modern Count of Monte Cristo." His mythical reputation rested precariously on a foundation of bribes. Illicit payoffs smoothed Meiggs's contract negotiations with the Peruvian government and ensured that rival bids had little chance of success. At one point, Meiggs's brother John bragged to a friend, "We have the *whole of Peru Boots and Breeches.*" Manuel Gonzáles Prada—the iconoclastic literary critic and director of Peru's National Library—was far less exultant about Meiggs's reputation, writing, "He built many bridges and tunnels in the Andes but wrecked many homes and reputations in Lima. He had a great harem of the most aristocratic ladies and girls in Lima. In the corrupt spirit of guano enrichment, the people were willing to throw themselves into a sewer if, at bottom, they glimpsed a golden [coin]." Lechery and loan-sharking were not among Meiggs's more admirable traits.[29]

Obstinacy was another of his less attractive qualities. As James E. Montgomery had suggested, Meiggs's Andean railways were "Herculean labours" that reached metaphorical heights and literal altitudes unchallenged by any of the world's other engineers. Don Enrique reputedly told the Peruvian legislature, "Anywhere a llama goes, I can take a train." Meiggs proved stubborn, even adamant, when it came to the details of his lofty plans for crisscrossing the Cordillera with tracks. "The Oroya road is a very remarkable piece of engineering work, executed perhaps not wisely but too well. The difficulties surrounding it are enormous," wrote *Harper's* correspondent Theodore Child in 1891. "The constructor, an American, Henry Meiggs, used to say, I was told, at certain arduous points, 'The line has to go there, and if we can't find a road for it, we'll hang the track from balloons.'"[30]

Metaphors of suspension did little to keep the Peruvian economy from sinking to new lows. As with Chile's nitrate mining operations several decades later, Meiggs's railroads depended on the importation of nearly every constitutive element. James Orton, a Vassar natural history professor who trekked through the Peruvian highlands during the 1870s, observed, "Peruvians may be proud of their guano; but certainly they cannot hold up their heads when they remember that not a thing has entered into the construction of their railways but what is foreign, save, perhaps, dirt, stones, lime, and powder, which last article, so indispensable, Mr. Meiggs is obliged by contract to buy of the government. The timber, iron, rolling stock, labor, fuel, and nearly all the food, are imported. Even the money which pays for it is foreign—bank bills engraved in New York, and Bolivian silver!" Extending his lumber empire down the Cordillera, Meiggs even had his engineers use California redwood ties on many of their lines.[31]

Peru's dependence on foreign materials for railroad building was hardly unusual among Latin American nations. Historian John Coatsworth noted that in 1910, Mexico spent 60 percent of its railroad revenues on imported construction materials. In fact, as with most nineteenth-century railroad projects south of the Rio Grande, Latin Americans shipped iron to the United States to be made into track that was then reimported. It is little wonder that railroads came to represent debilitating loops of fiscal dependency in which raw materials flowed north only to return south as far costlier value-added commodities.[32]

Meiggs's railroad projects affected the lives of tens of thousands of Chilean workers and had sweeping repercussions for the entire Chilean nation. Few of Meiggs's admirers recognized that their hero introduced a debt-peonage strategy, known as the enganche, to Chile and Peru. Although Meiggs built on centuries-old unfree labor systems throughout Latin America, his particular innovation was the transportation of workers en masse to large-scale project sites. Laborers signed contracts before departure that, on paper, guaranteed them a small cash advance, a wage paid in company scrip, housing, and rudimentary supplies. This agreement also tied them to a debt for their passage to the distant job site and a fixed term of service for the employer. Meiggs was, in many ways, standardizing the ad hoc arrangements that had characterized Chilean debt peonage in California. Between 1868 and 1872, *enganchadores*, literally "ones who press or trick others into performing a service," convinced thirty thousand Chilean *rotos* (itinerant landless peasants) to sign debt contracts and travel north to Peru, where they toiled in the perilous terrain of Honest Harry's railroad-building schemes. As one of Meiggs's contemporaries put it, "There was not a steamboat on the broad waters of the Pacific that did not pour into Peru as many *peones* as potatoes from Chile."[33]

Meiggs claimed that his fondness for Chilean laborers derived from their deferential nature. At an 1863 banquet, he announced, "Every time I undertake railroad work, I prefer to work with five hundred Chilean workers than with one thousand Irishmen. These [Irishmen] regularly rebel and often fight their superiors when they see the least reason for complaint of the food, or when the contract is not followed to the letter." According to economic historian Manuel Fernández Canque, Meiggs frequently praised "the Chilean rotos who are willing to work with me for a plate of beans and for a little justice." Meiggs's claims about the roto's docility—whether feigned or sincere—were at odds with popular Chilean portrayals of the archetypal migrant laborer. One scholar of Chilean literature maintained that the traits of the roto in the national mythology were "his fatalism, the legacy of Araucanian and Mapuche ancestors; his vigorous physique; his predominantly mestizo blood; and a restless disposition that led him into the armies, to the California Gold Rush, and to the work-camps of the Panama Canal."[34]

Beyond such mythologized depictions, careful historical analysis suggests that mid-nineteenth-century rotos were pragmatic individuals, adjusting to the new realities of transnational wage labor. In addition to *porotos* (a Chilean colloquialism for beans) and fair treatment, the prospect of significant wage increases was a powerful attraction. As day laborers on Chilean *haciendas*, or later on smaller *fundos*, landless seasonal laborers commonly made only ten to twenty-five *centavos* per day (one hundred Chilean centavos, or one Chilean peso, was equal to roughly sixty-four American cents in 1880). For the prospect of sixty-two centavos per day, these migrant peasants left their homeland to carry out the grueling task of Andean railroad construction. The notion of rational choice should not obscure the fact that enganche was a form of unfree labor. Peons toiled to pay off the debts incurred for their passage to distant landscapes of labor beyond the boundaries of their homelands and far from the few protections that nineteenth-century Chilean law afforded them.[35]

As it had during California's gold rush, the northward exodus of Chilean laborers caused widespread anxiety among the national aristocracy. Debates over the consequences of this mass departure filled the pages of the *Boletín de la Sociedad Nacional de Agricultura*. In 1871, several prominent politicians drafted a law to prevent the emigration of Chilean workers to Peru, but the initiative failed to pass in either house of Chile's National Congress. That year, members of the sociedad publicly warned of the deceptions awaiting peons who headed north with Meiggs. As they wrote, "If it is true that [the Chilean peon] receives a salary three times higher [in railway construction in Peru than in Chile], it is also true that he will suffer the bad influences of a tropical country, where healthy food is scarce and everything sells at exorbitant prices." In 1904, Chilean agricultural official Teodoro Schneider estimated that the emigration of seasonal agricultural workers with Meiggs's enganche cost the Chilean economy three million pesos per year during the late 1860s and early 1870s. More recently, Latin American historian Arnold J. Bauer argued that such figures were an exaggeration, noting, "There is no evidence that agricultural wages were driven up because of the emigration to Peru. Nor did agriculture suffer; on the contrary, the years between 1868 and 1872 were ones of peak cereal output." Neither Schneider nor Bauer got it entirely correct. Bauer did not acknowledge that much of this yield increase resulted from the mechanization of Chilean agriculture and the decisions by *hacendados* (landowners) to pursue vast irrigation projects in the countryside during the 1860s and 1870s. On the other hand, Schneider's cost estimates of out-migration are redolent of the ceaseless complaints lodged by *agricultores* (large-scale agriculturalists) who unpersuasively grumbled about a dearth of workers and exorbitant labor costs.[36]

Government bureaucrats resisted Chilean labor migrations to Peruvian railroad-building sites, complicating matters for Meiggs's labor recruiters. Charles Watson, one of Meiggs's most trusted subcontractors, faced many hurdles when enlisting Chilean peons for construction ventures. In a July 12, 1871, letter from Valparaíso, Watson wrote to Meiggs about the "enganche de peones" (recruitment of peons) for the Oroya project. He noted that during planting and harvest seasons, "[Chilean] peons are scarce and I have to sweep the area thoroughly to find them." In the agricultural zones around Melipilla (southwest of Santiago) and Quillota (northeast of Valparaíso), Watson encountered inflexible local officials who refused to permit workers to leave their provinces. At one point, a government officer even ordered his men to detain a train that was scheduled to transport sixty peons to their Peru-bound steamship.[37]

Spatial dislocation has long been a key feature of many debt peonage regimes. As historian Gunther Peck demonstrated in *Reinventing Free Labor*, work bosses in the late nineteenth- and early twentieth-century North American West used their "control of labor mobility" as a way to commodify the labor power of immigrant workers in remote locations. Likewise, the recruiters and supervisors who ran Meiggs's enganche system found that moving workers far away from their home environments undermined traditional repertoires of economic, political, and social alternatives for these men and the family members who later joined them. Relocation to remote locations also made escape difficult and helped to enforce the price monopolies of the company store; with few alternatives for acquiring food, shelter, and basic services, Meiggs's supply chain served as the workers' lifeline.[38]

Undoubtedly, Meiggs's railroad-building operations rearranged the geography of Chile's working class. At the end of 1871, as a direct result of his labor recruitment, at least 4,442 Chileans resided in the Peruvian district of Iquique. By the late 1870s, more than 15,000 Chileans were mining sodium nitrate in Peruvian and Bolivian territory as part of the labor migration initiated by Meiggs. Millions of metric tons of this salitre traveled to California by sea and ended up fertilizing the state's citrus operations. Shifting demographic realities from the northward flow of Chilean workers also helped Chile's government establish political hegemony in the Norte Grande after the War of the Pacific. The population explosion in these northern provinces reflects the demographic transition sparked by the continuation of the enganche system during the nitrate era. In 1890, fewer than 180,000 people lived in the nitrate regions, whereas by 1925 the population of these areas had nearly doubled, reaching 345,000.[39]

Chileans were not the only foreign-born workers that Meiggs employed on his Peruvian projects, however. Approximately six thousand Chinese debt peons labored to construct the Chimbote-Huaraz line and the Trans-Andean Central Railroad. The Peruvian government banned slavery in 1854 but offset potential labor shortages with *la trata amarilla*, the so-called yellow trade in coerced Chinese workers. Between 1847 and 1874, at least one hundred thousand "coolies" from China came to Peru aboard an estimated 276 vessels. Although many of these workers toiled on coastal cotton and sugar plantations, found employment as domestic servants, or dug guano on the Chincha Islands, thousands labored on Meiggs's railroad projects. Anglo-Irish explorer Thomas Joseph Hutchinson visited Meiggs's construction site at San Bartolomé in the mountains northeast of Lima and observed, "Few things on my journey up here gave me so much pleasure as an inspection of the 480 to 500 Chinese that were working at this camp." Hutchinson continued, "Before starting in the morning for their work, they all get bread and tea, and the whole arrangement here plainly indicates that John Chinaman would have little to complain of, if he were treated everywhere in Peru as he is on the Oroya railway line by the employés of Mr. Meiggs."[40]

Not all accounts were as flattering about the working conditions on Meiggs's project sites. James E. Montgomery noted in *Scribner's Monthly*, "Notwithstanding the great care and attention paid by Mr. Meiggs to the well-being of his workmen, who have been principally Chilians and Chinese, at least 10,000 persons are computed to have died thus far in the progress of the work." Among the worst killers was a mysterious disease known as Oroya Fever. During the 1880s, the Peruvian medical student Daniel Carrion established the patterns of this so-called verruga disease. We now know it is caused by the bacterium *Bartonella bacilliformis*, which is transmitted by a sand fly (*Lutzomyia verrucarum*) and features stages that lead from skin lesions to immunodeficiency and death.[41]

Exposure to devastating disease was just one of the many perils that Chinese workers faced during their itinerant lives in the Pacific World. The maritime journey from China to Latin America could be equally harrowing. In 1853, a *New York Daily Times* correspondent described the ships that transported Chinese workers to Peru: "Vessels, it appears, are equipped for the business upon the model of slave ships. The victims are crowded down between low decks, where any other than a prone or sitting posture is out of the question." Workers frequently responded to these dreadful conditions by rebelling during the transpacific passage. Over the three decades of the coolie trade between China and Peru, sixty-eight ships—or nearly 10 percent of all voyages—experienced mutinies.[42]

The persistence of such horrifying conditions did not dissuade the corporate sponsors of the coolie trade from pursuing their lucrative endeavors. Meiggs worked closely with W. R. Grace and Company, the leading inter-American shipping house, to arrange for a constant supply of Chinese workers. William Russell Grace wrote to his brother Michael in the early 1870s, "There is lots of money in the business. 600 men in China costs $60,000." After calculating a 10 percent death rate during the transpacific passage, William continued, "That cargo of 540 men can be sold the moment they are shipped [at] $340 hard dollars each or say $183,660." International outrage over the conditions that plagued such ventures eventually caused the governments of Peru and China to shut down this brutal transpacific labor trade. On July 26, 1874, representatives of the Qing government and Peruvian officials signed the Tratado de Paz, Amistad, Comercio y Navegación (Treaty of peace, friendship, commerce, and navigation), which formally ended the coolie trade.[43]

Once again, a California connection emerged to alter the outcome of a transnational process along the Cordillera. Undaunted by the Qing government's treaty with Peru, the Grace Brothers turned to the US West as a source for recruits. Their sibling, John W. Grace, arrived in San Francisco in 1873 to open a West Coast branch of the family business. John subsequently coordinated the passage of workers from California to Latin America. In the five years before the War of the Pacific, Grace Brothers' ships carried hundreds of Chinese laborers from the Golden State to Peru under three-to-five-year contracts for labor on sugar plantations and railroads. As a result, railroad construction in the Americas was truly an interhemispheric endeavor. Men from southern China who had driven spikes and dynamited tunnels on North

America's first transcontinental railroad in the 1850s and 1860s later worked on Meiggs's trans-Andean railways during the 1870s.[44]

Meiggs not only helped to transform the landscapes of labor in California, Chile, and Peru but also invested heavily in two of the fertilizers that shaped nineteenth-century agriculture. In 1869, Meiggs purchased all of Bolivia's "Mejillones" guano deposits between 23°S and 25°S latitude. Seven years later, his brother John leased the Tocopilla sodium nitrate deposits from Bolivia and transferred their lucrative resources to Peru's government. Such investments contributed to Meiggs's apprehensions about the mounting tensions among Chile, Peru, and Bolivia during the 1870s. Writing from Arica to his brother in Lima on April 7, 1870, Meiggs confided, "I am very anxious because I hear that Bolivia is also preparing for war." Perhaps anxieties about impending conflict among his adopted nations—and his desire to return to the United States if necessary—prompted Meiggs to come to terms with his own financial malfeasance. He finally settled most of his California debts in 1873. The California legislature subsequently passed An Act to Remove from Henry Meiggs Certain Legal Disabilities. On the morning of September 30, 1877, Meiggs died of heart disease in Lima, having never returned to San Francisco. Newspapers across the United States printed accolades to his accomplishments, while an estimated twenty thousand people attended Meiggs's Peruvian funeral, attesting to his popularity there.[45]

Honest Harry achieved the fame he had so avidly pursued, but his aspirations for fortune remained elusive. As a front-page story in the October 13, 1877, *Sacramento Daily Union* noted, "W. R. Grace, head of the chief Peruvian firm in [New York], speaking of the financial condition of the late Henry Meiggs at the time of his death, says he thinks that really nothing except a mass of worthless securities and contracts is left behind by Meiggs, and says he should be very sorry to be a creditor of the estate." During the years following Meiggs's death, debates over his legacy intensified. In 1890, the editors of the Philadelphia-based journal *Railway World* concluded that Meiggs "was more like the ancient monarch who built merely for display than the modern investor, who does not begin an undertaking without a fair hope that it will be profitable." That said, Meiggs died before his carefully laid financial schemes could come to fruition.[46]

Whether he deserves the label of ostentatious emperor or hardheaded visionary, Meiggs unquestionably launched an era of railroad expansion throughout Latin America. In the War of the Pacific, the Chileans who had adopted him as a fiscal refugee from California defeated the Peruvians who had granted Meiggs his fame. It was no coincidence that one-time California visitor Benjamín Vicuña Mackenna founded a newspaper called *El Nuevo Ferrocarril* (The new railroad) at the end of the war. During this moment of heady nationalism and martial bravado, celebrations of Chile's technical prowess seemed apt.[47]

Many of the Yankee managers who began their careers with Meiggs supervised similar feats of railway building elsewhere in the Americas. New Yorker Thomas Braniff, who met Meiggs in California during the gold rush and later joined him in South America, eventually amassed a fortune building the railroad that linked Mexico City and Veracruz. Other Anglos who advised Latin America's governments on railroad building, such as Archer Harmon and George Earl Church, consciously followed in Honest Harry's footsteps.[48]

Even California's nascent petroleum industry piggybacked on the connections that Meiggs had forged in South America. At the turn of the century, Los Angeles oil tycoon Edward Doheny used the example of Peruvian train engines that burned petroleum to cajole California's railway companies into adopting similarly petro-powered systems. In turn, Peruvian trains burned oil from drilling operations that had initially been launched by Henry Meiggs. Before his death, Meiggs had invested $150,000 in the first wells and refinery on Peru's northern coast. In the early 1900s, California's oil barons also found a significant market for their product in Chile. By October 1913, Chile had become the leading international client for fuel oil shipped from Northern California's ports. The nitrate industry, with its heavy transportation demands, generated much of this demand. Their economies linked in an enduring commodity exchange, California's oil went south as Chile's nitrates traveled north.[49]

Henry Meiggs also bequeathed a legacy of railroad enterprises to his immediate family. In 1871 the Costa Rican government signed a £1.6 million contract with Henry to construct a railroad between the inland capital of San José and the Caribbean port of Limón. Costa Rica's dictator Tomás Guardia Gutiérrez envisioned this line as a crucial artery between the coffee-growing regions of the country's central valley and the transatlantic markets. Meiggs entrusted the project to his nephews, Henry Meiggs Keith and Minor Cooper Keith. After Henry Keith died of dysentery in 1873, Minor Keith used the Costa Rican project as a stepping-stone on his ascent to becoming "the Cecil Rhodes of Central America." As it had with his uncle, Keith's personal fortune came at the expense of an entire national economy. The same year (1876) that the Peruvian government bankrupted the state treasury in building its railways, Costa Rica defaulted on its loans because of heavy debts incurred from railroad construction. On lands ceded to the railroad, Keith grew vast monoculture forests of bananas, which eventually became a lucrative export of their own. In 1899,

Keith's company merged with the Boston Fruit Company to become the United Fruit Company (UFCO), the world's largest banana producer.[50]

The UFCO used its railroads to globalize commodity trading, bringing inland environments and peoples into contact with capitalist middlemen and consumers in Europe and North America. Similar patterns emerged elsewhere in Latin America at the turn of the century. In northern Chile, almost all of the railroad lines ran from east to west, linking inland mines and *oficinas* to Pacific harbors. Few regional north-south Chilean rail links ever emerged. As a trans-continental tendency, the dominance of such east-west transportation pathways stultified Latin America's domestic economies. Writing of such patterns, poet and journalist Eduardo Galeano noted: "The tracks were laid not to connect internal areas one with another, but to connect production centers with ports. The design still resembles the fingers of an open hand: thus railroads, so often hailed as forerunners of progress, were an impediment to the formation and development of an internal market." In Galeano's visceral imagery, not only did railroads constitute the visible hand of the market, but they also acted as "venas abiertas" (open veins) that drained the wealth of the continent's economies into the coffers of the United States and western Europe.[51]

Railroads standardized and homogenized space. Before the railroad era, inland regions without canals, rivers, or other navigable waterways could be served only by terrestrial traffic where the fairly low speeds of draft animals—such as horses, llamas, or oxen—prohibited the rapid movement of people and goods. Railroads accelerated the pace of transportation by shifting thermody-namic dependency toward new elements of "organic nature," namely the wood and fossil fuels that powered steam engines. Before the 1870s, most railroads in the Americas used wood for fuel. Likewise, until the advent of timber preserva-tives in the 1920s, railroad crossties—known as "sleepers" in the United States and *traviesas* throughout Latin America—had to be replaced every few years. As a result, wherever the railroad went, deforestation followed.[52]

As the noted US horticulturalist Andrew Samuel Fuller wrote about North America in 1866, "Even where railroads have penetrated regions abundantly supplied, we soon find that all along its track timber soon becomes scarce. For every railroad in the country requires a continued forest from one end to the other of its line to supply it with ties, fuel, and lumber for building their cars." In the United States, the expansion of railroads occurred at a frenetic pace during the 1800s, leading to environmental anxieties about an impending "timber famine." In 1905, President Theodore Roosevelt addressed the American Forest Congress on this issue: "The railroads must have ties. . . . The miner must have timber [for tunnel supports]. . . . If the present rate of forest destruction is allowed to continue, with nothing to offset it, a timber famine in the future is inevitable."[53]

Chile also experienced lumber shortages in the regions served by its railroads. Before the twentieth-century development of a domestic forest products industry, Chileans imported much of the wood used for track construction. These demands were considerable. Each mile of track required an average of 1,055 railroad ties. Chile's north-south railroad, from Santiago to Puerto Montt, was 2,051 miles long and required over 5.6 million ties. As the US consul in Valparaíso told the *San Francisco Call* in 1911, shortages of suitable lumber for replacement crossties plagued government railroads, causing many of the nation's railway officials to advocate for continued imports of wood.[54]

Although railroad companies found few substitutes for wooden crossties, when it came to fuel, coal provided a convincing alternative to wood. Coal was less bulky and produced much more energy per unit burned than wood. Aboard a late nineteenth-century steam train, a single ton of coal could replace four tons of firewood. During the late 1800s, Chile experienced a coal boom that allowed it to supply consumers throughout Latin America and the Pacific World. In 1852, Matías Cousiño bought the Lota mines. One century later, Conservative Party official and mining company administrator Octavio Astorquiza described Lota's coal mines as "el nervio que anima la marcha del país" (the nerve that animates the progress of the nation). Railroads and steamships were the primary customers for Chilean coal. In the early 1850s, the skipper of the steamer *Yankee Blade*, which plied the sea-lane between Valparaíso and Panama, noted, "The quality of the Lota coal is excellent, far superior to the one generally used in Chile and known under the name 'Carbón de Talcahuano.'" Not surprisingly, Cousiño held 10 percent of the stock in Henry Meiggs's Santiago-Valparaíso Railway Company. Indeed, by 1871, Meiggs was purchasing Lota's *carbón de piedra* (mineral coal) to fuel trains on the first leg of his Oroya line.[55]

In addition to encouraging deforestation and stimulating coal mining, railroads triggered an agricultural reorientation toward monoculture throughout the Americas. Large landowners producing single-crop commodities for export benefited from increased access to coastal outlets and new international markets for their products. Effectively, capitalist railroad systems promoted economies of scale throughout the Latin American countryside. This shift affected crops as diverse as Mexican henequen, Brazilian coffee, and Cuban sugar.[56]

In Chile, wheat barons reaped similar benefits from commercial railway expansion. The third major Chilean railroad built after the Copiapó-Caldera and Santiago-Valparaíso lines was the southward extension of the railway through the Central Valley. Known as the Ferrocarril del Sur (FCS), its construction began in the late 1850s. As hacendados shifted production away from the declining export markets of California and Australia and toward the wheat trade with Great Britain, they counted on a new railroad to link their haciendas to Valparaíso's seaport and more generally enhance the region's economic development. Indeed, by the 1860s, the landed elites of Chile's north-central valley were using the FCSV and FCS to outcompete small farmers near Talca.[57]

Railway lines also opened corridors for the rapid transplantation — intentional or accidental — of nonnative species. In this case, a botanical displacement from California to Chile exemplified such processes. Toward the end of the nineteenth century, the California poppy (*Eschscholzia californica*) found a receptive habitat in Chile's Mediterranean soils. Endemic to the West Coast, this tenacious flower is a member of an extremely invasive group of plants, the Papaveraceae family. In the 1890s the German Chilean botanist Friedrich Johow explained, "This plant is very interesting for its rapid naturalization in Chile. Originating from California, it was introduced into the gardens of Valparaíso and Viña del Mar in the 1890s where it escaped immediately from cultivation, becoming established first along railroad lines." In the California poppy's case, the displacement seems to have been deliberate. Railroad builders used the colorful poppies — California's state flower — to stabilize roadbeds and mark the rights-of-way for their tracks.[58]

People spread alongside poppies. The paradigmatic dictum of nineteenth-century Argentine political theorist and diplomat Juan Bautista Alberdi (1810–84) was "gobernar es poblar" (to govern is to populate). This became a continent-wide maxim for Latin America's nineteenth-century leaders. Linked to the extension of railroads, the drive to colonize frontier regions with settlers of European descent was deeply intertwined with transcontinental discourses of modernity. Like the men and women who followed the railroad's advances, Meiggs was both a pioneer and a refugee. For the Yankee Pizarro, fortune and failure were always just beyond the next mountain range.[59]

Exoneration proved elusive, not occurring until a century after Meiggs's death. On July 19, 1977, the following item appeared in the *New York Times*: "San Francisco, July 18 — One hundred years after his death in South America, Henry 'Honest Harry' Meiggs has been exonerated of stealing nearly half a million dollars from this city in the crash of 1854." As the story continued, "Henry Meiggs has gone before 'a higher court than here on this earth,' said Judge Harry W. Low as he granted the motion to quash an indictment for theft of public funds issued after Mr. Meiggs fled."[60]

Posthumously, Meiggs became a part of the Cordillera where he had resurrected his idiosyncratic career. Soaring to an altitude of 15,700 feet, the highest rock formation along Peru's Ferrocarril Central Transandio bears the name Mount Meiggs. Today, Avenida Enrique Meiggs bisects downtown Lima, Peru, and a foursquare block called Barrio Meiggs is a thriving commercial district next to the Central Railway Station in Santiago. The story of Henry Meiggs, embellished with salacious details about his 1854 flight from California, retains its time-honored place on popular tours of the San Francisco waterfront. Much like the myriad fables surrounding the California gold rush, tales of Meiggs's accomplishments and shortcomings retain their mythical persuasion along the Pacific corridor between Chile and California.[61]

7

MOUNTAINS OF INFAMY, VINES OF PLENTY

As Ramón Gil Navarro's ship carried him back to Chile in 1852, the one-time prospector reflected on what he had left behind in the Golden State: "With the last rays of sunshine we lost sight of the golden land of California, the country of marvels, the country of the thousand and one nights, the country that was the scene of so much happiness and so much suffering of mine." He concluded, "The last hills of Monterey with their beautiful pine trees disappeared with yesterday's light of day." Little did the Argentine Chilean migrant know that in half a century, California's native Monterey pine (*Pinus radiata*) would take root in Chile. By the late twentieth century, this species became the preeminent softwood in Chilean silviculture, and plantation forestry was the country's second most profitable export division, behind only the long-established copper mining industry. As conservative politician Joaquín Lavín declared in 1988, "Wood is Chile's new copper." Colossal piles of Monterey pine wood-chips, destined for paper mills and particleboard factories in China, Europe, Japan, and the United States—notably California—became regular features of Chile's ports. Critics of the country's aggressive forest policy referred to these heaps as "montañas de infamia," or mountains of infamy, symbolizing Chile's Faustian bargain of short-range economic gain for long-term environmental degradation (fig. 16).[1]

The success of California's Monterey pine in Chile contrasts markedly with a potential ecological displacement that never transpired between the two regions. Although California's wine industry has suffered successive outbreaks of grape phylloxera (*Daktulosphaira vitifoliae*), an aphidlike insect that destroys so-called Old World grapevines (*Vitis vinifera*), the blight has never afflicted Chilean vineyards. This is surprising, given that phylloxera has devastated

Figure 16. A Monterey pine plantation. *Courtesy of Christopher J. Earle,*
Gymnosperm Database (www.conifers.org).

grapevines from Australia and South Africa to France and Argentina. In fact,
Chile is the only major wine-producing country on earth to remain phylloxera
free. Chile's relative geographic isolation, a Chilean vintner's fortuitous importation of French rootstock just before Europe's first phylloxera outbreak in
the 1860s, and a series of botanical quarantine policies have protected Chile's
vineyards from the microscopic pest.

This environmental seclusion has not prevented Chilean and Californian
winemakers from engaging in countless exchanges of technologies and ideas
related to their craft, however. Capital flows in the viticulture business have
also created a labyrinthine network of transnational links that connect Chile
and California with the world's other Mediterranean-type ecosystems where
wine grapes thrive. Although Chilean forestry and viticulture might seem unre-
lated, economic policies emphasizing the advantages of nontraditional exports
shaped both. Such strategies have come at a price. Monterey pines and grape
phylloxera exemplify intensifying "environmental globalization," or the increasingly rapid movement of nonnative species among the world's ecosystems. In
Chile's case, such phenomena threaten biodiversity and cultural resilience.[2]

The sudden transformation of Chile's forests dislocated indigenous Mapuche
communities, revealed an unprecedented shift in Chilean modes of environmental governance, and represented a dramatic expansion of export-oriented

economic strategies. The ongoing replacement of Chile's autochthonous and biologically diverse temperate rainforests with agrarian monocultures—the cultivation of one plant to the exclusion of all others—was the hallmark of a centuries-long effort to transform south-central Chile into an industrial agrarian landscape that resembled California. Since the mid-nineteenth century, supporters of this agenda have focused on removing Mapuche people from their forest homelands and replacing these inhabited landscapes with commercial farms and industrial forestry operations. In the words of historian and anthropologist José Bengoa, "The dream of a Chilean California was the motor behind the 'Pacification of Araucania.'" Indeed, by the year 2000, Monterey pine and eucalyptus (*Eucalyptus globulus* and *E. nitens*) plantations covered more than 3.7 million acres of ancestral Mapuche lands. In this way California's Monterey pine became the symbolic and material foundation for the rise of plantation forestry while serving as the primary biotic agent in the destruction of the world's second largest coastal temperate forest.[3]

The Monterey pine's astonishingly successful Chilean career has undergone five phases. First, in the late nineteenth century, this tree species served as an ornamental plant in and around Concepción. Second, during the early 1900s, German Chilean scientist Federico Albert recommended it for reforestation and erosion control. Third, from the 1930s to the 1970s, Monterey pine plantations expanded to meet mounting demand for paper-pulping and coal-mining fuel. Fourth, under the Pinochet dictatorship (1973–90), private companies used massive state subsidies to dramatically expand Monterey pine exports. Finally, from 1990 onward, multiple actors—ranging from environmental nongovernmental organizations to indigenous activists—contested the future of Chilean silviculture. Meanwhile, California has served, at every turn, as a model for how Chileans would implement their forestry programs and policies.[4]

The Monterey pine is a shade-intolerant, closed-cone conifer that matures to an average height of 49–98 feet in the wild but can reach up to 200 feet on plantations. It is endemic to the central California coast and possesses many advantages for industrial forestry, including a rapid maturation rate of fifteen to twenty years under optimal conditions. Monterey pinewood exhibits cellular uniformity, durability, and low resin content, making it an ideal material for fiberboard and paper manufacturing. Dispersal by humans has transformed it into the world's most widely distributed pine tree, yet it has become a relict species in its home environment, surviving on only a few thousand acres in the central coastal California regions of Año Nuevo, Monterey, and Cambria and on two islands off Mexico's Baja California peninsula, Guadalupe and Cedros. Throughout these limited zones, the Monterey pine has come under considerable threat from the often-fatal disease known as pitch canker (caused by the fungal plant pathogen *Fusarium circinatum*).[5]

During the late nineteenth century, the Monterey pine became an increasingly valuable element of California's expanding urban landscape. As state promoter Titus Fey Cronise wrote in 1868, "The streets of San Francisco, formerly planked with Oregon lumber, are now laid with the Monterey Pine." *Pinus radiata* also provided a softwood substitute for timber species typically used by builders on the Eastern Seaboard. In the 1870s, writer Rolander Guy McClellan discussed the utility of the Monterey pine before remarking: "California has many species peculiar to her soil, not to be found in any other part of the globe; indeed *all* her trees, flowers, and shrubs seem to be different from those in any other country, many of the former supplying the finest quality of cabinet and house timber."[6]

Monterey pine timber soon found its way to various regions of the Pacific World. By the end of the nineteenth century, California was exporting this wood to Hawai'i and Australia. The Golden State also became the source for a seed diaspora that stretched westward. As the editors of the *Pacific Rural Press* wrote in 1911, "Hundreds of thousands of Pinus radiata (Monterey pine) [from California] have been raised from seed in New Zealand." Similarly, in Australia, Monterey pine cultivation met with great success, in large part because of the crusading efforts of Victoria's government botanist the German Australian Ferdinand von Mueller.[7]

During the late nineteenth and early twentieth centuries, planters introduced the Monterey pine to other Mediterranean-type ecosystems, including South Africa's Cape Province, Spain, Portugal, and, most successfully, Chile. The global dispersal of *Pinus radiata* followed a series of circuitous routes. In the case of its displacement from California to Chile, the tree traveled to Europe's botanical gardens before reaching South America. During his 1602 expedition along the California coast, the Basque merchant Sebastián Vizcaíno depicted Monterey Bay, which featured "a great extent of pine forest from which to obtain masts and yards." Vizcaíno was unaware that he was describing a landscape transformed by humans for at least five thousand years. For millennia, coastal California Indians had managed their hunting and foraging terrain through selective burns. These low-intensity fires not only controlled underbrush but also caused the Monterey pines along California's coast to adapt gradually by producing much thicker bark than those found on the islands of Baja California.[8]

It was not until the eighteenth century that scientists collected and preserved Monterey pine specimens. After offering the Chilean potato to the residents of the Mission San Carlos Borromeo in Carmel in 1786, La Pérouse expedition members obtained the seeds of a curious tree that they called "pine-apple fir." Their gardener Colladon (also spelled Collignon) mailed an envelope containing these specimens to the Museum of Natural History in Paris, where botanist Jean-Louis-Auguste Loiseleur-Deslongchamps cataloged them as *Pinus californiana* in 1812. Nurserymen at the Jardin des Plantes, the principal French botanical garden, germinated twelve of these samples, but all of the saplings perished before reaching maturity. In the 1830s, the Irish physician Thomas Coulter (1793–1843) collected California conifer specimens during an expedition to Alta California. The cones he gathered provided British taxonomist David Don with enough biotic material to classify *Pinus radiata* and present his findings to London's Linnaean Society in 1835. Still, the Monterey pine remained unestablished beyond its native range.[9]

Scottish botanist David Douglas (1799–1834) was among the most audacious plant hunters of the nineteenth century. From 1824 to 1833 he served as a collector for the London Horticultural Society. Douglas scoured the Pacific Northwest in search of new botanical varieties and eventually introduced more than 240 plant species to Britain. His most long-lived and significant contributions were a diverse array of conifers, which included the Douglas fir (*Pseudotsuga menziesii*), Sitka spruce (*Picea sitchensis*), noble fir (*Abies procera*), grand fir (*Abies grandis*), and Monterey pine. As Douglas joked to his patron, Sir William Hooker, "You will begin to think that I manufacture pines at my pleasure." The progeny of Douglas's *Pinus radiata* seeds arrived at London's Kew Gardens in 1833 and eventually became the stock that supplied Monterey pine seedlings to Europe's plant nurseries.[10]

Half a century later, the amateur botanist Arturo Junge Sahr imported *Pino insigne*—or "distinguished pine" as Chileans call it—to his garden in Concepción, thus expanding the Monterey pine's geographical range to South America. Junge's parents had come to southern Chile from Germany during the colonization campaign organized by California gold rush chronicler Vicente Pérez Rosales. In 1887, Junge established a 193-acre ornamental plant nursery in Concepción known as the Quinta Junge.[11]

Local legend has it that Monterey pine seeds arrived at Junge's garden by accident. As a journalist for the Concepción-based newspaper *El Sur* contended, "Arthur Junge, an amateur botanist and zoologist and a member of a respected German family residing in Concepcion, ordered douglas fir seeds from France in 1886. By mistake, the Valmorin exporting house sent radiata pine seeds instead of the ones he requested." This incident may have occurred, but Junge's own meticulously kept ledgers show no such transactions until 1890, when he paid nine German marks for a half pound of *"Pinus insignis"* (Monterey pine) seeds from the G. Porzel Nursery in Erfurt, Germany. Junge was so impressed with the decorative attributes of his California conifers that in 1910 he donated several Monterey pines to be planted atop Cerro Caracol, or Caracol Hill, six blocks from the city of Concepción's Independence Plaza. Hybridizing Chilean botany with Prussian realpolitik, Junge also erected a monument at the site to Germany's Iron Chancellor, Otto von Bismarck.[12]

The subsequent spread of the Monterey pine in Chile benefited from the efforts of two other influential Germans. In 1889, President José Manuel Balmaceda hired Federico Albert to collaborate with the esteemed German Chilean paleontologist and zoologist Rodolfo Amando Philippi in establishing Chile's Natural History Museum. Raised and trained in Berlin, Albert had already gained considerable experience in Berlin's Botanical Museum before arriving in Santiago. Albert's introduction of German scientific forestry principles to his adopted country built on an emerging nineteenth-century awareness of deforestation and its consequences for economic growth and soil erosion. This knowledge eventually led to the creation of Chile's first national forest reserves. Peter Schmidtmeyer, an English traveler who toured South America in the 1820s, wrote about how timber shortages resulting from unconstrained wood harvests had inhibited copper mining operations around Chile's Coquimbo Province (north of Santiago). Without adequate fuel for their smelters, Chilean mining operations had to send their raw ores to Europe for further refining.[13]

Other accounts of deforestation's startling consequences followed these initial observations. In 1838, the French Chilean botanist Claudio Gay published an article "Sobre las causas de la disminución de los montes de la Provincia de Coquimbo" (On the causes of the decay of the mountains of the Province of Coquimbo), which discussed soil erosion from local deforestation in Coquimbo and anticipated—by nearly three decades—many of the conclusions reached by US conservationist George Perkins Marsh in his influential text *Man and Nature* (1864). In 1872, the Chilean government finally responded by regulating miners' rights to cut trees for fuelwood. The following year, the state formalized these restrictions with the Reglamento General de Corta (General felling rules), which limited the species, ages, heights, and regions for tree harvests. These regulations also codified a system of fines for illegal lumbering and established a ranger corps to enforce these new laws.[14]

Building on these ecological and legal shifts, Albert offered a prescriptive response to concerns about widespread soil loss in Chile's mining and agricultural zones. In his 1913 monograph, *El problema forestal en Chile* (The forest problem in Chile), Albert recommended that Chileans plant rapidly maturing tree species, such as Monterey pine and Tasmanian blue gum eucalyptus (which arrived from Australia in 1823) to restore vegetative cover and curtail erosion. He repeatedly referred to Californian tree-planting regimes as models for Chilean acclimatization of *Pinus radiata*, noting, "In California [the Monterey pine] is employed on a grand scale for the replanting of dunes, mixing it with Monterey Cypress. . . . It prefers fresh soil and humid air, for this produces the natural state in which [the Monterey pine] is encountered in California." For Albert, California supplied a familiar template for influencing Chilean environmental practices.[15]

The unprecedented proliferation of the Monterey pine in Chile was due, at least in part, to biological factors. As forest ecologist Roger Sands has pointed out: "Exotics often grow faster in their introduced environment than their home environment. *Pinus radiata* (radiata pine) is a good example. It is the dominant conifer in the southern hemisphere while of little consequence in its home environment of California and adjacent islands." The Monterey pine is truly a stranger on familiar soil in Chile. Although intolerant of severe frosts, it possesses unparalleled adaptability to variances in soil pH, elevation, and nutrient availability in temperate ecosystems. Ivan Castro Poblete, the executive director of the government forestry agency, Corporación Nacional Forestal, told a *New York Times* reporter in 1988, "Here, the radiata pine has found a better place to grow than in its place of origin. . . . It can be cut here in 25 years, a fraction of the time it takes to grow in the Pacific Northwest." In capitalist forestry, the conversion of trees into commodities is constrained by an array of environmental factors. Among the most important is the time trees require to reach harvestable size. Because the Monterey pine grows faster in southern Chile than almost anywhere else on earth, firms can shorten production times by simply relying on the "natural advantages" that this ecosystem provides.[16]

The tree's success as a botanical migrant also built on earlier social and economic exchanges between Chile and California. The demand for flour that accompanied California's mining boom, the subsequent gold rush that began in New South Wales, Australia, in 1851, and the rapid expansion of British demand in the 1870s all provided crucial stimuli to Chilean wheat cultivation. During the 1850s, Chilean hacendados opened areas for wheat farming by clearing hundreds of thousands of acres of native southern beeches (*Nothofagus glauca*)—colloquially known as *hualo*—in the central Cordillera, especially Concepción and Ñuble Provinces. Soils in this region were generally unfit for farming, and intensive agriculture soon led to declining fertility and soil erosion. This made these regions especially adaptable to Monterey pine silviculture; the

Monterey pine is well suited to sites that have experienced soil degradation caused by intensive agriculture.[17]

Expansion of wheat farming—along with its eventual transition to plantation forestry—had widespread ramifications for regional development and was explicitly connected to the notion of creating a "nueva California" in Chile. Chile's temperate rainforests, concentrated in the southern regions of the country between 35°S and 55°S latitude, have been the site of conflict and contested use since the Spanish arrived in the sixteenth century. Chilean elites identified the clearing of these native forests and the removal of their long-term human inhabitants as aspects of a larger "neuva California" project. In 1866, the editors of *El Meteoro*, a newspaper based in Los Ángles, Chile, the capital of Biobío Province, discussed their hopes for the colonization of the La Araucanía Region, south of Concepción: "Those lands can be ceded to Chileans or foreigners, or one part to the former and one to the latter. In this manner, the territory between the Bío-Bío and Imperial rivers will gradually be conquered: the industries, the population, the settlements will flourish; Araucanía will disappear with time and in its place a new California will rise." This "new California" would be one of large-scale, irrigated agriculture, on the order of the wheat boom that California was experiencing in the 1860s.[18]

While California offered a paradigm for Chilean land-use change, it also provided the wood with which shipbuilders constructed Chile's maritime fleets throughout the late 1800s. At the turn of the century, English geographer and Royal Geographical Society president Sir Thomas Hungerford Holdich observed: "I was a little surprised to learn from the naval authorities at Talcahuano that the forests of Southern Chile do not supply the greater part of the timber used in naval construction. These forests are so immense, the variety of timber contained in them is so great, the growth of it so splendid in height and girth, that it seemed almost incredible that the chief source of supply for the dockyards should be California." Because of regional labor shortages in the country's south-central region and the dearth of softwoods for construction before the arrival of the Monterey pine, timber was the most important commodity by monetary value that the United States sent to Chile in 1889. That year Chile was the destination for a million dollars' worth of wood exports from West Coast ports.[19]

Ironically, coal, the substance that eventually replaced wood as railroad engine fuel, provided an impetus for the expansion of Chilean forestry. In the early 1900s, stands of nonnative Monterey pine and eucalyptus became crucial materials for both construction and combustion in Lota's coal mines (twenty-four miles south of Concepción). By 1920, mining companies in that region had planted 1,977 acres of Monterey pines. Fifteen years later, the hills around Lota were covered in 61,776 acres of *Pinus radiata*. Eucalyptus and Monterey pine tree plantations of the Compáñia Carbonifera e Industrial de Lota (Coal Mining and Industrial Company of Lota, or CCIL) eventually spread beyond Lota, occupying so much land that they displaced many of the region's farmers. Often, these marginalized smallholders had few avenues of employment other than becoming miners for the CCIL.[20]

In 1931, the government passed the Ley de Bosques (Forest law), which encouraged harvesters to rely on Monterey pine plantations instead of native forests. The law promoted plantation forest exploitation by levying steep tariffs on imported wood products while offering tax breaks to domestic lumber producers. As of 1943, Chile was home to 354,596 acres of Monterey pine plantations, containing over a million new trees, from which foresters eventually harvested sizable saw logs at twenty-year intervals. Monterey pines have a far lower rotation age—the time it takes for newly planted species to become mature enough for harvesting—than Chile's native trees. The southern beech (*Nothofagus* spp.) ranges from 80 to 120 years, the monkey puzzle tree (*Araucaria araucana*) takes more than 500 years to grow to full stature, and the Patagonian cypress (*Fitzroya cupressoides*) needs more than 1,000 years to reach harvestable size. According to the market-driven calculus of investment and return, the relatively short time to harvest dictated the replacement of these slow-growing species with fast-growing Monterey pine plantations.[21]

In 1951, officials from the Compañia Manufacturera de Papeles y Cartones (Paper and Carton Manufacturing Company, or CMPC) decided to construct a pulping plant and a paper mill along the Biobío River, which opened at the end of the decade. The CMPC sawmill, built in 1961 at Concepción, allowed the company to exploit surrounding Monterey pine forests. Meanwhile, the Corporación de Fomento de la Producción de Chile (Production Development Corporation of Chile, or CORFO) played a major role in developing the nation's forestry industry. Founded in 1939 by President Pedro Aguirre Cerda, CORFO provided credit guarantees and direct funding to many of the forestry ventures that emerged at midcentury. One such endeavor involved forty-four thousand private shareholders who invested in the founding of the paper company Industrias Forestales S.A. in 1956.[22]

During the 1950s, the Monterey pine also got a promotional boost from foreign sources. Under the Plan Chillán—a United States–Chile cooperative rural development initiative that began in 1953—US agronomists advised central Chile's farmers to plant this California native tree for soil erosion control. As part of these efforts, Chilean filmmaker Armando Parot shot a sixteen-minute documentary film about the Monterey pine, *El pino insigne* (1956). Authorities held screenings in villages and towns throughout the region. It is unlikely that a more arboreal propaganda movie has ever been made.[23]

Pivotal to Chile's plantation forestry boom were economic policies instated by the Pinochet dictatorship, which offered financial incentives to privately owned forest product companies. After the 1973 coup, the new dictatorship drafted the Decreto Ley No 701: De fomento forestal. Passed on October 15, 1974, the so-called Forestry Development Act heavily subsidized tree-planting expenses. The government reimbursed 75 percent of the costs for establishing new plantations and expanding silvicultural practices (article 2) and provided a 50 percent tax reduction on profits from the exploitation of man-made or natural woodlands (article 14). This far-reaching state promotion of pine and eucalyptus monocultures, coupled with an increased Japanese demand for woodchips during the 1980s, resulted in the rapid expansion of exotic tree cultivation.[24]

As a consequence of these corporate-friendly policies, the area covered by *Pinus radiata*—and to a lesser extent *Eucalyptus globulus*—grew at an explosive rate, increasing by 770 percent from 72,187 acres in 1975 to 555,285 acres in 2007. Chile's old-growth forests bore the brunt of this shift. In the decade from 1985 to 1995 alone, logging companies cut down 4.5 million acres of native woodlands to make way for industrial tree farms. In 1970, the value of Chile's forest products exports was $40 million, while by the year 2000 it had reached $2.2 billion. A devastating reduction in biodiversity was among the many prices of Chile's export-driven economic growth.[25]

A few elites gained enormous wealth from lumber operations. The undisputed patriarch of the twentieth-century Chilean wood pulp industry was billionaire Anacleto Angelini. Don Cleto, as he was known before his death in 2007, was born in 1914 near Ferrara, Italy. Before immigrating to Chile in 1948, Angelini spent the late 1930s fighting in Benito Mussolini's fascist army during its brutal occupation of Abyssinia (modern-day Ethiopia). In addition to owning the oil firm Compañía de Petróleos de Chile, he purchased the wood pulp producer Celulosa Arauco y Constitución.[26]

In contrast to Don Cleto's soaring fortunes, an increasingly disenfranchised population of forestry workers have fought for a shrinking share of the value that their labor produces. Since the 1980s, Chile's forestry sector has developed elaborate subcontracting hierarchies. These relations of dependency transfer the environmental costs to taxpayers and shift the risks of doing business to lower levels of the employment hierarchy. Signs of resistance to this lopsided arrangement emerged in 2009. That year, a *movimiento obrero subcontratistas* (contract labor movement) began to play a major role in the Central Única de Trabajadores

(Unitary Federation of Workers), a resilient labor organization that was suppressed by Pinochet but has rebounded in the postdictatorship period. Meanwhile, state promotion of Monterey pine plantations continues unabated. Highway billboards in southern Chile repeat the mantra, "Si el bosque crece, Chile crece; obedezca a la ley de la silvicultura" (If the forest grows, Chile grows; obey the forestry law).[27]

Some commentators have framed the global expansion of monoculture timber production in a positive light. In a 2000 issue of *Foreign Affairs*, political scientist David G. Victor and environmental scientist Jesse H. Ausubel made an impassioned argument for high-yield plantation forestry:

> The main benefit of the new approach to forests will not reside within the planted woods, however. It will lie elsewhere: in the trees spared by more efficient forestry. An industry that draws from planted forests rather than cutting from the wild will disturb only one-fifth or less of the area for the same volume of wood. Instead of logging half the world's forests, humanity can leave almost 90 percent of them minimally disturbed. And nearly all new tree plantations are established on abandoned croplands, which are already abundant and accessible.

The claim that increasing industrial wood production from plantations will leave "wild" old-growth forests intact is one that a number of pundits and policy makers have endorsed. A second argument is that tree plantations are productive carbon dioxide sinks, absorbing greenhouse gases while producing valuable timber in the process.[28]

Despite the optimistic assessments of its supporters, plantation tree farming in places like Chile has had disastrous ecological and cultural consequences. Among the many negative environmental impacts of such arboreal monocultures are soil degradation, increased vulnerability to pests and parasites, massive intensifications of groundwater consumption, and chemical runoff from heavy pesticide and petrochemical fertilizer applications. In addition, biodiverse natural forests provide a complex mosaic of goods and services for local human populations, which include firewood, sustainably harvested food and game, and medicinal plants. Tree plantations do not offer any of these "ecosystems services." Even if timber companies establish their plantations on marginal soils or denuded farmland, invasion of old-growth forests by introduced species remains an ongoing threat. In Chile, the high-yielding Monterey pine long ago escaped the boundaries of plantation silviculture, invading stands of native forest with great alacrity. Chilean ecologists Pablo Becerra and Ramiro Bustamante call *Pinus radiata* and *Eucalyptus globulus* "invasive forestry species."[29]

Complex cultural issues also frustrate simple models of a wood-harvesting future based on plantation monocultures. The forestry industry has used the sustainable development discourse to justify what a number of commentators and indigenous activists refer to as an "eco-ethnocide" of the Mapuche. Aucán Huilcamán, a leader of the Temuco-based Mapuche Council of All Lands, pointed out in 2004, "From the moment the Chilean state annexed Mapuche territory, and used violence to do so, the rule of law has never existed south of the Bio-Bio. . . . The state refuses to recognize that we are a people with rights that were in force even before Chile existed as a nation and which remain in force today." Mapuche communities have begun referring to the endless straight rows of Monterey pine as the "new green army," an occupier akin to the military forces that subjugated their ancestors after the War of the Pacific.[30]

Pablo Neruda famously declared, "Quien no conoce el bosque chileno no conoce este planeta" (Whoever does not know the Chilean forest does not know this planet). The forest Neruda knew during his lifetime (1904–73) was certainly different from one that future generations of Chileans will experience.[31]

The Monterey pine is not the only introduced species that has shaped Chile's environmental and social history, however. Grapevines have also rearranged the country's landscapes. As they had done in California, religious pilgrims created Chile's first vineyards. To provide wine for the Eucharist, the Spanish padres Bartolomé de Terrazas and Francisco de Carabantes brought grapevines to Peru in the 1540s. During the late sixteenth century, the Viceroyalty of Peru became the Spanish Empire's prime viticulture region in the Americas. Early wine production efforts along South America's Pacific coast relied on Spanish País and Criolla varietals, Mediterranean cultivars that transferred effortlessly to a new ecosystem with similar geologic and climate characteristics.[32]

Two and a half centuries later—just before Peru and Chile achieved their independence from Spain—the Prussian naturalist Alexander von Humboldt claimed that these lands were distant enough from the Iberian Peninsula to pose no significant threat to Spain's monopoly on grapes and olives: "If the commerce of wines and indigenous oils has been tolerated in Peru and Chili, it is only because those colonies, situated beyond Cape Horn, are frequently ill provisioned from Europe, and the effect of vexatious measures is dreaded in provinces so remote." Ironically, Chile's geographic isolation saved its nascent wine industry from the insect invasion that devastated vines throughout the rest of the world.[33]

Phylloxera's devastation of wine grapes began in the nineteenth century. In 1866, five acres of vineyard in France's lower Rhône Valley fell victim to a previously unknown scourge that caused European *Vitis vinifera* grapevine varieties to wither and die. Two years later, after the mysterious infection had over-whelmed French viticulture, a three-member commission inspected stricken vines in the western Rhône. As Félix Cazalis reported to readers of the new entomological journal *L'Insectologie Agricole* (*Agricultural insectology*), the commission examined infected vines with microscopes: "Suddenly under the magnifying lens of the instrument appeared an insect, a plant louse of yellowish color, tight on the wood, sucking the sap. One looked more attentively; it is not one, it is not ten, but hundreds, thousands of the lice that one perceived, all in various stages of development." *La nouvelle maladie de la vigne* (the new vine disease) had arrived in Europe.[34]

Since at least 1831, the French had been importing American vines, in part to develop hybrid varieties that could resist another menace, the fungal disease known as powdery mildew (*Uncinula necator*). Phylloxera, a microscopic sap-sucking insect native to the Mississippi River Valley that destroys the roots of vines, traveled across the Atlantic on some of these vines, possibly in 1858 (fig. 17). Between 1857 and 1875, Western Europe experienced warmer than average weather, which may have contributed to phylloxera's rapid spread during those decades. In 1870, with nearly 40 percent of the French grape vines devastated, entomologist Charles Valentine Riley sent phylloxera-resistant *Vitis labrusca* rootstock from the midwestern United States to botanist Jules-Émile Planchon at the Jardin des Plantes, the same botanical garden where horticul-turalists had attempted to germinate Monterey pine samples taken by the La Pérouse expedition. Over the next fifty years, the French grafted nearly all

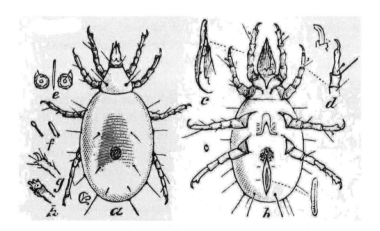

Figure 17. "Phylloxera Mite," illustration in Chas. V. Riley, "More about the Grape-Vine Pest," *Popular Science Monthly* 5 (June 1874): 164.

of their vines to phylloxera-resistant North American rootstock (*Vitis aestivalis,
V. berlandieri, V. labrusca, V. riparia,* and *V. rupestris*). As one might expect,
this development caused chagrin among the nation's cultural elite.[35]

During the nineteenth century, however, more immediate measures of
biological control took precedence. The threat posed by phylloxera was so great
that Austria-Hungary, France, Germany, Italy, and Switzerland held a summit
in 1878 and agreed to regulate the international plant trade to protect their vineyards. This was among the first steps toward creating a global agricultural order.
In 1913, Uruguay, Brazil, Chile, and Argentina followed suit, cofounding the
organization Defensa Agrícola, or Agricultural Defense, which established
means for phytosanitary certification of agricultural products moving across
their shared national borders. These prophylactic measures came too late for
most of the world's vineyards, however.[36]

To the great relief of its vintners, Chile was spared the phylloxera outbreaks
that devastated other nations' grapevines. In large part this was due to the valiant
efforts of a French immigrant. During the 1830s, recently arrived botanist
Claudio Gay—who would later write about the relation between deforestation
and soil erosion—established a state-run nursery in Santiago called the Quinta
Normal. Chilean winemakers used cuttings from these gardens to experiment
with thousands of vines and varieties of grapes from foreign vineyards. Because
the Quinta Normal's centralized facilities regulated arrivals of seeds and plant
tissues from other parts of the world, they curbed the ad hoc influx of flora and
associated microorganisms that had previously typified Chilean agriculture.[37]

French grape varieties made their first Chilean appearance in 1851, when
Silvestre Ochagavía Errázuriz planted *Vitis vinifera* cuttings on his vineyard at
Talagante in the Maipo Valley, south of Santiago. Because Ochagavía and
others had imported their French rootstock before the phylloxera outbreak, the
wine louse spared the South American nation. "With no subsequent need to
import vines, and with Chile's unique situation, bounded by the Pacific Ocean
to the west, the Andes to the east, vast deserts to the north and the Antarctic to
the south, the dreaded phylloxera has not found its way to any of this country's
vineyards," wrote noted wine authority Tom Stevenson. Following award-
winning appearances at the Vienna Exposition of 1873 and the Paris Exposition
of 1889, Chilean wines found new markets in Europe. By 1903, Chile had
become South America's leading wine exporter.[38]

Nearly a century later, Chilean vintners began marketing their "pre-phylloxera
wines," grown on ungrafted vines. Because Chile's Central Valley remained
isolated from phylloxera, it is one of the few regions on earth producing the
Carménère grape. This dark-hued variety of Cabernet—originally cultivated in

the Médoc region of Bordeaux—succumbed to the root-destroying epidemic in the 1860s and 1870s. Fortunately, Carménère vines had already arrived in Chile during the 1840s and have thrived there ever since. For more than a century, Chilean vintners confused Carménère with Merlot grapevines, which have virtually identical leaves. Thus, the production of invisibility occurred in botanical contexts as well as social ones. Not until the 1990s was Carménère's trans-equatorial journey rediscovered. After French oenologist Jean-Michel Boursiquot correctly identified Chile's Carménère plantings in 1994, the pre-phylloxera wine became an iconic variety for Chile's vintners, analogous to New Zealand's Sauvignon Blanc, Australia's Shiraz, and Argentina's Malbec. Chile had found its signature contribution to the wine world. As a *New York Times* headline announced, "Chilean Vineyards Have Outgrown Their Jug Wine Stage."[39]

North American vintners also experienced a "jug wine stage" before finding their own specialty varieties. Although French Huguenots in Florida and British settlers in Virginia made valiant attempts to cultivate wine grapes, their efforts largely failed. Mediterranean grape cultivation experienced its real success on the Pacific coast. Hernán Cortés brought wine grape cuttings to Mexico in 1520. More than two hundred years later, Spaniards established vineyards in and around the California missions, where the grapevines thrived. During the 1850s and 1860s, pioneering Hungarian-American winemaker Agoston Haraszthy imported 165 varieties of grapevines from Europe's best-known vineyards and planted them at his Buena Vista winery in Northern California. Thus began California's wine renaissance. The editors of the *California Farmer* proclaimed in 1855, "California may become the vineyard of the world."[40]

Dreams of a viticultural paradise in California did not remain unchallenged for long. In 1858, the same year John Patchett opened the state's first commercial winery in Napa Valley, grape phylloxera reached California from the eastern United States. This outbreak occurred at the same time that botanical collectors accidentally introduced the louse to Europe. Growers experimented with a staggering variety of techniques to curtail the spread of phylloxera. These included applying toad venom and tobacco juice to the plants and soils, spraying vines with sulfocarbonate, injecting roots with liquid carbon bisulfide, and flooding vineyards in the off season. Such attempts proved prohibitively expensive and rarely prevented future outbreaks. Sonoma County was among the hardest-hit regions. Its growers dug up more than four hundred thousand afflicted vines between 1873 and 1879.[41]

Federal legislation added insult to the injury of recurring phylloxera epidemics for winegrowers. The 1919 passage of the Eighteenth Amendment to the Constitution prohibited "the manufacture, sale, or transportation of intoxicating liquors with the United States." Not repealed until December 5, 1933, Prohibition put 560 of California's 700 wineries out of business. Those that did survive eked out a meager existence by manufacturing grape juice, medicinal "tonics," and sacramental wines for churches and synagogues. Beginning in 1933, California's wine industry began the slow but steady process of rebuilding. Not until 1986 did California have as many bonded wineries operating as had been in business in the years before Prohibition.[42]

During the late twentieth century, the major California wineries completed their transition from a "lifestyle industry" to a "scientific approach." Through a series of technological advances, including the introduction of stainless steel tanks, bladder presses, new aging processes, sophisticated bottling lines, drip irrigation, frost protection, and mechanical harvesting, Californian vintners revolutionized the efficiency of their processes and the consistency of their products. Even so, Californian winegrowers remain susceptible to new outbreaks of phylloxera.[43]

Although they embodied divergent entomological experiences, Californian and Chilean winemaking traditions have thrived on dense circuits of exchange since the nineteenth century. Unlike contemporary European wine production, which features cooperative wineries and family vineyards protected under systems like the French *appellation d'origin contrôlée* (controlled designation of origin), viticulture in California, Chile, Argentina, New Zealand, South Africa, and Australia has tended to favor large-scale, petrochemically dependent, and vertically integrated production in which companies own the entire supply chain. Santiago-based Viña Concha y Toro is among the leading players on the international wine market, owning vineyards, production facilities, and distribution outlets in 135 countries.[44]

Before the emergence of such corporate behemoths, the first exchanges between Californian and Chilean vintners were surprisingly informal. During their stint in Chile on a 1960s Peace Corps assignment, a pair of Stanford University graduates, Frederick Louis "Fritz" Maytag III and Paul Draper, leased a bodega, sourced Cabernet grapes from four local vineyards, and produced two vintages of wine. Finding Chilean viticulturists unreceptive to their unconventional experiments, the two returned to California. Draper eventually became the chief winemaker at Northern California's Ridge Vineyards, while Maytag bought York Creek Vineyards in Saint Helena and Anchor Brewing Company in San Francisco.[45]

Increasingly capital-intensive ventures followed suit. During the mid-1980s, the Chilean Agustin Huneeus, a former Seagram Company executive and owner of Concha y Toro, purchased several California vineyards, including

Franciscan Estate in Napa Valley. Robert Mondavi, one of California's premier vintners, moved in the other direction, toward Chile. In March 1996, he partnered with Chilean wine company Viña Errazuriz in a twelve-million-dollar joint venture. Viña Errázuriz, founded in 1870, occupies over 2,500 acres of the Aconcágua Valley and is one of the world's largest private vineyards.[46]

In similar fashion, Baroness Philippine Mathilde Camille de Rothschild, owner of the French winery Château Mouton Rothschild, partnered with Concha y Toro to produce Almaviva, a blend of Bordeaux varieties that retailed in the United States for sixty dollars per bottle. "Two things about the word 'Chile,' the quality of their wines and the quality of their soil," she told an interviewer in 1998. "It reminds me of California 30 years ago." Like so many developers and investors in the past, the baroness envisioned Chile as a *"nueva California."* Imagining Chile as a primitive California was part of the process that *New York Times* reporter Christian Wright has called "the Napa-fication of an ancient Spanish wine region."[47]

Yet not all winemaking operations in Chile or California hewed to predictable agribusiness models. At the end of the twentieth century, the roots of rebellion against industrial viticulture emerged from another transcontinental connection. In 1998, Álvaro Espinoza, one of Chile's most innovative winemakers, spent six months working at Mendocino County's Bonterra Vineyards. There he met Alan York, a well-known viticulture consultant who had previously helped California's Fetzer winery eliminate synthetic fertilizers and pesticides from its grape production processes. York gave Espinoza the text of Austrian philosopher Rudolf Steiner's 1924 lectures on biodynamic farming, *Spiritual Foundations for the Renewal of Agriculture.* Steiner pioneered modern organic farming, emphasizing "the farm as organism," advocating polyculture, and developing a series of soil and plant "preparations" of compost fertilizers. Although the long-term efficacy of such approaches for enhanced soil fertility remains under dispute, grape growers around the world have increasingly adopted biodynamic approaches.[48]

Espinoza was an instant convert. "Traditional viticulture artificializes the vineyards," Espinoza explained. "The result is that the wines are similar to those from other places." Wine journalist Monty Waldin added: "A vineyard which is part of the landscape, or the habitat, is less likely to be attacked by that habitat's pathogens. Biodynamics does work on a large scale, if, like Álvaro, you do it properly." With the support of parent company Viña Santa Emiliana, Espinoza began Viñedos Organicos Emiliana (Emiliana Organic Vineyards) on 593 acres in the Maipo, Casablanca, and Colchagua regions of Chile's wine country. As of 2014, Emiliana had expanded its operations to 2,760 acres in five Chilean valleys.[49]

Espinoza's California-inspired advocacy for an alternative agricultural model is a growing yet still young movement at odds with the prevailing trends in global food production. The dominant approach reduces ecosystem complexities through monocultures in an attempt to achieve ever-elusive control over planting, growth, and harvesting. In *Seeing Like a State*, anthropologist and political scientist James C. Scott pointed out that "agriculture is . . . a radical reorganization and simplification of flora to suit man's goals. Whatever their other purposes, the designs of scientific forestry and agriculture . . . seemed calculated to make the terrain, its products, and its workforce more legible— and hence manipulable—from above and from the center."[50]

This predisposition toward legibility and pliability, especially when driven by expanding commodity production, has homogenized the earth's surface. Coupled with the rapid dispersal of a few invasive species that have overwhelmed previously biodiverse environments, the result is an expanding uniformity of nonhuman nature. Agricultural ecologist Gábor Lövei has labeled this phenomenon "the McDonaldization of the biosphere." Almost every Mediterranean-type ecosystem on the planet now features vast single-crop plantations of Monterey pine and large-scale, chemically dependent commercial vineyards. These landscapes—exemplified by Chile and California—were not outcomes of some inexorable process. They were shaped by cultural, political, and economic factors at every turn.[51]

8

THE DAVIS BOYS AND THE FRUITS
OF NEOLIBERALISM

On October 31, 1967, California governor Ronald Reagan addressed seventy-three diplomats, businesspeople, and academics who had assembled in Sacramento for the fourth annual Chile-California Conference. As the former Hollywood actor and future US president told his audience, "Well, Chile is something special to California, and to Californians for a lot of reasons. We have had a long relationship with this friend of ours to the South." Reagan continued: "Our similarity of climates, our common Spanish heritage, which leaves us with cities of the same names, our sharing of the favored Pacific currents, give us much in common. This is the reason a Chile-California Program was started. This is why we, today, can easily answer the question, 'Why Chile?' Our friendship cannot be disregarded."[1]

As he so often did, Reagan spun nostalgic tales about an illustrious past to distract his audience from a disheartening present. The governor paired his laudatory opening remarks with the dispiriting announcement that he had rejected federal funding to continue the Chile-California Program. This inter-continental initiative, signed by President John F. Kennedy shortly before his 1963 assassination, was subsidized by the United States Agency for International Development (USAID) and lasted until partisan wrangling between Governor Reagan and State Department officials led to its demise in 1968.[2]

The ambitious scheme was one of two major programs developed between the Golden State and Chile during the Cold War era. The other, known as the Convenio, was a formal academic agreement between the University of Chile and the University of California, which received $9.75 million in support from the Ford Foundation between 1965 and 1978. The University of California at Los Angeles served as the Convenio's coordinating institution, arranging for student and faculty exchanges, facilitating shared course credits, and organizing mutual recognition of academic degrees from participating Chilean and Californian universities. During its fourteen-year existence, the program involved 287 participants from University of California campuses and 323 students and professors from the University of Chile.[3]

Both the Chile-California Program and the Convenio advanced Chile's "Californianization" while also shaping the ideological confrontations that preceded and followed Chile's 1973 *golpe de Estado* (coup d'état). The Convenio bore some similarities to an educational exchange between the Pontificia Universidad Católica de Chile, commonly called La Católica, and the University of Chicago. While the Chilean students who studied under the University of Chicago's right-wing economists Arnold Harberger and Milton Friedman during the 1950s and 1960s returned home and restructured Chile's economy around the neoliberal mantra "Stabilize, privatize, and liberalize," those involved with the University of California exchange produced far more diverse political, environmental, and social outcomes.[4]

The Chile-California Program and the Convenio emerged within the context of the Alliance for Progress, a sweeping strategic initiative launched by President Kennedy in 1961. As Kennedy announced on March 13 that year at a White House reception for 250 Latin American diplomats and US Congress members, "Therefore I have called on all the people of the hemisphere to join in a New Alliance for Progress—*Alianza para Progreso*—a vast cooperative effort, unparalleled in magnitude and nobility of purpose, to satisfy the needs of the American people for homes, work and land, health and schools—*techo, trabajo y tierra, salud y escuela.*" After listing ten specific steps the United States would take when administering this Marshall Plan for the Western Hemisphere, Kennedy declared, "We propose to complete the revolution of the Americas—to build a hemisphere where all men can hope for the same high standard of living—and all can live out their lives in dignity and freedom. To achieve this goal political freedom must accompany material progress." Intended as a decade-long, twenty-billion-dollar effort to bolster market-based development strategies throughout Latin America, the alliance was a watershed in US attempts to use economic aid as a foreign policy tool. In August 1961, members of the Inter-American Economic and Social Council of the Organization of American States gathered at the resort town of Punta del Este, Uruguay, where North American officials and representatives from nineteen Latin American countries issued the charter that officially launched the Alliance for Progress.[5]

Many of its initial goals were laudable. Agrarian reform, adult literacy, low-cost housing, equitable income distribution, price stability, and trade diversification made the list, but Cold War strategic priorities overshadowed these objectives. Frightened by Cuba's 1959 revolution and Soviet premier Nikita Khrushchev's support for leftist movements in the Western Hemisphere, Kennedy called Latin America "the most dangerous area in the world." Under Kennedy's leadership and the subsequent guidance of President Lyndon B. Johnson, the Alliance for Progress linked development assistance to counterinsurgency. As a result, the program suffered from contradictions between rhetoric and realpolitik. Former Central Intelligence Agency consultant Chalmers Johnson coined the term *blowback* to describe the long-term consequences of such covert foreign policy strategies.[6]

In the formal assessments of US lawmakers and the informal appraisals of Latin American popular opinion, the Alliance for Progress was a resounding failure. After taking office in 1969, President Richard M. Nixon appointed fellow Republican and New York governor Nelson Rockefeller to study the effectiveness of the program's first eight years. Rockefeller and twenty-three advisers made four trips to Latin America. In Argentina and the Dominican Republic, crowds violently protested their visit; in Chile and Venezuela, officials gave them the cold shoulder; and in Haiti, Rockefeller appeared in photographs, hobnobbing with the brutal dictator François "Papa Doc" Duvalier. In the preface to his 1969 report, Rockefeller explained, "There is general frustration over the failure to achieve a more rapid improvement in standards of living. The United States, because of its identification with the failure of the Alliance for Progress to live up to expectations, is blamed."[7]

Despite this disappointing outcome, the early years of the alliance were optimistic ones for US policy makers. In 1963, a confident President Kennedy suggested the idea for the Chile-California Program to California governor Edmund Gerald "Pat" Brown Sr. This state-based foreign exchange initiative was among Kennedy's final policy proposals before his assassination that November. After US administrative task forces visited Chile three times to determine the project's feasibility, officials from California, USAID, and Chile signed a contract of technical cooperation in December 1963. The parties agreed to focus on developing Chilean agriculture, education, water resources, highway transportation, and fiscal planning. Program officers established a headquarters in Santiago with a secondary bureau in Sacramento. By 1965, forty-five consultants from California had completed more than fourteen thousand hours of work on Chilean field projects, which ranged from upgrading standards and regulations for agricultural commodities to carrying out feasibility studies for national transportation schemes. To generate public awareness about these efforts, the program's second deputy director, Alan Sieroty, appeared in a series of radio announcements and on-air interviews in both Chile and California.[8]

The Chile-California Program's approach to foreign policy was not without precedent. Its forerunner, the Plan Chillán, was a decade-long development initiative launched in 1953. This technical cooperation program linked US agricultural extension agencies with the Chilean Ministries of Agriculture, Education, Health, and Public Works and the Corporación de Fomento de la Producción de Chile (Production Development Corporation of Chile, or CORFO) in an effort to improve rural food production, housing, transportation, and hygiene in central Chile's Maule, Ñuble, and Concepción Provinces. Centered on the city of Chillán—coincidentally, the same municipality where Henry Meiggs had taken refuge after his arrival in Talcahuano—the program differed from previous international financial aid efforts that had relied on capital grants, direct loans, or material assistance. Instead, Plan Chillán encouraged direct technical exchanges between comparable institutions in the two countries.

Supported by the Rockefeller Foundation, the United Nations Children's Fund (UNICEF), the United States Institute of Inter-American Affairs, and the University of California, Plan Chillán paired more than one hundred Chilean technicians with agronomists, economists, veterinarians, and urban planners from US institutions. Through collaborative fieldwork, these groups vaccinated cows against hoof-and-mouth disease, modernized the region's milk-processing facilities, developed a soil conservation plan for central Chile's agricultural zones, and instituted cooperative farming initiatives in rural areas. In addition, with the assistance from University of California agronomists, the University of Concepción opened a School of Agronomy in 1954. Plan Chillán's forestry programs also fostered the widespread planting of Monterey pine and eucalyptus trees throughout Concepción's coastal zones while promoting a suite of "green revolution" technologies, including petrochemical fertilizers, pesticides, harvest mechanization, and irrigation techniques.[9]

Although the Chile-California Program built on these efforts, its leaders were more overtly politicized than their predecessors. Operating in conjunction with Lyndon B. Johnson's Democratic administration, Chile-California Program bureaucrats paired hardnosed anticommunist propaganda with lofty declarations about modernization. In Johnson's words, Chile served as "a showcase for the Alliance for Progress." Symbolically, this 2,653-mile ribbon of a country was the front line in the Cold War struggle for Latin America. In 1964, reformist Christian Democrat Eduardo Frei Montalva defeated socialist candidate Salvador Allende Gossens in Chile's presidential election by 56 percent to

39 percent of the popular vote. Frei, who promised a "revolution in liberty," received support from a coalition of traditional right-wing parties and centrist constituencies. He also benefited from four million dollars in secret aid, which the CIA provided to his campaign between 1962 and 1964.[10]

United States officials cautiously celebrated Frei's victory and hailed California's impact on that outcome. As Preston N. Silbaugh, the first Chile-California Program director, remarked in September 1964, "Although the elections have proved that communism was not wanted in Chile, this does not mean that the danger has passed. Chile's struggle has just begun and it is our hope that California will be instrumental in helping this country achieve its goal of economic development and thus contribute to democracy's victory and communism's demise." A month later, an article in the *Modesto Bee* claimed, "The [Chile-California] program has reached the point where Californians are given the opportunity to take part in the final defeat of Communism in Chile." Three years onward, a *Los Angeles Times* reporter contended, "[The] California initiative has had a hand in preventing communism from making greater inroads in Chile." Such assessments were in many ways accurate.[11]

In its role as a bulwark against socialism and communism, the Chile-California Program sheltered the interests of US capital. During the twentieth century, North American mining corporations acquired immense sodium nitrate and copper holdings in Chile's Norte Grande, and their executives were anxious that a left-leaning government would nationalize these profitable operations. American firms had been acquiring mines in Chile for decades. In 1905, New York–based Braden Copper Company bought the El Teniente Copper Mine fifty miles north of Santiago. In 1909, the Guggenheim Exploration Co. (Guggenex) purchased a controlling share of the company. Two years later, the Guggenheims bought the Chuquicamata mines in the Atacama Desert. In 1916, the Anaconda Copper Company—which also owned extensive copper mines in Butte, Montana—acquired the Potrerillos mine seventy-five miles inland from the port of Chañaral in the Atacama region. By 1918 United States investors controlled 87 percent of Chile's copper output. Likewise, between 1925 and 1932, the Guggenheim family was the principal foreign investor in Chile's nitrate industry. Under Carlos Ibañez del Campo's military dictatorship (1927–31), the Guggenheims consolidated their corporate monopoly, the Compañía de Salitre de Chile (Chilean Sodium Nitrate Company), South America's single largest business enterprise at the time.[12]

As the demand for sodium nitrate declined in the era of industrially synthesized nitrogen, copper became Chile's leading export commodity. Because of its high thermal and electrical conductivity, its malleability, and its resistance to

corrosion, copper is a crucial element in electrical wiring, plumbing, and industrial applications. Formed by the seismic activities along South America's west
coast, the Chilean copper deposits at Chuquicamata, Escondida, Collahuasi,
and El Teniente are among the planet's most expansive reserves. For many
decades, Chile has been the world's top supplier of the red metal.[13]

Shortly after his 1964 election, President Frei offered US copper mining
companies the compromise of "Chileanization" through which the state would
increase its investments in these firms and expand production quotas but would
leave management in the hands of foreign owners. The Chilean left and the
country's miners' unions rejected Frei's plan and called for full nationalization
of the industry. The resulting strikes and civil unrest further radicalized Chile's
working class in the years before the 1970 presidential contest.[14]

By then, more than one hundred US corporations held $1 billion in invest-
ments in Chile. Chile was also a major trade destination for US commodities.
In 1966, it provided the third largest South American market—behind only
Brazil and Argentina—for US farm exports, notably wheat, tobacco, dairy products, and cotton. Both for its symbolic importance and for its economic significance, Chile received more Alliance for Progress funds on a per capita basis
than any other Latin American nation. More than $1.5 billion in US loans
flooded into Chile between 1961 and 1970.[15]

Much of this financial support subsidized raw materials exports and agricultural enterprises. In 1964, officials of Frei's newly elected government, along with
visiting advisers from the Department of Agriculture and Resource Economics
at the University of California Davis and the California State Department of
Agriculture, conducted an extensive review of Chile's agricultural marketing
process. Two years later, President Frei's administration implemented the Plan
de Desarollo Frutícola (Plan for fruit development), which included eight core
areas: (1) an exhaustive survey of existing fruit orchards; (2) analysis of contemporary and future demand patterns; (3) introduction of new varieties; (4) development of nurseries; (5) research into postharvest cold storage; (6) a system of
phytosanitary inspection for exports; (7) partially subsidized credit facilities
for orchard investments; and (8) "drawback" payments to stimulate exports.
The Chilean Banco del Estado (State Bank) provided credits for agricultural
development, while the Chile-California Program and the Convenio supplied
extensive consulting resources and technology transfers. Chile thus became the
primary supplier for meeting US demand for off-season produce. Shortly after
the meteoric rise of its fruit and vegetable sectors in the 1970s, Chile began to
dominate global produce markets during the Northern Hemisphere's winter
season, when US and European production volumes drop.[16]

These developments were contingent on a series of earlier revolutions in counterseasonal production and commodity transportation. During the late nineteenth century, the advent of refrigerated shipping enabled the dramatic intensification of the global food trade. In 1882, the SS *Dunedin* became the first vessel to transport frozen meat successfully from New Zealand to Britain. When the iron sailing ship arrived in London ninety-eight days out of New Zealand, the five thousand mutton carcasses in its cooling container were in flawless condition and quickly sold at the Smithfield Market, netting a healthy profit for their vendor. A new era in the global commodities trade had begun.[17]

The inauguration of the Panama Canal in 1914 provided the next windfall for long-distance food shipping companies. Although the opening of this inter-oceanic route curtailed Cape Horn traffic between the Atlantic and the Pacific, it created opportunities for Chilean exporters to move their goods rapidly to Atlantic ports. Four months after the canal's inauguration, a *Boston Daily Globe* reporter asked: "How would you like to have luscious peaches at Christmas, ripe plums, pears and cherries in the heart of mid-Winter, and great white muskmelons when the ground is covered in snow? This is what you may expect from Chile now that the Panama Canal is completed and the war demand for American goods is turning our shipping that way." By linking Chile's rich farmlands to North Atlantic ports via a fast new shipping route, the canal's promoters could promise US consumers access to a cornucopia of foods from the Southern Hemisphere.[18]

Six years on, this tantalizing prospect became reality. The San Francisco–based *Pacific Rural Press* published a report by US vice-consul S. Reid Thompson in Valparaíso that detailed the successes of a trial shipment of melons, plums, apples, grapes, peaches, and tomatoes from Valparaíso to New York in April 1921. Reid noted, "As the months of the greatest fruit production in Chile are just the opposite of those in the northern hemisphere, Chilean fruit can be placed in the United States during the months of January, February, March, and April, while the demand cannot be filled by productions in the United States." For North American markets, this Chilean fruit influx represented a retail revolution as important as Joseph Wolfskill's 1877 shipment of California oranges via railcar to Saint Louis. Both gave consumers unprecedented access to previously scarce off-season produce.[19]

Just as Chile's sodium nitrate mines had supplied a crucial infusion of nutrients to California's citrus orchards during the early 1900s and the interwar period, so the University of California's institutions provided a range of botanical materials, equipment, and expertise to Chilean agricultural enterprises in the postwar era. These resources helped to transform Chile's farming sector from a string of sprawling haciendas into an array of consolidated, high-tech agribusinesses. More than fifty Chilean exchange students and professors studied at UC Davis—California's premier agricultural university—in the 1960s and 1970s. Many of them returned to Chile, where they became known as the Davis Boys. The nickname referred to their counterparts, the Chicago Boys, the Chicago University–trained technocrats who returned to Chile and implemented an aggressive program of neoliberal economic and social restructuring in 1975. Scholars have devoted much energy to analyzing the Chicago Boys but have written next to nothing about their Davis counterparts. Both groups produced enduring, yet divergent legacies for Chilean society.[20]

As a force shaping Chile, the Convenio was an *exchange* and an *influence*, working in both directions to promote structural changes. Fulfilling one part of the agreement, California academics also traveled to Chile. The first wave of visiting University of California professors worked with their Chilean counterparts to launch modern fruit research programs and to develop a master's degree curriculum in fruit agriculture at the University of Chile. Californian agronomists also helped their Chilean counterparts implement irrigation schemes, which allowed Chilean farmers to transform the deserts of the Norte Grande into a bountiful *uva de mesa* (table grape) production zone.[21]

The Mediterranean-type ecosystems of Chile and California decisively shaped Convenio interactions. According to Anthony Wylie, a prominent Chilean agronomist who completed his graduate studies at UC Davis in the 1960s, "It is important to point out that the similarity in species cultivated and in growing conditions in Chile with those found in the American states such as California . . . has meant that the varieties and technologies available in these areas could be readily adopted and utilized in Chile." Yet numerous species previously untested on Chilean soil also played key roles in the nation's agricultural development. During the first two years of the Convenio, scientists at the University of Chile's Maipú Agronomic Experimental Station tested 228 varieties of nonnative fruits and nuts—ranging from gooseberries and papayas to loquats and chestnuts—from University of California agricultural research facilities. Many of these species became staple export commodities for Chilean fruit growers. As historian Arnold Bauer told the *UC Davis Magazine* in 2005: "The Davis boys were important in providing the technical expertise in the fruit and grape sectors. I think that the *convenio* with the University of California and the University of Chile was, in the terms expressed, very successful, even 'fruitful' if you don't mind the pun." Clearly, the exchange shaped multiple dimensions of the modern Chilean fruit sector.[22]

Some Chilean academics, however, criticized the program for not emphasizing the long-term development of Chilean science and technology. As sociologist Edmundo Fuenzalida argued, "Whatever the Convenio is able to create
in the University of Chile in the area of science and technology lacks roots
in the Chilean soil. . . . Instead of producing a modern higher education
institution capable of self-sustained growth, the Convenio contributed to the
creation of a subsidiary of the international centers of higher education (particularly the University of California)." Such dependency struck some as another
symptom of neocolonial relations between the United States and its southern
neighbors.[23]

Despite these criticisms, the Convenio fostered an era of transnational scientific
collaboration. One beneficiary of this partnership, ecologist Harold Mooney, was
among the first to recognize the opportunities that Chile and California afforded
for comparative ecosystems studies. Through the International Biological
Program (1964–74)—an initiative sponsored by the Paris-based International
Council of Scientific Unions—Mooney and an international team of scientists
developed a series of large-scale environmental comparisons for "Mediterranean
climate" zones, of which Chile and California became two principal test cases. As
similar ecosystems with distinct patterns of long-term historical development,
central Chile's and central California's ecosystems made an elegant pairing for
tracking long-term evolutionary trends of convergence and nonconvergence of
species. Such studies, facilitated through Convenio exchanges, encouraged widespread research relationships among biologists, geographers, land-use specialists,
and ecologists from both ends of the Cordillera and inaugurated a new phase of
global ecological investigations.[24]

The Convenio's advancements in scientific partnerships and educational
exchanges matched the Chile-California Program's innovations in matters of
policy. As a technical assistance triangle linking Sacramento, Santiago, and
Washington, DC, the Chile-California Program provided a pioneering example
of a US state coordinating an assistance program with a foreign country. It also
represented an unprecedented federal cession of development aid and educational exchange duties to a regional government. The advantages of this
strategy were notable. As UC Davis agricultural economist Jerry Foytik told the
Modesto Bee, "A program run by a state stands a much better chance of drawing
personnel. There are people, good experts, who will go abroad if the program is
not run entirely out of Washington." Richard N. Goodwin, adviser and speech-
writer to Democratic presidents Kennedy and Johnson, had strongly advocated
for devolving the responsibilities of US foreign aid programs to the states,
thereby "involving communities and citizens directly in our relationships with

the underdeveloped continents." The Chile-California Program not only did this but also championed President Johnson's conviction in the viability of various levels of government as quasi-autonomous entities. Under the auspices of the Alliance for Progress, other US states and regions followed California's lead. For example, the government of Oakland County, Michigan, established a technical assistance program with corresponding institutions in Colombia, and Utah officials developed a person-to-person exchange project with their Bolivian counterparts.[25]

In California's case, partisan politics undermined this novel approach to foreign policy. Disagreements between USAID officials in Washington and California administrators plagued the Chile-California Program from its inception. In 1967, Reagan's cabinet secretary William P. Clark argued that the Chile-California Program risked violating "the U.S. Constitution provision that 'no state shall enter into any treaty, alliance or confederation.'" Such an objection rang hollow. Despite numerous ideological shifts during his career, Reagan rarely refused federal largesse in support of state-based initiatives. A more likely reason for Reagan's rejection of the $250,000 in federal funds was the State Department's distaste for his nominee to head the program. After Reagan became governor in 1967, he fired Robert B. Keating, the acting head of the Chile-California Program, and named Raymond S. Long, former assistant to the California Agriculture Department, as Keating's replacement. According to State Department officials, Long neither spoke Spanish nor possessed adequate foreign policy experience for the job. This dispute hastened the program's demise. As Governor "Pat" Brown later told an interviewer, "We were the agent of the United States government in the AID program in Chile and we worked very closely with President Frei of Chile. I went down there and it was an excellent program. Reagan cut it out very unceremoniously and it was really an insult to the Chileans who liked the program."[26]

The Convenio outlived the Chile-California Program, but it faced numerous challenges that resulted from seismic shifts in Latin America's political landscape. In August 1969, California's Convenio officials conveyed similar frustrations to those expressed in Nelson Rockefeller's Alliance for Progress assessment that same year. As Convenio administrators noted, "The general Latin American opposition to North American exploitation makes any significant relationship with higher education difficult anywhere in South America." Apprehensive about the political upheaval preceding Chile's 1970 presidential election, members of the Convenio's California-based Policy Committee met on March 14, 1969, and reiterated their "willingness to work with the duly constituted authorities of that University, regardless of political affiliation or belief, whose academic goals, programs and methods are compatible with those of the University of California." Little did they know what turbulent times lay ahead.[27]

September 4, 1970, marked a major shift in US relations with Chile. That day, Salvador Allende Gossens, the leader of the Unidad Popular (Popular Unity) coalition of leftist parties, won 36 percent of the popular vote in a three-way race for the presidency, defeating former president Jorge Alessandri and Christian Democrat Radomiro Tomic. During the three years that followed, Allende achieved advances toward a more equitable and participatory democracy in a country beset by deep-seated class prejudices and profound structural inequalities. Allende's government instituted an agenda known as *La vía chilena al socialismo*, or the Chilean path to socialism. This program included extensive land reforms, the nationalization of mining industries, and the establishment of a government-administered health care system. It also involved substantial increases to the minimum wage, price freezes on consumer goods, widespread campaigns against illiteracy, the encouragement of mass participation in political decision-making, a new wave of public works projects, low-income housing initiatives, free milk distribution to schools and *poblaciones* (poor urban neighborhoods), expansions of organizing rights for workers, and a series of solidarity campaigns with other Third World countries.[28]

Despite experiencing notable successes, Chile suffered multiple crises, ranging from hyperinflation and public sector financial losses to social discontent among the wealthy. Allende and his cabinet committed policy blunders, but external factors contributed significantly to these challenges. Richard Nixon and his fervently anticommunist foreign policy team were among the most severe obstacles to social change in Chile. On June 27, 1970, just before Allende's election, National Security Adviser Henry Kissinger declared to a crisis group meeting in Washington, "I don't see why we need to stand by and watch a country go Communist due to the irresponsibility of its own people." That same year, Nixon instructed CIA director Richard Helms to "make [Chile's] economy scream." But Nixon's campaign against Allende did not stop there.[29]

Between 1970 and 1973, the CIA spent $8 million on covert action campaigns to sabotage Allende's social and economic programs. Referring to Nixon's Chile policy, Senator Frank Church of Idaho later remarked, "The attitude in the White House seemed to be, 'If in the wake of Vietnam I can no longer send in the Marines, then I will send in the CIA.'" A substantial portion of this money went toward propaganda. During the seven months between September 9, 1971, and April 11, 1972, the United States poured $1.5 million into anti-Allende campaigns by the right-wing Chilean newspaper *El Mercurio*.[30]

Corporate influence also drove US policy in Chile. International Telephone and Telegraph (ITT) and PepsiCo had been clients of Nixon's California-based law firm in the 1960s and retained their insider status when Nixon entered the White House in 1969. The leadership at both corporations regarded Allende as a threat to their Chilean business interests. Because of their Oval Office access, ITT and PepsiCo directors could act on these anxieties. ITT executives, charged with protecting their 70 percent interest in the highly profitable Chilean telephone company, Chiltelco, were disturbed by Allende's assertion that a nationalized phone system could provide Chileans with cheaper, more efficient service. Directors John A. McCone and Eugene R. Black, former heads of the CIA and the World Bank, respectively, ran ITT in a manner that journalist Jack Anderson likened to "a virtual corporate nation in itself with vast corporate holdings, access to Washington's highest officials, [and] its own intelligence apparatus." McCone and Black were accustomed to getting their way.[31]

Likewise, PepsiCo CEO Donald Kendall worried about the consequences of Allende's policies for his company's Chilean operations and feared that the democratic election of Allende's socialist government might encourage left-wing movements throughout the world. Executives from ITT and PepsiCo met privately with top-level US policy makers and spent millions in corporate funds, orchestrating campaigns to undermine Chile's economy. Similarly, international financial institutions withdrew aid for Chile after Allende's election. World Bank and International Monetary Fund officials openly opposed Allende's "politicized" economic agenda but later had no reservations in assisting Pinochet's dictatorship with $3.7 billion in bailout aid during the financial crises of the 1980s.[32]

Combined with the domestic campaigns of a highly organized and resistive right-wing coalition known as the Gremialistas, these efforts culminated in the violent termination of Allende's peaceful parliamentary transition to socialism. On Tuesday, September 11, 1973, the Chilean navy seized Valparaíso's port, the Chilean air force bombed the presidential Palacio de La Moneda, while the Chilean army shut down radio and television stations and occupied strategic facilities throughout the country. These coordinated actions effectively severed the president and his cabinet from strategic resources and reinforcements.[33]

United States involvement in the coup was multifaceted. Nearly all of the military officers involved in the golpe had attended the School of the Americas, a counterinsurgency training center established by the US Army in Panama in 1946. In 2000, Bill Clinton's administration declassified approximately sixteen thousand Cold War era documents about Chile, which revealed widespread US participation in Chilean political affairs during the run-up to the coup.

Three years later, Secretary of State Colin Powell publicly stated, "With respect to . . . Chile in the 1970s and what happened with Mr. Allende, it is not a part of American history that we're proud of."[34]

Allende's death in the Palacio de La Moneda and the seizure of power by General Augusto Pinochet's military junta ended one of the longest stretches of democratic governance in Latin American history. Scholars have puzzled over how a country steeped in open electoral traditions could plummet so precipitously into violent dictatorship. After a period of political turmoil ended in 1932, Chile experienced half a century of democratization. An index of democratic performance for 1965, which measured variables such as press freedom, freedom of group opposition, and fairness of elections, ranked Chile ahead of the United States, France, Italy, and West Germany.[35]

In *Polyarchy: Participation and Opposition*, published a mere two years before the coup, Yale University political scientist Robert Dahl hypothesized a geographical predisposition toward democracy: "In Switzerland the mountains, in Norway and New Zealand the mountains and fjords, the continental proportions and the enormous length of Chile—all reduced the prospects for a successful monopoly of violence by any one stratum of the population." Chile's extensive latitudinal range was no match for the 1973 putsch. The bloody coup d'état promptly disqualified Dahl's theory and ruptured the facade of Chilean exceptionalism vis-à-vis the rest of Latin America.[36]

After the coup, Pinochet turned "the enormous length of Chile" into a landscape of terror. A geographer by training, Pinochet made the production of invisibility a trademark of his regime. Santiago's National Stadium, the navy's warship *Esmeralda*, and the infamous complex called Villa Grimaldi became sites where the Dirección de Inteligencia Nacional (National Intelligence Directorate, DINA) interrogated and tortured tens of thousands of suspected "subversives." These locations remain synonymous with anguish, intimidation, perpetual detention, torture, and disappearance today. A number of US citizens were among those killed immediately following the golpe. Some of them were from California. University of California at Santa Barbara student Frank Teruggi and his colleague journalist Charles Horman were among thousands executed in the National Stadium, which served as an improvised concentration camp for the DINA. Their deaths, which became the subject of the 1982 Costa-Gavras film *Missing*, constituted a grim incarnation of the California-Chile connection.[37]

Such widespread repression provoked reassessments on the part of California's Convenio administrators. From January 19 to January 26, 1974, Phillip E. Johnson, chairman of the University Academic Freedom Committee, visited Santiago at the behest of Convenio officials. On his return, Johnson reported "that the California delegation was very concerned about the degree of support that the Chilean government intended to provide for academic activities at the University of Chile in the future, and about whether the academic freedom that scholarship requires would be guaranteed." He continued, "A number of the Chileans involved in the discussion fully appreciated that concern and indeed shared it themselves. Others responded that it would have been more appropriate for us to express a similar concern when scholarly activity was threatened by the extreme politicization within the University before the coup."[38]

Between 1973 and 1975, many University of California faculty and students contended that Convenio administrators should terminate the program to protest the junta's repression. Others, including the chairman of the University of California Senate Committee on Academic Freedom, proposed using the Convenio to assist Chilean scholars who faced persecution. In the final analysis, the University of California Academic Senate voted on May 29, 1975, to maintain the program's status quo as an apolitical academic exchange. By this time, the Ford Foundation's support for the Convenio had begun to wither; the program's official capacities ended in 1978.[39]

At the same time that Californian academics debated the final stages of the Convenio, University of Chicago scholars watched their ideological agenda attain unprecedented prominence. The Chilean military officers who rose to power in the golpe found themselves bereft of a comprehensive economic strategy. A group of US-trained Chilean economists stepped into the breach and secretly formulated a plan to replace Allende's social democracy with a program of privatization, tariff reductions, and austerity measures. Sergio de Castro, a recent graduate of the University of Chicago's economics doctoral program, led the Chicago Boys.[40]

Their program was well organized. A few weeks before the coup, the group completed a five-hundred-page book, fittingly called *El ladrillo: Bases de la política económica del gobierno militar chileno* (The brick: Foundations of a political economy for Chile's military government). In the prologue, de Castro contended that he and his colleagues intended to "help lift the country out of the economic prostration into which it was plunged: from the hopelessness and from the generalized poverty in which we were enveloped and imprisoned by the Popular Unity regime!" The text unfolded like a rambling discourse on Milton Friedman's 1962 defense of limited government and market-based economics, *Capitalism and Freedom*.[41]

The resemblance was hardly accidental. Friedman had trained the authors of *El ladrillo*. Until his death in 2006 at age ninety-four, Friedman was an avowedly public intellectual, a warrior for free-market fundamentalism. In the *New Republic*, economist Melville J. Ulmer called Friedman "a tireless, peppery advocate of liberalism in the 19th century European sense, perhaps the nation's outstanding intellectual exponent of laissez-faire." Chile's *golpe* offered Friedman and his colleagues a unique opportunity to test their radical economic theories.[42]

A group of Chilean graduate students provided the Chicago economist and his colleagues with an avenue for this experimentation. Between 1955 and 1964, USAID financed an exchange program that funded scholarships for students from Chile's Catholic University, La Católica, to study at the University of Chicago's Department of Economics. The initiative also provided US economists with fellowships to teach at La Católica.[43]

Friedman's colleague Arnold Harberger directed the Chicago-Chile exchange. Fluent in Spanish and married to a Chilean woman, Harberger made frequent visits to Chile throughout the program's duration. Like Friedman, Harberger was an ardent exponent of unbridled capitalism. He argued that the Chicago approach to economics was an ideologically neutral enterprise, which emphasized "a robust, simple, strong, theory" built on "studying facts [and] measuring things." For all intents and purposes, the exchange program transformed La Católica's economics department into a satellite of the University of Chicago. By 1964, twelve of the thirteen full-time professors at La Católica's School of Economics had earned their postgraduate degrees from the University of Chicago.[44]

The Chicago Boys belied the typical profile of the global power elite. As historian Bethany Moreton put it, they "were, in their own words, 'freaks,' 'computer nerds,' a distasteful crowd of parvenus. Excluded from the graces of the Ivies, with only their grubby technical skills to barter for prestige, the Chicago Boys developed economic theories that relied on arid mathematical models in the face of contradictory real-world evidence." Indeed, it was this outcast identity that fostered their claims to impartiality and supported their assertions that their program was a technical, scientific, and rational correction to Allende's wild, utopian plans.[45]

Harberger and Friedman not only trained a generation of Chilean economists but also exerted direct influence on Chilean policy makers. Visiting Santiago in March 1975, Friedman told a University of Chile audience that the nation needed a "shock treatment" of harsh economic measures to curtail the public sector, privatize government functions, and institute fiscal austerity. A month later, newly appointed finance minister Jorge Cauas followed Friedman's prescription. Cauas cut the national budget by over 20 percent, slashed the number of public employees in half, slowed the rate of money supply expansion, auctioned off state-owned enterprises (railroads, electricity, and mines) to private firms, instituted an aggressive deficit reduction regime, and suppressed union organizing. This was the opening act in what would become known as Chile's "neoliberal phase."[46]

This transition implemented an ideological formula that Chilean diplomat Orlando Letelier derisively referred to as "authoritarian capitalism." The Chicago Boys offered few objections to this characterization. In 1980, another of Friedman's students who went on to serve as Pinochet's minister of the economy remarked: "I have no doubts that as of 1973 and for many years before in Chile an authoritarian government—absolutely authoritarian—that could implement reform despite the interests of any group, no matter how important it was, was needed." In a 1982 *Newsweek* editorial, Friedman agreed, stating that Pinochet's junta "has supported a fully free-market economy as a matter of principle. Chile is an economic miracle." In reality, the miraculous was yoked to very real poverty, draconian suppression of dissent, and an ever-expanding web of murders, tortures, and disappearances.[47]

Despite propaganda to the contrary, most statistics did not paint a rosy picture of economic life in Pinochet's Chile. Two periods of severe recession, 1975–76 and 1982–83, yielded long-term trends of aggregate unemployment. Meanwhile, real wages fell nearly 13 percent between 1981 and 1987 as Pinochet's ministers reduced the minimum wage by 33 percent in an attempt to attract foreign investment. During the same period, per capita consumption fell by 25 percent and was 22 percent lower than it had been in 1972. Wealthier Chileans continued to purchase luxury items, but their spending came at a price. Between 1975 and 1982, the number of cars in Chile tripled, but so did the country's foreign debt, reaching $16 billion. By the end of 1986, per capita GDP barely equaled that of 1970. As Heraldo Muñoz—Chile's ambassador to the United Nations from 2003 to 2010 and an exile from the regime—pointed out, the economy had gotten so bad under the dictatorship that "Pinochet had to nationalize banks and industries on a scale unimagined by the Allende government."[48]

Such glaring contradictions aside, Pinochet's transformation of the Chilean economy involved a radical departure from precedent. Following the Great Depression of 1929–33, Latin America's dominant economic tendencies were protectionism and skepticism of foreign direct investment. This combination of approaches came to be known as *desarrollo hacia adentro* (inward-looking growth). From the 1940s through the 1960s, domestically oriented industrial development policies predominated. These strategies emphasized the replacement of foreign imports with nationally produced goods and services. Economists called this model import substitution industrialization (ISI).[49]

The Chicago Boys turned ISI on its head, aggressively promoting exports of primary commodities—copper, wood, fish, and fruit—unprocessed materials with low added value. As ecological economists Rayén Quiroga Martínez and Saar Van Hauwermeiren have pointed out, "The economic growth experienced in Chile is sustained upon the indiscriminate and deregulated exploitation of the country's natural resources and in particular the extractive activities, namely mining, fruit production, forestry and fishing." By 1985, unprocessed natural resources constituted 75 percent of Chile's exports. The Davis Boys had, perhaps unwittingly, built a model export sector for the Chicago Boys to use when implementing their extreme vision for Chile's future.[50]

During the first decade of Pinochet's military rule, the junta's austerity economics previewed the global economic order that was soon to emerge. After World War II, Keynesianism—a macroeconomic position advocating the significant involvement of the government and the public sector in regulating the business cycle—attained global dominance. This changed during the 1970s and 1980s, when right-wing governments led by Ronald Reagan, Margaret Thatcher, Helmut Kohl, and Brian Mulroney came to power in the United States, Great Britain, West Germany, and Canada. These neoliberal leaders privatized public goods and advocated for the management of social functions through free-market mechanisms. Their agendas of social marketization supported the expansion of capital by eradicating so-called distortions of the welfare state. Curiously, the key tenets of this ideological program exhibited a conspicuous inconsistency. As geographers Jamie Peck and Adam Tickell have pointed out, neoliberalism "exists in a self-contradictory way as a form of 'metaregulation,' a rule system that paradoxically defines itself as a form of *anti*regulation."[51]

Despite the complex and diverse ways in which this ideological formula has been applied, the neoliberal blend of metaregulation and antiregulation assumed its most terse formulation during the 1990s with economist John Williamson's technocratic notion of a "Washington consensus." This seemingly commonsense rubric became shorthand for the aggressive promotion, by any means necessary, of core neoliberal principles and policies throughout the developing world. Such structural adjustment programs, revealingly called SAPs, entailed violent suppression of dissent, egregious violations of economic and political sovereignty, and environmentally destructive practices, justified by the rhetoric of *free* trade, market *liberalization*, and *sustainable* development. Chile served as a valuable test case for such measures. In the words of sociologist Philip McMichael, "Chile was structurally adjusted before structural adjustment became fashionable."[52]

Although neoliberal ideologues advocated democratization through privatization, they were overwhelmingly comfortable with authoritarian regimes, as long as the leaders of these autocracies demonstrated unflinching loyalty to free-market fundamentalism. In the wake of the 1944 Bretton Woods Agreement, the International Monetary Fund and the World Bank funded right-wing military dictatorships in dozens of countries, from Kenya and Brazil to Indonesia and Pakistan. Such despotic administrations forcibly dismantled social welfare programs and created political spaces where the cancellation of elections, bans on public assembly, and suppression of dissent became familiar means of "safeguarding freedoms."[53]

Likewise, Pinochet and the Chicago Boys implemented brutal structural adjustments in Chile. In a 1978 letter to the *Times of London*, neoliberal political philosopher and one-time University of Chicago professor Friedrich von Hayek wrote, "In Modern times there have of course been many instances of authoritarian governments under which personal liberty was safer than under democracies. . . . More recently I have not been able to find a single person even in the much maligned Chile who did not agree that personal freedom was much greater under Pinochet than it had been under Allende." In his imaginary survey, Hayek forgot to visit the families of the disappeared.[54]

Resistance to Chile's neoliberal order was never far below the surface. The Movimiento de Izquierda Revolucionaria (Revolutionary Left Movement), led by students from the University of Concepción, emerged as the leading guerrilla group in the armed struggle against Pinochet's junta. Social movements also coalesced in streets and shantytowns throughout Chile. Historian Alison Bruey has investigated the direct action tactics that *pobladores* (residents of poor neighborhoods) used to assert their right to affordable housing during the dictatorship. Likewise, Chilean exile Marjorie Agosín spent decades documenting the stories of working-class women who stitched *arpilleras* (patchwork tapestries) to chronicle everyday suffering and memorialize their disappeared or murdered relatives. Dissidents smuggled many of these woven works of art out of Chile, thereby calling worldwide attention to the horrors of life under the dictatorship.[55]

Expressions of support for ordinary Chileans' struggles during the dictatorship also materialized in California. During the summer of 1978, stevedores from the San Francisco branch of the International Longshore and Warehouse Union refused to load US weaponry onto ships destined for Pinochet's military. This work stoppage, designed to show solidarity with persecuted Chilean trade unionists, harkened back to a moment in May 1850 when a group of Yankee miners from Calaveras County spoke out in support of Chileans who faced Anglo aggression.[56]

Other connections also brought Chileans and Californians together during Pinochet's reign of terror. During the darkest days of the dictatorship, California served as a haven for Chilean political refugees and a home for dissident voices. Among the most prominent of these was Santiago-born writer, activist, and teacher Fernando Alegría, who served as Allende's s cultural attaché from 1970 to 1973 and taught at Stanford University from 1967 to 1998. A few miles south of campus, a community of one hundred Chilean families built an exile enclave in Silicon Valley. Most of these women and men were rank-and-file supporters of the Unidad Popular government who lived with "las maletas listas" (the suit-cases ready) to return to their homeland at a moment's notice. As strangers inhabiting the country that had helped overthrow their president, they faced a predicament similar to that of Cuba's national hero, the nineteenth-century revolutionary José Martí, who signed his letters from New York: "en las entrañas del monstruo" (in the belly of the monster). Like Martí, Chilean ex-patriots lived with the knowledge that their host nation had willfully undermined the democratic self-determination of their homeland.[57]

Members of California's Chilean exile community also turned their energies toward assisting refugees from similarly brutal regimes. After the golpe, José Quiroga, a cardiologist who had served as Allende's personal physician, arrived in Los Angles. He secured a position at the UCLA School of Public Health, brought his wife and children to California, and cofounded the Program for Torture Victims, which works with refugees of political violence. In 1999, Quiroga told a *Los Angeles Times* reporter that his years of dislocation had produced profound existential uncertainties:

> The kids have grown up abroad. It is impossible to go back with them. You are basically lost. You try to rediscover your country. You lose your family if you go back, and you lose all your friends if you stay here. You can't win. It is funny because you always think that this is a transition period, that you are going to go back. Slowly you realize that the more time you remain here, the more difficult it will be to [leave]. I never in my life thought to emigrate. I always thought I would leave for a short period. This wasn't my plan in life, never.

For many, Quiroga's story evoked a familiar transpacific tale. By the year 2000, around twenty-two thousand Chileans were residing in California. An unplanned diaspora had become the norm for many of these émigrés, and in the process it helped shape California's cultural life.[58]

The Chilean expatriates and their allies who founded Berkeley's La Peña Cultural Center in June 1975 had similar aims to Quiroga's. They attempted to transform the devastating experience of exile into a positive force for social change. As one of the center's volunteer coordinators, Paul Flores, remarked in 2001, "We've created this international relationship with folks who know that it is a place where you can have not only international music and art, but reach out to different political environments that are undergoing serious oppression." The center's street-side façade features a three-dimensional mural titled *La Canción de la Unidad* (Song of unity), which depicts cultural icons of the left, including Chilean folk singer Victor Jara, United Farm Workers leader Cesar Chavez, and songwriter-activist Malvina Reynolds. Designed by artists Ray Patlán, O'Brian Thiele, Anna de Leon, and Osha Neumann, the painted sculpture pays homage to the Nueva Canción (New Song) Movement, a politicized tradition of folk music whose exponents faced repression and exile under the dictatorships that dominated Latin America during the 1970s and 1980s (fig. 18). The campaigns of Nueva Canción artists crossed continents and oceans, carrying messages of defiance and solidarity through song. Acts of resistance, like those expressed at La Peña Cultural Center, revealed deep fissures in the dictatorship's veneer of public support and ultimately helped to weaken US support for the junta.[59]

Assassinations committed by Pinochet's henchmen also unraveled official US backing of the dictatorship. In September 1974, the DINA used a car bomb to kill former army officer and Allende's vice president Carlos Prats and his wife in the Palermo district of Buenos Aires. The assassination was part of a string of terrorist attacks that DINA agents committed on foreign soil. The following year, they gunned down exiled Christian Democratic politician Bernardo Leighton and his wife in Rome; the couple barely survived the attack. Then, on September 21, 1976, DINA agents assassinated Orlando Letelier and his US coworker Ronni

Figure 18. The Song of Unity Mural at La Peña Cultural Center, Berkeley, California. *Photograph by author.*

Figure 19. Monument to Orlando Letelier and Ronni Moffitt, victims of Augusto Pinochet's overseas terror campaign. Sheridan Circle, Washington, DC. *Photograph by author.*

K. Moffitt in Washington, DC. DINA terrorists set off a car bomb, killing Letelier and Moffitt and injuring Moffitt's husband. Letelier, a former official at the Inter-American Development Bank, had been the Chilean foreign minister and ambassador to the United States during Allende's presidency (fig. 19).[60]

At the other end of this sinister arc, Pinochet's thugs publicly murdered Rodrigo Andrés Rojas De Negri, a young photojournalist who had graduated from a US high school, during a 1986 street demonstration in Santiago. After the 1973 golpe, relatives sent ten-year-old Rojas to live in Canada. He and his mother, the Chilean Communist Party activist Verónica DeNegri, eventually reunited in Washington, DC, where Rojas attended Woodrow Wilson High School. Rojas returned to his homeland in 1986 to photograph the widespread protests against the dictatorship. As Rojas and his friend Carmen Gloria Quintana were setting up a tire barricade during a demonstration in Santiago's Estación Central municipality, an army patrol intercepted the two. The soldiers severely beat them, doused them with gasoline, set them aflame, and dumped their charred bodies in an irrigation ditch twelve miles away. Four days later, Rojas died from second- and third-degree burns and extensive internal injuries, while Quintana survived the assault with scars covering 62 percent of her body. Through such acts of state-sponsored terrorism abroad and murders of Chileans at home, the Pinochet regime mutated into a diplomatic pariah.[61]

These wanton acts of outward aggression prefaced a devastating encounter with rebellious elements of a reenergized civil society at home. In February 1988, a coalition of parties, including the Socialist Party, the Pro-Democracy Party, the centrist Christian Democratic Party, and several smaller center-left parties joined forces to form the Concertación de Partidos por la Democracia (Alliance of Parties for Democracy). On October 5 of that year, the Concertación—as it is commonly known—defeated Pinochet in a national plebiscite over whether the dictator should extend his rule for another eight years. The "No" votes in the referendum carried the day with 56 percent of the total. As writer and activist Ariel Dorfman commented, "The erosion that Pinochet has suffered since the plebiscite can . . . be seen as foretelling . . . a day when he is no more than a sad synonym in some dictionary of horror."[62]

In the wake of this negative evaluation of his regime, Pinochet agreed to step down as supreme leader, but not before securing privileges as commander-in-chief of the army until March 1998, senator-for-life, and immunity from prosecution. Chile's first free elections in nearly two decades followed, and on March 11, 1990, Patricio Aylwin Azócar became the first postdictatorship president of Chile. In an address to the nation on New Year's Eve 1990, Aylwin framed the transition as "Chile's re-encounter with history."[63]

Yet the new leader also suggested that a clean break with the dictatorship's policies would not be forthcoming. The Concertación's catchphrase was the paradoxical slogan "Continuidad y Cambio" (Continuity and change). A writer for *Forbes* magazine reiterated this outlook in 1992: "The dictatorship has gone, but the free market policies it implemented live on in Chile. As a demonstration project for the developing world, Chile is priceless." Four sequential Concertación governments—those of Aylwin, Eduardo Frei Ruiz-Tagle (Eduardo Frei Montalva's son), Ricardo Lagos Escobar, and Verónica Michelle Bachelet Jeria—championed a truth-and-reconciliation process and oversaw significant civil liberties reforms but posed few major challenges to the Chicago Boys' neoliberal economic policies. For example, Chile is Latin America's only country to have privatized its sanitation sector and its entire urban water supply, projects carried out predominantly by postdictatorship governments.[64]

Nowhere was Chile's neoliberal economic model more self-consciously on display than in its fruit and vegetable sectors. With substantial assistance from the Chile-California Program and the Convenio, Chile engaged in an unprecedented expansion of its range of export commodities. Between the early 1970s and mid-1980s, the volume of Chilean fresh fruit and vegetable exports quadrupled.[65]

The benefits of this transformation did not distribute themselves evenly, however. Small farmers earned few profits from the shift toward high-volume export agriculture. In contrast, the large fruit-growing operations in Chile's

Central Valley and the vast wheat and livestock estates in the south reaped the yields of this reorientation. In the years immediately following the dictatorship, Chilean exporters sourced only 10 to 15 percent of their fruit from small farmers.[66]

The rise of a California-style agricultural export sector also depended upon a vast expansion of cultivated land. Chile's fruit-producing areas grew by 660 percent between 1965 and 2007, increasing from 116,000 acres to 762,184 acres. The corresponding labor requirements led to an unprecedented growth in the agricultural workforce. As of 2008, 450,000 Chileans worked in fruit production and packing. Beginning in the 1980s, these ranks swelled with part-time female workers—known as *temporeras*—who comprised more than 60 percent of the labor force in Chile's vineyards, orchards, and fruit-packing plants. Much of this seasonal labor involved twelve- to fourteen-hour days at minimum wages without benefits. Such arrangements left many Chilean farmworkers with little choice but to settle in shantytowns on the fringes of agro-export production areas.[67]

On numerous occasions, outsiders with a stake in the perceived success of Chile's neoliberal experiments reinforced the notion of Chile's economic exceptionalism in Latin America. On December 6, 1990, visiting US president George H. W. Bush told a joint session of Chile's National Congress, "Chile has moved farther, faster, than any other nation in South America toward real free-market reform." Bush elaborated: "This explosive growth has secured for Chile a growing impact on the world economy. Today the farmer in San Fernando labors not just to feed his family, or even his village, but to deliver products to the dinner tables of Japan, Europe, and the United States. From the miner in Calama, the world obtains the raw materials it puts to use in everything from new homes to skyscrapers to space shuttles." Bush's encomium celebrated a global neoliberal order. While the "developed world" conquers the skyline with high-rises and deploys satellites from spaceships, Chilean workers barely survive on falling wages as they extract and export the nation's wealth to enrich a global elite.[68]

Such trends have characterized the nation's long-term history. As Chilean economist Marcel Claude noted, "A factor intrinsic to the creation of income in Chile, from the time of independence until today, is the extraction and export of natural resources." In 1993, almost 36 percent of Chilean exports consisted of natural resources, such as forest products, fish, fruits and vegetables, and dairy and meat. One of the many pitfalls of trading out of poverty is what researchers Benoit Daviron and Stefano Ponte have called the "coffee paradox," in which a commodity "boom" in consuming countries is paired with a commodity "crisis" in its production zones. The exporting countries have little control over how value is added to raw materials, and thus the cost of the final product hardly ever corresponds to returns for producers.[69]

As cultural theorist Stuart Hall has reminded us, "Hegemonizing is hard work." Dominant ideologies do not reproduce themselves. They require intellectual commitment, political will, and military leverage to globalize their agendas. After leaving Chicago, Friedman and Harberger continued to promote laissez-faire economics from new positions in California. Friedman left the Midwest in 1976 to become a senior research fellow at Stanford University's conservative Hoover Institution. Since the late 1950s, the Hoover Institution—whose name honors the laissez-faire Republican US president who presided over the beginnings of the Great Depression—has pumped out studies with reliably conservative viewpoints. It has incubated dozens of Republican Party candidates, developed issue-oriented campaigns, and nourished a government-to-be when electoral politics have swung to the right. Freidman held his appointment at Hoover from 1977 until his death in 2006. In a similar relocation, Harberger moved from Chicago to UCLA, where he has remained since 1984. He continues to train Latin American economists in the doctrinal tenets of trade liberalization, public-resource privatization, and marketization of social interactions. As of 2012, Harberger had mentored twelve of Latin America's central bank presidents, and more than forty of the region's budget directors and cabinet ministers were once his students.[70]

Friedman and Harberger were not the only prominent policy makers to link Chicago, California, and Chile. In June 2008, two of Chile's most prominent citizens visited the United States. Eliodoro Matte Larraín, a Chilean billionaire and beneficiary of the dictatorship's free-market policies, delivered the convocation address at the University of Chicago's Graduate School of Business. Concurrently, Verónica Michelle Bachelet Jeria, Chile's democratic socialist president and a victim of torture under the Pinochet regime, spent several days touring and speaking at California's universities and meeting with California officials to resurrect the Chile-California program and the Convenio in a new hybridized form.[71]

In many ways, these two Chileans could not have had more divergent personal histories. Eliodoro Matte departed Santiago for Chicago in 1970, ten days after Salvador Allende's election. He received his master's degree in business administration in 1972 and returned to Chile to help orchestrate the right-wing transformation of his home country. As he told the class of Chicago graduates in 2008, neoliberal economics found immediate vindication after Allende's death: "First, Chile went from decades of stagnation to arguably the most progressive, most successful, and fairest economic environment in Latin America. This transformation was underway before Reagan and Thatcher made free markets an international model." Matte continued, "Second, and more significantly, the Chicago school (and the Chicago boys) believed that a free market model would drive demand for more democratic choice in the broader political environment. And they were right." Perhaps this pun was inadvertent, but it summarized the speaker's ideological commitments.[72]

Under the regime's corporate-friendly policies, the Matte family profited from a displaced California species. They built their fortune on the export of millions of tons of Monterey pine from Chile's tree plantations. As heir to one of Latin America's largest forest products companies, the paper and pulp firm CMPC, by 2014 Eliodoro Matte had a net wealth exceeding $2.5 billion. Matte also served as chairman of the board of the Centro de Estudios Públicos, the right-wing think tank that republished *El ladrillo* in 1992. His family business, the Matte Group, was one of two primary investors in a controversial $3.2 billion hydroelectric project, HidroAysén, which would have dammed the Baker and Pascua Rivers and flooded 12,500 acres of wilderness and Mapuche territory in Chilean Patagonia. In June 2014, the Council of Ministers—Chile's top admin-istrative authority—unanimously overturned the environmental permits issued in 2011 for the HidroAysén dams. Among the key organizers of the transnational opposition to the project was the Berkeley-based group International Rivers.[73]

In stark contrast to Matte, Michelle Bachelet is a pediatrician, a single mother of three, and a religious agnostic, factors that make her an outlier in rigidly Catholic Chile. Her father, Alberto Bachelet Martínez, served as briga-dier general of the Chilean air force under Allende. After Alberto Bachelet opposed the coup, Pinochet's agents tortured him for several months in Santiago's Public Prison, an ordeal that caused the cardiac arrest from which he died in March 1974. The following January, DINA agents kidnapped Michelle Bachelet and her mother, blindfolded them, and drove them to Villa Grimaldi for prolonged interrogation and torture. Eventually, the two escaped to Australia and then to East Germany, where Bachelet earned a medical degree. She later returned to Chile and served as minister of health and minister of defense before campaigning for president in 2006. In a run-off election, Bachelet defeated center-right candidate Sebastián Piñera with almost 54 percent of the vote, becoming the country's first female president.[74]

Pundits tended to contextualize Bachelet's election within a larger Latin American "left turn" of the early twenty-first century, which included victories for Hugo Chávez in Venezuela, Luiz Inácio Lula da Silva in Brazil, Néstor Kirchner in Argentina, Evo Morales in Bolivia, Rafael Correa in Ecuador, Tabaré Vázquez in Uruguay, and Bharrat Jagdeo in Guyana. Despite superfi-cial similarities, these victors offered diverse ideological stances. Bachelet generally fell to the right of her leftist colleagues. Her administration instituted a host of progressive social changes for women, minorities, and immigrants but maintained many neoliberal policies.[75]

This was most visible in Bachelet's attitude toward Chile's workers. As she stated in her election manifesto: "The principal source for generating employment is growth. There is no public policy, government subsidy or labor reform that can compete with the capacity of a healthy economy for generating employment." During her first term, Bachelet's devotion to neoliberal modernization manifested itself in the gap between campaign rhetoric about sustainable development and her administration's sustained support for the environmentally destructive salmon-farming industry and a series of catastrophic hydroelectric projects, which proceeded with little government oversight. Since the 1990 elections, behind-closed-door compromises between reformist organizations and Chile's military and business elites have dominated the nation's environmental politics.[76]

In *Chile and the Neoliberal Trap* (2012), economist Andrés Solimano posed the question: "Why did the four social-democratic (Concertación) administrations that came after the Pinochet regime choose to maintain, on the whole, albeit with some variations, economic and social policies so close to the spirit of the Washington-consensus paradigm?" A similar blend of neoliberal economic policies, paired with nominally progressive social stances, also prevailed in California. In a 2003 recall election, Californians chose as their governor—for the second time—an actor-turned-Republican politician. Former action film megastar and professional bodybuilder Arnold Schwarzenegger opposed public sector unions, advocated for privatizing the state's higher education system, argued for dismantling California's social safety net, and defended Reagan's trickle-down economics. He also made a splash by supporting gay rights, regulations on gun ownership, universal access to birth control, and climate change legislation. This amalgam of economic austerity measures and progressive social policies caused great anxiety among Christian Conservatives and right-wing talk radio hosts. As both Bachelet and Schwarzenegger demonstrated, a civil liberties agenda could coexist with doctrinaire free-market economic policies. This "third way" neoliberalism, promoting a kinder and gentler annihilation of the public sphere, held sway along the Cordillera.[77]

On June 12, 2008, forty-one years after Reagan addressed a gathering of Chilean and Californian dignitaries, Schwarzenegger and Bachelet met in Sacramento to sign a series of bilateral agreements on scientific, agricultural, and educational exchanges (fig. 20). These memoranda of understanding, titled *Chile—California, A Strategic Association for the 21st Century*, channeled the spirits of the Chile-California Program and the Convenio while leaving practical matters of funding and protocol in the hands of private organizations. In

Figure 20. Chilean president Michelle Bachelet (second from right) and California governor Arnold Schwarzenegger (right) tour the UC Davis Hopkins Vineyard in 2008 with student Alysha Stehly (left) and viticulture and enology professor Andy Walker (second from left). *Courtesy of the University of California, Davis.*

true neoliberal fashion, the agreements devoted few government resources to the attainment of their goals. Instead, they offered a vision of international aid where matters of diplomacy and mechanisms of accountability are removed from arenas of democratic process.[78]

At the press conference following the signing ceremony, Schwarzenegger spoke glowingly of Bachelet's biography, remarking, "It reads like a script to a Hollywood blockbuster except that people might not believe it is all true, but the fact is that it is all true." Just as Matte had conveniently excluded any discussion of the dictatorship's atrocities from his convocation remarks, the governor failed to mention the brutal acts that the Pinochet regime had committed against Bachelet and her family. Such unsavory elements did not fit his cinematic vision of life in the Pacific World or the enduring California-Chile connection.[79]

9

BREAKING THE RULE OF EXCEPTIONS

"California is not an Island," declared King Ferdinand VI of Spain in 1747. Thus he disclosed to his European counterparts the connection of Spain's northernmost American colony to continental terra firma. Before Ferdinand's pronouncement, European mapmakers had depicted California as a bulbous isle, set apart from North America by a "Red Sea" (fig. 21). The king's revelation confirmed his control over the social production of space, demonstrating how innovative cartography had long protected Spanish interests in the Pacific by making California seem inaccessible to Spain's rivals.[1]

An analogous myth of Chile's territorial isolation also emanated from Spain two and a half centuries later. At the 1992 World's Fair in Seville, the Chilean pavilion showcased a colossal chunk of iceberg shipped by refrigerated container from the Antarctic province to which the nation maintains a territorial claim. This translucent, sixty-ton glacial mass, named *El blanqueo* (The whitening), symbolized the nation's attempt to cleanse itself of the "dirty work" of the recently defunct Pinochet dictatorship while emphasizing Chile's cool detachment from its steamy, tropical neighbors, Peru and Bolivia. Eugenio García, the director of the Santiago-based marketing firm that devised the $850,000 government-backed scheme, told the Chilean magazine *Paula*, "We form part of an imprecise thing that is called Latin America, and there are negative judgments about that. . . . We are trying to shed that image."[2]

Islands and icebergs are just two of the potent images contrived by the residents and rulers of California and Chile to assert their exceptionalism, the notion that their histories and destinies are distinct from those of other nations or regions in the Americas. Ironically, both California and Chile are relatively recent inventions with imposed borders that bear little correspondence to the

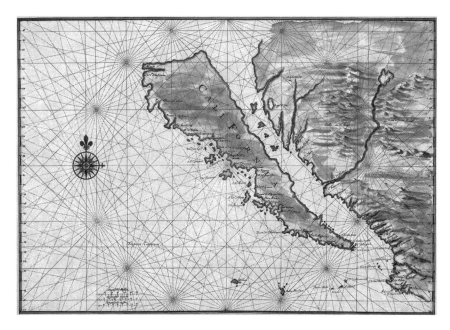

Figure 21. Johannes Vingboons, map of California shown as an island, 1639. *Courtesy of the Library of Congress.*

cultural zones inhabited by indigenous peoples before Spanish conquest. Narratives of exceptionalism are, indeed, deeply intertwined with processes of invasion and subjugation.

Despite these recurring claims of disconnection from their continental neighbors, neither Chile nor California has ever functioned as a self-contained entity. Instead, such assertions of autonomy conceal the ecological and cultural border crossings that have historically linked both places to countless displacements, exchanges, and influences from beyond their boundaries. Between the eighteenth and twenty-first centuries, many of these linkages occurred because of the fundamental roles that Chile and California played in an increasingly interconnected Pacific World. For residents of both places, the ocean that washed their western shores became an aquatic embodiment of future greatness, a zone of destiny in which former peripheries would develop into epicenters of capitalist commerce during a "Pacific age."[3]

From the eighteenth century onward, dominant groups in Chile and California forged their exceptionalist arguments from a heady amalgam of environmental, racial, and geopolitical elements. European-descended settlers in both places asserted that Providence had endorsed their colonization of the

Mediterranean-type landscapes along the eastern Pacific Rim. In such narratives, indigenous and dark-skinned populations had squandered the agricultural and economic potential of these fertile zones. According to this line of thinking, only after being "whitened" and "modernized" could either region realize its promise as a dominant force in the Pacific World. Although Chilean and Californian discourses of exceptionalism diverged in significant ways, they shared numerous features. Both mingled unstable racial taxonomies with geographical determinism, and both merged cultural mythology with political propaganda. More important, at key junctures, Chileans and Californians repeatedly contributed to each other's claims of incomparability.

Chilean elites have been distancing themselves from the rest of Latin America for more than a century. Since the late 1800s, members of Chile's upper class have touted their urbane distinctiveness, referring to themselves as the "English of Latin America." As if a tectonic snafu during the Jurassic period had unfairly wrested their homeland from the temperate embrace of Europe, Chile's privileged few have imagined their whiteness and modernity in contrast to the country's Mapuche people and the Indian-dominated populations of Peru and Bolivia, the two nations that Chile defeated in the War of the Pacific. This discourse of racial and cultural superiority helps to explain a Chilean preoccupation with the threat of "exotic" waterborne diseases—such as cholera, typhoid, and hepatitis—from Peru and Bolivia. As a representative of Chile's Ministry of Health announced in 1993, "In 1992 there was an impressive decrease of enteric infectious diseases [in Chile] as a result of the massive educational and information campaign triggered by the *existence of cholera in neighboring countries.*" Bolivians and Peruvians, many of whom work in Chile's fruit and vegetable industry as seasonal guest laborers, face persistent discrimination. In 2001, graffiti appeared on walls in downtown Santiago that read, "Chileno, los peruanos traen el cólera y la tuberculosis. Cuídate" (Chilean, the Peruvians bring cholera and tuberculosis. Beware).[4]

Framing Chile as "una buena casa ubicada en un mal barrio" (a good house located in a bad neighborhood) is a hallmark of exceptionalist Chilean assertions. Xenophobia and faith in Chile's supremacy over its continental neighbors are ideologies that take root at an early age. A 2004 study conducted by UNICEF and the Chilean Ministry of Education found that 46 percent of children and adolescents in Chile's public schools saw themselves as far superior to other Latin Americans. In the words of sociologist Jorge Larraín, "Once Chile considered itself part of a project shared with the rest of Latin America; now many Chileans begin to believe that they share in an exceptional character that separates them from Latin America. The entrepreneurial public version of

Chilean identity compounds this belief by insisting very much on the idea that Chile is different, a winner country that has become a model for Latin America." As Larraín argued, a Chilean discourse of exceptionalism flourished after the 1973 golpe, a period associated with the nation's neoliberal "miracle."[5]

Despite the fresh veneer it acquired under the Pinochet regime, this narrative has deeper origins. During the mid-1800s, racial superiority and strident nationalism permeated Chilean society. In 1858, the editors of the joint liberal-conservative newspaper *La Actualidad* referred to Chileans of European ancestry as "People of invincible spirit! Privileged race in Spanish America!" Twelve years later, the pamphleteer Domingo Morel opined, "Our country is destined by Providence to fulfill a magnificent mission in the South American continent: the regeneration of its races, nobly stimulating them by the example of our work and displaying to them the wealth and riches thus won."[6]

Bluster about Chile's "magnificent mission" received reinforcement from external sources, too. Throughout the 1800s, British commentators described Chile as South America's *república modelo* (model republic), and British merchants flocked to its port cities. Turn-of-the-century British naval writer Charles William Domville-Fife referred to Valparaíso as "the most English of the South American cities, the Liverpool of the Pacific." In turn, Chile's nineteenth-century upper class looked to Europe for inspiration, developing a *clase derrochadora* (spendthrift class) of decadent, belle époque elites. In art and fashion, these men and women followed the French while taking Britain as their model of commerce and deferring to Prussia in military matters. Meanwhile, the United States served as the yardstick by which Chile's ruling class measured their political prowess. In 1881, journalist Mauricio Cristi penned a tribute to his country's advancement: "Our progress even rivals that of the United States. The north and the south of America join hands on the path of civilization. . . . Such progress and such glory!" Cristi's accolade, which anticipated the Chilean victory in the War of the Pacific, also foreshadowed aggressive nationalist claims to come.[7]

Such assertions paralleled those made by many Yankees after the U.S.– Mexican War (1846–48). Few historians have compared the War of the Pacific with this earlier conflict in the Americas. Reading hemispheric history along a longitudinal axis reveals many similarities in how these two struggles altered the boundaries, identities, and fortunes of their respective winners and losers. In addition to subsisting on jingoistic fervor, both conflicts involved the control of a defeated country's capital city by the victorious power. In the US war with Mexico, General Winfield Scott's expeditionary force entered Mexico City on September 14, 1847. Similarly, during the War of the Pacific, Chilean troops under General Manuel Baquedano González seized control of Lima, Peru, on January 17, 1881. Both occupations were short-lived, but each concluded with the victor's emergence as the dominant regional power and heralded its rise as a Pacific World force. The two triumphant nations also conquered zones laden with valuable minerals—gold for the United States and sodium nitrate (nicknamed *oro blanco*, or white gold) for Chile—that launched their respective economies into eras of unprecedented economic growth.[8]

Chile's escalating military might aroused mistrust elsewhere in the Americas. In 1881, Columbian writer Adriano Páez published *La Guerra del Pacífico y deberes de la América* (*The War of the Pacific and the duties of America*), in which he warned: "Chile . . . will have a coastline more extensive than that of Brazil on the Atlantic. And since neither Ecuador nor Colombia has a fleet, Chile will dominate from the Strait [of Magellan] to the Panamanian Isthmus." Páez continued, "[Chile] will dominate commerce in the Pacific with the largest naval fleet in the Americas, with the exception of the United States." Such expressions of concern spread throughout Latin America. Critics derided Chile as "the Prussia of the Pacific," a ruthlessly expansionist power, hell-bent on regional dominance.[9]

Steeped in the chauvinism of postwar Chile, the physician and writer Nicolás Palacios published *La raza chilena* (The Chilean race) in 1904. This manifesto explained how a distinctive Chilean race had formed through the fusion of bellicose Mapuches and virile Germanic Visigoths from northern Spain. Such imagery displayed a paradoxical wistfulness that anthropologist Renato Rosaldo has termed "imperialist nostalgia," at once a celebration and a denial of indigenous culture in which "agents of colonialism long for the very forms of life they intentionally altered or destroyed."[10]

Many foreigners sanctioned the Chilean elite's claims of racial exceptionalism. In 1907, the US writer J. Gilbert van Marter called Chile "the New England of South America" and contended, "Chile is the only country in South America that is neither Latin nor negroid. . . . The rest of the Southern continent is the turbulent home of half-breeds of varying kinds, of Indians and negroes." Such endorsements of Chile's unmatched racial blend persisted. Dutch American geostrategist Nicholas John Spykman reiterated Palacios' notion of the Visigothic strength of the Chilean population. In his widely read *America's Strategy in World Politics* (1942), Spykman noted, "Chile seems to have drawn on the Basque provinces and the northern sections of the Iberian peninsula for her Spanish immigration. She thereby obtained a hardier and more energetic type of people than the Andalusians who seemed to favor other parts of Latin America." Then, in 1965, historian Robert N. Burr emphasized

Chilean ethnogenesis: "By the time of the republic's establishment, Chile's population was the product of a miscegenation so complete that almost no Chilean, however 'blue' his blood, could deny the presence of an Araucanian Indian somewhere in his family tree. . . . Chile's ethnic uniformity and lack of class conflict were the silver spoons with which it was born into republican life." Burr's assertions that the Chilean past displayed "ethnic uniformity" and exhibited a "lack of class conflict" depended on the erasure of racial discord and social strife from the nation's history, as well as the omission of Chile's indigenous people from the historical record. The choreography of these disappearing acts has long been a crucial function of exceptionalist discourses.[11]

Here, the cross-pollination of ideological strains from US and Chilean frontiers was at its most overt. In the mid-1800s, both Chile's well-respected geologist Ignacio Domeyko and one of its most eminent politicians, Antonio Varas, referenced United States military campaigns against Indians in the trans-Mississippi West as models for how Chile should "remove" its own native populations. Pedro Ruiz Aldea—a liberal newspaper editor who had spent time in California as a refugee from Manuel Montt's conservative government—used US history as a guide for how Chile could usurp Mapuche lands. Ruiz Aldea advocated a program of "commercial colonization" whereby Europeans would replace indigenous communities: "The plan to buy [Indian] land and colonize it with industrious settlers was adopted by the United States to populate the immense regions around the Mississippi, the Missouri and the Ohio Rivers. When you take a look at Araucanía it seems destined to play a similar role, since the unspoiled nature and fecundity of its territory offers the colonizers the best fruits possible." Once again, Chile's racial exceptionalism drew on historical precedents imported from the United States.[12]

During the twentieth century, the drive to displace the Mapuche from their ancestral territories acquired new fervor. In 1956, the editors of *El Diario Austral*, a Chilean paper from the southern city of Valdivia, wrote, "What would the United States have been if that great country had permitted the criterion of red skin to predominate over the mission of progress?" The editorial continued, "Among us, tolerance for the Indian hovers on the brink of lunacy. This is no longer romantic sensitivity but foolishness." This high modernist variant of nineteenth-century racism, counterpoising indigeneity and advancement, has permeated Chilean rhetoric for decades. Fernando Léniz, Pinochet's former economic minister and the commissioner general for the 1992 Chilean exposition in Seville, expressed the cleansing ambitions of his country's iceberg exhibit in equally blunt terms: "The idea is that Chile is seen as a modern country. Here there are no ethnic problems, we don't have a great pre-Columbian tradition.

Chile is basically a new country." The denial of ethnic conflict and the omission of Chile's rich pre-Columbian indigenous civilizations were, of course, lies. Despite the recurrence of such falsehoods, the drive to sanitize the national past of internal discord and ethnic difference has informed a persistent exceptionalist ideology in Chilean politics.[13]

Chile's history is replete with instances of official racism, underwritten by claims of biological superiority. On the country's northern frontier, the indigenous-dominated populations of Peru and Bolivia provided convenient foils for tales of a purer, whiter, more modern Chile. On September 5, 1882, an editorial in the Valparaíso newspaper *La Patria* contended that Peru "was a savage dressed like a European. Civilization, culture, progress of the century are phrases found on their lips but not in their spirit." A century later, one of the founding members of Pinochet's junta, Admiral José Toribio Merino, called Bolivians "metamorphosized camelids [*auquénidos metamorfoseados*], who have learned to speak, but not to think." One of the few successful attempts to chronicle Chilean racism is historian Florencia Mallon's *Courage Tastes of Blood* (2005), which examined a century of relations between a Mapuche community and the Chilean state. Otherwise, histories of racial prejudice in Chile remain rare.[14]

At other times, far more benign manifestations of Chilean exceptionalism have drawn on environmental premises. Some of Chile's most famous authors have asserted the uniqueness of their nation's geography to set it apart from the rest of Latin America. In her novel *Hija de la fortuna* (Daughter of fortune, 1999), California-based Chilean writer Isabel Allende described her homeland's "wild geography of imposing mountains, cliff-lined coasts, fertile valleys, ancient forests, and eternal ice." Allende was channeling Chilean poet Gabriela Mistral (1889–1957), Latin America's first Nobel laureate in literature, who had spent 1946–48 in Los Angeles, California. Mistral offered a similar synopsis of Chile's stunningly diverse landscapes: "It starts with the desert, which is like beginning with a sterility that loves no man. It is humanized in the valleys. It creates a home for living beings in the ample fertile agricultural zone. It takes on a grandiose sylvan beauty at the end of the continent, as if to finish with dignity, and finally crumbles, offering half life, half death, into the sea."[15]

Chile's apparent territorial remoteness and geographical uniqueness have captivated a wide range of commentators. In his startling, and often prescient, portrait of 1930s Argentina, writer Ezequiel Martínez Estrada gazed westward across the Andes and mused, "Chile is perhaps the worst constructed and worst located nation on this planet: it is like a plant that sprouts between two stones. All along one side runs the Pacific Ocean, which leads nowhere, since one must try to avoid it while navigating to the Straits of Magellan or the Panama Canal. The Andes enclose Chile at its back and the country lies like the prisoner of nature, for it is not more than the juncture of sea and mountain range." In the same vein, US historian Alfred Crosby remarked that Chile's inhospitable environment had made the colony unattractive to eighteenth- and nineteenth-century Europeans. As Crosby put it, "Mountainous Chile . . . produced few things in quantity or cheaply that Europe wanted, and in 1907 only 5 percent of her people were foreign-born, as compared with more than 25 percent on the pampa."[16]

Despite their virtues, Martínez's and Crosby's remarks gave an incomplete picture. Foreigners had long been captivated by Chile's rich farmlands, flourishing Pacific ports, and nascent industrial centers. As Chilean economist Marcial González wrote in 1848, "A phalanx of peaceful immigrants, of industrious settlers, brings in its customs and habits more civilization than the best books, more wealth than a thousand ships loaded with manufactures." New arrivals from Germany, Italy, Spain, and Great Britain often succeeded in Chile's fertile Central Valley and thrived in its coastal metropolises. During the second half of the nineteenth century, the Chilean upper class included many Europeans who had recently landed on South America's Pacific shores. The 1875 census recorded a total Chilean population of fewer than 2 million, with 4,109 Britons, 4,033 Germans, 2,330 French, and 15,000 residents of other nationalities. An observer in Chile during the years before World War I could not have missed the European immigrant population who dominated in economic terms, if not in actual numbers. As of 1914, foreign-born residents owned 32 percent of Chile's businesses and 49 percent of its industry.[17]

A similar brand of settler capitalism shaped California during the late nineteenth and early twentieth centuries. In the words of writer Wallace Stegner, "The boosters have been there from the beginning to oversell the West as the Garden of the World, the flowing well of opportunity, the stamping ground of the self-reliant." Examples of such Edenic advertising strategies abounded. Comparing California's agricultural zones to biblical depictions of the Fertile Crescent, a 1912 pamphlet from the Sunset Magazine Homeseekers' Bureau exclaimed to its eastern readers, "California is not Palestine excepting in that it is a promised land." A California Water Development Company pamphlet from the same period told an even more intricate story of westward progress:

> For more than Four Centuries American Civilization has been wending its
> way across the continent from east to west. . . . During the past five decades
> it has been banking up against the Pacific Coast, where, in the future, the

culmination of the highest type of American development will be found, and this growth will be assisted and accentuated by the next great development of the world's commerce having its basis of operation on the Pacific Ocean. Now is California's accepted time, and now is your opportunity, dear reader, to move with the tide.

As the promotional literature suggested, colonization of the Pacific coast would fulfill Anglo dreams of transcontinental hegemony.[18]

The dark side of *New York Tribune* editor Horace Greeley's midcentury exhortation to "Go West, young man" was the contention that these newly acquired territories had to undergo a thorough racial transformation. During the 1830s, Yankee observers often argued that "indigent" Hispanics and "lazy" Indians had mismanaged California's abundant lands. One of the earliest proponents of this view was Richard Henry Dana Jr. (1815–82), a young Harvard dropout who in 1834 left to sail around Cape Horn. Dana chronicled his ship's visits to the Mexican California settlements of San Diego, San Pedro, Santa Barbara, Monterey, and Santa Clara. On arriving in California, Dana wrote, "The Californians are an idle, thriftless people, and can make nothing for themselves." As far as Dana was concerned, these brown-skinned laggards were squandering nature's bounty. His views found currency among many easterners.[19]

For countless white commentators, the remedy for this failed land steward-ship lay in the application of a Puritan work ethic and a dose of Anglo-Saxon ingenuity. According to Frederick Hastings Rindge, another Massachusetts native who migrated to California during the 1800s: "Had it not been for the coming of the white men, this southland would perhaps never have been aroused from its lethargy; and its resources would never have been developed but for their enterprise. In Southern California, which was once a sleepy place, the coming of the Anglo-Saxon has turned inactivity into bustle. The old way was to say, 'Mañana sera otro dia' (To-morrow will be another day), but now it is, 'Work while it is day.'" By the late 1840s, the replacement of Spanish with English, brown skin with white, and Hispanic laziness with Anglo productivity were the central tropes of California boosterism.[20]

Therefore, it is unsurprising that the state's nineteenth-century Anglo promoters were reluctant to embrace evidence of Hispanic influences on California's development. To acknowledge the contributions of dark-skinned, poncho-clad Spanish-speakers to the transformation of a purportedly self-contained paradise would have been an admission that California was not, and never had been, independent of environments and cultures throughout the Pacific World. Much like the "imperialist nostalgia" that emerged in Chile to celebrate the archetypal Mapuche warrior while repressing the contemporary indigenous population, an Anglo tendency arose in the early twentieth century that romanticized the bygone Spanish past while denigrating the Mexican present.[21]

By no means did all of the Anglo migrants to California in the nineteenth century vehemently deny Latino contributions to the thirty-first state. As critical race theorists John Garvey and Noel Ignatiev have noted, "The white race is a historically constructed formation," one that is constantly being disrupted by legions of nonconformists, or "race traitors." At different times, and in a variety of situations, individuals and groups rebelled against the dominant racial and imperialist narratives of the day and found common cause with these "other Americans" from the Southern Hemisphere. Such stories of dissent and inter-racial solidarity undercut the temptation to make undifferentiated blocs out of diverse historical actors. In the words of Welsh cultural critic Raymond Williams, "There are in fact no masses; there are only ways of seeing people as masses." Yet, for the most part, the prevailing trends of nativism and manifest destiny succeeded in erasing the evidence of so many of these inter-American connections between Chile and California.[22]

Just as Chile's dominance of South America's Pacific coastline shifted Latin America's balance of power in the late 1800s, so California's commercial and strategic ascendency in the Pacific World bolstered the exceptionalist claims wrought by its promoters. During the mid-nineteenth century, boosters placed newly annexed California in the middle of the imagined geographies they created to entice prospective immigrants. Ernest Seyd, an agent of the Bank of England, wrote a pamphlet to attract British citizens to California in which he pointed out, "On glancing at a map of the Pacific, and the countries washed by its waters, one is forcibly struck by the commanding position of California, and its principal harbour, San Francisco, for the purposes of commerce. Almost the whole trade of the west coast of America, extending north and south some thousands of miles, and far inland eastward, passes through San Francisco." Promoters such as Seyd had discovered their own axial alignments of power. At the center lay the Golden Gate.[23]

Years before Seyd cajoled his compatriots into leaving Britain's rainy archipelago for California's sunny shores, Karl Marx and Friedrich Engels stressed the exceptionalism of the California gold rush in world history. In the Cologne-based newspaper *Neue Rheinische Zeitung*, they demonstrated an acute awareness of the reconfigured spatial and economic relations resulting from the gold discovery in the Sierra Nevada. As the two theorists of revolution explained: "Even taken by itself the Californian market is very important; a year ago there were 100,000 people there; now there are at least 300,000 people, who are producing almost nothing but gold, and who are exchanging this gold for their basic living requirements from foreign markets." They continued by placing the gold rush in its transpacific context: "But the Californian market itself is unimportant compared to the continual expansion of all the markets on the Pacific coast, compared to the striking increase in trade with Chile and Peru, western Mexico and the Sandwich Islands, and compared to the traffic which has suddenly arisen between Asia, Australia and California. Because of California, completely new international routes have become necessary, routes which will inevitably soon surpass all others in importance." Marx and Engels rightly emphasized the rapidity with which the gold rush had transformed global commerce, but they also called attention to a more general nineteenth-century Pacific World renaissance in which California and Chile served as two nodes in a vast circuit of human migrations, commodity flows, and biological linkages.[24]

For other commentators, rhetoric about California and its unique historical position vis-à-vis the rest of the United States drew on a litany of sources. Nineteenth-century proponents of exceptionalism found ample evidence for their claims about the state's unusual environment. As historian Simon Schama noted, during the Civil War, "Yosemite became a symbol of landscape that was beyond the reach of sectional conflict, a primordial place of such transcendent beauty that it proclaimed the gift of the Creator to his new Chosen People." Similarly, historian Linda Nash has shown how boosters extolled the salubrity of California's nineteenth-century coastline and claimed that its healing atmosphere, mild climate, and rejuvenating hot springs were a panacea for ailing easterners.[25]

This exceptionalist discourse only expanded in scope and scale during the twentieth century. At various turns, proponents of California exceptionalism have argued that the state's public higher education system, its labor history, its patterns of scientific research, its modes of urbanization, its architecture and fashion, and even its brand of conservative activism have developed in unique and unprecedented ways. Chronicling the rise of Orange County right-wing activism in the 1960s, historian Lisa McGirr demonstrated how the state's southern counties became the epicenter of an anticommunist, "national heritage" vision of Anglo renewal after World War II. Drawing on similar notions of conservative rejuvenation in the Golden State, the editors of Ronald Reagan's letters waxed poetic about the bellwether function of the birthplace of Reaganomics, "a social laboratory and harbinger for the nation."[26]

Others have been more measured in their admiration for the California anomaly. Civil rights leader W. E. B. Du Bois returned from a trip to Los Angeles and praised the city in 1913: "Out here in this matchless Southern

California there would seem to be no limit to your opportunities, your possi-bilities." Yet he cautioned readers about overindulging in euphoric appraisals of the Golden State: "Los Angeles is not Paradise, much as the sight of its lilies and roses might lead one at first to believe. The color line is there sharply drawn." California as a mythical land of opportunity—commemorated in verses that span more than a century from the gold miner's version of Stephen Foster's "Oh! Susanna" to Led Zeppelin's 1971 hit "Going to California"—has always been stitched through with color lines. Referring to race relations on the Pacific coast, historian-activist Lawrence Dunbar Reddick noted in 1945, "Either this will be a land of human democracy or else in letters large enough for the world's passing planes to read should be written the words 'Keep Out, For Whites Only.'" California's economic growth from the gold rush of the 1840s through the high-tech boom of the 1990s has left the past buried beneath economic peaks and troughs, seismic demographic upheavals, and shifting land-use patterns. Newcomers from Latin America and throughout the Pacific World were vital to these developments. These women and men helped to remake their surroundings time and again by contributing elements of their homelands to the reconstitution of California.[27]

For the most part, however, the Anglo boosters have carried the day. The roles of nonwhite immigrants in remaking the western United States remain outside the margins of the dominant historical narratives. Even those who have worked diligently to expose the racial fault lines of California's economic domi-nance have simultaneously endorsed exceptionalist stances. In 1939, the jour-nalist Carey McWilliams suggested that the Golden State's harvests depended on the widespread exploitation of migrant Asian and Latino farmworkers who "eke out a miserable existence, intimidated by their employers, homeless, starving, destitute. Today they are restless but quiet; tomorrow they may be rebellious." His exposé, *Factories in the Field*, was among the first widely read revelations of the expropriations that underwrote California agriculture. Ten years later, however, McWilliams remarked in *The California Exception*: "The nation needs to understand this tawny tiger by the western sea, and to under-stand all the rules must be laid to one side. All the copybook maxims must be forgotten. California is no ordinary state; it is an anomaly, a freak, the great exception among the American states."[28]

The discourse of Californian exceptionalism took a turn toward the Pacific in the 1980s. In 1984, Republican governor George Deukmejian told an audi-ence at the Los Angeles World Affairs Council, "California has the potential to be the capital of the world's fastest-growing economic community (the Pacific Rim), as well as its leading supplier and customer." "Pacific" and "Pacific Rim" quickly proliferated as key words in California's corporate lexicon. As of 1994, nearly three hundred California-based firms and limited partnerships included the words *Pacific Rim* in their names.²⁹

Likewise, visions of a new global order have emphasized Chile's ascendency in the Pacific World. In 1989, the executive director of the Asociación de Exportadores de Frutas de Chile (Chilean Fruit Exporters Association), Ronald S. Bown, framed Chile's export-orientation as the nation's passport to transoceanic connections: "Chile has a good position in the Pacific Rim, not only from the geographic point of view, but also because of the resources it can offer. We not only have a good export volume, but also in the past decade Asian companies have begun investing in Chile, in fishing, mining and forestry." This claim coincided with vigorous assertions of an emerging "Pacific century," the notion that the global economy was shifting its center of gravity toward an integrated Pacific Region.³⁰

During the late 1980s, a popular cartoon character—a kangaroo wearing a cowboy hat with dollars and financial documents in its pouch—made frequent cameos in Chilean newspapers. According to a *New York Times* reporter, "The kangaroo is a sign of the times as Chile's fast-growing, free-market economy increasingly looks across the Pacific—to Asia, Australia, and New Zealand—for trade and investments." Hopping in the direction of this new Pacific community seemed, to many observers, like Chile's preordained trajectory. In 2006, Chilean political scientist and politician Ignacio Walker wrote, "We have discovered a new neighbourhood. Our natural neighbourhood is Latin America. But, Asia, the Asia-Pacific basin, and what it represents in world economics and in politics today is a very promising region. . . . Chile, with 4,000 miles of coasts, looks face to face with Asia and the Asia-Pacific." Such assertions posited the Pacific World as a future zone of westward expansion. They also marked a spurning of Latin American trading partners and a reorientation toward Asian markets.³¹

By the 1990s, pundits had replaced the symbol of a happy-go-lucky kangaroo with one of an intrepid jaguar, suggesting that Chile was South America's counterpart to the ascendant "Asian tiger economies" of Hong Kong, Singapore, South Korea, and Taiwan. As a *Boston Globe* reporter remarked in 1995, "Stretched along the Pacific Ocean on an area roughly twice the size of California, Chile has become the Latin American jaguar, an economic powerhouse that in the past decade has recorded the world's fourth-fastest growth rate." The *Toronto Star* even claimed that Chile's jaguar economy could serve as a model for Canada's financial development.³²

Critics of the jaguar paradigm were hardly in short supply, however. As writers Stephanie Rosenfeld and Juan Luis Marré pointed out, "So the Chilean economy works, but it does not work for everyone. In fact, Chile's much-touted 'jaguar' economy may be less like the wild cat and more like the British auto-mobile—a symbol of both luxury and unreliability." Lurking beneath the mirage of sleek feline analogies and macroeconomic statistics were unprece-dented wealth disparities driven by perpetually shrinking working- and middle-class incomes, widespread environmental destruction, reduced civil society capacity, and massive expansions of national debt.[33]

Tigers and jaguars offer tempting metaphors of exceptionalism. Yet, when looked at with an eye toward transnational connections, California and Chile appear quintessentially *American* in its broadest sense. Their landscapes were shaped by resourceful indigenous peoples, transformed by ambitious Conquistadors, wrested from Iberian control by determined revolutionaries, expanded by aggressive nineteenth-century military campaigns, and remade by waves of immigrants. Both places have faced the vicissitudes of postwar economic cycles, experimented with radical alternatives, and experienced the vagaries of neoliberal globalization. Seen along a longitudinal axis, islands and icebergs look more like peaks and valleys in a cordillera.

EPILOGUE: WORLDS NOT REALIZED

The idea of a "Latin" America was born in the revolutionary crucible of nineteenth-century Paris. Speaking to an agitated crowd during the summer of 1856, the fiery Chilean liberal Francisco Bilbao (1823–65) became the first to use the geopolitical designation *América Latina*. This incendiary notion of a culturally unified continent ignited imaginations and declared independence from the baroque constraints of the Spanish Empire. In addition, it asserted a radical, democratic vision for the newly liberated nations of the Americas. Bilbao, the cofounder of Chile's militant Sociedad de la Igulidad (Society of Equality), drew inspiration from the French Revolutions of 1789 and 1848, encouraging artisans in his homeland to overthrow the Conservative Party regime of Manuel Montt.[1]

In a cruel rhetorical inversion, the French monarchy appropriated the notion of *Latin America* for decidedly imperialist and undemocratic purposes. In 1865, Emperor Napoléon III attempted to justify his transatlantic conquests by demonstrating the "Latin" linguistic heritage shared by the Spanish-, French-, and Portuguese-speakers who had colonized the Americas. His dream of hegemony in Mexico withered with the 1867 execution of his protégé Emperor Maximilian I, but the potent concept of Latin America survived. Thus, the idea of *América Latina* emerged as a blistering contradiction; it served a revolutionary's anti-imperialist ambitions for continental solidarity while also fulfilling a monarch's symbolic justification for colonial rule.[2]

Time and again, exiles, emperors, liberators, slaves, and free peoples have remade the Americas in complex and contradictory ways. As boundaries have come and gone, so too have the maps that claimed to solidify these divisions. Despite the ephemeral quality of official borders, the defining lines separating one political zone from another have never failed to shape the experiences of those living within or across them. For some, these cartographic perimeters are akin to the hyphen in the midst of their ethnic identity, simultaneously connecting and dividing. "Mexican-American" was an absurd redundancy until the United States seized half of its southern neighbor's territory at the end of the U.S.-Mexican War, sweeping California into the obligatory embrace of the Union.

As a borderland of perpetual paradoxes and endless incongruities, California proves difficult to fix in space and time. Many who revisit the Golden State after an absence feel that its former landscapes have been irredeemably engulfed by waves of unprecedented expansion. Richard Henry Dana Jr., the young Boston Brahmin who first sailed to California in 1835, returned in 1859 and found it altered beyond recognition. Of this geographical vertigo Dana wrote, "When I saw all these things, and reflected on what I once was and saw here, and what now surrounded me, I could scarcely keep my hold on reality at all, or the genuineness of anything, and seemed to myself like one who had moved in 'worlds not realized.'" Despite such relentless historical upheavals, remnants of past influences lie strewn about the state. Traces of a Chilean presence are scattered across maps of California. Place-names, such as Chili Gulch (Calaveras County), Chili Bar (El Dorado County), Chileno Valley (Marin County), Chileno Creek (Merced County), and Chileno Canyon (Los Angeles County) attest to the sites where Chilean pioneers established mining camps or longer-term settlements.[3]

Other vestiges of "worlds not realized" also remain. They include a memorial at the Carmel Mission, which celebrates La Pérouse's 1786 visit and a brass plaque embedded in the concrete sidewalk of San Francisco's Columbus Avenue, marking the location of "Little Chile." Forty minutes south of San Francisco on the 101 Freeway, a street named Valparaiso Avenue commemorates Faxon D. Atherton's mercantile and personal ties to Chile's famous port city. Likewise, a hotel built entirely with Chilean mahogany perches awkwardly amid a row of single-family homes in the Sutter County town of Verona. In 1849, stevedores loaded the wood on a ship bound for the upscale markets of New York, but the captain—besotted by gold fever—transported his expensive cargo northward instead. In Calaveras County, between Mokelumne Hill and San Andreas, State Landmark number 265 records the battle that took place between Chileans and Yankees at that spot on December 28, 1849, while the headstones in Marysville's Catholic graveyard bear the epitaphs of many Chilean pioneers. A well-worn tombstone in the Sonora City Cemetery reads, "Here lies Pasqual Gonzales, a Chilian, who ended his life by hanging himself in his cell, in the county jail." If, as the poet Adrienne Rich once suggested, "A place on the map is also a place in history," a motley assortment of gravestones, monuments, street signs, and historical markers may remind careful observers of a long-distant Chilean presence. Even so, such fragments hardly do justice to the profound Chilean influences on California's development.4

The production of invisibility is a trenchantly material process. Mark Twain, who spent the 1860s *Roughing It* in California, mused, "No real estate is permanently valuable but the grave." Yet many California cemeteries did not offer reliable, long-term lodging. At the turn of the century, the San Francisco Board of Supervisors yielded to the demands of land speculators and banned further burials in the city. They also ordered officials at the Laurel Hill and Calvary Cemeteries to remove the interments and deposit the bodies elsewhere. Developers turned the Golden Gate Cemetery into Lincoln Park Golf Course in 1906 and summarily dumped the grave markers in a heap at Ocean Beach. Over the following three decades, tombstones from the Masonic Cemetery became landfill for the vehicle approach to Golden Gate Bridge, and builders used the remains of the monuments from the Odd Fellows Cemetery to shore up the Aquatic Park seawall at Fisherman's Wharf, the breakwater that replaced the original wood-planked Meiggs' Wharf. As Chilean diplomat and historian Benjamín Vicuña Mackenna noted, "The dead have no friends in San Francisco."5

The surviving burial sites have fared no better. Only two cemeteries remain in the city, the San Francisco National Cemetery at the Presidio and the Mission Dolores Cemetery from which the New York–born author and poet Bret Harte wrote his paean to a charming, yet highly embellished Spanish past. During the summer of 1993, while excavating the ground around the Palace of the Legion of Honor for the renovation and expansion of the museum, construction crews found "about 300 corpses from the Gold Rush era—two of them still clutching rosaries, others . . . wearing dentures and Levis." There were, no doubt, anonymous Chileans among the bodies in this potter's field. After a short hiatus from the digging, during which archaeologists scrambled to identify artefacts and bones, the excavation continued. The episode served as a poignant reminder that as Californians disinter their past to develop their future, the dead become outlaws.6

Others have exhumed the deceased for more creative purposes. Chilean writers have long contended that the gold rush era Californian bandit Joaquín Murieta was not a Mexican horse thief but rather their countryman. French writer Roberto Heyene first introduced this alluring idea to Chileans in his 1879 novel, *El bandido chileno Joaquín Murieta en California.* In a 1966 play, *Fulgor y muerte de Joaquín Murieta* (Splendor and death of Joaquín Murieta), the

Chilean writer Pablo Neruda celebrated Murieta's legendary defiance of Anglo manifest destiny. The operatic drama, in which Murieta appeared as a nineteenth-century Robin Hood figure resisting North American belligerents, offered Neruda a platform from which to criticize the US war in Vietnam. More recently, the Chilean novelist Isabel Allende—who lives in the Bay Area—resurrected Murieta in *Hija de la fortuna* (Daughter of fortune). The novel, set during the gold rush, follows Chilean-born protagonist Eliza Sommers as she stows away onboard a ship bound for San Francisco in pursuit of her departed lover, Joaquín Andieta. The elusive Andieta, rumored to have become an outlaw, unmistakably conjures Murieta's spirit. Through literary reclamations such as these, Chileans have reinvented their place in California history.[7]

Still, the most durable legacies of Chile's influence on California remain etched in terra firma, invisible to most casual observers. Below the streets of San Francisco, the mud-sealed hulls of Chilean ships serve as a subterranean skeleton for the city's shoreline district. Farther inland, alfalfa, Chile club wheat, and potatoes grown in the Sacramento and San Joaquin Valleys reconstitute the genetic legacy of ecological transfers from Chilean soil. The crags and crevices of California's Sierra Nevada Range and the tunnels beneath the Santa Clara Valley bear the markings of Chilean miners, while Chile's sodium nitrate leaves its legacy among the roots, trunks, and branches of California's vast fruit orchards. Beyond such earthbound contingencies, we are left with the rhetorical question posed by the Chilean historian Gilberto Harris Bucher: "How many Chileans were deposited in tombs that did not have any other epitaph than a name or a date written in blood?" Thousands of these women and men altered the state's rural mining regions and metropolitan neighborhoods in far-reaching ways, yet the violent actions of Yankees in the thrall of manifest destiny prompted most Chileans to return home within a few years.[8]

Evanescence is a recurring theme in California history. "It is an odd thing, but everyone who disappears is said to be seen in San Francisco," quipped the Irish author and poet Oscar Wilde in *The Picture of Dorian Gray*. "It must be a delightful city, and possess all the attractions of the next world," Wilde continued. Indeed, the Golden State offers innumerable fables of abundance and pairs them with ostentatious displays of wealth as proof. This ceaseless layering of myth and matter beguiles formal interpretive schemes. The Boudin Bakery, a bustling tourist destination along Fisherman's Wharf, advertises its founder's 1849 discovery that "wild yeasts in the San Francisco air had imparted a unique tang to their traditional French bread." In a land where even the sourdough loaves are leavened with a mystical Pacific fog, the ethereal possibilities seem endless.[9]

Despite its enticements, such an approach to history obscures the social and environmental relations on which all myths and miracles depend. Chile's landscapes underwent profound transformations to supply the ingredients for California's increasingly ravenous metabolic cycles. Hacendados reshaped Chile's Central Valley to grow the wheat that fed prospectors during the California gold rush. Likewise, the arid Atacama Desert bears the scars of the sodium nitrate mining that fueled California's citrus boom. Much of the lumber used in California's housing industry is cut from Chile's monoculture plantations, which grow a species of tree endemic to the California coast. In a perpetual rhythm of counterseasonal agricultural exports, Chile and California provide the world with the produce of their Mediterranean-type ecosystems, while low-wage workers from Bolivia, Peru, and Mexico ceaselessly traverse national borders to sustain this transhemispheric food production regime. Such boundary crossings are part of a much longer chain of migrations and relocations. From adventurer Vicente Pérez Rosales to sex worker Rosario Améstica, fugitive debtor Henry Meiggs to coal miner Manuel Oyarzo, physician José Quiroga to novelist Isabel Allende, the Davis Boys to Michelle Bachelet, these women and men joined the thousands of other anonymous Chileans and Californians who made transequatorial journeys along the Cordillera.

The mountain ranges that span the western regions of the Americas and the Pacific waters that wash their shores have long suggested a deep connection between Chile and California. Before the nineteenth century, these two endpoints of empire remained hinterlands to Spanish colonial administrative centers in Mexico City and Lima. The botanical displacement of the potato, orchestrated by the La Pérouse expedition, transformed a potential relation into an actual biological and cultural connection. It was gold—discovered along the mountainous backbone of the Americas—that eventually drew the two ends of the Cordillera into sustained contact. In 1926, Chile's first diplomatic minister to Washington, DC, recalled the frosty words of Henry Clay, secretary of state under John Quincy Adams: "Chile had nothing to give us, nor have we anything to give her." Over the centuries that followed, Clay's assertion proved resoundingly hollow.[10]

South of the equator, stretches of iron railroad track, omnipresent clusters of poppies, and ubiquitous stands of Monterey pines serve as tangible reminders of the Californian presence in Chile's landscapes. Building on scientific investigations that were first funded by the Chile-California Program and the Convenio, ecologists have attempted to quantify the breadth of the botanical exchanges between the two Mediterranean-type ecosystems. In 2008, a team of Chilean scientists "recorded 1212 alien plant species in California and 593 in central Chile, of which 491 are shared between the two regions. These figures include 25 species that are native to California and 37 that are native to Chile." But complementary zones, when connected by cultural encounters, are not reducible to numerical summaries.[11]

As the scholar Benedict Anderson argued, the formation of national identity involves the emergence of "an imagined community," a perception of group coherence that develops in the minds of its members through narratives of fraternity and rules about inclusion or exclusion from the body politic. In this book I have suggested that other imagined communities exist beyond the confines of nation-states. They are literal Pacific Worlds and metaphorical cordilleras composed of transported landscapes, ideological imperatives, scientific collaborations, commercial transactions, and even acts of violence. People make transnational connections, but not always under circumstances of their choosing.[12]

Unseen elements provide the scaffolding behind such "imaginary geographies." These traces might include Latinos hanging from a lynching oak, bales of alfalfa in a dark ship's hold, molecules of nitrogen coursing through an orange grove, or gangs of debt peons mining *salitre* from the driest desert on earth. Likewise, there are the incongruous elements, the symbolic detours that structure the narrative: a pope who partitioned the earth with an edict, a gold rush metropolis that turned pulverized gravestones into profitable real estate, Governor Schwarzenegger's comparison of President Bachelet's life to a Hollywood movie, a sixty-ton iceberg on display in Seville, or a menagerie of neoliberal kangaroos and jaguars.[13]

Some relations along the Cordillera seem more sincere. In 1973, as Pablo Neruda gazed across the Pacific from his house on Chile's Isla Negra, he drew on a deep-seated bond with another American poet who had penned "Facing West from California's Shores," more than a century earlier. Writing against the right-wing visions of Nixon and Pinochet, Neruda exclaimed, "Comienzo por invocar a Walt Whitman" (I begin by invoking Walt Whitman). Neruda had a carpenter hang a portrait of Whitman on the wall of his Valparaíso home. When the man asked if the picture was of Neruda's grandfather, the poet replied that it was, indeed, him.[14]

Ideologies are ways of reading, and thereby deciphering or encrypting, experience. Following Neruda, in this book I have made a case for the virtues of reading displacements, exchanges, and influences along the longitudinal axis of the Americas. In fact, issues that US and Latin American historians typically cast in national, regional, or even local terms—lynching, unfree labor, agricultural extension, turbulent political upheaval, waterfront development, or railroad expansion—acquire greater resolution and richness when also examined from transnational perspectives. The hallmark of a transnational approach to the past, observed American studies scholar Micol Seigel, is that "without losing sight of the 'potent forces' nations have become, it understands them as 'fragile, constructed, imagined.' Transnational history treats the nation as one among a range of social phenomena to be studied, rather than the frame of the study itself." Much like Braudel's advocacy for historicizing at multiple timescales, these are not either/or arguments. They are, instead, encouragements of a diasporic approach to the past, one that focuses on migrations, flows, and connections across time and space.[15]

The eastern shores of the Pacific Ocean, encompassing the vast coastlines of Chile and California, make up half of a basinwide tectonic arc known to geologists as the Ring of Fire. Earthquakes and volcanic activity have continually reconstituted this seismically active region. For millennia this zone has also been transformed by turbulent cross-cultural encounters and concentrated episodes of biological interchange. Even at their most volatile, the geographies of Chile and California exhibit an intractable eloquence. When read with an eye for the unexpected, the Cordillera divulges countless possible *sitios de memoria*, or memory sites, places where the disappeared can once again emerge into the realm of the living.

ABBREVIATIONS

AHA	Atherton Heritage Association, Atherton, California
ARNAD	Archivo Nacional de Chile de la Administración (National Archives of Chile), Santiago
BANC	Bancroft Library, University of California, Berkeley
BC	Biblioteca Central "Luis David Cruz Ocampo," University of Concepción, Chile
BLYU	Beinecke Library, Yale University, New Haven, Connecticut
CHS	California Historical Society, San Francisco
CSA	California State Archives, Sacramento
CSL	California State Library, Sacramento
HCRL	Helen Crocker Russell Library of Horticulture, San Francisco
HL	Huntington Library, San Marino, California
KPFK	KPFK Radio, North Hollywood, California
LoC	Library of Congress, Washington, DC
MHS	Massachusetts Historical Society, Boston
NAQMM	New Almaden Quicksilver Mining Museum, New Almaden, California
SCP	Society of California Pioneers, San Francisco
SFMM	San Francisco Maritime Museum
UCD	Shields Library Department of Special Collections, University of California, Davis
UCh	University of Chile, Santiago
UCon	University of Concepción, Concepción, Chile
USNA	US National Archives, College Park, Maryland

NOTES

1. Neruda, *Canto General.*
2. "Chile: What Help for the Temporeras?" *Economist,* February 15, 2001, 41.
3. Costa, *Crowns of Glory, Tears of Blood,* xviii.
4. Benjamin, *Origin of German Tragic Drama,* 45.
5. For example, Chileans and Chile receive no mention in Butler and Lansing, *American West*; Street, *Beasts of the Field*; Lamar, *New Encyclopedia of the American West*; and Phillips and Axelrod, *Encyclopedia of the American West.* They receive only passing reference in Milner, O'Connor, and Sandweiss, *Oxford History of the American West,* 169, 199. One of the few exceptions is Mary Marki, "Chileans and the California Gold Rush," in *Encyclopedia of Immigration and Migration,* ed. Bakken and Kindell, 140–44. In Chile, Cristián Guerrero Yoacham kindly shared his unpublished bibliography of readings relevant to the Chile-California connection: "Notas criticas para una bibliografía Chilena."
6. For examples, see Limerick, *Something in the Soil*; Robinson, *New Western History*; Cronon, Miles, and Gitlin, *Under an Open Sky*; White, *"It's Your Misfortune"*; Worster, *Rivers of Empire*; Limerick, *Legacy of Conquest*; and Armitage and Jameson, *Women's West.* Among the primary goals of the "New Western History" has been the redefinition of the American West as a coherent region rather than a frontier process. For a critique of this assertion of regional exceptionalism, see Johnston, "Beyond 'The West.'"
7. Limerick, Milner, and Rankin, *Trails,* 144–45. On the overland routes to California and the West, see Faragher, *Women and Men on the Overland Trail*; and Unruh, *Plains Across.*
8. Delgado, *To California by Sea,* ix. The statistic is from Rice, Bullough, and Orsi, *Elusive Eden,* 194. For more on these themes, see Dening, "Performing on the Beaches."
9. The origins of the *Annales* approach lie in the work of Lucien Febvre and Marc Bloch. For a statement of their intellectual agenda, see Fernand Braudel, "History and the Social Sciences: The *Longue Durée,*" in Braudel, *On History,* 25–54. The quotation is

from Braudel, *Mediterranean and Mediterranean World*, 1:20–21. For more on disciplinary constraints to knowledge production, see Wallerstein, "Time of Space." For cautions about exploding disciplinary divisions entirely, see Massey, "Negotiating Disciplinary Boundaries."

10. "Unequal exchange" has been a central concept of both world systems analysis and dependency theory. For examples, see Wallerstein, *Modern World System*; Frank, *World Accumulation*; and Frank, *Capitalism and Underdevelopment in Latin America*. Alf Hornborg has added the crucial dimensions of *energy* and *ecology* to theories of unequal exchange. See, e.g., Hornborg, "Zero-Sum World."

11. Thanks to Chris Boyer for his suggestions about employing such a framework.

12. Di Castri and Mooney, *Mediterranean Type Ecosystems*, 11–19; Aschmann, "More Restrictive Definition"; Monero and Oechel, *Global Change and Mediterranean-Type Ecosystems*; M. Kat Anderson, Michael G. Barbour, and Valerie Whitworth, "A World of Balance and Plenty: Land, Plants, Animals, and Humans in a Pre-European California," in *Contested Eden*, ed. Gutiérrez and Orsi, 18–19; Komareck, *Proceedings*; and Cowling et al., "Plant Diversity in Mediterranean-Climate Regions," 362.

13. See Rockman and Steele, *Colonization of Unfamiliar Landscapes*.

14. The geographers Ellen Churchill Semple, Thomas Griffith Taylor, and Ellsworth Huntington were well-known twentieth-century proponents of environmental determinism. Some scholars have argued that Jared Diamond is the most prominent inheritor of their legacy. On this point, see McNeill, "History Upside Down."

15. Groves and di Castri, *Biogeography of Mediterranean Invasions*, 33. Crosby, *Columbian Exchange*. For a substantial elaboration on the Columbian Exchange, see Mann, *1493*. Crosby, *Ecological Imperialism*, 2; Bahre, *Destruction of Natural Vegetation*, 38; and Richard H. Groves, "Exchanges of Weeds between the Americas and Mediterranean Europe," in *Global Land Use Change*, ed. Turner et al., 324.

16. Rindge, *Happy Days in Southern California*, 21. On the passage of Mediterranean species from Spain to the Americas, see Dunmire, *Gardens of New Spain*.

17. Luis Llambi, "Opening Economies and Closing Markets: Latin American Agriculture's Difficult Search for a Place in the Emerging Global Order," in *From Columbus to ConAgra*, ed. Bonano et al., 203; Blank, "Perspective," 23. On the roles of women workers in the new labor regimes that accompanied Chile's economic reorientation toward export agriculture, see Barrientos et al., *Women and Agribusiness*; Bee and Vogel, "Temporeras and Household Relations"; and Diaz A., *Investigación participativa acerca de las trabajadores temporeras de la fruta*.

18. Braudel, *Mediterranean and Mediterranean World*. Also see the revision of Mediterranean history in Horden and Purcell, *Corrupting Sea*. For writings on the Indian Ocean, see Das Gupta, *World of the Indian Ocean Merchant*; and Chaudhuri, *Asia before Europe*. For examples of Atlantic World scholarship, see Linebaugh and Rediker, *Many-Headed Hydra*; Rodgers, *Atlantic Crossings*; Roach, *Cities of the Dead*; Gilroy, *Black Atlantic*; Thornton, *Africa and Africans in the Making of the Atlantic World*; and Curtin, *Rise and Fall of the Plantation Complex*.

19. Dennis O. Flynn and Arturo Giráldez, "Introduction," in *Environmental History in the Pacific World*, ed. McNeill, ix. For early examples of European-oriented Pacific

history, see Spate, *Pacific since Magellan*; and Prieto, *El Océano pacífico*. The quotation is from Matsuda, "AHR Forum," 759. Recent exceptions include: Chang, *Pacific Connections*; Cumings, *Dominion from Sea to Sea*; Dening, *Beach Crossings*; and Blank and Spier, *Defining the Pacific*. On the multiple diasporas in Pacific World history, see Lee, "'Yellow Peril.'"

20. Cushman, *Guano and the Opening of the Pacific World*; Igler, *Great Ocean*; Matsuda, *Pacific Worlds*. On "trans-localism," see ibid., 5.

21. For discussions of the analytical possibilities that emerge from an emphasis on transnational connections, see Melillo, "Global Entomologies"; and Pomeranz, *Great Divergence*, 3–27. Over the past three decades, scholars have taken diverse approaches to global environmental history. For recent examples, see Penna, *Human Footprint*; Hughes, *Environmental History of the World*; Simmons, *Global Environmental History*; Radkau, *Nature and Power*; Hornborg and Crumley, *World System and Earth System*; Richards, *Unending Frontier*; Chew, *World Ecological Degradation*; Davis, *Late Victorian Holocausts*; and McNeill, *Something New under the Sun*.

22. Tyrell, *True Gardens of the Gods*.

23. For an example of another historical account that traces the connections between migrants from a single nation to California—albeit only during the years of the gold rush—see Rohrbough, *Rush to Gold*.

24. Trouillot, *Silencing the Past*, xix.

CHAPTER 1. CORDILLERAS IN MIND

1. For more on this market-driven "world hunt," see Richards, *Unending Frontier*, 463–616. On the illicit trade that developed between Yankee whalers and sealers and Chileans who were resisting Spanish colonial trade restrictions, see Johnson, "Early Relations of the United States with Chile." Historian Greg Grandin focuses on nineteenth-century Yankee whalers and sealers off the coast of Chile when framing his account of the transnational history of slavery in the Americas. Grandin, *Empire of Necessity*.

2. Rodriguez, "True West," 43.

3. The *Inter Caetera* was the third of the bulls issued by Alexander VI on this topic. For an English translation, see Davenport, *European Treaties*, 75–78. The Treaty of Tordesillas made no mention of dividing the Atlantic waters on either side of the demarcation line. With the 1529 Treaty of Zaragoza, the Spanish and Portuguese established a north-south counter-meridian in the Pacific Ocean, seventeen degrees east of the Moluccas. See Steinberg, "Lines of Division, Lines of Connection."

4. For an account of the conquest of Mexico, see Cortés, *Letters from Mexico*. Among the most distinctive accounts of Incan life is Vega, *First Part of the Royal Commentaries of the Yncas*.

5. For firsthand accounts from this period, see Beebe and Senkewicz, *Lands of Promise and Despair*.

6. Manuel de Salas quoted in Collier and Sater, *A History of Chile, 1808–1994*, 3. On colonial Chile's isolation, see Burr, *By Reason or Force*, 13. On the tribunal's

sentence, see Clayton, "Trade and Navigation in the Seventeenth-Century Viceroyalty of Peru," 15.

7. Padre Junípero Serra to Viceroy Antonio María de Bucareli y Ursúa, Mexico, June 11, 1773, quoted in Garr, "Rare and Desolate Land," 134. Sánchez, *Telling Identities*, 50.

8. Bengoa, *Historia del pueblo mapuche*; Sergio Villalobos Rivera, "Guerra y paz en la Auraucania: Periodificación," in *Auraucania*, ed. Villalobos Rivera and Pinto Rodríguez, 7–30. Bío-Bío is alternatively spelled Biobío or Bio Bio.

9. Sando, "'Because He Is a Liar and a Thief'"; Murray, *Modocs and Their War*.

10. Chapman, *Republican Hispanic America*, 353.

11. Callahan, *American Relations in the Pacific and the Far East*, 10; Paine, *Ships of the World*; Smith, *Empress of China*; Ver Steeg, "Financing and Outfitting the First United States Ship to China"; and Caruthers, *American Pacific Ocean Trade*, 77.

12. Sultan (ship) account book, 1815–1819, MHS. Jean Heffer, *United States and Pacific*, 11. Heffer's terminology and basic concepts build on Arrell Morgan Gibson's landmark study: *Yankees in Paradise*.

13. Pratt, *Imperial Eyes*, 15–37. For an elaboration on the concept of a "portmanteau biota," see Crosby, *Ecological Imperialism*, 89–90. Joseph Banks quoted in Nigel Rigby, "The Politics of Seaborne Plant Transportation, 1769–1805," in *Science and Exploration in the Pacific*, ed. Lincoln, 81. Even so, commercial motives never receded far over the horizon. See Mackay, *In the Wake of Cook*. McNeill, "Of Rats and Men," 313–14. On the role of botany in shaping European colonial expansion during this era, see Brockway, *Science and Colonial Expansion*.

14. James Scott uses the term *legibility* to describe the standardization and simplification that states attempt to impose on unknown entities. See Scott, *Seeing Like a State*, 2–3. Commissioners for the Admiralty, "Instructions," in Cook, *Journals*, 1:cclxxxii. Sorrenson, "Ship as a Scientific Instrument," 223.

15. Malcolm Margolin, "Introduction," in *Monterey in 1786*, ed. Margolin, 10–11; and John Dunmore, "Introduction," in La Pérouse, *Journal*, 1:liv–lvi.

16. Allen, "La Pérouse." Eyer, "French Expansion into the Pacific," 12.

17. Annick Foucrier, "The French Presence in the Pacific Ocean and California, 1700–1850," in *French and Pacific World*, ed. Foucrier, 19.

18. Margolin, *Monterey in 1786*, 7. The earliest record of a maritime expedition tasked with transporting living plants is preserved on the walls of a temple at Deir el-Bahri, dating to ca. 1500 BCE. The image records the voyage of Egyptian queen Hatshepsut's ships, which she sent to the land of Punt on the northeastern coast of Africa to obtain frankincense (*Boswellia*) and myrrh (*Commiphora*) trees. See Janick, "Plant Exploration," 191.

19. Brossard, "Laperouse's Expedition to the Pacific Northwest," 44.

20. For the records of this earlier expedition, see Frézier, *Relation du voyage de la Mer du Sud*. Frézier's map of Concepción prior to the earthquakes of 1730 and 1751 appears in Barros Arana, *Historia general de Chile*, 6:74. La Pérouse, *Journal*, 1:41.

21. Ambrosio O'Higgins soon became the Spanish governor of Chile (1788–96) and later served as the viceroy of Peru (1796–1801). His son, Bernardo O'Higgins (1778–1842), led Chile's struggle for independence and became the country's first head of state.

22. Salaman, *History and Social Influence of the Potato*, 63; B. Pickersgill and C. B. Heiser, "Origins and Distribution of Plants Domesticated in the New World Tropics," in *Origins of Agriculture*, ed. Reed, 208–36; Spooner et al., "Single Domestication for Potato"; Henry Hobhouse, *Seeds of Change*, 237; Kenneth Pomeranz and Steven Topik, *The World that Trade Created*, 143; Zimmerer, "Ecogeography of Andean Potatoes," 447; Hawkes, "Chilean Wild Potato Species," 671.

23. Salaman, *History and Social Influence of the Potato*, 69.

24. Among the most extensive treatments of California's Franciscan missions and their relations with the region's native peoples is Hackel, *Children of Coyote, Missionaries of Saint Francis*.

25. The most influential early essay on Spain's New World missions was Herbert E. Bolton, "Mission as a Frontier Institution." Bolton's theses have been superseded, yet the "borderlands" concept that he developed retains its potency. See Weber, *Mexican Frontier*; and Radding, *Wandering Peoples*. The most comprehensive work on the Spanish colonial administrator is Priestley, *José de Gálvez*.

26. La Pérouse, *Journal*, 1:173, 192.

27. Dlugosch and Parker, "Founding Events in Species Invasions"; Hunt, *California Firsts*, 117.

28. Williams, "Much Depends on Dinner," 69; Peters, *San Francisco*, 22. For more on the diets of Northern California's tribes, see Heizer, *Handbook of North American Indians*, vol. 8: *California*.

29. Dowsett, *Start in Life*, 101.

30. Skinner, *Historical Review*, 155; Adele Ogden, "New England Traders in Spanish and Mexican California," in *Greater America*, ed. Ogden and Sluiter, 396. La Pérouse to Charles Claret de Fleurieu, Macao, January 26, 1787, in La Pérouse, *Journal*, 2:502.

31. Gibson, *Feeding the Russian Fur Trade*, 28. John Ledyard quoted in Bockstoce, *Opening of the Maritime Fur Trade*, 1. Also see Dudden, *American Pacific*, 3–4.

32. Ogden, "New England Traders in Spanish and Mexican California," 395. Kenneth J. Bertrand, "Geographical Exploration by the United States," in *Pacific Basin*, ed. Friis, 257. Hitchman, *Maritime History of the Pacific Coast*, 10. Cleveland, *Voyages of a Merchant Navigator*, 9.

33. Hart, *New Englanders in Nova Albion*, 3–4.

34. Ogden, "New England Traders in Spanish and Mexican California," 396. Bancroft, *History of California*, 2:32–33.

35. Shaler, *Journal of a Voyage*, 156. Prevost quoted in Cleland, *History of California*, 29–30.

36. Cleland, *History of California*, 141–42. Atherton, *California Diary*, xix, xxiv. Eventually, Chileans living in the area founded the town of Atherton. See López Urrutia, *Los Atherton*; and miscellaneous letters and papers at the AHA.

37. Greenberg, *Wicked War*, 102; Smith, *War with Mexico*, 1:334–35.

38. On the moral and racial justifications for war made by supporters of the invasion of Mexico, see Slotkin, *Fatal Environment*, 175. For *Californio* resistance to the US takeover of California, see Haas, *Conquests and Historical Identities in California*. Martínez Caraza, *Intervención norteamericana en México*.

39. Thomas O. Larkin quoted in Rohrbough, *Days of Gold*, 16. *Californian*, March 15, 1848. For more on Sutter, see Hurtado, *John Sutter*.
40. Larry Schweikart and Lynne Pierson Doti, "From Hard Money to Branch Banking: California Banking in the Gold-Rush Economy," in *Golden State*, ed. Rawls and Orsi, 212.
41. *California Star*, June 10, 1848.
42. The quotation is from Larkin, *Papers*, 7:353. Bunster, *Chilenos en California*, 87; Beilharz and López, *We Were 49ers!*, xiii.
43. Polk, *Message from the President*, 10. *El Commercio de Valparaíso*, February 5, 1849. The Sierra Nevadas are four hundred miles long and fifty miles wide, making them one of the world's largest mountain ranges. Schoenherr, *Natural History of California*, 1.
44. Perkins, *Three Years in California*, 222.
45. These figures are based on my own calculations using the extensive data from Goodman, *Key to the Goodman Encyclopedia*. Goodman's figures generally verify the estimates of older, less-comprehensive sources. See, e.g., Clark, *Clipper Ship Era*.
46. Henry David Cooke to "Henry C.," November 29, 1848, folder 3, box 15, CSL.
47. Gardiner, *In Pursuit of the Golden Dream*, 67. George Bruce Upton Jr. to George B. Upton Sr., April 1–7, 1852 (at sea and at Valparaíso on the seventh), HL. For more on the political situation in Chile during 1848 and its relation to the California gold rush, see Gazmuri, *El "48" chileno*, 61–63.
48. Pedro Feliz Vicuña, "Movimiento de población," *El Mercurio*, December 28, 1848, as cited in Hernández Cornejo, *Chilenos en San Francisco de California*, 1:79. On the play, see ibid., 1:75; and José Pelaéz y Tapia, *Historia de El Mercurio*, 82–83.
49. Uribe Orrego, *Nuestra marina mercante*, 2. Elias P. Overton, "Elias P. Overton's Book, Patchogue, Long Island, New York. Writen [*sic*] on Board the Bark Keoka James McGuire Capt.," June 20, 1849, BANC. Hernández Cornejo, *Chilenos en San Francisco de California*, 1:69.
50. Historians Simon Collier and William Sater simply contended, "At the height of the rush there were thousands of Chileans in California"; Collier and Sater, *History of Chile, 1808–1994*, 81. At the other extreme, political scientist F. LaMond Tullis contended, "No less than 50,000 Chileans arrived in California between 1848 and 1852"; Tullis, "California and Chile in 1851," 294. In his doctoral dissertation on California's Sonora mining region, William R. Kenny cited Enrique Bunster's factually flawed "Vida y milagros de los Chilenos en California" to conclude that "it is perhaps safe to estimate a maximum of 20,000 Chileans present in California by 1850"; Kenny, "History of the Sonora Mining Region of California," 217. Without any supporting evidence, Juan Guzmán Cruchaga estimates "our early settlers in California" at "thirty-thousand Chileans"; Guzmán Cruchaga, "Chilenos en California," Santiago, December 12, 1947, mimeograph of seven-page typed manuscript in English and Spanish, stamped with seal: *Consulado de Chile en San Francisco*, CHS. Similarly, historian Ramón Pérez Yañez wrote that "tens of thousands of Chileans" came to California, but provided no evidence for this conclusion; Pérez Yañez, *Forjadores de*

Chile, 259. On the 1850 census, see Thompson, *Growth and Changes in California's Population*, 9; and Bowman, *Index to the 1850 Census of California*, i.

51. Horace Rumbold, "Report by Mr. Rumbold on the Progress and General Condition of Chile," in Foreign Office of Great Britain, *Reports by Her Majesty's Secretaries of Embassy and Legation*, 317. The Chilean government carried out censuses in 1831–35, 1843, 1865, 1875, and 1895. See Mamalakis, "Historical Statistics of Chile," 129. For examples of these pseudonyms, see López, *Chilenos in California*.

52. Gilberto Harris Bucher has produced the most comprehensive work on immigration to and emigration from Chile in the nineteenth century. See Harris Bucher, *Tres estudios sobre marineria nacional*; Harris Bucher, *Emigrantes e inmigrantes en Chile*; and Harris Bucher, *Emigración y políticas gubernamentales en Chile*. López, *Chilenos in California*, xvii–xx. Giacobbi, *Chile and Her Argonauts*, 22. Historian Brian Loveman concludes that at least 5,500 Chileans were in California as of 1852; Loveman, *Chile*, 132.

53. *Daily Alta California*, April 10, 1851.

54. Dunmore, *Where Fate Beckons*, 259–64. The first of these efforts is chronicled in Dillon, *Narrative and Successful Result*.

CHAPTER 2. A VENICE OF PINE

1. W. H. Auden, "Journey to Iceland," in *Collected Shorter Poems*, 100. Frémont suggested that he renamed the strait *Chrysopylae* [Golden gate], "on the same principle that the harbor of *Byzantium* (Constantinople afterward) was called *Chrysoceras* (Golden horn)." Frémont, *Geographical Memoir upon Upper California*, 32. Barth, *Instant Cities*.

2. Juan Guzmán Cruchaga, "Chilenos en California," Santiago, December 12, 1947, mimeograph of seven-page typed manuscript in English and Spanish, stamped with seal: *Consulado de Chile en San Francisco*, CHS.

3. Wheat cultivation in California began with the arrival of Franciscan missionaries in the late eighteenth century. Franciscans and their California Indian laborers also grew barley, corn, legumes, and various fruits and vegetables. See Jackson and Castillo, *Indians, Franciscans, and Spanish Colonization*, 13–14.

4. Shew's daguerreotype is plate 62 in Newhall, *Daguerreotype in America*. For a discussion of the origin of the expression "forest of masts," see Burgess and Burgess, *¡Viva California!*, 188–89. The quotation is from Thomas Reid, "Diary of a Voyage to California in the Bark Velasco," October 9, 1849, BANC. For more on the San Francisco Harbormaster's Records, see Delgado, *To California by Sea*, 19. Arthur H. Clark contends that during 1849, 91,405 passengers arrived in San Francisco aboard nearly eight hundred ships; Clark, *Clipper Ship Era*, 101.

5. On abandoned ships, see Bancroft, *History of California*, 7:125. Anonymous, letter published in *El Mercurio*, May 15, 1849, in Hernández Cornejo, *Chilenos en San Francisco de California*, 1:106. For another example, see Lucett, *Rovings in the Pacific*, 2:352.

6. Mulford, *Life by Land and Sea*, 46. Also see Carl Nolte, "Experts Dig up Nautical Past of Long-Buried 1818 Whaler," *San Francisco Chronicle*, January 28, 2006; and Dale

Champion, "Gold Rush Fleet's Muddy Ghosts," *San Francisco Chronicle*, July 4, 1988. Williams, *Pioneer Pastorate and Times*, 45.

7. For a comprehensive treatment of gold rush era ships moored in San Francisco Harbor, see Harmon, Soeten, and Kortum, *Notes on the Gold Rush Ships*. Hall, *Around the Horn in '49*, 244–45. Albion, *Rise of New York Port*, chap. 7.

8. William Kelly, *Stroll through the Diggings of California*, 177. Barry and Patten, *Men and Memories of San Francisco*, 133–34. For a full account of the *Niantic*'s history, see McCollum, *California as I Saw It*, 66–77.

9. Ayers, *Gold and Sunshine*, 32–33. Delgado and Frank, "Gold Rush Enterprise," 324. Ellis, *From the Kennebec to California*, 44. McCollum, *California as I Saw It*, 76. For more on the archaeology of the *Niantic*, see Mary Hilderman Smith, "An Interpretive Study of the Collection Recovered from the Storeship *Niantic*," ms., SFMM, 1981; and Bullen, "Glimpse into the *Niantic*'s Hold."

10. Bonyun and Bonyun, *Full Hold and Splendid Passage*, 160. "Miscellaneous Documents of the ship *Balance*, 1848–1849," CHS (bill of lading for goods shipped from Talcahuano, Chile, to San Francisco, August 25, 1849, for José Ignacio Palma).

11. Casey, "Oakland's Redwood Retreat"; Isenberg, *Mining California*, 8.

12. The quotation is from Raven, *Golden Dreams and Leaden Realities*, 248. Pickens, "'Marvel of Nature,'" 17.

13. Vicuña Mackenna, "Páginas de mi diario durante tres años de viaje, 1853–1854–1855," in Vicuña Mackenna, *Obras Completas*, 1:26. The statistic is from López Urrutia, *Breve historia naval de Chile*, 67. For more on the destruction of the Chilean merchant marine during the gold rush, see Loópez Urrutia, *Historia de la marina de Chile*, 191–92.

14. On Urbistando, see Encina, *Historia de Chile*, 8:506; Hernández Cornejo, *Chilenos en San Francisco de California*, 1:176; and Pérez Rosales, *Times Gone By*, 269.

15. Seasholes, *Gaining Ground*. For a history of New York's water lots, see Hartog, *Public Property and Private Power*. For more on water-lot expansion in San Francisco Bay, see Booker, *Down by the Bay*, 33–68. Over thousands of years, many societies have modified their terrestrial-aquatic margins. For an example of landmaking at Constantinople in 330 CE, see Bury, *History of the Later Roman Empire*, 1:69–70. Similarly, Venetians built their island municipality upon millions of alder, oak, elm, and larch piles sunk deep into the anoxic mud of the surrounding lagoons. See Donnici et al., "Caranto Paleosol"; and Appuhn, *Forest on the Sea*. The Dutch spent centuries constructing dikes to hold back rivers and the ocean. Half the country's terra firma is below sea level. For an overview of hydraulic engineering in the Netherlands until 1960, see Van Veen, *Dredge, Drain, Reclaim*.

16. Walter J. Thompson, "The Armada of Golden Dreams," *San Francisco Chronicle*, July 2, 1916; Erin Pursell, "Modern City Surrounds What Was Once Forest of Ships," *Oakland Tribune*, March 10, 2006; Carl Nolte, "Few Clues Unearthed about Mystery Ship Buried after Gold Rush," *San Francisco Chronicle*, September 8, 2005;

Kenneth J. Garcia, "Muni Diggers Uncover Bit of S.F.'s Past," *San Francisco Chronicle*, December 7, 1994.

17. "Reminiscences: The Last of the Storeships," *Daily Alta California*, May 22, 29, June 5, 1882.

18. Lorena L. Hays, "Personal Journal (1852–1859)," October 8, 1853, p. 29, BANC. Davis, "California Breadstuffs," 524. For figures on nineteenth-century Chilean wheat exports, see Barros, *Historia diplomática de Chile*, 191–93. Strain, *Cordillera and Pampa*, 21. Evans, *Mexican Gold Trail*, 195. Tinkham, *History of San Joaquin County*, 326.

19. Knower, *Adventures of a Forty-Niner*, 138; Helper, *Land of Gold*, 77; Vicuña Mackenna, "Páginas de mi diario," 33.

20. For cautions about overestimating the corresponding expansion of Chilean agriculture, see Bauer, *Chilean Rural Society*, 64. Coffin, *Pioneer Voyage to California*, 36.

21. Morison, *By Sea to San Francisco*, 20. For an overview of how regional grain trading networks became globally integrated in the eighteenth and nineteenth centuries, see Mercier, "Evolution of World Grain Trade."

22. Evans, *Chile and Its Relations with the United States*, 74. Balie Peyton, "Legation of the United States, Santiago, Chile. To: Hon. John M. Clayton, Secretary of State of the United States," March 24, 1850, Despatch No. 2 of "Despatches from U.S. Ministers to Chile, 1823–1906," M10, roll T9, vol. 9 (July 20, 1849–October 2, 1851), USNA. Peyton, a former congressman from Tennessee, spent four years (1849–53) as US Minister to Chile. After coming to San Francisco in the fall of 1853, he opened a law office with William Duer and went on to win the election for city attorney of San Francisco on May 18, 1854. See Durham, *Volunteer Forty-Niners*, 142.

23. Calculated from "U.S. Customs House, San Francisco—Records. 1849–1897, Key to Arrangement," part 1, BANC. "U.S. Customs House, San Francisco—Records. 1849–1897," part 1, box 1, 1849–1850 (A-Gen), BANC. Sepúlveda G., *El Trigo chileno en el mercado mundial*, 41–46.

24. Charles L. Ross, "Experiences of a Pioneer of 1847 in California," p. 14, BANC. For a superb account of the symbolic and material transformation of marketplaces, see Agnew, "Threshold of Exchange."

25. James R. Garniss, "The Early Days of San Francisco—Reminiscences for the Bancroft Library, 1877," pp. 10–11, BANC. Newmark, *Sixty Years in Southern California*, 332.

26. Ryan, *Personal Adventures in Upper and Lower California*, 1:407. Letts, *California Illustrated*, 134. Revere, *Keel and Saddle*, 160. Also see Buck, *Yankee Trader in the Gold Rush*, 56. For an account of flour shortages in the mines near Stockton, see Dexter, *Early Days in California*, 23–26.

27. Decker, *Fortunes and Failures*, 37. Thomas Reid, "Diary of a Voyage to California in the Bark Velasco," October 7, 1849, BANC. Derbec, *French Journalist in the California Gold Rush*, 208n53.

28. "U.S. Customs House, San Francisco—Records. 1849–1897," box 1, 1849–1850 (A-Gen), and box 2, 1849–1850 (Geo-Z), BANC. Player-Frowd, *Six Months in California*, 130. John. O. Earll, "Statement of John O. Earll, A Pioneer of 1849—Bancroft Library, 1877," page 2, BANC.

29. Ibid., 7–8. For a different account of this incident, see Bancroft, *History of California*, 7:169 n36. On Chilean provisions and wheat shipped to and sold in California, see Hernández Cornejo, *Chilenos en San Francisco de California*, 1:86–87, 196–200.

30. On Australia's nineteenth-century wheat agriculture and grain trade, see Dunsdorfs, *Australian Wheat-Growing Industry*. For a comprehensive account of Australia's gold rush, see Blainey, *Rush that Never Ended*. For figures on Chilean wheat exports, see Sepúlveda G., *El trigo chileno en el mercado mundial*, 48; and Encina and Castedo, *Resumen de la historia de Chile*, 2:1176. During the eighteen-year period between 1844 and 1861, 1855 was the peak year for Chile's combined wheat and flour export trade. See Cariola Sutter and Sunkel, *Un siglo de historia económica de Chile*, 119–20.

31. Kuhlmann, *Development of the Flour-Milling Industry*, 96–101; and Evans, *Young Mill-Wright and Miller's Guide*. On Evans's many accomplishments as an engineer and inventor, see Ferguson, *Oliver Evans*.

32. Cunningham, "Gold Rush Journal: 1852–1854," August 30, 1853, BANC; Levi Floyd Walker, "Journal of a Trip to the California Mines and Back: 1849–1850," March 15, 1850, BLYU; Collier and Sater, *History of Chile, 1808–1994*, 81; Bauer, *Chilean Rural Society*, 83n12.

33. "The Wonders of California," *New York Daily Times*, November 3, 1851. For a comparison between the costs of producing wheat in California and Chile, see "Agriculture," *Sacramento Daily Union*, December 9, 1851. After losing their markets in California, Chilean wheat growers developed a short-lived, but enormous, market in Britain. James Douglas Jr. notes that in 1873, Chile exported $11,347,599 of wheat to Britain. This followed the repeal of the Corn Law, which had forbidden the importing of lower-priced foreign wheat—known as corn—in the 1800s. Douglas, "Chile," 91.

34. Gates, *California Ranchos and Farms*, 51. For the emergence of small famers following California's mining boom, see Kindell, "Settling the Sunset Land." Davis, "California Breadstuffs," 525. Williams, *Pioneer Pastorate and Times*, 212–13. For figures on California's wheat cultivation, see Wik, *Steam Power on the American Farm*, 51–52. This quotation is from Alexander B. Grogan to Faxon Dean Atherton, May 19, 1857, box 4, folder 22, p. 2 of 3, CHS.

35. Hittell, *Resources of California*, 170, 172. On the history of Chilean wheat, see David and David, *Trigo en Chile*.

36. Rasmussen, "Diplomats and Plant Collectors," 30.

37. Marten, "Development of Wheat Culture." Hayes, *Pioneer Notes*, 127. "Bearded Chili Wheat," *Banner*, June 10, 1871, reprinted in *Daily Alta California*, June 14, 1871. For other examples, see "Permanent Exposition Building," *Sacramento Daily Union*, June 20, 1888; George Martin, "Jottings Round San Jose," *Pacific Rural Press*, June 28, 1873; and "To Grain Growers," *California Farmer and Journal of Useful Sciences* 6, no. 14 (October 31, 1856): 108.

38. Gunn and Gunn, *Records of a California Family*, 179.

39. On the fires, see Berglund, *Making San Francisco American*, 19. Williams, *Pioneer Pastorate and Times*, 48. On the city's building spree, see Cross, *Financing an Empire*, 1:149; and Lotchin, *San Francisco*, 18.

40. Deverell, *Whitewashed Adobe*, 131. Pitt, *Decline of the Californios*, 53.

41. McCollum, *California as I Saw It* (1850), 36. Ryan, *Personal Adventures in Upper and Lower California*, 1:406; Kirker, "El Dorado Gothic," 35.
42. Charles B. Turrill, *California Notes*, 61; Ethington, *Public City*, 259.

CHAPTER 3. CHILECITO AND SPANISHTOWN

1. Bret Harte, "Letter 6: *Christian Register* [Boston], May 19, 1866—written from San Francisco, April 10, 1866," in *Bret Harte's California*, ed. Scharnhorst, 34. Harte became the founding editor of the *Overland Monthly* in 1868. Three years later, the *Atlantic Monthly* offered him the most lucrative contract any author in the United States had received up to that point; Scharnhorst, *Bret Harte*, xiii. Mission Dolores, originally known as the Misión San Francisco de Asis, was founded in 1776. It was the sixth mission of the twenty-one built in California by the Franciscan Missionaries between 1769 and 1823.
2. Royce, *California*, 218.
3. Boyd, *Wide-Open Town*, 4. For an example of an article that discusses Anglo and Chinese sex work in San Francisco but makes no mention of Latina/o prostitution, see Shumsky and Springer, "San Francisco's Zone of Prostitution, 1880–1934." North Beach remained the city's central sex-work district until the 1960s. See Boyd, *Wide-Open Town*, 87.
4. Sears, "All That Glitters," 383–402. Boyd, *Wide-Open Town*, 2. Also see Johnson, *Roaring Camp*, 169–70.
5. Felix Paul Wierzbicki, *California As It Is*, 65. Lucett, *Rovings in the Pacific*, 2:338. "The Golden Emigration," *Placer Times*, December 8, 1849. On the role of gender in shaping San Francisco during the decade following the Mexican War, see Jolly, "Inventing the City."
6. Bederman, *Manliness and Civilization*, 11. On these Victorian archetypes, see Halttunen, *Confidence Men and Painted Women*, 1–32; and Barnhart, *Fair but Frail*, 10. For an account of the criminalization of prostitution in San Francisco, see Pillors, "Criminalization of Prostitution." Clark, *Lectures*, 191.
7. For more on Dominga de Goñi, see Ester Edwards Orrego, "The Chilean Athertons," AHA. The quotations are from "Women in California," *Daily Alta California*, November 3, 1851; and Fondo del Ministerio de Relaciones Exteriores de Chile, ARNAD. Cónsules Chilenos en el Extranjero, vol. 73 (September 2, 1851).
8. Soulé, Gihon, and Nisbet, *Annals of San Francisco*, 412.
9. Hutchison, *Labors Appropriate to Their Sex*, 13. López Urrutia, *Chilenos in California*. "Love and Jealousy: A Chileno Woman Shoots Her Seducer on the Public Streets," *Daily Alta California*, October 15, 1867. On Lee and Ryland's Circus, see Slout, *Olympians of the Sawdust Circle*, 263.
10. Margaret DeWitt to her mother, September 28, 1849, folder 4, box 3, DeWitt Family Papers, BANC. Wyman, "California Emigrant Letters, Concluded," 354.
11. López Urrutia, *Chilenos in California*, xxi. Such designations were likely made by census takers, not by the Chilenas they enumerated.
12. Kimball, *Nell Kimball*, 217–18.

13. Limerick, *Legacy of Conquest*, 49. Among the best-researched accounts of prostitution in the American West is Butler, *Daughters of Joy, Sisters of Misery*.

14. Timothy Coffin Osborn, "Timothy Coffin Osborn Journal," transcript, p. 162, BANC. Megquier, *Apron of Gold*, 59 (emphasis added). Chandler, *California Gold Rush Camps*, section 1:2.

15. The quotation is from Barnhart, *Fair but Frail*, 20. Christman, *One Man's Gold*, 198. Young, *Days of '49*, 41.

16. Benemann, *Year of Mud and Gold*, 86. "Disorderly House," *Daily Alta California*, April 1, 1852; "City Items: Dance Houses," *Daily Alta California*, November 22, 1857.

17. Hurtado, *Intimate Frontiers*, 16. Dana, *Two Years before the Mast*, 215.

18. Coffin, *Pioneer Voyage to California*, 57. Asbury, *Barbary Coast*, 34–35. Crosby, *Memoirs*, 109. For two divergent interpretations of Chinese prostitution in California, see Benson Tong, *Unsubmissive Women*; and Hirata, "Free, Indentured, Enslaved."

19. Palmer, *New and the Old*, 34–35. "Murder of a Chilian," *Sacramento Daily Union*, September 7, 1854; *Daily Alta California*, September 9, 1854.

20. Pérez Rosales, *Times Gone By*, 218, 228. Rosario Améstica reappears in Eduardo Galeano's poetic history of Latin America, *Faces and Masks*, 167.

21. Langley, *San Francisco Directory for 1864*. On the concept of "the walking city," see Warner, *Streetcar Suburbs*, 15–21. Pérez-Rosales, *Times Gone By*, 227. The 1854 census recorded Chile's national population as 1,439,000. See Oficina Central de Estadísticas, *Censo general*.

22. Decker, *Fortunes and Failures*, 32. Kahn, *Imperial San Francisco*, 25. Kahn notes that the only exceptions were a few Massachusetts mill towns.

23. Bancroft, *California Inter Pocula*, 261–62.

24. Stoddard, *Footprints of the Padres*, 59. Holinski, *Californie et les routes interocéaniques*, 122. Holinski was a Lithuanian who wrote in French. The translation is mine.

25. Tchen, *New York before Chinatown*, 63–96. Soulé, Gihon, and Nisbet, *Annals of San Francisco*, 472. Lapp, *Blacks in Gold Rush California*, 103.

26. Harlow, *California Conquered*, 398–99n34, 299. William Heath Davis lists the officers of the regiment and their companies in the appendix of *Seventy-Five Years in California*, 382–83.

27. Ryan, *Personal Adventures in Upper and Lower California*, 1:258. On the Old Shades Tavern, see Cross, *Early Inns of California*, 99–101. Oehler, "Nantucket to the Golden Gate," 168. Historian Charles Bateson contended that the Hounds were predominantly "Australians, mainly ex-convicts who had been shipped to New South Wales or Tasmania under sentence of transportation"; Bateson, *Gold Fleet for California*, 120. I have found no evidence to support his conclusion. Historian Donald C. Biggs disputed the notion that the New York Volunteers constituted the core membership of the Hounds and argues that the criminal intent of the Regulators was a ruse orchestrated by the authors of *The Annals of San Francisco*. Unfortunately, Biggs had not done thorough research when he argued that "almost nothing was written of [the Hounds] in journals and letters" and that "the conclusion is irresistible that the myth of the Hounds sprang full-blown from the head of journalist Frank Soulé"; Biggs, *Conquer and Colonize*, 203.

28. Evans, À la California, 295.

29. Ryan, Personal Adventures in Upper and Lower California, 1:261–62. Ryan's service with the New York Volunteers is mentioned in Rohrbough, Days of Gold, 14. Palmer, "Pioneer Days in San Francisco," 554.

30. Asbury, Barbary Coast, 42. White, Picture of Pioneer Times in California, 106. Eldredge, Beginnings of San Francisco, 2:600n1; Oehler, "Nantucket to the Golden Gate," 168. For the contrasting viewpoint—namely, that Leavenworth was not allied with the Hounds—see Mullen, Let Justice Be Done, 62–71.

31. Bancroft, Popular Tribunals, 92. Williams, Pioneer Pastorate and Times, 58; Cross, Early Inns of California, 101–2; Eldredge, Beginnings of San Francisco, 2:600; Mullen, Let Justice Be Done, 58; Nasatir, "Chileans in California during the Gold Rush Period," 70n1; Asbury, Barbary Coast, 41.

32. White, Picture of Pioneer Times in California, 106.

33. Lotchin, San Francisco, 376–77n76. On the Hounds' "constitutional convention," see Mullen, Let Justice Be Done, 58. James Findla, "Statement of a Few Events in Early Days of Cal. as Given by James Findla, for Bancroft Library, 1878," p. 10, BANC.

34. Daily Alta California, June 28, 1849. Charles Frederick Winslow also mentions the shooting. See Oehler, "Nantucket to the Golden Gate," 168. Ryan, Personal Adventures in Upper and Lower California, 1:265–66. Daily Alta California, August 2, 1849.

35. Daily Alta California, August 9, 1849.

36. Soulé, Gihon, and Nisbet, Annals of San Francisco, 557. Alta California, August 9, 1849, testimonies of Felica Alvarez (the Alta's editors spelled her name incorrectly), Alfred Miller, Leopold Blankenschmidt, María Alvarez, and Pedro Danino. In its steamer edition for August 2, 1849, the Alta California published a seventeen-column review of the trial. The testimonies listed are excerpted from records of the court proceedings. The Alta's account differs substantially from the one presented in the Annals of San Francisco. Daily Alta California, August 9, 1849. Ryan, Personal Adventures in Upper and Lower California, 1:263. Thorne, "Bound for the Land of Cannan, Ho!," 264.

37. Oehler, "Nantucket to the Golden Gate," 169. Dr. Charles Frederick Winslow's letters to his wife, Lydia, on the island of Nantucket offer one of the most detailed accounts of the Hounds' attack on Little Chile. Winslow, a graduate of Harvard Medical School, sailed to California in 1849. Before his arrival in San Francisco, he had practiced medicine on Tahiti and Maui for five years. Alta California, August 9, 1849; Soulé, Gihon, and Nisbet, Annals of San Francisco, 559.

38. Davis, Seventy-Five Years in California, 310–11. William Heath Davis had close ties to the Latino community of San Francisco. His wife, María de Jesus Estudillo, was a Mexican Californian from a prominent San Diego family. Davis spoke Spanish, he had visited Chile on several occasions, and he maintained ties with the leading commercial houses in Valparaíso. On Davis's adventures involving the Chilean flour trade, see Rolle, American in California, 81. Cogswell, Gold Rush Diary of Moses Pearson Cogswell, 54.

39. Pérez Rosales, Times Gone By, 272.

40. Oehler, "Nantucket to the Golden Gate," 169. Mullen, Let Justice Be Done, 60.

41. *Daily Alta California*, August 2, 1849.

42. Samuel C. Upham, *Notes of a Voyage to California*, 222. On the trial, see Bagley, *Scoundrel's Tale*, 312–13.

43. On the Almadén mine, see Matilla Tascón, *Historia de las minas de Almadén*. In 1563, Spaniard Amador de Cabrera discovered cinnabar deposits at Huancavelica in the Viceroyalty of Peru. See Robins, *Mercury, Mining, and Empire*; and Lohmann Villena, *Las minas de Huancavelica*. On the use of mercury during the California Gold Rush, see Young, *Western Mining*, 93–94; Paul, *California Gold*, 59, 140; and Hittell, *Mining in the Pacific States*, 22, 133.

44. Moerenhout, *Inside Story of the Gold Rush*, v. Details of these developments can be found in P. Della Torre, *United States vs. Andrés Castillero*.

45. Coomes, "From Pooyi to the New Almaden Mercury Mine," 5.

46. Dorrance, "Legacy of the Red Ore," 7–8. Downer, "Quicksilver Mine of New Almaden," 220.

47. For numbers of workers, see Valencia, "New Almaden and the Mexican," 58; and "Work at the New Almaden Mines," *Daily Alta California*, March 21, 1866. Meagher, "Quicksilver, and Its Home," 507.

48. Wells, "Visit to the Quicksilver Mines," 34.

49. *Gallipolis Journal*, May 1, 1851. Wells, "Visit to the Quicksilver Mines," 31. James M. Hutchings, "Blessing the Mine," in *Scenes of Wonder and Curiosity*, ed. Olmsted, 186.

50. Hayes-Bautista et al., "Empowerment, Expansion, and Engagement," 14, 17. See "Demonstración de simpatía por Chile," *El Nuevo Mundo*, November 29, 1865; "Lista de donativos con que contribuyen las Sociedades Patrióticas Chilenas de California y Nevada, para auxilio de guerra que sostiene Chile contra España," *El Nuevo Mundo*, April 6, 1866; Hayes-Bautista et al., "Empowerment, Expansion, and Engagement," 17; and Pitti, *Devil in Silicon Valley*, 73.

51. For examples, see "From Our Exchanges," *California Farmer and Journal of Useful Sciences*, February 10, 1865, 32; "Strike at the New Almaden Mine," *Sacramento Daily Union*, April 11, 1866; and "The New Almaden Strike," *Daily Alta California*, March 21, 1868.

52. "Quicksilver Mines of Old and New Almaden," 338; "A Visit to the New Almaden Mines," *Daily Alta California*, December 28, 1857. California's annual gold yields also peaked in 1853, with the removal of $54.9 million in gold from California's mountains and rivers; "California Gold," *Journal of the American Geographical and Statistical Society* 1 (March 1859): 89. Chileans also extracted quicksilver from the Punitaqui mines but not in sufficient quantities to meet nineteenth-century demand. See Pinto Rodríguez, *Minas de azogue de Punitaqui*.

53. Brewer, *Up and Down California in 1860–1864*, 139, 142–43. Like New Almaden, New Idria was named after a European mercury mining town. Idrija, Slovenia, known as Idria when under Austrian rule, was a second major source of the mercury exported by Spain to the Americas.

54. Currently, the greatest risk of mercury exposure comes from fish consumption, dental amalgams, and vaccines. See Clarkson, Magos, and Myers, "Toxicology of Mercury";

Florentine and Sanfilippo, "Elemental Mercury Poisoning"; and Mulford, *Life by Land and Sea*, 103–4.

55. Wells, "Visit to the Quicksilver Mines," 39.

CHAPTER 4. MANIFEST DESTINY AT THE END OF A ROPE

1. Revere, *Keel and Saddle*, 143.

2. Pérez Rosales, *Times Gone By*, 212.

3. Marx, *Capital*, 1:280. For two preliminary attempts to address the varieties of unfree labor that persisted in California after its admission the union as a nominally free state, see Smith, *Freedom's Frontier*; and Magliari, "Cave Johnson Couts."

4. Paz Brownrigg, "Linchocracia." I have borrowed this definition of lynching from Carrigan and Webb, "Lynching of Persons of Mexican Origin or Descent," 413. Norton, *Life and Adventures of Col. L. A. Norton*, 293.

5. Storti, *Incident at Bitter Creek*. For Chinese minister Zheng Zaoru's report to Congress on the event, see "Memorial of Chinese Laborers at Rock Springs, Wyoming (1885)," in *Chinese American Voices*, ed. Yung, Chang, and Lai, 48–54. Bederman, *Manliness and Civilization*, 47. Carrigan and Webb, "Lynching of Persons of Mexican Origin," 413. Gonzales-Day, *Lynching in the West*, 207–16.

6. Goldsby, *Spectacular Secret*, 21.

7. "Judge Lynch in Contra Costa," *Sacramento Daily Union*, January 27, 1855.

8. Pérez Rosales, *Times Gone By*, 237.

9. Warren Sadler, "Warren Sadler Journal, Reminiscences and Miscellaneous Papers, 1849–1867," vol. 2, p. 76, BANC.

10. Enrique Bunster, "Vida y milagros," 59–60.

11. Revere, *Keel and Saddle*, 160–61.

12. Woods, *Sixteen Months at the Gold Diggings*, 99–100.

13. Clappe, *Shirley Letters*, 121.

14. Pedro Ruiz Aldea quoted in *We Were Forty-Niners!*, 225. Ruiz Aldea was a journalist and activist from Concepción who had rebelled against Manuel Montt's conservative government and fled to California in 1859. He returned to Chile in 1861 and founded several newspapers in the south. For more on Ruiz, see Bengoa, *Historia del pueblo Mapuche*, 166.

15. Perkins, *Three Years in California*, 103. On clothing differences among Latino miners from various countries, also see Sucheng Chan, "A People of Exceptional Character: Ethnic Diversity, Nativism, and Racism in the California Gold Rush," in *Rooted in Barbarous Soil*, ed. Starr and Orsi, 57.

16. Shaw, *Golden Dreams and Waking Realities*, 64.

17. Kelly, *Excursion to California*, 2:19.

18. Stephen L. Fowler, "Journal of Stephen L. and James E. Fowler of East Hampton, Long Island," October 29, 1849, p. 31, BANC. Ward, *Sam Ward in the Gold Rush*, 31, 46. For example, see "Letter from Sonora," *Daily Alta California*, November 28, 1853, 1.

19. Paul, *California Gold*, 135. Hittell, *Resources of California*, 279.

20. Paul, *Mining Frontiers in the Far West*, 31–32; Farish, *Gold Hunters of California*, 36. Delano, *Alonzo Delano's California Correspondence*, 136. For an example of the Chile mill's role in prolonging small-scale California mining, see "Letter from Tuttletown," *Daily Alta California*, April 16, 1858. Baxley, *What I Saw*, 426. For illustrations of the *arrastre* and Chile mill, see Rickard, *Journeys of Observation*, 122–23; and Coy, *Pictorial History of California*, 140. On North Carolina miners' uses of the Chilean Mill, see *Athens Post*, May 5, 1854.

21. Webster, *Gold Seekers of '49*, 105. McKinstry, *California Gold Rush Overland Diary*, 368, 370.

22. Monaghan, *Chile, Peru, and the California Gold Rush*, 112–14; Grivas, *Military Governments in California*, 201. Smith quoted in McGuinness, *Path of Empire*, 34–35.

23. On rising anti-immigrant sentiment, see Bancroft, *History of California*, 6:403. William R. Wheaton, "Statement of Facts on Early California History," p. 6, BANC. Benigno Gutiérrez, "Account of Benigno Gutierrez for the Society of California Pioneers," p. 3, Alice Phelan Sullivan Library, SCP. *Placer Times*, July 21, 1849.

24. Tyson, *Diary of a Physician in California*, 82–83.

25. "An Act for the Better Regulation of the Mines and the Government of Foreign Miners," quoted in Wood, *California's Agua Fría*, 61. Morrell, *Gold Rushes*, 108.

26. Hutton, *Glances at California*, 44. George Enoch Jewett, "George E. Jewett's Journal—1849–50," May 19, 1850, BANC.

27. Taylor, *Eldorado*, 394.

28. Colton, *California Diary*, 203. Carson, *Early Recollections of the Mines*, 25. On lawyers and merchants who resisted the tax, see Ellison, *Self-Governing Dominion*, 126.

29. *Stockton Times* quoted in Peterson, "Anti-Mexican Nativism in California," 312. For more on "An Act to Provide for the Protection of Foreigners, and to Define Their Liabilities and Privileges," see McClain, "Chinese Struggle for Civil Rights," 539.

30. More generally, Michael Denning has recast American exceptionalism as a complex of contradictions specific to settler capitalism. Denning, "'The Special American Conditions,'" 365.

31. John O'Sullivan in *United States Magazine and Democratic Review* 17, no. 85 (1845): 5. Pratt, "John L. O'Sullivan and Manifest Destiny," 225.

32. Benton, "Speech to the United States Senate, May 28, 1846." Saxton, *Rise and Fall of the White Republic*, 146.

33. White, *Picture of Pioneer Times in California*, 16. Buck, *Yankee Trader in the Gold Rush*, 128.

34. Sasnett, "United States—Her Past and Her Future," 629. From 1859 to 1861, Sasnett served as Auburn University's first president.

35. For more on the debate over resource extraction in the western United States, see DeVoto, "The West"; and Robbins, "'Plundered Province' Thesis." For two approaches to the intersection of labor and nature in North America's Pacific Coast history, see Igler, *Industrial Cowboys*; and White, *Organic Machine*. On the decline of small-scale, entrepreneurial mining and the rise of capital-intensive hydraulic excavation, see Isenberg, *Mining California*, 23–52.

36. Lomas, "Dennis Kearney."

37. For the state constitution's ban of slavery, Browne, *Report of the Debates*, 4. On Indian labor in California ranchos and households during the mid-1800s, see Hurtado, "'Hardly a Farm House.'" The quotation is from White, *"It's Your Misfortune,"* 339. For a history of unfree California Indian labor under US rule, see Madley, "'Unholy Traffic in Human Blood and Souls.'"

38. Tyler, "Fugitive Slaves in Mexico," 1.

39. Morse, "The Story of a Gold Miner," 223. For examples of self-employed Blacks, see Peters, *Autobiography*, 192. Garrison quoted in Lapp, *Blacks in Gold Rush California*, 13.

40. For Los Angeles, see Beasley, *Negro Trail Blazers of California*, 90. For Redding, see Lapp, *Blacks in Gold Rush California*, 70. For the Sierras, see *Grass Valley Telegraph*, December 4, 1855. The quotations are from T. Dwight Hunt in the *Liberator*, June 29, 1849; and *Alta California*, May 4, 1850.

41. William H. Seward quoted in Foner, *Free Soil, Free Labor, Free Men*, 41.

42. In 1811 the first Chilean congress decreed that the children of slaves born in Chilean territory would be free. See Luis Galdames, *History of Chile*, 169–70. Chile had no more than five thousand slaves of African descent at the time of its independence. See Feliú Cruz, *Abolición de la esclavitud en Chile*, 39–40. Gil Navarro, *Gold Rush Diary*, 46 (quotation), 1.

43. Collier and Sater, *History of Chile*, 12, 42. On nineteenth-century Chilean rural peonage, see Salazar Vergara, *Labradores, peones y proletarios*; Bauer, "Chilean Rural Labor," 1069–70; Bauer, "Rural Workers in Spanish America"; and Loveman, "Critique."

44. Case quoted in Lyman, "Reminiscences of Wm. M. Case," 281. John Lacourt to Gov. (Riley) of California, March 24, 1849, Concepcion (Chili), in Archives of California, vol. 63, p. 327, BANC. Sepúlveda G., *El trigo chileno en el mercado mundial*, 42; Pérez Yañez, *Forjadores de Chile*, 250; and Hernández-Cornejo, *Chilenos en San Francisco de California*, 1:20. Statistics on Chile's merchant marine are from López Urrutia, *Breve historia naval de Chile*, 67.

45. Recardo Tornero quoted in Ruiz Esquide, "Migration, Colonization and Land Policy," 387.

46. Buckelew quoted in Beasley, *Negro Trail Blazers of California*, 69. David Brody, "Free Labor, Law, and American Trade Unionism," in *Terms of Labor*, ed. Engerman, 218.

47. Contrata D. José Manuel Ramirez y Don Juan Sampson y otros, January 5, 1849, ARNAD, Colección Notarial (Valparaíso), vol. 83, no. 9, fol. 12–14, and no. 10, fol. 14–15; Pérez Rosales, *Times Gone By*, 217; Harris Bucher, *Emigración y políticas gubernamentales*, 134–36; Gil Navarro, *Gold Rush Diary*, 280n47. For more on Chilean debt peons in California, see Sisson, "Bound for California"; and Fernando Purcell, "'Too Many Foreigners for My Taste': Law, Race and Ethnicity in California, 1848–1852," in *Evil, Law and the State*, ed. Parry, 17–29. The quotation is from B., "For the Placer Times," *Placer Times*, June 2, 1849.

48. Contrato de peónaje entre Don Santiago King con varios peones, ARNAD, Colección Notarial (Valparaíso), vol. 82, no. 384, folder 372v–373. Also aboard were eight peons who sailed with their *patrón* Carlos Armstrong and his wife. See Sepúlveda G., *El trigo*

chileno en el mercado mundial, 42. For the *Virjinia* passenger list, see "Movimiento Maritimo," *El Commercio de Valparaíso*, September 12, 1848. For more on King of William, see Millard, *History of the San Francisco Bay Region*, 3:59–62, 71. For other peonaje contracts, see Convenio de Don Manuel Barañas con Jacinto Celis y otros, ARNAD, Colección Notarial (Santiago), vol. 198, no. 307, fol. 347–48; Don G. Jagerschmidt y otros, May 21, 1849, ARNAD, Colección Notarial (Valparaíso), vol. 83, no. 278, fol. 293v–95v.

49. Bancroft, *History of California*, 6:403n64.

50. Ayers, *Gold and Sunshine*, 46. For a Chilean version of the confrontation, see Gil Navarro, *Gold Rush Diary*, 68–71. For a contrasting explanation, see *Alta California*, December 31, 1849.

51. The Chilean War is discussed briefly in Johnson, *Roaring Camp*, 196–208; Monaghan, *Chile, Peru, and the California Gold Rush*, 243–48; and Faugsted, *Chilenos in the California Gold Rush*, 37–38.

52. Gil Navarro, *Gold Rush Diary*, 84.

53. Morton McCarver quoted in Browne, *Report of the Debates*, 138. Millard, *History of the San Francisco Bay Region*, 3:61.

54. Edward Gilbert quoted in Browne, *Report of the Debates*, 150.

55. In 1882 former Scottish banker David Jacks started producing and marketing a cheese in the Monterey area that came to be known as "Monterey Jack." See Jerry Hirsch, "California Cheese Ripens into an Art," *Los Angeles Times*, May 30, 2004. On Gilbert and Stevenson's regiment, see Upham, *Notes of a Voyage to California*, 495.

56. Zerbe and Anderson, "Culture and Fairness," 114. Data are from Johnson, "Vigilance and the Law," 560.

57. For the statistic, see Marks, *Precious Dust*, 250. Theodore Kimball, "Journal of Theodore Kimball," pp. 5–6, BANC; Russailh, *Last Adventure*, 15; and Shinn, *Mining Camps*, 141.

58. Francisco P. Ramírez quoted in Paz Brownrigg, "Linchocracia."

59. Jackson, *Diary of a Forty-Niner*, 105. Canfield (1843–1909) claimed that his book reprinted the diary of Alfred T. Jackson of Norfolk, Connecticut, during his mining adventures in Rock Creek, Nevada County, California, from 1850 to 1852. "Rough Abstract of a Forty-Niner Diary" quoted in Kenny, "History of the Sonora Mining Region," 257. "Calaveras Correspondence—Another Man Hung," *Sacramento Daily Union*, July 29, 1853. Marjorie Tisdale Wolcott, editor's note in Hayes, *Pioneer Notes*, 160n1.

60. Carson, *Early Recollections of the Mines*, 35; Ayers, *Gold and Sunshine*, 132; Henry Veel Huntley, *California*, 118.

61. Newmark, *Sixty Years in Southern California*, 141. Borthwick, *Three Years in California*, 233–34.

62. "Summary of the Fortnight Ending March 1st," *Daily Alta California*, March 1, 1854. "The Rancheria Tragedy: The Work of Revenge Going On—Mexicans and Chileans Being Hung and Shot Down Like Coyotes," *Daily Alta California*, August 11, 1855.

63. Heyde Wiggins Stewart to Peter H. Burnett, "From Heyde Wiggins Stewart and Others from Calaveras County concerning Foreign Miners, May 2nd 1850," letter 2, CHS. Whitman, *Democratic Vistas*, 414.

64. Nasatir, "Chileans in California during the Gold Rush Period," 60. Kip, *California Sketches*, 57.
65. Pérez Rosales, *Times Gone By*, 294.
66. Farwell, "Society of California Pioneers, Part III," 366.

CHAPTER 5. SUPPLEMENTING THE SOIL

1. On Berwick, see "The Fruit-Growers," *Los Angeles Times*, November 22, 1893; "The Land and Its Fruits," *Los Angeles Times*, January 4, 1896; and Barratt, *Carmel Valley*, 49. In *Looking Backward*, a nineteenth-century Bostonian named Julian West lapsed into a 113-year mesmeric trance. On awakening—Rip Van Winkle–style—in the year 2000, West found himself in a world without war or poverty. A scientist named Doctor Leete greeted the time traveler and showed him around this radically transformed society; Bellamy, *Looking Backward*. Berwick, "Farming in the Year 2000, A.D.," 571. Bird guano from Peru's Chincha Islands and sodium nitrate from Chile's northern deserts were the key ingredients of a "First Green Revolution" in which farmers throughout Europe and the United States began depending on imported commodity fertilizers from distant landscapes to reinvigorate exhausted soils. See Melillo, "First Green Revolution."
2. For California's dairy industry, see the Real California Milk website, available at: http://www.realcaliforniamilk.com/products/dairy/.
   On the California citrus industry as the engine of Southern California's economic growth from the 1880s through World War II, see Sackman, *Orange Empire*, 5.
3. Rejmanek and Richardson, "What Attributes Make Some Plant Species More Invasive?" 1659. John D. Gerlach, "How the West Was Lost: Reconstructing the Invasion Dynamics of Yellow Starthistle and Other Plant Invaders of Western Rangelands and Natural Areas," in *California Exotic Pest Plant Council*, ed. Kelly, Wagner, and Warner, 68. On alfalfa's role in restoring soil fertility, see Chorley, "Agricultural Revolution in Northern Europe," 71.
4. Salo, "Red brome"; and Sumner and Buck, *Exotic Pests and Diseases*, 227. For more information on red brome, see the Summary List of Accessioned Plants at HCRL.
5. Other macronutrients include: phosphorus, potassium, calcium, magnesium, and sulfur. Brady, *Nature and Property of Soils*, 21; Galloway et al., "Nitrogen Fixation."
6. Brady, *Nature and Property of Soils*, 436.
7. On the early history of alfalfa cultivation, see McNeill and McNeill, *Human Web*, 84–85. On the ethnohistory and distribution of alfalfa, see Réal Michaud, W. F. Lehman, and M. D. Rumbaugh, "World Distribution and Historical Development," in *Alfalfa and Alfalfa Improvement*, ed. Hansen, Barnes, and Hill, 25–31; D. K. Barnes, et al., *Alfalfa Germplasm in the United States*, 1–21; Bolton, *Alfalfa*; and Ridley, *Dispersal of Plants*, 648. On alfalfa's failure to thrive in eastern North America, see Sprague, Alexander, and Dudley. "Plant Breeding and Genetic Engineering," 18; and Ivanov, *Alfalfa [Lyutserna]*, 9.
8. *California Farmer* quoted in "Alfalfa or Chili Clover," *Ohio Farmer* 48, no. 3 (July 17, 1875): 35; Rasmussen, *San Francisco Ship Passenger Lists*, vol. 1.

9. "The Late Drowning Case near San Pablo," *Sacramento Daily Union*, December 1, 1874. In the Marin County 1850 Census, solicitor L. B. Miznor listed Oyarzo's home as "Valperazo" [Valparaíso]. Cameron, "Quintay Ranch," 363; Wickson, *Rural California*, 116; Raven, "Amphitropical Relationships," 161; Wing, *Alfalfa Farming in America*, 53; Jelinek, *Harvest Empire*.

10. The Assessor of Monterey County, "Annual Report for 1869," quoted in Hittell, *All about California*, 60. Nordhoff, *California*, 130. Blayney, *Changing Landscape of U.S. Milk Production*, 5. Mark Fiege, *Irrigated Eden*, 52–53.

11. Stegner, *Where the Bluebird Sings*, xix; and Smythe, *Greatest Irrigated Farm*, 6. Salvator, *Los Angeles in the Sunny Seventies*, 74.

12. Hubert Howe Bancroft, "Biographical materials relating to John Bensley," folder 1, fol. 4, p. 8, BANC; and Delgado, *Bensley Water System*, 1–3. For more about Bensley's financial dealings, see Igler, *Industrial Cowboys*, 72–74. Also see Sullivan, *Early Days in California*, 186–88. On Chile's waterworks, see Collier and Sater, *History of Chile*, 82–83. California's irrigated landscapes long predate Spanish colonial incursion. Owens Valley Paiute Indians in east-central California practiced extensive irrigation of wild plant communities for large-scale food production. See Lawton, Wilke, DeDecker, and Mason, "Agriculture among the Paiute of Owens Valley," 13–49. On irrigation practices during the Spanish period (1769–1821), see Frederick W. Roeding, *Irrigation in California*, 33.

13. Putnam, "History, Importance, and Production Dynamics of Alfalfa," 3; Hoover et al., *Historic Spots in California*, 568; and Gilbert, *Illustrated Atlas and History of Yolo County*, 82. For more on the concept of a "hydraulic West," see Worster, *Rivers of Empire*, 406.

14. Fradkin, *Seven States of California*, 236. Gregory, *History of Yolo County*, 62.

15. Dondlinger, *Book of Wheat*, 113.

16. "Alfalfa or Chilian Clover Seed," *Southern Planter*, no. 10 (October 1853): 310. Cox and Megee, *Alfalfa*, 27, 93. On the transfer of alfalfa from California to Colorado and Kansas, see Wing, *Alfalfa Farming in America*, 70–71; and Smith, "Upsetting the Balance of Nature," 652.

17. "A Los Angles dairy farmer" quoted in Madden, *Lands of the Southern Pacific Railroad Company*, 40. I. D. O'Donnell, "At the Great New York Land Show in Madison Square Garden," quoted in Raban, *Bad Land*, 26–27.

18. I use the term *soil degradation* to denote "the temporary or permanent lowering of the soil's productive capacity." Decreasing soil fertility is one aspect of soil degradation. Others include erosion, salinization, acidification, pollution, and compaction. J. K. Syers et al., "Managing Soils for Long-Term Productivity," 1012. Melillo, "First Green Revolution," 1045. In 1860, the Chilean José Santos Ossa discovered salitre deposits in the Antofagasta regions. See H. Iglesias, *José Santos Ossa*.

19. During the nineteenth and early twentieth centuries, sodium nitrate was known as salitre, saltpeter, saltpetre, nitre, nitrate(s), and nitrate of soda. San Bernadino County was founded in 1853, while Riverside became a county in 1893.

20. A summary of the war can be found in Kiernan, "Foreign Interests." For a Bolivian interpretation, see Querejazu Calvo, *Guano, salitre, sangre*. For a Peruvian perspective, see Bonilla, *Un siglo a la deriva*. For an analysis of the effects of Latin American

mining on labor relations and environmental degradation, see Dore, "Environment and Society."

21. On the hyper-aridity of the Atacama Desert, see Veblen, Young, and Orme, *Physical Geography of South America*, 160.

22. "Nitrate of Soda," *Southern Cultivator* (September 1877): 348. M. G. Ellzey, "Nitrogen and Phosphates," *American Farmer*, September 1, 1884, 237. Gustafson, *Soils and Soil Management*, 322.

23. "On the Saltpetre of Chile, (Nitrate of Soda)," *Journal of the Franklin Institute* 11 (June 1833): 401. Darwin, "*Origin of Species*," 374. Alfredo Leubel quoted in Oscar Bermúdez, *Historia del salitre*, 154. *Report of the Consul General of Chile at San Francisco*, 13.

24. Sater, "Chile and the World Depression of the 1870s," 99.

25. Mosier, Syers, and Freney, *Agriculture and the Nitrogen Cycle*, 234. On the atmospheric origins of the sodium nitrate deposits in Chile's Atacama Desert and California's Mojave Desert, see Böhlke, Ericksen, and Revesz, "Stable Isotope Evidence." Garcés Feliz, *Ciudades del salitre*.

26. Monteón, "*Enganche* in the Chilean Nitrate Sector," 67. For more on the nitrate workers who toiled in the Antofagasta and Tarapacá Provinces during the second half of the nineteenth century, see Pinto Vallejos, *Trabajos y rebeldías en la pampa salitrera*.

27. Wright, *Republic of Chile*, 270.

28. Reid, *Nitrate Fields of Chile*, 13–15.

29. Crookes quoted in Galloway and Cowling, "Reactive Nitrogen and the World," 64. Wright, *Republic of Chile*, 282.

30. MacCurdy, *History of the California Fruit Growers Exchange*, 2, 7; and Towne and Wentworth, *Shepherd's Empire*, 318. Also see Steen, *Cooperative Marketing*, 39.

31. Chandler, *Railroads*, 3. For a more recent history of the transcontinental railroads, see White, *Railroaded*. Geographer David Harvey included the development of railroads in the second phase (1850–1930) of the phenomenon that he has termed "space-time compression." See Harvey, *Condition of Postmodernity*, 241. Wolfgang Schivelbusch discusses railroads and the "annihilation of space and time" in *Railway Journey*, 33. On the building of the Southern Pacific Railroad and the sale of western produce to eastern markets, see Orsi, *Sunset Limited*.

32. Warner, *Our Italy*, 119; MacCurdy, *History of the California Fruit Growers Exchange*, 5; and California State Board of Horticulture, *Culture of the Citrus in California*, 54.

33. Salvator, *Los Angeles in the Sunny Seventies*, 156. Zierer, "Citrus Fruit Industry," 54.

34. Ackerman, "Influences of Climate," 298. Southern California's orange and lemon growers purchased shipments of "inferior grades of alfalfa" from the north for fertilizer. See, e.g., John A. Armstrong, "Grapes, Giants and Guano," *Los Angeles Times*, January 27, 1935. The *California Fruit Grower* quoted in "Thick Rind and Coarse-Fleshed Oranges," *Los Angeles Times*, February 1, 1896, 14.

35. California State Board of Horticulture, *Culture of the Citrus in California*, 138.

36. Luther Burbank quoted in Balfour, Gutherie, and Co., *Nitrate of Soda and Thomas' Phosphate Powder*, 13.

37. "First Steamer of Many Brings Load of Fertilizer," *Los Angeles Herald*, February 12, 1907. Wright, *Republic of Chile*, 282.
38. Haskell, "Fertilizer Use in the United States," 265–66.
39. *California Citrograph* quoted in David Danelski, "Perchlorate in Fertilizer Contaminates Water," *Riverside Press-Enterprise*, February 28, 2004.
40. Hillman, *Cultivation of Citrus Fruits*, 24. For more examples, see Meyers, *Food for Plants*.
41. "Mines and Mining," *Los Angeles Times*, May 28, 1902.
42. McWilliams, *Factories in the Field*. On Mexican citrus workers' experiences in Southern California, see González, *Labor and Community*.
43. Curtis and Pepper, "Our Nitrogen Problem," 173.
44. California Nitrate Development Company of San Francisco, *Story about Nitrate of Soda*; and Forney, *Nitre Beds of the United States*. Vandercook, *California Nitrates*, 3. Anonymous, "Nitrate Deposits in the United States," *Science* 44, no. 1146 (1916): 864. "The Nitrate Problem," *Washington Post*, November 27, 1916.
45. Fritz Haber quoted in Smil, "Detonator of the Population Explosion," 415.
46. Smil, *Enriching the Earth*, 47.
47. Whitbeck, "Chilean Nitrate and the Nitrogen Revolution," 273; and Knight, "Research in the Bureau of Chemistry and Soils," 315; and Brand, "Fertilizer Industry," 22.
48. J. A. Wood, "Chilean Nitrate Figures: Synthetic Equivalents, It Is Held, Have Not Supplanted Natural Product," *New York Times*, November 21, 1944; "Chile's Great Nitrate Industry Needs Funds to Avert Collapse," *New York Times*, April 11, 1955; David Pimentel and Marcia Pimentel, "Comment," 330–31.
49. Wines, *Fertilizer in America*, 125. For examples of well-received histories of California agriculture that make no mention of Chilean fertilizer, see Vaught, *Cultivating California*; Stoll, *Fruits of Natural Advantage*; Pisani, *From the Family Farm to Agribusiness*; and Jelinek, *Harvest Empire*.
50. William D. Boyce quoted in Melillo, "First Green Revolution," 1053. Fiona Ortiz, "Chile's Ghost Towns Done Up for Tourists; Areas around Nitrate Mines Restored," *Washington Post*, November 22, 2005.

CHAPTER 6. A RAILROAD IN THE CLOUDS

1. Montgomery, "Railroad in the Clouds," 463.
2. This estimate is the result of an extensive search of the California Digital Newspaper Collection, a public database of major California newspapers published since 1846, available at: cdnc.ucr.edu.
   Stewart, *Henry Meiggs: Yankee Pizarro*, translated as *Henry Meiggs: Un Pizarro yanqui*. For an earlier biographical sketch of Meiggs, which Stewart did not consult, see Simon Camacho, *El ferrocarril de Arequipa*. Scholars wanting to expand on Stewart's work now have access to the extensive correspondence in Meiggs's epistolary, published and annotated in Salinas Sánchez, *Estudio socio-histórico*.
3. For a popular global history of railroads, see Wolmar, *Blood, Iron and Gold*.

4. "Henry Meiggs," 15. Rousseau, "Jacksonian Monetary Policy," 457–88. The *New York City Directories for 1838–39* lists Meiggs's lumberyard at 605 Greenwich Street in Manhattan. See Lawrence, "Henry Meiggs," 28n4.

5. Meiggs's first wife, Gertrude Burns, died on November 13, 1833. Their son, William Wardell, died in September 1850. Meiggs married his second wife, Caroline Doyle, on September 7, 1835. She died in Santiago, Chile, on December 25, 1861. Caroline and Henry had six children, three of whom survived to adulthood. These details can be found in "The Will of Henry Meiggs: All Legal Debts to Be Paid His Heirs Mentioned," *New York Times*, November 4, 1877. Baumgardner, *Yanks in the Redwoods*, 64, 71. Details about the *Ontario* can be found in McNairn and MacMullen, *Ships of the Redwood Coast*, 4; and Baumgardner, *Yanks in the Redwoods*, 66. Before it became Mendocino, the area around the mill was known as "Meiggsville."

6. A century later, North Beach became the home of San Francisco's Beatnik movement, which had its epicenter at City Lights Bookstore on Columbus Avenue. See James Vernando Gatewood, "City Lights Books: The History of a Community" (PhD diss., Brown University, 2008). Soulé, Gihon, and Nisbet, *Annals of San Francisco*, quoted in Dickson, *San Francisco Kaleidoscope*, 19. For detailed histories of Meiggs's sponsorship of both New York's and San Francisco's music scenes, see Lawrence, "Henry Meiggs," 26–41; and Hopkins, "California Recollections of Hopkins," 335. "Fresh American Forgeries," *Bankers' Magazine* (January–December 1854): 731. In 1881 Meiggs Wharf became part of Fisherman's Wharf. Sherman, *Recollections of California*, 90; Baumgardner, *Yanks in the Redwoods*, 71; Harker, "'Honest Harry' Meiggs," 196–97.

7. The quotation is from Camp, *San Francisco*, 93. Also see Upham, *Notes of a Voyage to California*, 142–52; and Tinkham, *California Men and Events*, 124–26.

8. "Astounding Developments! $1,000,00 Comptroller's Warrants Forged! Over-Issue of $300,00 of Stock! Schuylerism in San Francisco! Flight of Henry and John Meiggs," *Daily Alta California*, October 8, 1854.

9. On attempts by Governor John Bigler to extradite Meiggs to California, see "Probable Arrest of Harry Meiggs!" *Daily Alta California*, November 1, 1855. Ironically, Bigler made his own transpacific journey south, serving as the US ambassador to Chile (1857–61). On Meiggs's early years in Chillán, see Donoso, *Una amistad de toda la vida*, 22. On the Maipó Bridge, see Stewart, *Henry Meiggs*, 23.

10. William G. Delano to Faxon Dean Atherton, July 9, 1863, box 4, folder 29, p. 3 of 4, CHS. For more on the project, see María Edwards, "Construcción de los ferrocarriles en Chile," 149.

11. Samuel W. Brown to his wife, September 16, 1849, in "Samuel W. Brown diary and letters," CHS 236, folder 1, CHS. In 1821 the Chilean government granted a license to two British men, Charles Neville and Joseph Moss, to run a weekly stage line between Santiago and Valparaíso. See Edmundson, *History of the British Presence in Chile*, 175. For the list of investors in the Copiapó-Caldera line, see *El Mercurio*, September 27, 1849. On the problems Wheelwright faced when constructing the Santiago-Valparaíso line, see Rivera Jofre, *Reseña histórica del ferrocarril*, 9, 47, 51; and Bautista Albérdi,

Vida y los trabajos industriales, 182–86, translated the following year as: *Life and Industrial Labors*. Also see "Public Works," *El Ferrocarril*, January 8, 1858. *El Ferrocaril* of Santiago and *El Mercurio* of Valparaíso were Chile's leading nineteenth-century newspapers. On February 14, 1851, the Chilean government awarded Wheelwright the contract to build Chile's first telegraph lines. See Johnson, *Pioneer Telegraphy in Chile*, 15. Wheelwright eventually moved to Argentina, where he supervised the construction of the Argentine Central Railroad between Rosario and Córdoba (1863–70). See Goodwin, "Central Argentine Railway," 628.

12. Wetmore was also involved in Meiggs's railroad projects. In addition, he developed South American guano mines, and he built the first Protestant church in Santiago. See "Pacific Coast Items," *Sacramento Daily Union*, June 27, 1873; and Van Dyke, Leberthon, and Taylor, *City and County of San Diego*, 114. The quotation is from Albert Claypool White, "A Yankee Monte Cristo," *Maine Farmer*, January 23, 1896. For more on Meiggs's lavish lifestyle in Santiago, see Pablo Figueroa, *Diccionario biográfico*, 136. The city demolished Meiggs's mansion in 1940 to make room for commercial expansion.

13. James Churchman, "Americans in Chile," *Daily Alta California*, December 26, 1861.

14. On Meiggs's replacement of Lima's city walls with new promenades, see David S. Parker, "Civilizing the City of Kings: Hygiene and Housing in Lima, Peru," in *Cities of Hope*, ed. Pineo and Baer, 154. For more on the 1868 earthquake and other *terremotos* that hit nineteenth-century Peru, see Silgado F., "Historia de los sismos." The letter that accompanied Meiggs's donation (August 20, 1868) and Balta's reply to this missive (August 21, 1868) can be found in Salinas, *Estudio socio-histórico*, 176.

15. Meiggs completed three of these lines—Mollendo to Arequípa, Arequípa to Puno (on the shores of Lake Titicaca), and Ilo to Moquegua—during his lifetime. For specifics on the eight projects, see J. Fred Rippy, "Henry Meiggs, Yankee Pizarro," in *History of Latin American Civilization*, ed. Hanke, 1:149. The year before his death, Meiggs published many of his contracts and related legislative documents in Meiggs, *Ferrocarriles del Perú*. On the costs of Meiggs's railways, see Rand, *Railroads of Peru*, 7; and Orton, *Andes and the Amazon*, 445.

16. Pike, *Modern History of Peru*, 125. On these anticolonial Indian uprisings, see Lynch, *The Spanish American Revolutions*, 170. José Bengoa, "Chile *Mestizo*, Chile *Indígena*," in *Manifest Destinies and Indigenous Peoples*, ed. Maybury-Lewis, Macdonald, and Maybury-Lewis, 132. For a discussion of the role of "Remington rifles and railroads" in Julio A. Roca's late nineteenth-century genocidal campaign against the indigenous populations in the Pampean and Patagonian regions, known as the Conquista del desierto (conquest of the desert), see Winn, *Americas*, 103–4. The concept of a "force multiplier" originates with Clausewitz, *On War*, book 6: chaps. 4, 12. This combination of trains and breech-loading rifles was not essential to the genocide of American Indians. The Pequot Genocide of the 1630s, for example, was accomplished without either. Thanks to Ben Madley for this caveat.

17. "The American Aladdin," *Sacramento Daily Union*, March 25, 1871. This story originally appeared in the *New York Sun* and circulated quite widely.

18. On the scope and scale of this tragedy, see Madley, "American Genocide."

19. Gootenberg, *Imagining Development*, 101. Meiggs quoted in Rippy, "Henry Meiggs, Yankee Pizarro," 152. Morley, "Bowling Green."

20. Sears, "Republic of Peru." For more on Gird, see Bancroft, *History of the Pacific States*, 19:23n51. On Thorndike, see Seaver, *Historical Sketches of Franklin County*, 782.

21. For Malinowski's report on the Callao-Lima-Oroya Railway, see Malinowski, *Ferro-carril central transandino*. For details about the Trans-Andean Central Railroad, see Lévesque, *Railways of Peru*, 2:16–21. Rippy, "Henry Meiggs, Yankee Pizarro," 150; and John Briley, "On a Train to Lima, It's about the Ride," *Washington Post*, December 6, 2009.

22. Malinowski quoted in Gootenberg, *Imagining Development*, 91. For a contrasting view, see Jacobsen, *Mirages of Transition*, 184. "The Railroads of Peru," *American Architect and Building News*, July 27, 1878, 35. On Meiggs's aspirations for control of the Cerro de Pasco mines, see Laite, *Industrial Development and Migrant Labor*, 55; and Dennis McCarthy, *International Business History*, 108–9.

23. For the ways in which railroads shaped sectional conflict in the nineteenth-century United States, see Thomas, *Iron Way*. On the connection between railroads and "informal empire" throughout the world, see Davis and Wilburn, *Railway Imperialism*. For an overview of Latin America's railroad history, see Sanz Fernández, *Historia de los ferrocarriles*. Annual Report of William Tecumseh Sherman, October 27, 1883, 48th Cong., 1st Sess., H. Exec. Doc. 1, part 2 (Serial 2182): 45–46. On Meiggs's debts to Sherman, see Sherman, *Memoirs*, 106–7.

24. Pardo quoted in Clayton, *Peru and the United States*, 54. For more on Pardo's ambitions for converting guano profits into railroads, see Bonilla, *Guano y burguesía*, 62. Rand, *Railroads of Peru*, 3.

25. Davelouis, *Informe que el que suscribe eleva a la consideración de los poderes legislativo y ejecutivo*, 15. For more on Davelouis, see Gootenberg, *Imagining Development*, 103; and Contreras, "El reeplazo del beneficio de patio." On the history of quicksilver mining in Peru, see Lang, "New Spain's Mining Depression." Average annual California quicksilver prices (in dollars per 76.5-pound flask) from 1850–1890 can be found in California State Mining Bureau, *California Mineral Production for 1916*, 47. On California's quicksilver exports, see Hubert Howe Bancroft Collection, "The New Almaden Mine," p. 20 of 63, BANC. See also, St. Clair, "New Almaden and California Quicksilver"; and miscellaneous letters and documents in NAQMM.

26. Frémont quoted in Stewart, "Notes on an Early Attempt," 121.

27. Basadre, *Historia de la República del Perú*, 5:136. For a similar argument that railroads were by no means the solution to all of Peru's development problems, see Contreras, *Aprendizaje del capitalismo*, 172. O'Brien, *Century of U.S. Capitalism*, 16. For more on the national debate over the "Meiggs Bonds" see Clarke, *Peru and Its Creditors*, 57–60. On Peru's mounting national debt in the nineteenth century, see Palacios Moreyra, *Deuda anglo-peruana*.

28. Salinas, *Estudio socio-histórico*, 3n1. For details about the Dreyfus contract, see Quiroz, *Corrupt Circles*, 152–61.

29. Wetmore, "Harry Meiggs in Peru," 179. John G. Meiggs quoted in Pletcher, *Diplomacy of Trade and Investment*, 198. On Meiggs's bribes, see Clayton, *Peru and the United*

States, 56; Stewart, *Henry Meiggs,* 47; and Arnaldo Márquez, *Orjía financiera del Perú,* 66. Manuel Gonzáles Prada quoted in Haine, *Railways across the Andes,* 238.

30. Meiggs quoted in Lansing, *Against All Odds,* 181. Child, "Impressions of Peru," 272.

31. Orton, *Andes and the Amazon,* 447. On shipments of California wooden railroad ties to Peru, see Montgomery, "Railroad in the Clouds," 461; and Wetmore, "Harry Meiggs in Peru," 182. This trade continued for decades. For examples, see "Railroad Ties for Peru," *San Francisco Call,* December 18, 1902; and Simmons, *Lumber Markets of the West and North Coasts,* 71.

32. Coatsworth, *Growth against Development,* 143–44. For a divergent perspective, see Van Hoy, *Social History of Mexico's Railroads.* On the export of iron to the US for reimportation as finished rails, see Pike, *United States and Latin America,* 166.

33. Bermúdez, *Historia del salitre,* 243; Monteón, "*Enganche* in the Chilean Nitrate Sector," 67; Manuel Fernández, "British Nitrate Companies and the Emergence of Chile's Proletariat, 1880–1914," in *Proletarianisation in the Third World,* ed. Munslow and Finch, 48; and Stewart, *Henry Meiggs,* 133. Among Chilean historians, these numbers vary. Gabriel Salazar Vergara suggests that thirty-five thousand workers accompanied Meiggs to Peru; Salazar Vergara, *Historia de la acumulación capitalista en Chile,* 73. Cecilia Osorio Gonnet contends that it was between twenty thousand and thirty thousand; Osorio Gonnet, "Chilenos, Peruanos y Bolivianos," 123. Watt Stewart gives a figure of twenty-five thousand; Stewart, *Henry Meiggs,* 115. The quotation is from Duffield, *Peru in the Guano Age,* 123 (emphasis added).

34. *La Union,* September 23, 1917. For a similar view of the merits of employing Chilean peons at mining sites, see Enock, *Great Pacific Coast,* 327–28. Manuel Fernández Canque quoted in González Miranda, *Hombres y mujeres de la Pampa,* 144. Chapman, "Observations on the Roto in Chilean Fiction," 310. For similar arguments about the stereotypical traits of this Chilean archetype, see Hernández Cornejo, *Roto chileno.*

35. Stewart, "Trabajador chileno," 136. Teodoro Schneider puts the number at thirty thousand. See Schneider, *Agricultura en Chile,* 11. The statistic on monetary equivalencies is from Fetter, *Monetary Inflation in Chile,* 13–14. The wage rates are from Brian Loveman, "Critique," 480n5. On the enganche labor system, see Bollinger, "Bourgeois Revolution in Peru," 41–42. In the 1880s Chile's large estates dissolved into smaller subdivisions known as *fundos,* which existed alongside the bigger haciendas. *Fundos* were generally at least 247 acres, while *haciendas* tended to be 2,470 hectares, or more. Often, these terms were interchangeable, making their differentiation even more difficult. For an early attempt to define these land tenure units, see S. Tornero, *Chile ilustrado,* 427. For a rebuttal of contentions that the Latin American enganche system did not constitute unfree labor, see Brass, *Towards a Comparative Political Economy of Unfree Labour,* 182–216.

36. For example, see "Crónica agrícola," *Boletin de la Sociedad Nacional de Agricultura* 2 (June 15, 1871): 286–87. On the attempt to outlaw Chilean emigration to Peru, see Aranguiz, "Situación de los obreros agrícolas," 28. *Boletin de la Sociedad Nacional de Agricultura* (1871) quoted by Ruiz Esquide, "Migration, Colonization and Land Policy," 352. Schneider, *Agricultura en Chile,* 11. Bauer, "Chilean Rural Labor," 1081. Robles-Ortiz, "Agrarian Capitalism and Rural Labour," 500; Collier and Sater, *History of Chile,* 82–83.

37. Charles Watson to Henry Meiggs, June 12, 1871, in Salinas, *Estudio socio-histórico*, 226. On the incident of the official detaining the train full of peons, see ibid., 232.
38. Peck, *Reinventing Free Labor*, 2. For a more extensive version of this argument, see Melillo, "First Green Revolution."
39. Pinto Vallejos, Valdivia O., and Venegas V., "Peones chilenos en las tierras del salitre," 69; Monteón, "*Enganche* in the Chilean Nitrate Sector," 67; Rector, *History of Chile*, 125.
40. Rodríguez Pastor, *Herederos del dragón*, 47–51; and Hu-DeHart, "Coolies, Shopkeepers, Pioneers," 106. Watt Stewart claims that 90,000 Chinese arrived in Peru during this period; Stewart, *Chinese Bondage in Peru*,74. Arnold J. Meagher puts the number at 109,000; Meagher, *Coolie Trade*, 222. For ship numbers, see Lai, "Chinese Indentured Labor," 120. Hutchinson, *Two Years in Peru*, 2:66.
41. Montgomery, "Railroad in the Clouds," 461. Pamo, "Daniel Carrion's Experiment."
42. "The Asiatic Slave Trade," *New York Daily Times*, July 22, 1853. Meagher, *Coolie Trade*, 191.
43. William R. Grace quoted in G. de Secada, "Arms, Guano, and Shipping," 698. The text of the treaty appears in Ministerio de Relaciones Exteriores, *Colección de los tratados*, 159–65. Such transpacific diplomatic arrangements occurred elsewhere in Latin America. Mexico and China signed a similar treaty (Tratado de Amistad, Comercio y Navegación entre China y México) on December 14, 1899. After the expiration of their indenture contracts, many Chinese laborers settled in Lima, where they established a thriving Chinatown known as the Barrio Chino. See Lausent-Herrera, "Chinatown in Peru," 69–113.
44. Stewart, *Chinese Bondage in Peru*, 66–67; Clayton, *Grace*, 74; and Chang-Rodríguez, "Chinese Labor Migration," 391.
45. United States Department of State, *Papers Relating to the Foreign Relations of the United States*, 271; Greenhill, and Miller, "Peruvian Government and the Nitrate Trade," *Journal of Latin American Studies* 5, no. 1 (1973): 124; and E. Simpson, "Chapter on Peru," 28. J. R. Brown, "Frustration of Chile's Nitrate Imperialism," *Pacific Historical Review* 32, no. 4 (1963): 386n8. Henry Meiggs to John Meiggs, April 7, 1870, in Salinas, *Estudio socio-histórico*, 206. Halsey, Railway Expansion in Latin America (New York, 1916), 35–36. Hittell, *History of the City of San Francisco*, 226. Governor Newton Booth vetoed the bill on the grounds that it violated the state's constitution, which did not grant pardoning power to the legislative branch. The legislature immediately overrode the governor's veto. The text of the bill and excerpts from the governor's veto can be found in "Harry Meiggs Pardoned," *Los Angeles Herald*, April 1, 1874. For more on the passage of the pardon, see "The Meiggs Bill," *Sacramento Daily Union*, March 30, 1874. Oddly, Meiggs's biographer Watt Stewart did not mention the California legislature's vote to override the governor's veto. See Stewart, *Henry Meiggs*, 328. Meiggs's flight from San Francisco and subsequent exploits in Chile and Peru commanded extensive attention in North American newspapers. For examples, see "A Modern Monte Christo," *Chicago Tribune*, February 10, 1871; and "A Remarkable Career," *New York Times*, October 12, 1877.
46. *Sacramento Daily Union*, October 13, November 5, 1877. "The Meiggs System of Peruvian Railways," *Railway World* 18, no. 22 (1890): 507.

47. The library of the Museo Nacional Benjamín Vicuña Mackenna in Santiago houses this newspaper's entire collection.

48. Haber, *Industry and Development*, 76. On Archer Harmon, see Clark, *Redemptive Work*. An account of Church's disastrous attempt to construct a railway connecting Brazil's border states of Rondônia and Acre to the Amazon River at Porto Velho can be found in Craig, *Recollections of an Ill-Fated Expedition*.

49. Jonathan C. Brown and Peter S. Linder, "Oil," in *The Second Conquest of Latin America*, ed. Topik and Wells, 132–33. Doheny arrived in Los Angeles in 1892 and invested a thousand dollars in a tar pit that turned out to be among the sources of the state's turn-of-the-century oil bonanza. In his 1927 novel *Oil!* Upton Sinclair modeled the character Vern Roscoe after Doheny. Jonathan C. Brown, "Jersey Standard and the Politics of Latin American Oil Production, 1911–30," in *Oil Business in Latin America*, ed. Wirth, 8. "Chile Wants California Oil," *Los Angeles Herald*, December 30, 1906; "California Oil Goes to All Pacific Ports," *Los Angeles Herald*, September 25, 1910; "New Steamer Building for Coast Oil Trade: It Will Ply from Chile to British Columbia," *San Francisco Call*, August 1, 1911; Arnold and Garfias, *Geology and Technology*, 404–5. On the nitrate industry's demand for oil, see Fanning, "Foreign Trade in Petroleum," 92.

50. Rankin, *History of Costa Rica*, 74; and Clayton, *Grace*, 76. On Minor Keith's role in shaping Central American history, see Dosal, *Doing Business with the Dictators*, 55–74.

51. Przeworski, *Decline of the Copper Industry*, 213–14; and Galeano, *Open Veins of Latin America*, 199.

52. On railroads and the acceleration of experience, see Schivelbusch, *Railway Journey*, 7; and Felipe Zegarra, "Ferrocarriles en el Perú," 213–59. On wood as the fuel for early railroads, see White, *History of the American Locomotive*, 83–89. On the need to constantly replace "sleepers," see McNeill, "Woods and Warfare in World History," 404. A general discussion of railroads and deforestation can be found in Williams, *Deforesting the Earth*, 314–15. On deforestation and railroad expansion in southern Chile, see Otero Durán, *Huella del fuego*, 100.

53. Fuller, *Forest Tree Culturist*, 12. For an account of the devastating interplay between railroads and deforestation in Appalachia, see Lewis, *Transforming the Appalachian Countryside*. Theodore Roosevelt quoted in Williams, *Forest Service*, 112.

54. Zaret, "Distribution, Use and Cultural Meanings of Ciprés de las Guaitecas," 15. "Chilean Railroads Find Ties Scarce: Government Considers Importing Owing to High Cost," *San Francisco Call*, March 14, 1911. For examples of early twentieth-century lumber exports to Chile from US West Coast ports, see "Chartered for Lumber," *San Francisco Call*, June 29, 1905; and "Send Lumber to Chile," *Los Angeles Herald*, August 25, 1906.

55. Williams, *Deforesting the Earth*, 314. For more on the mining history of Lota, see Astorquiza, *Lota*. On Lota's coal, see Luis Ortega, "First Four Decades," 4–6; and Pablo Figueroa, *Historia*, 18. Charles Watson to Henry Meiggs, June 10, 1871, in Salinas, *Estudio socio-histórico*, 224.

56. Allen Wells, "All in the Family," 159–209; Moyano Bazzani, *La nueva frontera del azúcar*; Mattoon, "Railroads, Coffee, and the Growth of Big Business"; and Funes Monzote, *From Rainforest to Cane Field in Cuba*.

57. Oppenheimer, "National Capital and National Development," 58; and Daitsman, "People Shall Be All," 40.

58. Rundel and Gustafson, *Introduction to the Plant Life*, 118. See also Leger, "Local Adaptation." This measurement accounts for the number of species in a family that become invasive. On invasive species and government regulation of biotic migration in Chile, see Agustin Iriarte, Lobos, and Jaksic, "Especies de vertbrados invasores." Friedrich Johow quoted in Mary T. Kalin Arroyo, Clodomiro Marticorena, Oscar Matthei, and Lohengrin Cavieres, "Plant Invasions in Chile: Present Patterns and Future Predictions," in *Invasive Species in a Changing World*, ed. Mooney and Hobbs, 388. Frías L. et al., "Polymorphism and Geographic Variation," 195.

59. Bautista Alberdi, *Escritos póstumos*, 8:266.

60. Les Ledbetter, "'Honest Harry' Regains His Name 100 Years Later," *New York Times*, July 19, 1977.

61. Buckman, *Under the Southern Cross*, 134. Bakalinsky, *Stairway Walks in San Francisco*, 19.

CHAPTER 7. MOUNTAINS OF INFAMY, VINES OF PLENTY

1. Gil Navarro, *Gold Rush Diary*, 251. Clapp, "Unnatural History of the Monterey Pine." The value of Chile's forestry exports grew ten times between 1973 and 1980. See Mamalakis, *Historical Statistics of Chile*, 3:261–62. Lavín, *Chile*, 60. On the "mountains of infamy," see Marc Lifsher, "New Agreements to Expand Ties between California, Chile," *Los Angeles Times*, June 13, 2008; Adriana Hoffmann, "Astillas, ¡No!," *El Mercurio*, October 11, 1995; and Claro and Wilson, "Trans-Pacific Wood Chip Exports." Chile first exported lumber to Japan in 1977; H. B. Lisboa, "The Chilean Radiata Pine Sector," in *Management of Radiata Pine*, ed. Lewis and Ferguson, 373.

2. I borrow the concept, but not the definition, of *environmental globalization* from William C. Clark, "Environmental Globalization," in *Governance in a Globalizing World*, ed. Nye and Donahue, 86–108.

3. Bengoa, *Historia del pueblo mapuche*, 352. Human Rights Watch and Observatorio de Derechos de los Pueblos Indígenas, "Undue Process," 14; and Haughney, "Neoliberal Policies, Logging Companies." The quotation is from Neira, Verscheure, and Revenga, *Chile's Frontier Forests*, 13.

4. For a comprehensive historical treatment of the contested landscape of Chile's southern forests, see Klubock, *La Frontera*.

5. Critchfield and Little, *Geographic Distribution of the Pines of the World*, 19. For more on relict species, see Habel and Assmann, *Relict Species*. On pitch canker, see Gordon, Storer, and Wood, "Pitch Canker Epidemic in California."

6. Cronise, *Natural Wealth of California*, 509. McClellan, *Golden State*, 163.

7. Wilson, "Port of Monterey and Vicinity," 205. T. W. Adams, "California Conifers in New Zealand," *Pacific Rural Press*, April 1, 1911. Chile's native temperate hardwood forests are very similar to those of New Zealand, having in common *Podocarpus*, *Nothofagus*, and *Weinmannia* genera. Lisboa, "Chilean Radiata Pine Sector," 368. For

an account of Mueller's efforts to promote *Pinus radiata* in Australia, see Tyrell, *True Gardens of the Gods*, 87–102.

8. Sands, *Forestry in a Global Context*, 61; Sutton, "Need for Planted Forests," 103–4; and Grut, *Pinus Radiata*, 1. Sebastián Vizcaíno quoted in Conway, *Monterey*, 31. In 1791, members of the Spanish scientific and ethnographic expedition led by Italian-born Alejandro Malaspina had described the Monterey pine but found it inadequate for making ships' masts and so paid it little heed; Beidleman, *California's Frontier Naturalists*, 67. On California Indian use of fire as a pine forest management tool, see Stephens and Libby, "Anthropogenic Fire and Bark Thickness"; and Keeley, "Native American Impacts on Fire Regimes."

9. Miller, "California Closed Cone Pines," 660–61; Peter B. Lavery and Donald J. Mead, "*Pinus radiata*: A Narrow Endemic from North America Takes on the World," in *Ecology and Biogeography of Pinus*, ed. Richardson, 433; and Coleman, *Report upon Monterey Pine*, 1. For more on Coulter's botanical expeditions, see Nelson and Probert, *Man Who Can Speak of Plants*.

10. David Douglas quoted in Murray, "David Douglas," 157. On Douglas and the introduction of exotic pines to Europe, see House, "Man Who Made Pines." On the arrival of *Pinus radiata* at Kew Gardens, see Den Ouden and Boom, *Manual of Cultivated Conifers*, 345.

11. For early observations on these colonization efforts, see Pérez Rosales, *Memoria*. In Chile, the term *Quinta* can refer to a country house, but it can also signify an orchard or tree plantation. Today, the Parque Residencial Quinta Junge has been turned into an upscale gated community in Concepción. For more on the Junge family, see Armando de Ramón, *Biografías de chilenos*, 2:D–K. On the German colonization of southern Chile, see Young, *Germans in Chile*; and Held Winkler, *Colonización alemana*.

12. Muñoz Villegas, "Chile's Distinguished Immigrant Takes Root," 24. The story is repeated in slightly different form in Otero Durán, *Huella del fuego*, 142. Also see Contesse Gonzalez, "Apuntes y consideraciones." Junge's ledgers are available at the UoC, Chile, as: Arturo Junge, Journals, BC. They are discussed in Krebs, "Monterey Pine," 45, 60. On Cerro Caracol, see "Cerros que dan identidad a las ciudades," *El Mercurio*, January 11, 2009; and Ulloa Valenzuela, "*Pinus radiata*," 10.

13. For more on Albert's role in the development of Chile's forestry policies, see Camus, "Federico Albert"; and Hartwig, *Federico Albert*. Schmidtmeyer, *Travels into Chile*, 70. On wood shortages around the copper mines of Coquimbo, also see Bahre, *Destruction of the Natural Vegetation*, 42.

14. Claudio Gay, "Sobre las causas de la disminución de los montes de la Provincia de Coquimbo," *El Araucano*. April 20, 1838. Marsh, *Man and Nature*. Camus, *Ambiente, bosques y gestión forestall*, 119; and Saelzer Balde, *Evolución de la legislación*, 7–16.

15. Navarro de Andrade, Yecchi, and Correa Montt, *Eucalipto*, 6n1. The quotations are from Albert, *Pino de Monterey*, 13, 22.

16. Sands, *Forestry in a Global Context*, 61; Sutton, "Need for Planted Forests," 103; Shirley Christian, "Chile Promotes Forestry Industry," *New York Times*, October 31, 1988; and Prudham, *Knock on Wood*, 14.

17. Antonio Prado and Weber, "Facilitating the Way for Implementation of Sustainable Forest Management," 5; Schlatter, "Fertilidad del suelo," 13; and Klubock, "Politics of Forests and Forestry," 562.

18. For histories of the anthropogenic transformation of Chile's native forests, see Claudio Donoso and Antonio Lara, "Utilización de los bosques nativos en Chile: pasado, presente y future," in *Ecología de los bosques nativos*, ed. Armesto, Villagrán, and Kalin Arroyo, 363–87; and Elena Cruz and Rivera, *Cambios ecológicos*. For comparisons to similar transformations of California's woodlands, see Philip W. Rundel, "Landscape Disturbance in Mediterranean-Type Ecosystems: An Overview," in *Landscape Disturbance and Biodiversity in Mediterranean-type Ecosystems*, ed. Rundel and Montenegro, 14. *El Meteoro*, December 15, 1866, quoted in Bengoa, *Historia del pueblo mapuche*, 160–61. On this land-use shift, see Degarrod, "Female Shamanism," 342, 345.

19. Holdich, *Countries of the King's Award*, 196. "Our Trade with Chile," *San Francisco Call*, September 24, 1891.

20. Thomas Klubock, "Labor, Land, and Environmental Change in the Forestry Sector in Chile, 1973–1998," in *Victims of the Chilean Miracle*, ed. Winn, 340; and Clapp, "Unnatural History," 5. On the CCIL's tree plantations, see Pavilack, *Mining for the Nation*, 15. For more on the CCIL's control of land around Concepción and Lota, see Astorquiza, *Lota*, 156–57.

21. Republica de Chile, *Decreto supremo 4.363*. Ramiro O. Bustamante, I. A. Serey, and S. T. A. Pickett, "Forest Fragmentation, Plant Regeneration and Invasion Processes Across Edges in Central Chile," in *How Landscapes Change*, ed. Bradshaw and Marquet, 147; Armesto, Villagrán, and Donoso, "Desde la era glacial a la industrial," 71; and Toro and Gessel, "Radiata Pine Plantations in Chile," 38.

22. Arze and Svensson, "Development of International Competitiveness," 189–90; Clapp, "Creating Competitive Advantage," 279.

23. Cisternas, Martinez, Oyarzun, and Debels, "Caracterización del proceso de reemplazo de vegetación nativa," 667; Vega, *Itinerario*, 125. Exceptions to this dubious distinction might include Hanns Springer's and Rolf von Sonjevski-Jamrowski's 1936 proto-Nazi film, *Ewiger Wald* (Eternal forest), which glorified a Germanic "forest feeling" of *Volksgemeinschaft* (people's community) rooted in ancient myths of pagan, woods-dwelling tribes.

24. Toro and Gessel, "Radiata Pine Plantations in Chile," 34; Aagesen, "Northern Fringe," 80; García Elizalde and Leyton, *Desarrollo frutícola y forestal*.

25. Statistics are from Nahuelhual et al., "Land-Cover Change to Forest Plantations," 12. FAO Global Forest Resources Assessment 2000, available at http://www.fao.org/forestry/site/fra2000report/en/.
    Among the most comprehensive surveys of vegetation in Chile is Universidad Austral de Chile, Pontificia Universidad Católica de Chile, y Universidad Católica de Temuco, *Catastro y evaluación de recursos vegetacionales nativos de Chile*. See also Neira, Verscheure, and Revenga, *Chile's Frontier Forests*, 6.

26. Adam Bernstein, "Billionaire Anacleto Angelini, 93; Started Empire in Chile with $100," *Washington Post*, August 31, 2007; "Anacleto Angelini: 1914–2007; Chilean

Industrialist; Italian-Born Billionaire Flourished during Pinochet Dictatorship," *Chicago Tribune*, August 31, 2007.

27. Escobar and López, *El sector forestal en Chile*; Maurizio Atenzi, Fernando Durán-Palma, and Pablo Ghigliani, "Employment Relations in Chile and Argentina," in *Research Handbook in Comparative Employment Relations*, ed. Barry and Wilkinson, 145.

28. Victor and Ausubel, "Restoring the Forests," 138. For an example of the carbon dioxide sink argument, see G. Mery and M. Kanninen, "Forest Plantations and Carbon Sequestration in Chile," in *Forest Transitions and Carbon Fluxes*, ed. Palo, 74–100. On the contradictions of this claim, see Cristián Alarcón Ferrari, "Forests: Capital Accumulation, Climate Change and Crises in Chile and Sweden," in *Ecology and Power*, ed. Hornborg, Clark, and Hermele, 222.

29. Clapp, "Tree Farming and Forest Conservation in Chile," 341–56; Goldbach and Müller-Hohenstein, "Ecosystems of the IX Region of Chile," 55; Giljum, "Trade, Materials Flows, and Economic Development," 255; Núñez, Nahuelhual, and Oyarzún, "Forests and Water," *Ecological Economics* 58, no. 3 (2006): 606–16; Bustamante and Simonetti, "Is *Pinus radiata* Invading the Native Vegetation?," 243–49; James K. Agee, "Fire and Pine Ecosystems," in *Ecology and Biogeography of Pinus*, ed. Richardson, 211; Richardson, Williams, and Hobbs, "Pine Invasions in the Southern Hemisphere," 514; and Becerra and Bustamante, "Effect of a Native Tree on Seedling Establishment," 2763.

30. Montalba Navarro and Carrasco Henríquez, "¿Desarrollo sostenible o eco-etnocidio?," 101–33. Aucan Huilcaman quoted in Larry Rohter, "Chile Uses Terror Law to Fight an Old Battle," *International Herald Tribune*, August 12, 2004. Du Monceau de Bergendal Labarca, "Role of Political Strategies of Mapuche Communities," 2. Also see Adam Henne and Teena Gabrielson, "Chile Is Timber Country: Citizenship, Justice and Scale in the Chilean Native Forest Market Campaign," in *Environment and Citizenship in Latin America*, ed. Latta and Wittman, 149–67.

31. Pablo Neruda, "El bosque Chileno," in *Confieso que he vivido*, 12.

32. Del Pozo, *Historia del vino chileno*, 28; R. George, "Drinking Wine," in *Wine*, ed. Sandler and Pinder, 1–20, 10; and Rice, "Archaeology of Wine," 188.

33. Humboldt, *Political Essay*, 2:367.

34. Félix Cazalis, as cited in Gale, "Saving the Vine from *Phylloxera*," 70. On the history of the phylloxera outbreak in France and subsequent attempts to control the spread of the louse, see Pouget, *Histoire de la lutte contre le Phylloxera*. For more on the phylloxera outbreak throughout Europe and the attempts to quell it, see Gale, *Dying on the Vine*; Campbell, *Phylloxera*; and Ordish, *Great Wine Blight*.

35. Ladurie and Baulant, "Grape Harvests"; and Smith, *Plant Resistance to Arthropods*, 2. In 1884 the French government awarded Riley its Grand Gold Medal and named him a Chevalier of the Legion of Honor for his efforts to save the nation's grapevines. The entomologist Victor Antoine Signoret suggested the name *Phylloxera* to Planchon. The term comes from the Greek for "dried leaf," which Signoret found fitting because the insect sucks the cells of the vine's root tissue dry. See Paul, *Science, Vine and Wine in Modern France*, 21n13.

36. For more on this development, see Castonguay, "Creating an Agricultural World Order"; and Jansen, "American Insect in Imperial Germany."

37. Ricardo Couyoumdjian, "Vinos en Chile," 30.

38. Del Pozo, *Historia del vino chileno*, 71; and Knowles and Sharples, "History and Development of Chilean Wines." Stevenson, *Sotheby's World Wine Encyclopedia*, 410. This argument is repeated in many official documents. For example, see Agosin and Bravo-Ortega, "Emergence of New Successful Export Activities," 14. William Foster and Alberto Valdés, "South America: Early History of Wine in Chile and Argentina," in *World's Wine Markets*, ed. Anderson, 211.

39. Overton and Murray, "Playing the Scales"; Philippo Pszczólkowski T. "Invención del cv. Carménère"; Dorothy J. Gaiter and John Brecher, "Tastings: Southern Exposure—At $10 and Less, Chile Gives Old Names a New Spin," *Wall Street Journal*, February 7, 2003. On "pre-phylloxera wines," see Goode, "Never the Same Since?"; Anthony Rose, "The Vineyard's Best-Kept Secret," *Independent*, January 26, 2002; and Nathaniel C. Nash, "Chilean Wineries Outgrow the Jug: Chilean Vineyards Have Outgrown Their Jug Wine Stage," *New York Times*, April 4, 1992.

40. McGinty, *Strong Wine*, 303; Fuller, *Religion and Wine*, 10; Pinney, *History of Wine in America*, 287. The *California Farmer* quoted in Leggett, *Early History of Wine Production in California*, 68.

41. Davidson and Nougaret, *Grape Phylloxera in California*, 122. In his multivolume history of California, Hubert Howe Bancroft mentions phylloxera on several occasions. See, e.g., Bancroft, *History of California*, 7:47–50. On the adaptability of the phylloxera louse, see Carosso, *California Wine Industry*, 110. For farmers' experiments with toad venom and tobacco juice, see Susana Iranzo, Alan L. Olmstead, and Paul W. Rhode, "Historical Perspectives on Exotic Pests and Diseases in California," in *Exotic Pests and Diseases*, ed. Sumner, 58. For sulfocarbonate as a preventative measure, see Gardner, "Phylloxera." On nineteenth-century attempts to flood California orchards as a control for phylloxera, see William Henry Bishop, "Southern California," 53. On Sonoma County in the 1870s, see Carosso, *California Wine Industry*, 111.

42. Sullivan, *Companion to California Wine*, 271–72. For the view that national Prohibition was not as detrimental to the California wine industry as many have supposed, see Meers, "California Wine and Grape Industry and Prohibition."

43. Geraci, *Salud!*, 43–46; MacNeil, *Wine Bible*, 630; Aylward and Turpin, "New Wine in Old Bottles," 512; and Crowley, "Chile's Wine Industry," 99n1. For examples of Californian winegrowers' continued susceptibility to phylloxera outbreaks, see Anne Schamberg, "Short Supply, Big Demand Sends Wine High," *Milwaukee Journal Sentinel*, March 3, 1996; and Frank J. Prial, "Phylloxera, Scourge of the 19th Century's Vineyards, Is Back in California," *New York Times*, July 11, 1990.

44. Sandra Ann Harris, "Wine's Newest Frontier Joint Ventures between Chilean and California Wineries Take Root and Take Off," *San Francisco Examiner*, February 8, 1998; Wolf, "Using Theoretical Models," 7. For more on the appellation system and tendency to reproduce forms of environmental determinism, see Moran, "Wine Appellation as Territory."

45. Andrew Jefford and Paul Draper, "The Art and Craft of Wine," in *Questions of Taste,* ed. Smith, 200–201. Sullivan, *Companion to California Wine,* 207–8.

46. Geraci, "Fermenting a Twenty-First Century California Wine Industry," 454. Jonathan Friedland, "Chile Juices Up Its Winemaking Image with the Support of Big U.S. Vintners," *Wall Street Journal,* April 5, 1996. Because of a weak dollar and a grape surplus in the United States, Mondavi decided to sell its 50 percent share in Viña Errazuriz's Caliterra in 2004. See Carol Emert, "Mondavi Writing off Its Chilean Venture," *San Francisco Chronicle,* January 23, 2004.

47. Philippine de Rothschild quoted in Craig Torres, "Chile Uncorks a Premium Wine Just as Global Economy Fizzles," *Wall Street Journal,* October 28, 1998. Christian L. Wright, "The Napa-fication of an Ancient Spanish Wine Region," *New York Times,* August 28, 2010.

48. Paull, "Attending the First Organic Agriculture Course"; Reeve et al., "Soil and Winegrape Quality."

49. Álvaro Espinoza quoted in Goode, *Science of Wine,* 72. Monty Waldin quoted in Goode and Harrop, *Authentic Wine,* 68. For more on biodynamic wine production, see Waldin, *Biodynamic Wines.* See the Emiliana Organic Vineyards regions map, available at http://www.emiliana.cl/vineyards-winery/?login=ok.

50. Scott, *Seeing Like a State,* 2.

51. Lövei, "Biodiversity." For more on biological invasions resulting from human dispersal, see Bradley et al., "Global Change, Global Trade"; and Vitousek, D'Antonio, Loope, and Westbrook, "Biological Invasions as Global Environmental Change."

CHAPTER 8. THE DAVIS BOYS AND THE FRUITS OF NEOLIBERALISM

1. Box F3721:572: Chile-California Program-Records of the Chile California Task Force (1967–68)—Press release containing the remarks by Governor Ronald Reagan at Chile-California Conference—Sacramento, October 31, 1967 (Released by the Governor's Office), pp. 1–2, CSA.

2. On Reagan's talent mythologizing the past and the future to dissuade his audiences from analyzing the material conditions of their present, see Wills, *Reagan's America.* Ray Zeman, "Reagan Rejects U.S. Poverty, Chile-California Program Aid," *Los Angeles Times,* August 3, 1967; David F. Belnap, "Chile Expands Despite Loss of California Ties: Program Was Orphaned by Reagan, but Industry, U.S. Government Keep It Alive," *Los Angeles Times,* January 18, 1968.

3. Agosin and Bravo-Ortega, "Emergence of New Successful Export Activities," 26–27; Svenson and Coleman, "U.C.L.A. Experience with Foreign Programs," 59–60. On the roles of the Rockefeller and Ford Foundations in funding development programs in Chile, see Puryear, *Thinking Politics, Intellectuals and Democracy in Chile, 1973–1988,* 11–15.

4. The quotation is from Alex Lo, "Last Rites for the Washington Consensus," *South China Morning Post,* June 5, 2008.

5. John F. Kennedy quoted in Plank, "Alliance for Progress," 802. For more on such development strategies, see Taffet, *Foreign Aid as Foreign Policy.* "Charter of Punta del

Este Establishing an Alliance for Progress within the Framework of Operation Pan America," as printed in US House Committee on Foreign Affairs, *Regional and Other Documents*, 101–3.

6. Michaels, "Alliance for Progress and Chile's 'Revolution in Liberty,'" 75; Rabe, *The Most Dangerous Area in the World*. Johnson, *Blowback*; Johnson, *Sorrows of Empire*; Johnson, *Nemesis*. For more on the connection between Kennedy's civic action programs and his support for counterinsurgency, see Gill, *School of the Americas*, 74–75.

7. Nelson Rockefeller quoted in Taffet, *Foreign Aid as Foreign Policy*, 187. The report was published as Rockefeller, *Rockefeller Report on the Americas*. Among the earliest critical assessments of the alliance is Levinson and Onís, *Alliance That Lost Its Way*.

8. Jerry Gillam, "California, Chile, U.S. Join in Alliance Pact," *Los Angeles Times*, December 7, 1963; Brown, "Agricultural 'Extension' in Chile," 202; and Dvorin, "Chile-California Experiment," 37. The quotation is from Edmund G. Brown, Sr., "Years of Growth, 1939–1966: Law Enforcement, Politics, and the Governor's Office," an oral history conducted in 1977–1981 by Malca Chall, Amelia R. Fry, Gabrielle Morris, and James Rowland, Regional Oral History Office, 1982, p. 575, BANC. For more on particular projects and initiatives, see Box F3721:1: Chile California Program—Task Force Records, General Information—"The Chile-California Program of Technical Cooperation" (November 1965): 1–15, CSA. On Sieroty's radio announcements, see "Chile, California, and KPFK," *KPFK Program Folio*, February 28–March 27, 1966, 2, KPFK.

9. For the Plan Chillán, see Benjamin Maluenda, "Servicios informativos del Plan Chillán," in *Información de extensión agrícola*, 19–21; Sergio Bonilla, "Proceso de formación y evolución del INIA en Chile," in *Organización y administración*, ed. Stagno and Allegri, 59–60; Glick, *Administration of Technical Assistance*, 140–41; Cisternas, Martinez, Oyarzun, and Debels, "Caracterización del proceso de reemplazo de vegetación nativa," 667; Herbert L. Matthews, "U.S. Project Aids Farmers in Chile: Technical Assistance Plan Helps Undeveloped Areas and Trains Agronomists," *New York Times*, April 16, 1955; and Phillips, *Recent Developments Affecting Livestock Production*, 52–53.

10. Lyndon Johnson quoted in Kornbluh, *Pinochet File*, 5. For more on Frei Montalva's electoral platform and Christian Democrats' views, see Frei's inaugural address, reprinted in Pinochet de la Barra, *Obras escogidos*, 299–305. Also see Gazmuri, *Eduardo Frei Montalva*, 2:559–65. On the loyalty of US ambassador Ralp Dungan to Frei's Catholic humanist political program, see Kirkendall, "Kennedy Men and the Alliance for Progress," 749. On CIA aid to Pinochet, see Kornbluh, *Pinochet File*, 4. In 1963, Frei had criticized the Alliance for Progress. See Edward C. Burks, "Liberal in Chile Says U.S. Aid Fails," *New York Times*, April 18, 1963. Four years later, Frei wrote a plea in *Foreign Affairs* for a spiritual revolution to renew flagging US commitment to the Alliance for Progress. See Eduardo Frei Montalva, "Urgencies in Latin America: The Alliance That Lost Its Way," *Foreign Affairs* 45, no. 3 (1967): 437–48.

11. Preston N. Silbaugh quoted in George Natanson, "California Ally of Chile in Red Fight: State's Project Significant with Election of Frei," *Los Angeles Times*, September 17, 1964. Robert J. Markson, "California Utilizes Economic Weapon in Helping Chile

Defeat Threat of Communism," *Modesto Bee*, October 15, 1964. George Natanson, "California Program Aids Chile: Plan Valuable in Helping Halt Communism," *Los Angeles Times*, February 5, 1967.

12. "Documents and Legislation Concerning the 'Chileanization' of Anaconda's Chile Exploration Company," *International Legal Materials* 9, no. 5 (1970): 921–74. On Chileanization versus nationalization, see Al Gedicks, "The Nationalization of Copper in Chile: Antecedents and Consequences," in *World as a Company Town*, ed. Idris-Soven, Idris-Soven, and Vaughan, 405–30. On the copper industry and the Guggenheim family's Chilean investments, see Finn, *Tracing the Veins*; O'Brien, "'Rich beyond the Dreams of Avarice'"; and Przeworski, *Decline of the Copper Industry in Chile*.

13. Radetzki, "Seven Thousand Years in the Service of Humanity."

14. Klubock, *Contested Communities*, 277. For more on the rising expectations of workers and peasants during the 1960s, see Oppenheim, *Politics in Chile*, 26.

15. William L. Alexander, "Introduction: Enduring Contradictions of the Neoliberal State in Chile," in *Lost in the Long Transition*, ed. Alexander, 5; US Department of Agriculture, *Foreign Agriculture* 5, no. 44 (1967): 3; and Michaels, "Alliance for Progress and Chile's 'Revolution in Liberty,' 1964–1970," 77.

16. Box F3721:230: Chile-California Program—Sacramento, Office—General Records—Task Order, Reports-T.O. #3-Agricultural Marketing (1964–67), pp. 2–3, CSA. On the *Plan de desarrollo frutícola*, see Barton and Murray, "Grounding Geographies of Economic Globalisation," 86; and Meller, "Review of the Chilean Trade Liberalization and Export Expansion Process," 166. For more on Banco del Estado funding of the program, see Murray, "Local Responses to Global Restructuring in the Chilean Fruit Complex," 27. On Chile and counterseasonal production, see Raper, Thornsbury, and Aguilar, "Regional Wholesale Price Relationships"; and Luis Llambi, "Opening Economies and Closing Markets: Latin American Agriculture's Difficult Search for a Place in the Emerging Global Order," in *From Columbus to ConAgra*, ed. Bonano et al., 203.

17. Farrer, *To Feed a Nation*, 54; Swatland, "Meat Products and Consumption Culture," 83.

18. Frank G. Carpenter, "Chile a Winter Fruit Garden," *Boston Daily Globe*, December 13, 1914.

19. "Many Chilean Fruits to the United States," *Pacific Rural Press*, November 25, 1922. For more on issues surrounding increases in transportation efficiency and historical changes in the perishable food trade, see William Coyle, William Hall, and Nicole Ballenger, "Transportation Technology and the Rising Share of U.S. Perishable Food Trade," in *Changing Structure of Global Food Consumption and Trade*, ed. Regmi, 31–40.

20. Biglaiser, "Internationalization of Chicago's Economics," 275; Valdés, *Pinochet's Economists*; Fontaine Aldunate, *Economistas y el Presidente Pinochet*. Among the few historical accounts to mention the Chile-California Program, the Convenio, and the Davis Boys are Andra Brosy Chastain, "Francis Violich"; and Tinsman, *Buying into the Regime*, 53.

21. AR–14: Convenio Archives, box 1, folder: Publications 1 of 4, UCD; Lovell S. Jarvis, "Changing Private and Public Roles in Technological Development: Lessons from the Chilean Fruit Sector," in *Agricultural Technology*, ed. Anderson, 247; Gastón Bruna Day and Fernando Silva Véira, "Factores determinantes de la modernización del subsector frutícola en Chile," in *Modernización de la agricultura en América Latin y el Caribe*, ed. Pomareda Benal and Torres Zorrilla, 45; and Rivera, "Institutional Conditions of Chilean Fruit Export Expansion."

22. Anthony Wylie, "Agricultural Development and Technology: The Growth of Chile's Fruit and Vegetable Export Industry," in *Sharing Innovation: Global Perspectives on Food, Agriculture, and Rural Development*, ed. Kotler, 157. "Final Report of R. S. Bringhurst, Resident Participant, Department of Pomology, Davis—September 1967–August 1968 and Annual Report, July 1, 1967–June 1968," AR-14: Convenio Archives, box 1, folder: Convenio 68–69, pp. 5–10, UCD. Arnold J. Bauer quoted in Kathleen Holder, "Chilean Fresh," *UC Davis Magazine Online* 22, no. 3 (2005), available at http://ucdavismagazine.ucdavis.edu/issues/sp05/feature_3.html.

23. Edmundo Fuenzalida quoted by Simon Schwartzman, "The Focus on Scientific Activity," in *Perspectives on Higher Education*, ed. Clark, 217.

24. Cody and Mooney, "Convergence versus Nonconvergence." For an account of the origins, controversies, and outcomes of the International Biological Program, see Hagen, *Entangled Bank*, 175–86. For more on the Convenio, the IBP, and the effect of such international exchanges on the global ecology, see Mooney, "Road to Global Ecology," 10–12; and Geisse G., "Medio ambiente como tema de cooperación Chile-California."

25. Dvorin, "Chile-California Experiment," 35; Jerry Foytik quoted in "Economist Cites Chile's Problem," *Modesto Bee*, June 26, 1966; James D. Ewing, "'Instant Capitalism' Idea," *Boston Globe*, November 26, 1966; Dvorin, "Foreign Aid by States," 622; William S. Broomfield, "Local Government Aid Experiment Promises Bright Future for Alliance for Progress," *Congressional Record*, 88th Cong., 1st Sess., October 29, 1963, 1–2; "Utahns Take on Projects of Aid to Bolivia," *Deseret News and Telegram*, January 31, 1964.

26. For evidence of these disagreements, see transcriptions of taped conversations among California planners in Box F3721: 25: Chile-California Program-Master Contract Records, Preliminary Plans-Contracts-Meetings, 1963, CSA. The quotation from Clark comes from Associated Press, "California Plans Assistance to Chile," *Tri-City Herald*, August 1, 1967, 14. For more on this tendency in Reagan's policy choices, see Jesse Jackson Jr., "Reagan: A Legacy of States' Rights," *Nation*, June 28, 2004, available at http://www.thenation.com/article/reagan-legacy-states-rights.
On the State Department's assessment of Long, see Zeman, "Reagan Rejects U.S. Poverty, Chile-California Program Aid," 3. The quotation is from Brown, "Years of Growth, 1939–1966," 317.

27. AR 23, Chancellor's Office, box 107, folder: Chile Program, 1968–69, "Coordinator's Status Report—Annual Meeting (August 1969)," p. 5, UCD; and *University of Chile-University of California Cooperative Program Comprehensive Report*, vol. 1, Narrative Report (July 1979), 54, as cited in Svenson and Coleman, "U.C.L.A. Experience with Foreign Programs," 61.

28. On October 24, the Chilean National Congress overwhelmingly confirmed Allende as the winner of the election. In addition to his 1964 bid for the presidency, Allende had unsuccessfully run in 1952 and 1958 as the leader of the Frente de Acción Popular (Popular Action Front), the predecessor of the Unidad Popular. Allende lost the 1958 presidential election by only 3 percent (34,000 votes) to conservative Jorge Alessandri Rodríguez, whose father, Arturo, had twice been president. Eduardo Frei Montalva placed third in the contest. Allende Gossens, *Nuestro camino al socialismo*; Pinto Vallejos, *Cuando hicimos historia*.

29. Henry Kissinger quoted in Hersh, *Price of Power*, 265. Nixon to Helms quoted in Qureshi, *Nixon, Kissinger, and Allende*, xi.

30. The statistic is from US Congress, *Covert Action in Chile, 1963–1973*, 148. Senator Frank Church quoted in Moyers, *Secret Government*, 55. On US funding for *El Mercurio*, see De La Barra and Dello Buono, *Latin America after the Neoliberal Debacle*, 231.

31. Jack Anderson, "Memos Bare ITT Try for Chile Coup," *Washington Post*, March 21, 1972.

32. Gregory Palast, "Inside Corporate America: A Marxist Threat to Cola Sales?," *Observer*, November 8, 1998; Qureshi, *Nixon, Kissinger, and Allende*, 50–51, 66–67; Kapur, Lewis, and Webb, *World Bank*, 1:300–301; and International NGO Forum, "World Bank and IMF Adjustment Lending in Chile," in *Fifty Years Is Enough*, ed. Dahaher, 52.

33. Valdivia Ortiz de Zárate, *Nacionales y gremialistas*; and Loveman, "Military Dictatorship and Political Opposition," 1. On struggles over the memory of the coup, see Stern, *Battling for Hearts and Minds*.

34. Gill, *School of the Americas*, 2, 80. The US military moved the SOA to Fort Benning, Georgia, in 1984. Although the school's stated mission is to "provide doctrinally sound, relevant military education and training to the nations of Latin America; to promote democratic values and respect for human rights; and to foster cooperation among multinational military forces," reports from journalists and human rights groups show a quit different reality. See US Office of the Inspector General, Department of Defense, "Evaluation Report on Training of Foreign Military Personnel," 8. As peace studies scholar Jack Nelson-Pallmeyer notes, "SOA graduates have played key roles in nearly every coup and major human rights violation in Latin America in the past fifty years"; Nelson-Pallmeyer, *School of Assassins*, 9. "The C.I.A.'s Chile Files," *New York Times*, November 17, 2000. Powell quoted in Mary Anastasia O'Grady, "Americas: Setting the Record Straight on Allende, Once More," *Wall Street Journal*, April 25, 2003. These interventions were part of Operation Condor (1973–80), during which much of Latin America was ruled by US-backed dictatorships. See Dinges, *Condor Years*; and Stella Calloni, *Años del lobo*.

35. William T. Cavanaugh, "Torture and Eucharist: A Regretful Update," in *Torture Is a Moral Issue*, ed. Hunsinger, 103; Cristian Fuentes and Manfred Wilhelmy, "De la reinserción a la diplomacia para el desarollo: Política exterior de Chile, 1992–1994," in *América Latina en el mundo*, ed. Van Klaveren, 233; and Bollen, "Issues in the Comparative Measurement of Political Democracy," 387.

36. Dahl, *Polyarchy*, 56. On this rupture, see Sigmund, "Chilean Military," 242.

37. On Pinochet's training as a geographer, see David Harvey, "What Kind of Geography?," 18. Comisión Nacional de Verdad y Reconciliación, *Report of the Chilean National Commission*. Patricio Guzman's 1997 film, *Chile: Obstinate Memory*, chronicles the anguish of Pinochet dictatorship survivors unable to verify the deaths of their relatives and loved ones as a result of the regime's 1978 self-amnesty law (Decree Law 2.191), which gave agents of the state penal impunity for crimes committed under military rule. In November 2004, the National Commission on Political Imprisonment and Torture issued the *Valech Report*. The investigative body, set up by the government of President Ricardo Lagos, registered thirty-five thousand cases of torture and proposed means of compensating the victims and their families. See *Comisión Nacional sobre Prisión Política y Tortura* (2004), available at http://www.indh.cl/informacion-comision-valech.

   Although *Missing* won an Academy Award and the Palme d'Or, Pinochet's government banned it in Chile. A sixty-million-dollar lawsuit by former US ambassador Nathaniel Davis alleging "public disgrace, scorn and ridicule" caused the film to be removed from the US market. A judge eventually dismissed the suit. In retrospect, Costa-Gavras's hard-hitting political accusations against the US government have been vindicated. See Martin Douglas, "Nathaniel Davis, Diplomat, Is Dead at 86," *New York Times*, May 23, 2011; and Fabiola Gutierrez and Chris Kraul, "Extradition Sought in '73 Chile Killing," *Los Angeles Times*, November 30, 2011.

38. "Report by Professor Phillip E. Johnson to the President, the Academic Council, the Assembly of the Academic Senate, and the Representative Assembly of the University of California (February 8, 1974)," AR-23: Chancellor's Office, box 131, folder: Chile Program, 1971–74, UCD.

39. Svenson and Coleman, "U.C.L.A. Experience with Foreign Programs," 64–65.

40. Silvia Bortzutzky, "The Chicago Boys: Social Security and Welfare in Chile," in *Radical Right and the Welfare State*, ed. Glennerster and Midgley, 88.

41. De Castro, "Prólogo," 9. Friedman, *Capitalism and Freedom*.

42. Ulmer, "Friedman's Currency," *New Republic*, November 6, 1976, 8–9.

43. For details of the program, see Valdés, *Pinochet's Economists*. On the relations among structural violence, social and natural disasters, and Friedman's economic philosophies, see Klein, *Shock Doctrine*.

44. Arancibia Clavel and Balart Páez, *Sergio de Castro*, 65; Jonathan Friedland, "U.S. Scholar Puts Stamp on Latin Markets—Arnold Harberger Nurtured Key Policy Makers," *Wall Street Journal*, September 12, 1996; and Friedman and Friedman, *Two Lucky People*, 403; Valdés, *Pinochet's Economists*, 165.

45. Moreton, "Soul of Neoliberalism," 118. For an analysis of how Chilean neoliberalization promoters framed their project in ideological terms, see Moulián and Vergara, "Estado, ideología y políticas económicas," 845–903.

46. Sigmund, "Rise and Fall of the Chicago Boys," 44; and Jarvis, *Chilean Agriculture under Military Rule*, 102. On the predominance the Chicago Boys eventually attained in the national economic planning agency (ODEPLAN), see Fontaine Aldunate, *Economistas y el Presidente Pinochet*, 46. For the stated goals of these measures, see

Jorge Cauas, "The Government Economic Recovery Program," in *Chilean Economic Policy*, ed. Méndez, 161. On the unfolding of the neoliberal development model in Chile, see Kurtz, "Chile's Neo-Liberal Revolution."

47. Letelier, "'Chicago Boys' in Chile"; Pablo Barahona quoted by Genaro Arriagada Herrera and Carol Graham, "Chile: Sustaining Adjustment during Democratic Transition," in *Voting for Reform*, ed. Haggard and Webb, 245; Friedman, "Free Markets and the Generals." For two thorough deconstructions of the "Chilean miracle," see Nef, "Chile"; and Eugenio Díaz-Corvalán, "Nuevo sindicalismo, viejos problemas." For a longer-term view examining the burdens borne by low-skilled workers under Chile's free trade orthodoxy, see Berg, *Miracle for Whom?*

48. Statistics are from: Elizalde Hevia and González Gutiérrez, "Chile: ¿autosuficiencia o 'autismo' energético?," 41; Altieri and Rojas, "Ecological Impacts of Chile's Neoliberal Policies," 56; Collins and Lear, "Free Market Miracle or Myth?," 157; and Skidmore and Smith, *Modern Latin America*, 137–38. The quotation is from Muñoz, *Dictator's Shadow*, 307.

49. Silva, "Import-Substitution Model"; Cristóbal Kay, "Latin America's Agrarian Transformation: Peasantization and Proletarianization," in *Disappearing Peasantries?*, ed. Bryceson, Kay, and Mooij, 126; Glade, *Latin American Economies*.

50. Schurman, "Uncertain Gains," 4; Quiroga Martínez and Van Hauwermeiren, *Tiger without a Jungle*, 18–19; Collier and Sater, *History of Chile*, 395.

51. For a representative statement of this period of "global Keynesianism," see Brandt Commission, *North-South*. On this paradox of neoliberalism, see Jamie Peck and Adam Tickell, "Neoliberalizing Space," in *Spaces of Neoliberalism*, ed. Brenner and Theodore, 37.

52. John Williamson, "What Washington Means by Policy Reform," in *Latin American Adjustment*, ed. Williamson, 7–20. For regional differences in the implementation of neoliberal agendas, see Brenner and Theodore, "Cities and the Geographies of Actually Existing Neoliberalism." McMichael, *Development and Social Change*, 130.

53. For a sampling of scholarship on this topic, see Melillo, "Spectral Frequencies," 147–61; Toussaint and Millet, *Debt, the IMF, and the World Bank*; Goldman, *Imperial Nature*; and Chomsky and Herman, *Washington Connection and Third World Fascism*.

54. Friedrich August von Hayek to *Times* (London), July 11, 1978.

55. For more on the MIR, see Naranjo, Ahumada, Garcés, and Pinto, *Miguel Enríquez y el proyecto revolucionario*; Bruey, "Limitless Land and the Redefinition of Rights"; and Agosín, *Tapestries of Hope, Threads of Love*.

56. Mills, "Dockers Stop Arms to Pinochet."

57. Juan Armando Epple, *Actas de Palo Alto*. Marita Eastmond, "Reconstructing Life: Chilean Refugee Women and the Dilemmas of Exile," in *Migrant Women*, ed. Buijs, 35–54. For an account of the persistence of unique Chilean cultural forms in the face of adversity, see Knudsen, "Dancing Cueca." Martí, *Entrañas del monstruo*.

58. José Quiroga quoted in Eric Pape, "Five Degrees of Exile; California Is Haven to Many Political Figures Forced to Flee Their Native Countries," *Los Angeles Times*, July 11, 1999. On post-1950 Chilean immigration to the United States, see Doña-Reveco, "Shadow of Empire and Nation."

59. Paul Flores quoted in Wilson, "Where Art Means Politics." On the mural, see Eva Sperling Cockcroft and Holly Barnet-Sánchez, "Introduction," in *Signs from the Heart*, ed. Cockcroft and Barnet-Sánchez, 13.

60. Freed and Landis, *Death in Washington*; Robert Pear, "Cuban Exile Pleads Guilty in the 1976 Bomb Slaying of Chilean Ambassador," *New York Times*, July 31, 1991; Vernon Loeb, "Documents Link Chile's Pinochet to Letelier Murder," *Washington Post*, November 14, 2000. For more on Letelier's legacy, see Letelier, Garcés, and Landau, *Orlando Letelier*.

61. Carla Hall, "Burn Victim Travels World to Decry Chilean Brutality," *Houston Chronicle*, April 24, 1988; Shirley Christian, "Burn Victim in Chile Confronts Army," *New York Times*, July 6, 1987. For evocative eulogies to Rojas by a Chilean and a North American, see Agosín, "Generals' Bonfires"; and James S. Gordon, "Remembering Rodrigo Rojas, Murdered in Chile," *Washington Post*, August 24, 1986.

62. In 2012, Chilean director Pablo Larraín released his film *No* about the plebiscite. See Charlotte Higgins, "Postcards from Cannes: Latin American Studies—The Adman Who Fought Pinochet with Happiness," *Guardian*, May 22, 2012. Larraín's movie provoked controversy in Chile. Some critics focused on the fact that Larraín's family were—and remain—*pinochetistas*. Additionally, the film ignored the difficult and dangerous work undertaken by activists who registered voters and encouraged them to vote. Disregarding this history, Larraín portrayed the plebiscite as an elaborate marketing campaign. Thanks to Ray Craib for his insights regarding the film. The quotation is from Ariel Dorfman, "Epilogue: October 1989," in *Chile from Within*, ed. Meiselas, 121.

63. Collier and Sater, *History of Chile*, 382.

64. Briggs, "Political Miracle," 108; Bauer, *Contra la corriente*. As historian Greg Grandin has shown, free-market fundamentalism has been one of Chile's most reliable long-term exports; Grandin, *Empire's Workshop*, 175.

65. Walter L. Goldfrank, "Fresh Demand: The Consumption of Chilean Produce in the United States," in *Cultural Politics of Food and Eating*, ed. Watson and Caldwell, 43.

66. Oscar Muñoz and Hugo Ortega, "Chilean Agriculture and Economic Policy," in *Modernization and Stagnation*, ed. Twomey and Helwage, 161–88. For a similar conclusion, see Gwynne and Kay, "Agrarian Change," 6. On Chilean exports from small versus large farming operations, see Carter and Mesbah, "Can Land Market Reform Mitigate?"

67. Statistics are from Goldfrank, "Chilean Fruit"; and Retamales and Sepúlveda, "Fruit Production in Chile," 173. As of 2014, the World Bank listed Chile's population as 17,773,000. See "World Development Indicators," available at http://data.worldbank.org/indicator/SP.POP.TOTL?cid=GPD_1.

On the *temporeras*, see Bain, "Structuring the Flexible and Feminized Labor Market," 349; Arce and Marsden, "Social Construction of International Food," 306–7; and Valdés, *Condiciones de vida y trabajo*. For more on the relation between women's wage work and neoliberal restructuring of Chile's fruit sector, see Tinsman, "Reviving Feminist Materialism." These zones are located in Chile's nine fruit-growing regions (from North to South): Atacáma, Coquimbo, Aconcágua, Metropolitana, Rancagua,

Maúle, Bío Bío, La Araucánia, and Los Lagos. Chile is 2,653 miles long. Approximately 1,000 miles of Chile's total length can sustain fruit and vegetable production.

68. George H. W. Bush, "Remarks to a Joint Session of the Congress in Valparaíso, Chile," December 6, 1990, available at http://bushlibrary.tamu.edu/research/public_papers. php?id=2533&year=1990&month=12.

69. Claude, *Vez más la miseria*, 24. The statistic is from Patricio Meller and Raul E. Sáez, "Lecciones y desafíos futuros del auge exportador Chileno," in *Auge exportador chileno*, ed. Meller and Sáez, 37. Daviron and Ponte, *Coffee Paradox*.

70. Stuart Hall quoted in Lipsitz, "Struggle for Hegemony," 146. P. T. Maiken, "Milton Friedman: The Free Market Monetarist Thrives in a New Locale," *Chicago Tribune*, July 20, 1980; Hoover Institution Fellows Profile, "Milton Friedman," available at http://www.hoover.org/fellows/10630.

   On the roles of the Hoover Institution and similar think tanks in the development of postwar US conservatism, see Stahl, "Selling Conservatism"; O'Connor, *Social Science for What?*; and Stefancic and Delgado, *No Mercy*. Harberger and Just, "Conversation with Arnold Harberger," 3.

71. For more on Bachelet's visit to the University of California, see Boas, "Bachelet Energizes Berkeley."

72. Matte, "Commencement Speech."

73. On Matte's wealth, see *Forbes Magazine* online, "The World's Billionaires (as of January 24, 2015)," available at http://www.forbes.com/profile/eliodoro-matte/.

   For the International Rivers press release about the defeat of the HidroAysén project, see http://www.internationalrivers.org/node/8338.

74. Quiroga, "Primera mujer presidenta."

75. For analyses of this ideological shift, see Castañeda, "Latin America's Left Turn"; and Seligson, "Rise of Populism," 81. On Bachelet's amalgam of social and economic stances, see Rudiger Dornbusch and Sebastian Edwards, "Exchange Rate Policy and Trade Strategy," in *Chilean Economy*, ed. Bosworth, Dornbusch, and Labán, 104.

76. Michele Bachelet quoted in Sehnbruch, "Record Number of Conflicts?," 2. For more on neoliberal continuities in labor policy during and after the dictatorship, see Taylor, "Labor Reform." On Bachelet's environmental policies, see Latta and Aguayo, "Testing the Limits"; Soluri, "Something Fishy"; and Carruthers, "Environmental Politics in Chile," 353.

77. Solimano, *Chile and the Neoliberal Trap*, 9. Broxmeyer, "Silver Screen to the Recall Ballot"; Richard R. Paddock, "Hardship Predicted for Students," *Los Angeles Times*, April 17, 2008; Brenner, "California Nurses Lead the Fight"; Mitchell, " 'They Want to Destroy Me' "; and Marc Sanalow, "Schwarzenegger's Liberal Views Leave GOP Flummoxed," *San Francisco Chronicle*, August 14, 2003. For more on this concept of a "Third Way" neoliberalism in Chile, see Taylor, *Pinochet to the "Third Way."*

78. California Chamber of Commerce, "Trading Partner Portal: Chile," available at http://www.calchamber.com/International/Portals/Chile/Pages/Default.aspx.

   For more on the privatization of international aid under neoliberalism, see Kamat, "Privatization of Public Interest."

79. Dave Jones, "Reporters Notebook from the Chilean President's Visit to UC Davis," June 27, 2008, available at http://dateline.ucdavis.edu/dl_detail.lasso?id=10480.

CHAPTER 9. BREAKING THE RULE OF EXCEPTIONS

1. Polk, *Island of California*, 326. Originally, this depiction stemmed from a portrayal of California in 1602 by the Spanish explorer Friar Antonio de la Ascensión, a member of Sebastián Vizcaíno's expedition to California in the years 1602–3, who described California as a formidable island occupying seventeen degrees of latitude in the northern Pacific Ocean. See Burrus, "Two Fictitious Accounts," 272–73. On the historical relations among cartography, imperialism, and state formation in Latin America, see Craib, *Cartographic Mexico*. Tyrolean Jesuit Eusebio Kino confirmed that California was part of the mainland during his explorations of the American Southwest (1698–1701). Despite this evidence, the myth of its separation from the continent continued to captivate the European imagination for nearly fifty years before Ferdinand VI's declaration. Mathes, "Mythological Geography of California," 333–34.

2. Chile maintains an Antarctic territorial claim through its Antártica Chilena Province. This territory, which stretches from 53°W to 90°W, is recorded in the *Main Antarctic Treaty* of June 23, 1961. See Pinochet de la Barra, *Antárctica chilena*. On the idea of "cleansing" Chile's past, see Gómez-Barris, *Where Memory Dwells*, 4. On Chile's assertions of separation from its neighbors, see Staab and Maher, "Dual Discourse," 105. For an analysis of both, see Richard, *Cultural Residues*, 116–17. Ariel Dorfman ridiculed the Chilean iceberg exhibition in his novel *The Nanny and the Iceberg*. On the "whitening" of Chilean history, see Moulian, *Chile actual*, 40–41. For more on the details of the exhibit, see Sam Dillon, "Chile's Icy Exhibit Starts a Hot Debate," *Toronto Star*, April 18, 1992. Eugenio García quoted in Sam Dillon, "Chile's Iceberg Message: We're Both Cool and Efficient," *Seattle Times*, April 26, 1992. One of the Chilean delegation's senior representatives told Chilean reporters, "We don't want to be confused with our neighbors"; Guillermo Tejeda, "Hielos mentales en la cultura chilena," *La Época*, September 8, 1991.

3. The idea of a Pacific Age first emerged in 1892, then reappeared in the 1920s, 1960s, 1980s, and 1990s. See Korhonen, "Pacific Age in World History."

4. The expression is from Andrés Benítez, quoted in Subercaseaux, *Chile*, 76. In a September 1998 interview with John Lee Anderson of the *New Yorker*, Augusto Pinochet explained, "The Chileans will tell you with pride they are often called the English of South America"; Pinochet quoted in O'Shaughnessy, *Pinochet*, 1. Ministerio de Salud quoted in Trumper and Phillips, "Give Me Discipline," 34n27. Cárdenas Casto, "'Y verás como quieren en Chile'"; and Stefoni Espinoza, *Inmigración peruana en Chile*. The graffiti is discussed in Universidad Alberto Hurtado–Centro de Ética, "¿Es *Chile* una sociedad *racista?*"

5. UNICEF, "Voz de los niños," 13. Larraín, "Changes in Chilean Identity," 332. For a similar claim about Chilean exceptionalism, see Stern, *Battling for Hearts and Minds*, xxvi.

6. *La Actualidad* quoted in Barr-Melej, *Reforming Chile*, 244n30. Morel, *Ensayo sobre el desarollo de la riqueza de Chile*, 3. For more on the transnational resonance of manifest destiny, see Maybury-Lewis, Macdonald, and Maybury-Lewis, *Manifest Destinies and Indigenous Peoples*.

7. *Times* (London), April 22, 1880, quoted in Blakemore, *British Nitrates and Chilean Politics*, 1. Domville-Fife quoted in Lorenzo S., Harris B., and Vásquez L., *Vida, costumbres y espíritu empresarial de los porteños*, 42. Monteón, "British in the Atacama Desert," 117. Prussian Emil Körner Henze served as commander-in-chief of the Chilean army from 1900 to 1910. His military philosophies can be found in Körner and Rivera, *Estudios sobre historia militar*. Mauricio Cristi quoted in Beckman, "Creolization of Imperial Reason," 73. Cristi was Benjamín Vicuña Mackenna's secretary.

8. On the "peasant nationalism" that arose in Mexico and Peru during these conflicts, see Knight, "Peasants into Patriots," 147. For more on the Chilean invasion as a watershed event in Peruvian history, see Larson, *Trials of Nation Making*, 178. On visions of Pacific hegemony among Chile's governing class, see Kiernan, "Chile from War to Revolution."

9. Páez, *Guerra del Pacifico*, 9–10. For more on Páez's pamphlet, see Burr, "Balance of Power," 54. Sater and Herwig, *Grand Illusion*, 31.

10. Palacios, *Raza Chilena*, 4, 32, 48–52. For more on Palacios's role in establishing Chilean bourgeois identity, see Barr-Melej, *Reforming Chile*, 51–76. Palacios's racial theories profoundly affected Francisco A. Encina, one of Chile's most distinguished historians; see Griffin, "Francisco Encina," 7–8. Rosaldo, "Imperialist Nostalgia," 107–8.

11. Marter, "New England of South America," 410. Spykman, *America's Strategy in World Politics*, 221. Burr, *By Reason or Force*, 13–14.

12. Domeyko, *Araucanía y sus habitantes*, 139; Antonio Varas, "Informe presentado a la Cámara de Diputados," in *Documentos relativos a la ocupación de Arauco*, ed. Saavedra, 45–46. Ruiz Aldea, *Aruacanos*, 82–83.

13. *El Diario Austral* quoted in Foerster and Montecino, *Organizaciones, líderes y contiendas mapuches*, 61. Fernando Léniz quoted in Javier Pinedo C., "Una metáfora de país: La discusión en torno a la presencia de Chile en el Pabellón Sevilla 1992," in *Ensayismo y modernidad en América Latina*, ed. Ossandón B., 92. On Chile's isolationism, see Alamos Varas, "Algunas fuentes históricas"; and Walter Sánchez G., "Las tendencias sobresalientes de la política exterior chilena," in *150 años de política exterior chilena*, ed. Sánchez G. and Pereira L., 374–90.

14. *La Patria*, September 5, 1882, cited in Sater, *Chile and the United States*, 49. Eduardo Mendoza, *Crisis de gobernabilidad*, 52n48. Suzanne Oboler and Anani Dzidzienyo, "Flows and Counterflows: Latinas/os, Blackness, and Racialization in Hemispheric Perspective," in *Neither Enemies nor Friends*, ed. Dzidzienyo and Oboler, 8. Mallon, *Courage Tastes of Blood*. For another recent exception to this trend, see Gaune and Lara, *Historias de racismo y discriminación en Chile*.

15. Allende, *Daughter of Fortune*, 14. For more on Mistral's political activism and her literary output during her time in Southern California, see Horan, "California Dreaming." Gabriela Mistral quoted in Winn, *Americas*, 317.

16. Martínez Estrada, *X-Ray of the Pampa*, 91. Crosby, *Ecological Imperialism*, 298.

17. González, *Europa y la América*, 18. Pike, "Aspects of Class Relations in Chile," 15–16. For immigrant population figures, see Dirección General de Estadística, *Sinopsis geográfico-estadística*. Solberg, "Immigration and Urban Social Problems," 217.

18. Stegner, *Where the Bluebird Sings*, xix. Rhea, *Turlock District*, 6. California Water Development Company, *"Do You Want a Ranch in California?,"* 5.

19. Greeley founded the *New York Tribune* and the Liberal Republican Party. On the controversy surrounding when he first made his famous pronouncement, see Shapiro, *Yale Book of Quotations*, 322–23. Dana, *Two Years before the Mast*, 94. Omar Valerio-Jiménez, "Race and Immigration in the Nineteenth Century," in *Companion to California History*, ed. Deverell and Igler, 149.

20. Rindge, *Happy Days in Southern California*, 32–33. On the ways Anglo booster literature concealed the countless historical connections between Los Angeles and the Mexican people who created the city, see Deverell, *Whitewashed Adobe*.

21. Kropp, *California Vieja*, 7.

22. Ignatiev and Garvey, *Race Traitor*, 9. Williams, *Culture and Society*, 319.

23. Seyd, *California and Its Resources*, 64.

24. Karl Marx and Friedrich Engels, "Review, May-October, 1850," in *Collected Works*, 10:504.

25. Schama, *Landscape and Memory*, 191. Nash, *Inescapable Ecologies*, 3.

26. On California's unusual model for expanding its public higher education system, see Robert C. Dynes, "High Stakes in Higher Education: California's Competitiveness Starts with Research Universities," *San Francisco Chronicle*, April 16, 2004; and Douglass, *California Idea and American Higher Education*. For arguments about how labor history developed differently in California from the rest of the nation, see Milkman, *L.A. Story*. On the state's novel trajectory of scientific development, see Smith, *Pacific Visions*. For an account of how the urbanization of Los Angeles proceeded differently from that of cities in the Midwest and on the East Coast, see Avila, *Popular Culture in the Age of White Flight*. For claims about California's unusual design and fashion trends, see Kaplan, *California Design*. On California as a model for foreign states, see Leadbeater, *Britain*. McGirr, *Suburban Warriors*, 20. The quotation is from Reagan, *Reagan*, 168.

27. W. E. B. Du Bois quoted in Susan Anderson, "A City Called Heaven: Black Enchantment and Despair in Los Angeles," in *The City*, ed. Scott and Soja, 342. Reddick, "New Race-Relations Frontier," 144. McWilliams, "Cultural Arts in California," 79.

28. For examples, see Deverell, *Whitewashed Adobe*; Pitti, *Devil in Silicon Valley*; and Almaguer, *Racial Fault Lines*. McWilliams, *Factories in the Field*, 9. McWilliams, *California*, 24.

29. "Cal 'Capital' of Pacific Rim?" *Asian Week*, May 11, 1984, 10; Karl Schoenberger, "In Search of the All-Important Pacific Rim Trade," *Los Angeles Times*, September 11, 1994. On California's place in the discourse of Asian Tiger economies, see "California: America's Tiger State," *BusinessWorld*, February 20, 2001, 1.

30. Ronald S. Bown quoted in Juanita Darling, "Chile's Export Strategy—Economy Benefits as Products Head West," *Orange County Register*, December 11, 1989. On the "Pacific Century," see Dixon and Drakakis-Smith, "Pacific Asian Region," 77–78; Abegglen, *Sea Change*; Elegant, *Pacific Destiny*; and Linder, *Pacific Century*.

31. "Trouble with the Neighbors: Can Chile Stay Different?" *Economist*, July 18, 2002, 30. For recent examples of Chilean exceptionalism, see Cavanaugh, "Making Enemies"; Mullins, *Shadow of the Generals*, 13–14; and Lisa Hilbink, "An Exception to Chilean Exceptionalism? The Historical Role of Chile's Judiciary," in *What Justice?*, ed. Eckstein and Wickham-Crowley, 64–97. On Chile's links to the Asia-Pacific, see Shirley Christian, "Chile's Growing Trans-Pacific Ties," *New York Times*, March 28, 1988; Salazar Sparks, *Chile y la comunidad del Pacífico*; and Walker, *Chile and Latin America*, 25.

32. Mario Sznajder, "The Chilean Jaguar as a Symbol of a New Identity," in *The Collective and the Public in Latin America*, ed. Roniger and Herzog, 285–98; Pietrobelli, *Industry, Competitiveness and Technological Capabilities in Chile*; and Raymundo Riva Palacio, "Chile: La otra cara del jaguar; La ilusion neoliberal," *El Norte*, October 13, 1996, 14. The quotations are from Diego Ribadeneira, "A Jewel in an Economic Rough: Revitalized Chile Looks to Join NAFTA," *Boston Globe*, January 18, 1995; and James Whelan, "What Canadians Could Learn from Chile's Strong Economy," *Toronto Star*, January 2, 1995.

33. Rosenfeld and Marré, "How Chile's Rich Got Richer," 20. For more on these socioeconomic and environmental problems, see the chapters in Winn, *Victims of the Chilean Miracle*.

EPILOGUE

1. Mix, "Bilbao y el hallazgo de América Latina"; Fox, *Hispanic Nation-Culture*, 13. Others attribute the phrase "América Latina" to the Columbian José María Torres Caicedo. See Bushnell and Macaulay, *Emergence of Latin America*, 3. On the meaning of Bilbao's claim, see Durán Corsanego, "¿Latinoamérica o Hispanoamérica?," 61. For a much more extensive, discussion of the origins of the concept of "Latin America," see Gobat, "Invention of Latin America."

2. Braudel, *History of Civilizations*, 427. For differing views on the historical controversy surrounding the naming of Latin America, see John L. Phelan, "Pan-Latinism, French Intervention in Mexico (1861–1867) and the Genesis of the Idea of Latin America," in *Conciencia y autenticidad históricas*, ed. Ortega y Medina, 279–98; and Paul Estrade, "Del invento de 'América Latina' en París por latinoamericanos (1856–1889)," in *París y el mundo ibérico e iberoamericano*, 179–88. Louis-Napoléon Bonaparte is better known for being the object of scorn in Victor Hugo's *Napoléon le petit*.

3. Dana, *Two Years before the Mast*, 465. Gudde and Bright, *California Place Names*, 76–77.

4. Hoover et al., *Historic Spots in California*, 494. Edna Bryan Buckbee, *Saga of Old Tuolumne*, 410. Rich, *Blood, Bread, and Poetry*, 27.

5. Twain, *Notebooks and Journals*, 3:Notebook 42 (1898). Twain, *Roughing It*. Benjamín Vicuña Mackenna quoted in Beilharz and and López, *We Were 49ers!*, 200.

6. Roy Rivenburg, "Forgotten Graves Yield Glimpse of the Past," *Los Angeles Times,* November 12, 1993.
7. Heyene, *Bandido Chileno Joaquín Murieta.* For more on Heyene and Murieta, see Pereira Salas, "Algo más sobre Joaquín Murieta," *El Bibliófilo Chileno,* no. 10 (December 1964): 137–41. Cherokee writer John Rollin Ridge, also known as Yellowbird, wrote the first English-language novel about Murieta; Ridge, *Life and Adventures of Joaquín Murieta.* Among the most evocative writing on Murieta (also spelled Murrieta) is Richard Rodriguez, "The Head of Joaquín Murrieta," in *Days of Obligation,* 133–48. For Chilean writings about Murieta, see Dorfman, *Americanos*; Pereira Poza, "Joaquín Murieta"; "Chileno poeta Sigue La Ruta de Joaquín Murieta en California," *El Rancagüino,* July 2, 1969; and Acevado Hernández, *Joaquín Murieta.*
8. Harris Bucher, *Emigrantes e inmigrantes en Chile,* 104.
9. Wilde, *Picture of Dorian Gray,* 234. Boudin Bakery Website, "Meet Boudin," available at: http://www.boudinbakery.com/meetboudin/.
10. Alberto Cruchaga Ossa, "Impressions of the First Chilean Minister to Washington," *Pan American Magazine,* no. 39 (1926): 157, quoted in Sater, *Chile and the United States,* 17.
11. Jiménez et al., "Do Climatically Similar Regions Contain Similar Alien Floras?" 614.
12. Anderson, *Imagined Communities,* 15. On issues of national identity in modern Chile, see Larraín, "Changes in Chilean Identity," 321–38.
13. Said, *Orientalism,* 54–55.
14. Walt Whitman, "Facing West from California's Shores," in *Leaves of Grass,* 116. Although *Leaves of Grass* was first published in 1855, this poem did not take its final title until the 1867 edition. The quotation is from Neruda, *Incitación al Nixonicidio,* 17–21. The anecdote about Neruda and the carpenter is from Nolan, *Poet-Chief,* 4. For more on the influence of Whitman on Neruda, see Alegría, *Walt Whitman en Hispanoamérica.*
15. Seigel, "Beyond Compare," 63.

BIBLIOGRAPHY

Aagesen, David L. "On the Northern Fringe of the South American Temperate Forest: The History and Conservation of the Monkey-Puzzle Tree." *Environmental History* 3, no. 1 (1998): 64–85.

Abegglen, James C. *Sea Change: Pacific Asia as the New World Industrial Center.* New York: Free Press, 1994.

Acevado Hernández, Antonio. *Joaquín Murieta: Drama en seis actos.* Santiago: Suplemento Excelsior, 1938.

Ackerman, Edward A. "Influences of Climate on the Cultivation of Citrus Fruits." *Geographical Review* 28, no. 2 (1938): 289–302.

Agnew, Jean-Christophe. "The Threshold of Exchange." *Radical History Review*, no. 1 (Fall 1979): 99–118.

Agosin, Manuel R., and Claudio Bravo-Ortega. "The Emergence of New Successful Export Activities in Latin America: The Case of Chile." *Inter-American Development Bank Working Paper No. 236.* Washington, DC: Inter-American Development Bank, 2009.

Agosín, Marjorie. "The Generals' Bonfires: The Death of Rodrigo Rojas in Chile." Translated by Janice Molloy. *Human Rights Quarterly* 9, no. 3 (1987): 423–25.

———. *Tapestries of Hope, Threads of Love: The Arpillera Movement in Chile.* Translated by Celeste Kostopulos-Cooperman. Albuquerque: University of New Mexico Press, 1996.

Agustin Iriarte, J., Gabriel A. Lobos, and Fabián M. Jaksic. "Especies de vertbrados invasores en Chile y su control y monitoreo por agencias gubernamentales." *Revista Chilena de Historia Natural* 78 (March 2005): 143–51.

Alamos Varas, Pilar. "Algunas fuentes históricas de la política exterior de Chile." *Estudios Internactionales* (Santiago), no. 126 (May–August 1999): 3–39.

Albert, Federico. *El pino de Monterey, pinus insignis o mejor pino radiata.* Santiago: Imprenta Cervantes, n.d.

Albion, Robert G. *The Rise of New York Port, 1815–1860.* New York: Charles Scribner's Sons, 1939.

Alegría, Fernando. *Walt Whitman en Hispanoamérica*. Mexico City: Ediciones Studium, 1954.

Alexander, William L., ed. *Lost in the Long Transition: Struggles for Social Justice in Neoliberal Chile*. Plymouth, UK: Lexington Books, 2009.

Allen, Edward W. "Jean-François Galaup de La Pérouse: A Checklist." *California Historical Society Quarterly* 20 (1941): 47–64.

Allende, Isabel. *Daughter of Fortune: A Novel*. Translated by M. Sayers Peden. New York: Harper Perennial, 1999.

Allende Gossens, Salvador. *Nuestro camino al socialismo: La vía chilena*. Buenos Aires: Ediciones Papiro, 1971.

Alliende Edwards, María Piedad. "La construcción de los ferrocarriles en Chile, 1850–1913." *Revista Austral de Ciencias Sociales*, no. 5 (Spring 2001): 143–61.

Almaguer, Tomás. *Racial Fault Lines: The Historical Origins of White Supremacy in California*. Berkeley: University of California Press, 1994.

Altieri, Miguel A., and Alejandro Rojas. "Ecological Impacts of Chile's Neoliberal Policies, with Special Emphasis on Agroecosystems." *Environment, Development and Sustainability* 1, no. 1 (1999): 55–72.

Anderson, Benedict. *Imagined Communities*. London: Verso, 1983.

Anderson, J. R. *Agricultural Technology: Policy Issues for the International Community*. Wallingford, UK: CAB International/World Bank, 1994.

Anderson, Kym, ed. *The World's Wine Markets: Globalization at Work*. Northampton, MA: Edward Elgar, 2004.

Angel, Myron. *History of Placer County, California, with Illustrations and Biographical Sketches of Its Prominent Men and Pioneers*. Oakland, CA: Thompson and West, 1882.

Antonio Prado, José, and Carlos Weber. "Facilitating the Way for Implementation of Sustainable Forest Management: The Case of Chile." Paper 21 of the UNFF Intersessional Experts Meeting on the Role of Planted Forests in Sustainable Forest Management, Wellington, New Zealand, March 23–27, 2003, 1–11.

Appuhn, Karl. *A Forest on the Sea: Environmental Expertise in Renaissance Venice*. Baltimore: Johns Hopkins University Press, 2009.

Arancibia Clavel, Patricia, and Francisco Balart Páez. *Sergio de Castro: El arquitecto del modelo económico chileno*. Santiago: Editorial Biblioteca Americana, 2007.

Aranguiz, Horacio. "La situación de los obreros agrícolas en el siglo XIX." *Estudios de Historia de las Instituciones Políticas y Sociales* 1, no. 2 (1967): 28–29.

Arce, A., and T. K. Marsden. "The Social Construction of International Food." *Economic Geography* 69, no. 3 (1993): 293–311.

Armesto, Juan J., Carolin Villagrán, and Mary Kalin Arroyo, eds. *Ecología de los bosques nativos de Chile*. Santiago: Editorial Universitaria, 1996.

Armesto, Juan, Carolina Villagrán, and Claudio Donoso. "Desde la era glacial a la industrial: La historia del bosque templado chileno." *Ambiente y Desarrollo* 10, no. 1 (1994): 66–72.

Armitage, Susan, and Elizabeth Jameson, eds. *The Women's West*. Norman: University of Oklahoma Press, 1987.

Arnaldo Márquez, José. *La orjía financiera del Perú: El guano i el salitre; Artículos publicados en "La Libertad Electoral."* Santiago: Imprenta de *La Libertad Electoral,* 1888.

Arnold, Ralph, and V. R. Garfias. *Geology and Technology of the California Oil Fields.* New York: American Institute of Mining Engineers, 1914.

Arze, Elias C., and Börje W. Svensson. "Development of International Competitiveness in Industries and Individual Firms in Developing Countries: The Case of the Chilean Forest-Based Industry and the Chilean Engineering Firm Arze, Recine and Asociados." *International Journal of Production Economics* 52, nos. 1–2 (1997): 185–202.

Asbury, Herbert. *The Barbary Coast: An Informal History of the San Francisco Underworld.* New York: Alfred A. Knopf, 1933.

Aschmann, H. H. "A More Restrictive Definition of Mediterranean Climates." *Bulletin, Botanical Society of France* 2–4 (1985): 21–30.

Astorquiza, Octavio. *Lota: Antecedentes históricos con una monografía de la compañía minera e industrial de Chile.* Concepción, Chile: Sociedad Imprenta y Litografía Concepción, 1929.

Atherton, Faxon D. *The California Diary of Faxon Dean Atherton.* Edited by Doyce B. Nunis, Jr. San Francisco: California Historical Society, 1964.

Auden, W. H. *Collected Shorter Poems (1927–1957).* New York: Random House, 1966.

Avila, Eric. *Popular Culture in the Age of White Flight: Fear and Fantasy in Suburban Los Angeles.* Berkeley: University of California Press, 2004.

Ayers, James Joseph. *Gold and Sunshine: Reminiscences of Early California.* Boston: Gorham, 1922.

Aylward, David, and Tim Turpin. "New Wine in Old Bottles: A Case Study of Innovation Territories in 'New World' Wine Production." *International Journal of Innovation Management* 7, no. 4 (2003): 501–25.

Bagley, Will, ed. *Scoundrel's Tale: The Sam Brannan Papers.* Spokane, WA: Arthur H. Clark, 1999.

Bahre, Conrad J. *Destruction of the Natural Vegetation of North-Central Chile.* Berkeley: University of California Press, 1979.

Bain, Carmen. "Structuring the Flexible and Feminized Labor Market: GlobalGAP Standards for Agricultural Labor in Chile." *Signs* 35, no. 2 (2010): 343–70.

Bakalinsky, Adah. *Stairway Walks in San Francisco.* 7th ed. Birmingham, AL: Wilderness, 2010.

Bakken, Gordon M., and Alexandra Kindell, eds. *Encyclopedia of Immigration and Migration in the American West.* Thousand Oaks, CA: Sage, 2006.

Balfour, Gutherie, and Co. *Nitrate of Soda and Thomas' Phosphate Powder as Fertilizers in California.* San Francisco: Balfour, Gutherie, 1905.

Bancroft, Hubert Howe. *California Inter Pocula.* San Francisco: History Co., 1881.

———. *California Pioneer Register and Index, 1542–1848.* Baltimore: Regional, 1964.

———. *History of California.* 7 vols. San Francisco: A. L. Bancroft, 1884–90.

———. *History of the Pacific States of North America: California.* 34 vols. San Francisco: A. L. Bancroft, 1882–90.

———. *Popular Tribunals.* San Francisco: A. L. Bancroft, 1887.

Barnes, D. K., et al. *Alfalfa Germplasm in the United States: Genetic Vulnerability, Use, Improvement, and Maintenance.* Washington, DC: Agricultural Research Service, 1977.

Barnhart, Jaqueline Baker. *The Fair but Frail: Prostitution in San Francisco, 1849–1900.* Reno: University of Nevada Press, 1986.

Barratt, Elizabeth. *Carmel Valley.* Charleston, SC: Arcadia, 2010.

Barrientos, Stephanie, et al. *Women and Agribusiness: Working Miracles in the Chilean Fruit Export Sector.* New York: St. Martin's, 1999.

Barr-Melej, Patrick. *Reforming Chile: Cultural Politics, Nationalism, and the Rise of the Middle Class.* Chapel Hill: University of North Carolina Press, 2001.

Barros Arana, Diego. *Historia general de Chile.* 2nd ed. 16 vols. Santiago: Editorial Nascimento, 1930–37.

Barros, Mario. *Historia diplomática de Chile.* Barcelona: Ediciones Ariel, 1971.

Barry, Michael, and Adrian Wilkinson, eds. *Research Handbook in Comparative Employment Relations.* Northampton, MA: Edward Elgar, 2011.

Barry, Theodore A., and Benjamin A. Patten. *Men and Memories of San Francisco, in the "Spring of '50."* San Francisco: A. L. Bancroft, 1873.

Barth, Gunther. *Instant Cities: Urbanization and the Rise of San Francisco and Denver.* New York: Oxford University Press, 1975.

Barton, Jonathan R., and Warwick E. Murray. "Grounding Geographies of Economic Globalisation: Globalised Spaces in Chile's Non-Traditional Export Sector, 1980–2005." *Tijdschrift voor Economische en Sociale Geografie* 100, no. 1 (2009): 81–100.

Basadre, Jorge. *Historia de la república del Perú, 1822–1933.* 7th ed. 11 vols. Lima: Editorial Universitaria, 1983.

Bateson, Charles. *Gold Fleet for California: Forty Niners from Australia and New Zealand.* Auckland, New Zealand: Minerva, 1963.

Bauer, Arnold J. "Chilean Rural Labor in the Nineteenth Century." *American Historical Review* 76, no. 4 (1971): 1059–83.

———. *Chilean Rural Society from the Spanish Conquest to 1930.* New York: Cambridge University Press, 1975.

———. "Expansión económica en una sociedad tradicional: Chile central en el siglo XIX." *Historia* (Universidad Católica de Chile) 9 (1970): 137–41.

———. "Rural Workers in Spanish America: Problems of Peonage and Oppression." *Hispanic American Historical Review* 59, no. 1 (1979): 34–63.

Bauer, Carl J. *Contra la corriente: Privatización, mercados de agua y el estado en Chile.* Santiago: LOM Ediciones, 2002.

Baumgardner, Frank H. *Yanks in the Redwoods: Carving Out a Life in Northern California.* New York: Algora, 2010.

Bautista Albérdi, Juan. *Escritos póstumos de J. B. Alberdi: América.* 16 vols. Buenos Aires: Imprenta Cruz Hermanos, 1895–1901.

———. *La vida y los trabajos industriales de William Wheelwright en la América del Sud.* Paris: Garnier hermanos, 1876.

Baxley, Henry Willis. *What I Saw on the West Coast of South and North America, and at the Hawaiian Islands.* New York: D. Appleton, 1865.

Beasley, Delilah L. *The Negro Trail Blazers of California: A Compilation of Records from the California Archives in the Bancroft Library at the University of California.* Los Angeles: Times Mirror, 1919.

Becerra, Pablo I., and Ramiro O. Bustamante. "Effect of a Native Tree on Seedling Establishment of Two Exotic Invasive Species in a Semiarid Ecosystem." *Biological Invasions* 13, no. 12 (2011): 2763–73.

Beckman, Erika. "The Creolization of Imperial Reason: Chilean State Racism in the War of the Pacific." *Journal of Latin American Cultural Studies* 18, no. 1 (2009): 73–90.

Bederman, Gail. *Manliness and Civilization: A Cultural History of Gender and Race in the United States, 1880–1917.* Chicago: University of Chicago Press, 1995.

Bee, Anna, and Isabel Vogel. "Temporeras and Household Relations: Seasonal Employment in Chile's Agro-Export Sector." *Bulletin of Latin American Research* 16, no. 1 (1997): 83–95.

Beebe, Rose Marie, and Robert M. Senkewicz, eds. *Lands of Promise and Despair: Chronicles of Early California, 1535–1846.* Berkeley, CA: Heyday Books, 2001.

Beidleman, Richard G. *California's Frontier Naturalists.* Berkeley: University of California Press, 2006.

Beilharz, Edwin A., and Carlos U. López, trans. and eds. *We Were 49ers! Chilean Accounts of the California Gold Rush.* Pasadena, CA: Ward Ritchie, 1976.

Bellamy, Edward. *Looking Backward, 2000–1887.* Boston: Ticknor, 1888.

Benemann, William. *A Year of Mud and Gold: San Francisco in Letters and Diaries, 1849–1850.* Lincoln: University of Nebraska Press, 1999.

Bengoa, José. *Historia del pueblo Mapuche (siglo XIX y XX).* Santiago: Ediciones Sur, 1985.

Benjamin, Walter. *The Origin of German Tragic Drama (Ursprung des Deutsches Trauerspiel).* Translated by John Osborne. London: Verso, 1998.

Benton, Thomas Hart. "Speech to the United States Senate, May 28, 1846." *Congressional Globe*, 29th Cong., 1st Sess., no. 58 (June 6, 1846): 917–18.

Berg, Janine. *Miracle for Whom? Chilean Workers under Free Trade.* New York: Routledge, 2006.

Berglund, Barbara. *Making San Francisco American: Cultural Frontiers in the Urban West, 1846–1906.* Lawrence: University of Kansas Press, 2007.

Bermúdez, Oscar. *Historia del salitre desde sus orígenes hasta la Guerra del Pacífico.* Santiago: Universidad, 1963.

Berwick, Edward. "Farming in the Year 2000, A.D." *Overland Monthly and Out West Magazine* 15 (June 1890): 569–73.

Biggs, Donald. *Conquer and Colonize: Stevenson's Regiment and California.* San Rafael, CA: Presidio, 1977.

Biglaiser, Glen. "The Internationalization of Chicago's Economics in Latin America." *Economic Development and Cultural Change* 50, no. 2 (2002): 269–86.

Bishop, William Henry. "Southern California." *Harper's New Monthly Magazine* 66, no. 391 (1882): 45–65.

Blainey, Geoffrey. *The Rush That Never Ended: A History of Australian Mining.* Melbourne: Melbourne University Press, 1963.

Blakemore, Harold. *British Nitrates and Chilean Politics, 1886–1869: Balmaceda and North.* London: Athlone, 1974.

Blank, Paul W., and Fred Spier, eds. *Defining the Pacific: Opportunities and Constraints.* Aldershot, UK: Ashgate, 2002.

Blank, Steven C. "Perspective: Is This California Agriculture's Last Century?" *California Agriculture* 54, no. 4 (2000): 23–25.

Blayney, Don P. *The Changing Landscape of U.S. Milk Production.* Statistical Bulletin no. 978. Washington, DC: United States Department of Agriculture, 2002.

Boas, Taylor. "Bachelet Energizes Berkeley." *Berkeley Review of Latin American Studies* (Fall 2008): 9–13.

Bockstoce, John. *The Opening of the Maritime Fur Trade at Bering Strait.* Philadelphia: American Philosophical Society, 2005.

Böhlke, J. K., G. E. Ericksen, and K. Revesz. "Stable Isotope Evidence for an Atmospheric Origin of Desert Nitrate Deposits in Northern Chile and Southern California, U.S.A." *Chemical Geology* 136, nos. 1–2 (1997): 135–52.

Bollen, Kenneth A. "Issues in the Comparative Measurement of Political Democracy." *American Sociological Review* 45, no. 3 (1980): 370–90.

Bollinger, William. "The Bourgeois Revolution in Peru: A Conception of Peruvian History." *Latin American Perspectives* 4, no. 3 (1977): 18–56.

Bolton, Herbert E. "The Mission as a Frontier Institution in the Spanish American Colonies." *American Historical Review* 23, no. 1 (1917): 42–61.

Bolton, J. L. *Alfalfa: Botany, Cultivation, and Utilization.* New York: Interscience, 1962.

Bonano, Alessandro, et al., eds. *From Columbus to ConAgra: The Globalization of Agriculture and Food.* Lawrence: University Press of Kansas, 1994.

Bonilla, Heraclio. *Guano y burguesía en el Perú.* Lima: Instituto de Estudios Peruanos, 1974.

———. *Un siglo a la deriva: Ensayos sobre el Perú, Bolivia y la guerra.* Lima: Instituto de Estudios Peruanos, 1980.

Bonyun, Bill, and Gene Bonyun. *Full Hold and Splendid Passage: America Goes to Sea, 1815–1860.* New York: Alfred A. Knopf, 1969.

Booker, Matthew Morse. *Down by the Bay: San Francisco's History between the Tides.* Berkeley: University of California Press, 2013.

Borthwick, John David. *Three Years in California.* London: William Blackwood and Sons, 1857.

Bosworth, Barry P., Rudiger Dornbusch, and Raúl Labán, eds. *The Chilean Economy: Policy Lessons and Challenges.* Washington, DC: Brookings Institution, 1994.

Bowman, Alan P. *Index to the 1850 Census of California.* Baltimore: Genealogical Publishing, 1972.

Boyd, Nan Alamilla. *Wide-Open Town: A History of Queer San Francisco to 1965.* Berkeley: University of California Press, 2003.

Bradley, Bethany A., et al. "Global Change, Global Trade, and the Next Wave of Plant Invasions." *Frontiers in Ecology and the Environment* 10, no. 1 (2012): 20–28.

Bradshaw, Gay A., and Pablo A. Marquet. *How Landscapes Change: Human Disturbance and Ecosystem Fragmentation in the Americas.* Berlin: Springer-Verlag, 2003.

Brady, Nyle C. *The Nature and Property of Soils.* 8th ed. New York: Macmillan, 1974.

Brand, Charles J. "The Fertilizer Industry." *Annals of the American Academy of Political and Social Science* 193 (September 1937): 22–33.

Brandt Commission. *North-South, a Programme for Survival: Report of the Independent Commission on International Development Issues.* Cambridge, MA: MIT Press, 1980.

Braudel, Fernand. *A History of Civilizations.* Translated by Richard Mayne. New York: A. Lane, 1994.

———. *The Mediterranean and the Mediterranean World in the Age of Philip II.* Translated by Siân Reynolds. 2 vols. New York: Harper and Row, 1972–73.

———. *On History.* Translated by Sarah Matthews. Chicago: University of Chicago Press, 1980.

Brass, Tom. *Towards a Comparative Political Economy of Unfree Labour: Case Studies and Debates.* Portland, OR: Frank Cass, 1999.

Brenner, Mark. "California Nurses Lead the Fight against Schwarzenegger's Anti-Union Ballot Initiatives." *Labor Notes,* February 18, 2006, available at http://labornotes.org/node/20.

Brenner, Neil, and Nik Theodore. "Cities and the Geographies of Actually Existing Neoliberalism." *Antipode* 34, no. 3 (2002): 349–79.

———, eds. *Spaces of Neoliberalism: Urban Restructuring in North America and Western Europe.* Oxford: Blackwell, 2002.

Brewer, William H. *Up and Down California in 1860–1864: The Journal of William H. Brewer.* Edited by Francis P. Farquhar. New Haven: Yale University Press, 1930.

Briggs, Jean A. "A Political Miracle." *Forbes,* May 11, 1992, 108–11.

Brockway, Lucile. *Science and Colonial Expansion: The Role of the British Botanic Garden.* London: Virago, 1980.

Brossard, C. R. Maurice de. "Laperouse's Expedition to the Pacific Northwest, 1785–1788." *Pacific Studies* 2, no. 1 (1978): 44–51.

Brown, C. A. "Alexander von Humboldt as Historian of Science in Latin America." *Isis* 35, no. 2 (1944): 134–39.

Brown, J. R. "The Frustration of Chile's Nitrate Imperialism." *Pacific Historical Review* 32, no. 4 (1963): 383–96.

Brown, Marion R. "Agricultural 'Extension' in Chile: A Study of Institutional Transplantation." *Journal of Developing Areas* 4, no. 2 (1970): 197–210.

Browne, J. Ross, ed. *Report of the Debates of the Convention of California—On the Formation of the State Constitution, in September and October, 1849.* Washington, DC: J. T. Towers, 1850.

Broxmeyer, Jeffrey. "From the Silver Screen to the Recall Ballot: Schwarzenegger as Terminator and Politician." *New Political Science* 32, no. 1 (2010): 1–21.

Bruey, Alison J. "Limitless Land and the Redefinition of Rights: Popular Mobilisation and the Limits of Neoliberalism in Chile, 1973–1985." *Journal of Latin American Studies* 44, no. 3 (2012): 525–52.

Bryceson, Deborah, Cristóbal Kay, and Jos Mooij, eds. *Disappearing Peasantries? Rural Labour in Africa, Asia and Latin America.* London: Intermediate Technology, 2000.

Buck, Franklin A. *A Yankee Trader in the Gold Rush: The Letters of Franklin A. Buck.* Boston: Houghton Mifflin, 1930.

Buckbee, Edna Bryan. *The Saga of Old Tuolomne.* New York: Press of the Pioneers, 1935.

Buckman, Williamson. *Under the Southern Cross in South America.* New York: Book Publishers, 1914.

Buijs, Gina, ed. *Migrant Women: Crossing Boundaries and Changing Identities.* Providence, RI: Berg, 1993.

Bullen, Isabel. "A Glimpse into the *Niantic*'s Hold." *California History* 58, no. 4 (1979/80): 326–33.

Bunster, Enrique. *Chilenos en California: Miniaturas históricas.* 4th ed. Santiago: Editorial del Pacifico, 1970.

———. "Vida y milagros de los Chilenos en California." *Antártica* 2 (May 1846): 56–67.

Burgess, Michael, and Mary Wickizer Burgess, eds. ¡*Viva California! Seven Accounts of Life in Early California.* San Bernardino, CA: Borgo, 2006.

Burr, Robert N. "The Balance of Power in Nineteenth-Century South America: An Exploratory Essay." *Hispanic American Historical Review* 35, no. 1 (1955): 37–60.

———. *By Reason or Force: Chile and the Balancing of Power in South America, 1830–1905.* Berkeley: University of California Press, 1965.

Burrus, Ernest J. "Two Fictitious Accounts of Ortega's 'Third Voyage' to California." *Hispanic American Historical Review* 52, no. 2 (1972): 272–83.

Bury, John Bagnall. *History of the Later Roman Empire from the Death of Theodosius I to the Death of Justinian (A.D. 395 to A.D. 565).* 2 vols. London: Macmillan, 1923.

Bush, George H. W. "Remarks to a Joint Session of the Congress in Valparaíso, Chile." December 6, 1990, available at http://bushlibrary.tamu.edu/research/public_papers. php?id=2533&year=1990&month=12.

Bushnell, David, and Neill Macaulay. *The Emergence of Latin America in the Nineteenth Century.* New York: Oxford University Press, 1988.

Bustamante, Ramiro O., and Javier A. Simonetti. "Is *Pinus radiata* Invading the Native Vegetation in Central Chile? Demographic Responses in a Fragmented Forest." *Biological Invasions* 7, no. 2 (2005): 243–49.

Butler, Anne M., and Michael J. Lansing. *The American West: A Concise History.* Malden, MA: Blackwell, 2008.

Butler, Judith. *Daughters of Joy, Sisters of Misery: Prostitutes in the American West, 1865–90.* Urbana: University of Illinois Press, 1985.

California Chamber of Commerce. "Trading Partner Portal: Chile." Available at http:// www.calchamber.com/International/Portals/Chile/Pages/Default.aspx.

California Nitrate Development Company of San Francisco. *A Story about Nitrate of Soda in Death Valley, California.* San Francisco: California Nitrate Development Company, 1910.

California State Agricultural Society. *Transactions of the California State Agricultural Society during the Year 1858.* Sacramento: Printed by John O'Meara, State-Printer for California, 1859.

California State Board of Horticulture. *Annual Report of the State Board of Horticulture of the State of California for 1892.* Sacramento: A. J. Johnston, Superintendent State Printing, 1892.

———. *The Culture of the Citrus in California.* Sacramento: A. J. Johnston, Superintendent State Printing, 1900.

California State Mining Bureau. *California Mineral Production for 1916.* Bulletin no. 74. Sacramento: California State Printing Office, 1917.

California Water Development Company. *"Do You Want a Ranch in California On Government Land? . . ."* Los Angeles: George Rice and Sons, 1901.

Callahan, James M. *American Relations in the Pacific and the Far East, 1784–1900.* Baltimore: Johns Hopkins University Press, 1901.

Calloni, Stella. *Los años del lobo: Operación Cóndor.* Buenos Aires: Ediciones Continente, 1999.

Camacho, Simon. *El ferrocarril de Arequipa: Historia documentada de su origen, construcción é inauguracíon.* Lima: Imprenta del estado, 1871.

Cameron, W. E. "Quintay Ranch—To the President and Directors of the California State Agricultural Society." *Transactions of the California State Agricultural Society during the Year 1858.* Sacramento: California State Agricultural Society, 1859.

Camp, William Martin. *San Francisco: Port of Gold.* New York: Doubleday, 1947.

Campbell, Christy. *Phylloxera: How Wine Was Saved for the World.* London: HarperCollins, 2004.

Camus, Pablo. *Ambiente, bosques y gestión forestall en Chile, 1541–2005.* Santiago: LOM Ediciones, 2006.

———. "Federico Albert: Artífice de la de la gestión de los bosques de Chile." *Revista de Geografía Norte Grande,* no. 30 (2003): 55–63.

Cárdenas Casto, Manuel. " 'Y verás como quieren en Chile': Un estudio sobre el prejuicio hacia los inmigrantes bolivianos por parte de los jóvenes chilenos." *Última Década* 14, no. 24 (2006): 99–124.

Cariola Sutter, Carmen, and Osvaldo Sunkel. *La historia económica de Chile, 1830 y 1930: Dos ensayos y una bibliografía.* Madrid: Ediciones Cultura Hispánica del Instituto de Cooperación Iberoamericana, 1982.

———. *Un siglo de historia económica de Chile, 1830–1930.* Santiago: Editorial Universitaria, 1990.

Carosso, Vincent P. *The California Wine Industry, 1830–1895: A Study of the Formative Years.* Berkeley: University of California Press, 1951.

Carrigan, William D., and Clive Webb. "The Lynching of Persons of Mexican Origin or Descent in the United States, 1848 to 1928." *Journal of Social History* 37 (Winter 2003): 411–38.

Carruthers, David. "Environmental Politics in Chile: Legacies of Dictatorship and Democracy." *Third World Quarterly* 22, no. 3 (2001): 343–58.

Carson, James H. *Early Recollections of the Mines, and a Description of the Great Tulare Valley.* 2nd ed. Tarrytown, NY: W. Abbatt, 1931.

Carter, M. R., and D. Mesbah. "Can Land Market Reform Mitigate the Exclusionary Aspects of Rapid Agro-Export Growth?" *World Development* 21, no. 7 (1993): 1085–100.

Caruthers, J. Wade. *American Pacific Ocean Trade: Its Impact on Foreign Policy and Continental Expansion, 1784–1860.* New York: Exposition, 1973.

Casey, Carrie. "Oakland's Redwood Retreat." *American Forests* 97 (November–December 1991): 55–57.

Castañeda, Jorge G. "Latin America's Left Turn." *Foreign Affairs* 85, no. 3 (2006): 28–43.

Castonguay, Stéphane. "Creating an Agricultural World Order: Regional Plant Protection Problems and International Phytopathology, 1878–1939." *Agricultural History* 84, no. 1 (2010): 46–73.

Caughey, John Walton. *Gold Is the Cornerstone*. Berkeley: University of California Press, 1948.

Cavanaugh, William T. "Making Enemies: The Imagination of Torture in Chile and the United States." *Theology Today* 63, no. 3 (2006): 307–23.

Chandler, Alfred D., Jr. *The Railroads: The Nation's First Big Business*. New York: Harcourt, Brace and World, 1965.

Chandler, Robert J. *California Gold Rush Camps: A Keepsake in Fourteen Parts*. San Francisco: Book Club of California, 1998.

Chang, Kornel S. *Pacific Connections: The Making of the U.S.-Canadian Borderlands*. Berkeley: University of California Press, 2012.

Chang-Rodríguez, Eugenio. "Chinese Labor Migration into Latin America in the Nineteenth Century." *Revista de Historia de América*, no. 46 (December 1958): 375–97.

Chapman, Arnold. "Observations on the Roto in Chilean Fiction." *Hispania* 32, no. 3 (1949): 309–14.

Chapman, Charles Edward. *Republican Hispanic America: A History*. New York: Macmillan, 1937.

Chastain, Andra Brosy. "Francis Violich and the Rise and Fall of Urban Developmental Planning in Chile, 1956–1969." *HIb: Revista de Historia Iberoamericana* 4, no. 2 (2011): 10–39.

Chaudhuri, K. N. *Asia before Europe: Economy and Civilization of the Indian Ocean from the Rise of Islam to 1750*. New York: Cambridge University Press, 1990.

Chew, Sing. *World Ecological Degradation: Accumulation, Urbanization, and Deforestation 3000 B.C.–A.D. 2000*. Walnut Creek, CA: AltaMira, 2001.

Child, Theodore. "Impressions of Peru." *Harper's New Monthly Magazine* 82, no. 488 (1891): 253–77.

Chomsky, Noam, and Edward S. Herman. *The Washington Connection and Third World Fascism*. Boston: South End Press, 1979.

Chorley, G. P. H. "The Agricultural Revolution in Northern Europe, 1750–1880: Nitrogen, Legume, and Crop Productivity." *Economic History Review* 34 (February 1981): 71–93.

Christman, Enos. *One Man's Gold: The Letters and Journal of a Forty-Niner*. Edited by Florence Morrow Christman. New York: McGraw-Hill, 1930.

Cisternas, Marco, Patricia Martinez, Carlos Oyarzun, and Patrick Debels. "Caracterización del proceso de reemplazo de vegetación nativa por plantaciones forestales en una cuenca lacustre de la Cordillera de Nahuelbuta, VIII Región, Chile." *Revista Chilena de Historia Natural*, no. 72 (1999): 661–76.

Clapp, Roger A. "Creating Competitive Advantage: Forest Policy as Industrial Policy in Chile." *Economic Geography* 71, no. 3 (1995): 273–96.

———. "Tree Farming and Forest Conservation in Chile: Do Replacement Forests Leave Any Originals Behind?" *Society and Natural Resources* 14, no. 4 (2001): 341–56.

———. "The Unnatural History of the Monterey Pine." *Geographical Review* 85, no. 1 (1995): 1–19.

Clappe, Louise Amelia Knapp Smith. *The Shirley Letters from the California Mines, 1851–52.* 2nd ed. New York: Alfred A. Knopf, 1949.

Clark, A. Kim. *The Redemptive Work: Railway and Nation in Ecuador: 1895–1930.* Wilmington, DE: Scholarly Resources, 1998.

Clark, Arthur H. *The Clipper Ship Era: An Epitome of Famous American and British Clippers Ships, Their Owners, Builders, Commanders, and Crews, 1843–1869.* New York: G. P. Putnam's Sons, 1911.

Clark, Burton R., ed. *Perspectives on Higher Education: Eight Disciplinary and Comparative Views.* Berkeley: University of California Press, 1984.

Clark, Rev. Rufus W. *Lectures on the Formation of Character, Temptations and Mission of Young Men.* Boston: J. P. Jewett, 1853.

Clarke, William. *Peru and Its Creditors.* London: Ranken, 1877.

Clarkson, Thomas W., Laszlo Magos, and Gary J. Myers. "The Toxicology of Mercury: Current Exposures and Clinical Manifestations." *New England Journal of Medicine* 349, no. 18 (2003): 1731–37.

Claro, Edmundo, and Geoff A. Wilson. "Trans-Pacific Wood Chip Exports: The Rise of Chile." *Australian Geographical Studies* 34, no. 2 (1996): 185–99.

Claude, Marcel. *Una vez más la miseria: ¿Es Chile un país sustentable?* Santiago: LOM Ediciones, 1997.

Clausewitz, Claus von. *On War.* Translated by James John Graham. London: N. Trübner, 1873.

Clayton, Lawrence A. *Grace: W. R. Grace & Co.; The Formative Years, 1850–1930.* Ottawa, IL: Jameson Books, 1985.

———. *Peru and the United States: The Condor and the Eagle.* Athens: University of Georgia Press, 1999.

———. "Trade and Navigation in the Seventeenth-Century Viceroyalty of Peru." *Journal of Latin American Studies* 7, no. 1 (1975): 1–21.

Cleland, Robert Glass. *A History of California: The American Period.* New York: Macmillan, 1926.

Cleveland, Richard J. *Voyages of a Merchant Navigator, of the Days That Are Past, Compiled from the Journals and Letters of the Late Richard J. Cleveland.* Edited by H. W. S. Cleveland. New York: Harper and Brothers, 1886.

Coatsworth, John H. *Growth against Development: The Economic Impact of Railroads in Porfirian Mexico.* DeKalb: Northern Illinois University Press, 1981.

Cockcroft, Eva Sperling, and Holly Barnet-Sánchez. *Signs from the Heart: California Chicano Murals.* Albuquerque: University of New Mexico Press, 1993.

Cody, M. L., and H. A. Mooney. "Convergence versus Nonconvergence in Mediterranean-Climate Ecosystems." *Annual Review of Ecology and Systematics* 9, no. 1 (1978): 265–321.

Coffin, George. *A Pioneer Voyage to California and Round the World, 1849 to 1852.* Chicago: Gorham B. Coffin, 1908.

Cogswell, Moses Pearson. *The Gold Rush Diary of Moses Pearson Cogswell of New Hampshire*. Concord: New Hampshire Historical Society, 1949.

Colectivo Oficios Varios, ed. *Arriba quemando el sol: Estudios de historia social chilena: Experiencias populares de trabajo, revuelta y autonomía (1830–1940)*. Santiago: LOM Ediciones, 2004.

Coleman, George Albert. *Report upon Monterey Pine, Made for the Pacific Improvement Company*. Berkeley: California Forest and Range Experiment Station, 1905.

Collier, Simon, and William F. Sater. *A History of Chile, 1808–2002*. 2nd ed. New York: Cambridge University Press, 2004.

———. *A History of Chile, 1808–1994*. New York: Cambridge University Press, 1996.

Collins, Joseph, and John Lear. "Free Market Miracle or Myth? Chile's Neoliberal Experiment." *Ecologist* 26, no. 4 (1996): 156–66.

Colton, Walter. *The California Diary: By Rev. Walter Colton, U.S.N. Late Alcalde of Monterey with Index and Illustrations*. Reprint ed. Oakland, CA: Biobooks, 1948.

Comisión Nacional de Verdad y Reconciliación. *Report of the Chilean National Commission on Truth and Reconciliation*. Translated by Phillip E. Berryman. 2 vols. Notre Dame: University of Notre Dame Press, 1993.

Contesse Gonzalez, D. "Apuntes y consideraciones para la historia del pino radiata en Chile." *Boletin de la Academia Chilena de la Historia* 97 (1987): 351–73.

Contreras, Carlos. *El aprendizaje del capitalismo: Estudios de historia económica y social del Perú Republicano*. Lima: IEP, 2004.

———. "El reeplazo del beneficio de patio en la minería peruana, 1850–1913." *Revista de Indias* 59, no. 216 (1999): 391–416.

Conway, J. D. *Monterey: Presidio, Pueblo, and Port*. Charleston, SC: Arcadia, 2003.

Cook, Captain James. *The Journals of Captain James Cook*. Edited by John Beaglehole. 3 vols. Cambridge: Hakluyt Society, 1968.

Coomes, Mary L. "From Pooyi to the New Almaden Mercury Mine: Cinnabar, Economics, and Culture in California to 1920." PhD diss., University of Michigan, 1999.

Cortés, Hernán. *Letters from Mexico*. Edited by Anthony Pagden. New Haven: Yale University Press, 1986).

Cowling, Richard M., et al. "Plant Diversity in Mediterranean-Climate Regions." *Trends in Ecology and Evolution* 11 (1996): 362–66.

Cox, George W. *Alien Species in North America and Hawaii: Impacts on Natural Ecosystems*. Washington, DC: Island Press, 1999.

Cox, J. F., and C. R. Megee. *Alfalfa*. New York: John Wiley and Sons, 1928.

Coy, Owen Cochran. *Pictorial History of California*. Berkeley: University of California Extension Division, 1925.

Craib, Raymond B. *Cartographic Mexico: A History of State Fixations and Fugitive Landscapes*. Durham, NC: Duke University Press, 2004.

Craig, Neville B. *Recollections of an Ill-Fated Expedition to the Headwaters of the Madeira River in Brazil*. Philadelphia: J. B. Lippincott, 1907.

Critchfield, William B., and Elbert L. Little. *Geographic Distribution of the Pines of the World*. Washington, DC: USDA Forest Service, 1966.

Cronise, Titus Fey. *The Natural Wealth of California.* San Francisco: H. H. Bancroft, 1868.

Cronon, William, George Miles, and Jay Gitlin, eds. *Under an Open Sky: Rethinking America's Western Past.* New York: W. W. Norton, 1992.

Crosby, Alfred W. *The Columbian Exchange: Biological Consequences of 1492.* Westport, CT: Greenwood, 1972.

——. *Ecological Imperialism: The Biological Expansion of Europe, 900–1900.* 2nd ed. Cambridge: Cambridge University Press, 2004.

Crosby, Elisha Oscar. *Memoirs of Elisha Oscar Crosby: Reminiscences of California and Guatemala from 1849 to 1864.* Edited by Charles Albro Baker. San Marino, CA: Huntington Library, 1945.

Cross, Ira B. *Financing an Empire: History of Banking in California.* 4 vols. Chicago: S. J. Clarke, 1927.

Cross, Ralph Herbert. *The Early Inns of California, 1844–1869.* San Francisco: Cross and Brandt, 1954.

Crowley, William K. "Chile's Wine Industry: Historical Character and Changing Geography." *Journal of Latin American Geography* 26, no. 1 (2000): 87–101.

Cumings, Bruce. *Dominion from Sea to Sea: Pacific Ascendancy and American Power.* New Haven: Yale University Press, 2009.

Curtin, Philip D. *The Rise and Fall of the Plantation Complex: Essays in Atlantic History.* 2nd ed. New York: Cambridge University Press, 1994.

Curtis, Harry A., and Charles M. Pepper. "Our Nitrogen Problem." *Annals of the American Academy of Political and Social Science* 112 (March 1924): 173–83.

Cushman, Gregory T. *Guano and the Opening of the Pacific World: A Global Ecological History.* New York: Cambridge University Press, 2013.

Dahaher, Kevin. *Fifty Years Is Enough: The Case against the World Bank and the International Monetary Fund.* Boston: South End, 1994.

Dahl, Robert A. *Polyarchy: Participation and Opposition.* New Haven: Yale University Press, 1971.

Daitsman, Andrew L. "The People Shall Be All: Liberal Rebellion and Popular Mobilization in Chile, 1830–1860." PhD diss., University of Wisconsin, Madison, 1994.

Dana, Richard Henry, Jr. *Two Years before the Mast.* Rev. ed. Boston: Houghton Mifflin, 1911.

Darwin, Charles. *"The Origin of Species" and "The Voyage of the Beagle."* New York: Alfred A. Knopf, 2003.

Das Gupta, Ashin. *The World of the Indian Ocean Merchant, 1500–1800: Collected Essays of Ashin Das Gupta.* Edited by Uma Das Gupta. Oxford: Oxford University Press, 2001.

Davelouis, Héctor. *Informe que el que suscribe eleva a la consideración de los poderes legislativo y ejecutivo, sobre el estado actual de la minería en el Perú.* Lima: Huerta, 1863.

Davenport, Frances Gardiner, ed. *European Treaties Bearing on the History of the United States and Its Dependencies to 1648.* Washington, DC: Carnegie Institution of Washington, 1917.

David, F. Jorge, and David Lebòn David. *Trigo en Chile: Una historia desconocida.* Santiago: Ediciones del Día, 1993.

Davidson, W. M., and R. L. Nougaret. *The Grape Phylloxera in California*. Washington, DC: US Department of Agriculture, 1921.

Daviron, Benoit, and Stefano Ponte. *The Coffee Paradox: Global Markets, Commodity Trade and the Elusive Promise of Development*. London: Zed Books, 2005.

Davis, Clarence B., and Kenneth E. Wilburn, Jr., eds. *Railway Imperialism*. New York: Greenwood, 1991.

Davis, Horace. "California Breadstuffs." *Journal of Political Economy* 2, no. 4 (1894): 517–35.

Davis, Mike. *Late Victorian Holocausts: El Niño Famines and the Making of the Third World*. London: Verso, 2001.

Davis, William Heath. *Seventy-Five Years in California*. San Francisco: John Howell, 1967.

De Castro, Sergio. "Prólogo." In *"El ladrillo": Bases de la política económica del gobierno militar chileno*, 1–12. Santiago: Centro de Estudios Públicos, 1992.

Decker, Peter R. *Fortunes and Failures: White-Collar Mobility in Nineteenth-Century San Francisco*. Cambridge, MA: Harvard University Press, 1978.

Degarrod, Lydia Nakashima. "Female Shamanism and the Mapuche Transformation into Christian Chilean Farmers." *Religion* 28, no. 4 (1998): 339–50.

De La Barra, Ximena, and Richard Alan Dello Buono. *Latin America after the Neoliberal Debacle: Another Region Is Possible*. Lanham, MD: Rowman and Littlefield, 2009.

Delano, Alonzo. *Alonzo Delano's California Correspondence: Being Letters Hitherto Uncollected from the Ottawa (Illinois) Free Trader and the New Orleans True Delta, 1849–1852*. Edited by Irving McKee. Sacramento: Sacramento Book Collectors Club, 1952.

Delgado, James P. *The Bensley Water System: The Politics, Planning, and Construction of San Francisco's First Water System*. San Francisco: Golden Gate National Recreation Area, 1980.

———. *To California by Sea: A Maritime History of the California Gold Rush*. Columbia: University of South Carolina Press, 1990.

Delgado, James P., and Russel Frank. "A Gold Rush Enterprise: Sam Ward, Charles Mersch, and the Storeship 'Niantic.'" *Huntington Library Quarterly* 16, no. 4 (1983): 321–30.

Della Torre, P. *The United States vs. Andrés Castillero: no. 420, "New Almaden": Transcript of the Record*. 4 vols. San Francisco: N.p., 1859–61.

Del Pozo, José. *Historia del vino chileno*. 3rd ed. Santiago: Editorial Universitaria, 2004.

Dening, Greg. *Beach Crossings: Voyaging across Times, Cultures, and Self*. Philadelphia: University of Pennsylvania Press, 2004.

———. "Performing on the Beaches of the Mind: An Essay." *History and Theory* 41(2002): 1–24.

Denning, Michael. "'The Special American Conditions': Marxism and American Studies." *American Quarterly* 38, no. 3 (1986): 356–80.

Den Ouden, P., and B. K. Boom. *Manual of Cultivated Conifers*. The Hague: Martinus Nijhoff, 1965.

De Ramón, Armando. *Biografías de chilenos, miembros de los poderes ejecutivo, legislativo y judicial, 1876–1973*, 4 vols. Santiago: Ediciones Universidad Católica de Chile, 1999.

Derbec, Etienne. *A French Journalist in the California Gold Rush: The Letters of Etienne Derbec*. Edited by Abraham P. Nasatir. Georgetown, CA: Talisman, 1964.

Deverell, William. *Whitewashed Adobe: The Rise of Los Angeles and the Remaking of Its Mexican Past*. Berkeley: University of California Press, 2004.

Deverell, William, and David Igler, eds. *A Companion to California History*. Malden, MA: Blackwell, 2008.

DeVoto, Bernard. "The West: A Plundered Province." *Harper's Magazine* 169 (August 1934): 355–64.

Dexter, A. Hersey. *Early Days in California*. Denver: Tribune-Republican Press, 1886.

Diaz A., Estrella. *Investigación participativa acerca de las trabajadores temporeras de la fruta*. San Bernardo, Chile: Centro El Canelo de Nos, Programa Mujer, 1991.

Díaz Bordenave, Juan, ed. *Información de extensión agrícola: Informe del seminario de información de extensión agrícola y economía doméstica para los países sudaméricanos*. Turrialba, Costa Rica: IICA, 1957.

Díaz-Corvalán, Eugenio. "Nuevo sindicalismo, viejos problemas: La concertación en Chile." *Nueva Sociedad*, no. 124 (March–April 1993): 114–21.

Di Castri, Francesco, and Harold A. Mooney, eds. *Mediterranean Type Ecosystems: Origins and Structure*. New York: Springer, 1973.

Dickson, Samuel. *San Francisco Kaleidoscope*. Stanford, CA: Stanford University Press, 1949.

Dillon, Peter. *Narrative and Successful Result of a Voyage in the South Seas Performed by Order of the Government of British India, to Ascertain the Actual Fate of La Pérouse's Expedition*. 2 vols. London: Hurst, Chance, 1829.

Dinges, John. *The Condor Years: How Pinochet and His Allies Brought Terrorism to Three Continents*. New York: New Press, 2004.

Dirección de Estadística. *Sinopsis estadística: Año 1920*. Santiago: Imprenta y Litografía Universo, 1921.

———. *Sinopsis geográfico-estadistica de la república de Chile, 1933*. Santiago: Imprenta y Litografía Universo, 1933.

Dixon, Chris, and David Drakakis-Smith. "The Pacific Asian Region: Myth or Reality." *Geografiska Annaler: Series B, Human Geography* 77, no. 2 (1995): 75–91.

Dlugosch, K. M., and I. M. Parker. "Founding Events in Species Invasions: Genetic Variation, Adaptive Evolution, and the Role of Multiple Introductions." *Molecular Ecology* 17, no. 1 (2007): 431–49.

Domeyko, Ignacio. *Araucanía y sus habitantes: Recuerdos de un viaje hecho a las provincias meridionales de Chile en los meses de enero y febrero de 1845*. Buenos Aires-Santiago: Editorial Francisco de Aguirre, 1971.

Doña-Reveco, Cristián Alberto. "In the Shadow of Empire and Nation: Chilean Migration to the United States since 1950." PhD diss., Michigan State University, 2012.

Dondlinger, Percy Tracy. *The Book of Wheat: An Economic History and Practical Manual of the Wheat Industry*. 2nd ed. New York: Orange Judd, 1919.

Donnici, Sandra, et al. "The Caranto Paleosol and Its Role in the Early Urbanization of Venice." *Geoarchaeology: An International Journal* 26, no. 4 (2011): 514–43.

Donoso, Ricardo. *Una amistad de toda la vida: Vicuña Mackenna y Mitre.* Santiago: Imprenta Cervantes, 1926.

Dore, Elizabeth. "Environment and Society: Long-Term Trends in Latin American Mining." *Environment and History* 6, no. 1 (2000): 1–29.

Dorfman, Ariel. *Americanos: Los pasos de Murieta.* Buenos Aires: Seix Barrel, 2009.

———. *The Nanny and the Iceberg.* New York: Farrar, Straus and Giroux, 1999.

Dorrance, John. "Legacy of the Red Ore: Almaden Quicksilver County Park." *Bay Nature* 2 (January–March 2002): 6–9.

Dosal, Paul J. *Doing Business with the Dictators: A History of the United Fruit Company in Guatemala, 1899–1944.* Wilmington, DE: SR Books, 1993.

Douglas, James, Jr. "Chile: Its Geography, People and Institutions." *Journal of the American Geographical Society of New York* 13 (1881): 59–92.

Douglass, John Aubrey. *The California Idea and American Higher Education: 1850 to the 1960 Master Plan.* Stanford, CA: Stanford University Press, 2000.

Downer, S. A. "The Quicksilver Mine of New Almaden." *Pioneer* 2 (October 1854): 220–28.

Dowsett, Charles Finch. *A Start in Life: A Journey across America; Fruit Farming in California.* London: Dowsett, 1891.

Dudden, Arthur Power. *The American Pacific: From the Old China Trade to the Present.* New York: Oxford University Press, 1992.

Duffield, Alexander James. *Peru in the Guano Age: Being a Short Account of a Recent Visit to the Guano Deposits with Some Reflections on the Money They Have Produced and the Uses to Which It Has Been Applied.* London: R. Bentley and Son, 1877.

Du Monceau de Bergendal Labarca, María Isabel. "The Role of Political Strategies of Mapuche Communities in Shaping Their Social and Natural Livelihoods." PhD diss., University of British Columbia, 2008.

Dunmire, William W. *Gardens of New Spain: How Mediterranean Plants and Foods Changed America.* Austin: University of Texas Press, 2004.

Dunmore, John. *Where Fate Beckons: The Life of Jean-François de la Pérouse.* Fairbanks: University of Alaska Press, 2007.

Dunsdorfs, Edgars. *The Australian Wheat-Growing Industry, 1788–1948.* Melbourne: University Press, 1956.

Durán Corsanego, Emilio. "¿Latinoamérica o Hispanoamérica?" *Razón Española,* no. 96 (July–August 1999): 61–62.

Durham, Walter T. *Volunteer Forty-Niners: Tennesseans and the California Gold Rush.* Nashville, TN: Vanderbilt University Press, 1997.

Dvorin, Eugene P. "The Chile-California Experiment." *Bulletin of the Atomic Scientists* 21, no. 9 (1965): 35–38.

———. "Foreign Aid by States." *National Civic Review* 53, no. 11 (2007): 585–622.

Dykstra, Robert R. "Body Counts and Murder Rates: The Contested Statistics of Western Violence." *Reviews in American History* 31, no. 4 (2003): 554–63.

Dzidzienyo, Anani, and Suzanne Oboler, eds. *Neither Enemies nor Friends: Latinos, Blacks, Afro-Latinos.* New York: Palgrave Macmillan, 2005.

Eckstein, Susan, and Timothy P. Wickham-Crowley, eds. *What Justice? Whose Justice? Fighting for Fairness in Latin America*. Berkeley: University of California Press, 2003.

Edmundson, William. *A History of the British Presence in Chile: From Bloody Mary to Charles Darwin and the Decline of British Influence*. New York: Palgrave Macmillan, 2009.

Eduardo Mendoza, Juan. *Las crisis de gobernabilidad y los conflictos vecinales desde la perspectiva de la seguridad y defensa: 2000–2006*. Santiago: Pontificia Universidad Católica de Chile, 2006.

Edwards, María Piedad Alliende. "La construcción de los ferrocarriles en Chile, 1850–1913." *Revista Austral de Ciencias Sociales* no. 5 (Spring 2001): 143–61.

Eldredge, Zoeth Skinner. *The Beginnings of San Francisco from the Expedition of Anza, 1774, to the City Charter of April 15, 1850; With Biographical and Other Notes*. 2 vols. San Francisco: Z. S. Eldredge, 1912.

Elegant, Robert S. *Pacific Destiny: Inside Asia Today*. New York: Crown, 1990.

Elena Cruz, M., and Rigoberto Rivera. *Cambios ecológicos y de poblamiento en el sector forestal chileno*. Santiago: GIA, 1983.

Elizalde Hevia, Antonio, and Mario González Gutiérrez. "Chile: ¿Autosuficiencia o 'autismo' energético? La tensión entre integración regional y sustentabilidad." *Revista Polis* 7, no. 21 (2008): 37–62.

Ellis, Henry Hiram. *From the Kennebec to California: Reminiscences of a California Pioneer*. Edited by Laurence R. Cook. Los Angeles: W. F. Lewis, 1959.

Ellison, William Henry. *A Self-Governing Dominion: California, 1849–1860*. Berkeley: University of California Press, 1950.

Encina, Francisco Antonio. *Historia de Chile: Desde la prehistoria hasta 1891*. 20 vols. Santiago: Editorial Nascimento, 1949.

Encina, Francisco Antonio, and Leopoldo Castedo. *Resumen de la historia de Chile*. 3rd ed. 3 vols. Santiago: Zig-Zag, 1959.

Engerman, Stanley L., ed. *Terms of Labor: Slavery, Serfdom, and Free Labor*. Stanford, CA: Stanford University Press, 1999.

Enock, Charles Reginald. *The Great Pacific Coast: Twelve Thousand Miles in the Golden West*. New York: Charles Scribner's Sons, 1910.

Epple, Juan Armando. *Actas de Palo Alto: La obra literaria de Fernando Alegría*. Santiago: Editorial Mosquito, 2000.

Escobar, Patricio, and Diego López. *El sector forestal en Chile: Crecimiento y precarizacion del empleo*. Santiago: Ediciones Tierra Mia, 1996.

Ethington, Philip J. *The Public City: The Political Construction of Urban Life in San Francisco, 1850–1900*. 2nd ed. Berkeley: University of California Press, 2001.

Evans, Albert S. *À la California: Sketch of Life in the Golden State*. San Francisco: A. L. Bancroft, 1873.

Evans, George W. *Mexican Gold Trail: The Journal of a Forty-Niner*. San Marino, CA: Huntington Library, 1945.

Evans, Henry Clay, Jr. *Chile and Its Relations with the United States*. Durham, NC: Duke University Press, 1927.

Evans, Oliver. *The Young Mill-Wright and Miller's Guide*. Philadelphia, 1795.

Eyer, Marguerite. "French Expansion into the Pacific in the 17th, 18th, and 19th Centuries." *Annual Publication of the Historical Society of Southern California* 11, no. 1 (1918): 5–23.

Fanning, L. M. "Foreign Trade in Petroleum." *Annals of the American Academy of Political and Social Science* 127 (September 1926): 84–93.

Faragher, John Mack. *Women and Men on the Overland Trail*. New Haven: Yale University Press, 1979.

Farish, Thomas Edwin. *The Gold Hunters of California*. Chicago: M. A. Donohue, 1904.

Farrer, Keith. *To Feed a Nation: A History of Australian Food Science and Technology*. Collingwood, Australia: CSIRO, 2005.

Farwell, Willard B. "The Society of California Pioneers, Part III." *Overland Monthly and Out West Magazine* 29, no. 172 (1897): 366–78.

Faugsted, George E., Jr. *The Chilenos in the California Gold Rush*. San Francisco: R&E Research Associates, 1973.

Felipe Zegarra, Luis. "Ferrocarriles en el Perú: ¿Qué tan importantes fueron?" *Revista Desarrollo y Sociedad* (Bogotá), no. 68 (July–December 2011): 213–59.

Feliú Cruz, Guillermo. *La abolición de la esclavitud en Chile: Estudio histórico y social*. Santiago: Universidad de Chile, 1942.

Ferguson, Eugene S. *Oliver Evans: Inventive Genius of the American Industrial Revolution*. Greenville, DE: Eleutherian Mills–Hagley Foundation, 1980.

Fetter, Frank. *Monetary Inflation in Chile*. Princeton, NJ: Princeton University Press, 1931.

Fiege, Mark. *Irrigated Eden: The Making of an Agricultural Landscape in the American West*. Seattle: University of Washington Press, 1999.

Finn, Janet L. *Tracing the Veins: Of Copper, Culture, and Community from Butte to Chuquicamata*. Berkeley: University of California Press, 1998.

Florentine, M. J., and D. J. Sanfilippo II. "Elemental Mercury Poisoning." *Clinical Pharmacy* 10, no. 3 (1991): 213–21.

Foerster, Rolf, and Sonia Montecino. *Organizaciones, líderes y contiendas mapuches (1900–1970)*. Santiago: Ediciones CEM, 1988.

Foner, Eric. *Free Soil, Free Labor, Free Men: The Ideology of the Republican Party before the Civil War*. 3rd rev. ed. New York: Oxford University Press, 1995.

Fontaine Aldunate, Arturo. *Los economistas y el Presidente Pinochet*. Santiago: Zig-Zag, 1988.

Forbes Magazine online. "The World's Billionaires (as of March 12, 2012)." Available at http://www.forbes.com/billionaires/#p_9_s_ao_All%20industries_All%20countries_All%20states_.

Foreign Office of Great Britain. *Reports by Her Majesty's Secretaries of Embassy and Legation on the Manufactures, Commerce, &c. of the Countries in Which They Reside, Part III*. London: Harrison and Sons, 1876.

Forney, J. M. *The Nitre Beds of the United States: Report on the Deposits of Nitrate of Soda Found in the Counties of Inyo and San Bernadino, State of California*. Los Angeles: W. A. Vandercook, 1892.

Foucrier, Annick, ed. *The French and the Pacific World, 17th–19th Centuries: Explorations, Migrations and Cultural Exchanges*. Burlington, VT: Ashgate, 2005.

Fox, Geoffrey. *Hispanic Nation-Culture, Politics, and the Constructing of Identity.* Tucson: University of Arizona Press, 1996.

Fradkin, Philip L. *The Seven States of California: A Natural and Human History.* Berkeley: University of California Press, 1995.

Frank, Andre Gunder. *Capitalism and Underdevelopment in Latin America: Historical Studies of Chile and Brazil.* New York: Monthly Review Press, 1967.

———. *World Accumulation, 1492–1789.* New York: Algora Press, 1978.

Freed, Donald, and Fred Landis. *Death in Washington: The Murder of Orlando Letelier.* Westport, CT: Lawrence Hill, 1980.

Frei Montalva, Eduardo. "Urgencies in Latin America: The Alliance That Lost Its Way." *Foreign Affairs* 45, no. 3 (1967): 437–48.

Frémont, John C. *Geographical Memoir upon Upper California, in Illustration of His Map of Oregon and California.* Washington, DC: Wendell and Van Benthuysen, 1848.

Frenkel, R. E. *Ruderal Vegetation along Some California Roadsides.* Berkeley: University California Press, 1977.

Frézier, Amédée François. *Relation du voyage de la Mer du Sud aux côtes du Chily et du Pérou, fait pendant les années 1712, 1713 & 1714. . . .* Paris: J. G. Nyon, 1716.

Frías L., D., et al. "Polymorphism and Geographic Variation of Flower Color in Chilean Populations of *Eschscholzia californica,*" *Plant Systematics and Evolution* 123, no. 3 (1975): 185–98.

Friedman, Milton. *Capitalism and Freedom.* Chicago: University of Chicago Press, 1962.

———. "Free Markets and the Generals." *Newsweek,* January 25, 1982, 59.

Friedman, Milton, and Rose D. Friedman. *Two Lucky People: Memoirs.* Chicago: University of Chicago Press, 1998.

Friis, Herman R., ed. *The Pacific Basin: A History of Its Geographical Exploration.* New York: American Geographical Society, 1967.

Fuller, Andrew Samuel. *The Forest Tree Culturist: A Treatise on the Cultivation of American Forest Trees, with Notes on the Most Valuable Foreign Species.* New York: Geo. E. and F. W. Woodward, 1866.

Fuller, Robert C. *Religion and Wine: A Cultural History of Wine Drinking in the United States.* Knoxville: University of Tennessee Press, 1996.

Funes Monzote, Reinaldo. *From Rainforest to Cane Field in Cuba: An Environmental History since 1492.* Translated by Alex Martin. Chapel Hill: University of North Carolina Press, 2008.

Galdames, Luis. *La evolución constitucional de Chile, 1810–1925.* Vol. 1. Santiago: Imprenta y Litografía Balcells, 1925.

———. *A History of Chile.* Translated by Isaac Joslyn Cox. Chapel Hill: University of North Carolina Press, 1941.

Gale, George. *Dying on the Vine: How Phylloxera Transformed Wine.* Berkeley: University of California Press, 2011.

Galeano, Eduardo. *Faces and Masks.* Translated by Cedric Belfrage. New York: Pantheon, 1987.

———. *The Open Veins of Latin America: Five Centuries of the Pillage of a Continent.* Translated by Cedric Belfrage. 2nd ed. New York: Monthly Review, 1997.

Galloway, James N., and Ellis B. Cowling. "Reactive Nitrogen and the World: 200 Years of Change." *AMBIO: A Journal of the Environment* 31 (March 2002): 64–71.

Galloway, James N., et al. "Nitrogen Fixation: Atmospheric Enhancement-Environmental Response." *Global Biogeochemical Cycles* 9 (June 1995): 235–52.

Gandy, Matthew. *Concrete and Clay: Reworking Nature in New York City.* Cambridge, MA: MIT Press, 2002.

Garcés Feliz, Eugenio. *Las ciudades del salitre: Un estudio de las oficinas salitreras en la región de Antofagasta.* Santiago: Editorial Universitaria, 1988.

García Elizalde, Pedro, and José Leyton. *Desarrollo frutícola y forestal en Chile y sus derivaciones sociales.* Santiago: CEPAL, 1986.

Gardiner, Howard C. *In Pursuit of the Golden Dream: Reminiscences of San Francisco and the Northern and Southern Mines, 1849–1857.* Edited by Dale L. Morgan. Stoughton, MA: Western Hemisphere, 1970.

Gardner, J. S. "Phylloxera." *Nature* 26, no. 654 (1882): 38.

Garr, Daniel J. "A Rare and Desolate Land: Population and Race in Hispanic California." *Western Historical Quarterly* 6, no. 2 (1975): 133–48.

Gates, Paul W. *California Ranchos and Farms, 1846–1862.* Madison: State Historical Society of Wisconsin, 1967.

Gatewood, James Vernando. "City Lights Books: The History of a Community." PhD diss., Brown University, 2008.

Gaune, Rafael, and Martín Lara, eds. *Historias de racismo y discriminación en Chile.* Santiago: Uqbar Editores, 2010.

Gay, Claudio. *Historia física y política de Chile.* 28 vols. Santiago: El Museo de Historia Natural, 1844–71.

Gazmuri, Cristián. *Eduardo Frei Montalva y su época.* 2 vols. Santiago: Aguilar Chilena de Ediciones, 2000.

———. *El "48" Chileno: Igualitarios, reformistas, radicales, masones y bomberos.* Santiago: Editorial Universitaria, 1992.

G. de Secada, C. Alexander. "Arms, Guano, and Shipping: The W. R. Grace Interests in Peru, 1865–1885." *Business History Review* 59, no. 4 (1985): 597–621.

Geisse G., Guillermo. "El medio ambiente como tema de cooperación Chile-California." *Ambiente y Desarrollo*, no. 64 (1994): 64–70.

Geraci, Victor W. "Fermenting a Twenty-First Century California Wine Industry." *Agricultural History* 78, no. 4 (2004): 438–65.

———. *Salud! The Rise of Santa Barbara's Wine Industry.* Reno: University of Nevada Press, 2004.

Gerber, Julien-François. "Conflicts over Industrial Tree Plantations in the South: Who, How and Why?" *Global Environmental Change* 21, no. 1 (2001): 165–76.

Giacobbi, Stephen. *Chile and Her Argonauts in the Gold Rush.* San Francisco: R and E Research Associates, 1974.

Gibson, Arrell Morgan. *Yankees in Paradise: The Pacific Basin Frontier.* Edited by John S. Whitehead. Albuquerque: University New Mexico Press, 1993.

Gibson, James R. *Feeding the Russian Fur Trade: Provisionment of the Okhotsk Seaboard and the Kamchatka Peninsula, 1639–1856.* Madison: University of Wisconsin Press, 1969.

Gilbert, Frank T. *The Illustrated Atlas and History of Yolo County*. San Francisco: DePue, 1879.

Giljum, Stefan. "Trade, Materials Flows, and Economic Development in the South: The Example of Chile." *Journal of Industrial Ecology* 8, nos. 1–2 (2004): 241–61.

Gill, Lesley. *The School of the Americas: Military Training and Political Violence in the Americas*. Durham, NC: Duke University Press, 2004.

Gil Navarro, Ramón. *The Gold Rush Diary of Ramón Gil Navarro*. Edited and translated by María del Carmen Ferreyra and David S. Reher. Lincoln: University of Nebraska Press, 2000.

Gilroy, Paul. *The Black Atlantic: Modernity and Double Consciousness*. London: Verso, 1993.

Glade, William P. *The Latin American Economies: A Study of Their Institutional Evolution*. New York: American Book, 1969.

Glennerster, Howard, and James Midgley, eds. *The Radical Right and the Welfare State: An International Assessment*. Hemel Hempstead, UK: Harvester-Wheatsheaf, 1991.

Glick, Philip. *The Administration of Technical Assistance: Growth in the Americas*. Chicago: University of Chicago Press, 1957.

Gobat, Michel. "The Invention of Latin America: A Transnational History of Anti-Imperialism, Democracy, and Race." *American Historical Review* 118, no. 5 (2013): 1345–75.

Goldbach, Heiner E., and Klaus Müller-Hohenstein. "Ecosystems of the IX Region of Chile: Influence of Land Use on Sustainability." In *Summary Reports of European Commission Supported STD-3 Projects (1992–1995)*. Wageningen, Netherlands: Technical Centre for Agricultural and Rural Cooperation, 1999.

Goldfrank, Walter L. "Chilean Fruit: The Maturation Process." Working Paper no. 16 of the Workshop on the Globalization of the Fresh Fruit and Vegetable System, University of California at Santa Cruz, December 6–9, 1991.

Goldman, Michael. *Imperial Nature: The World Bank and Social Justice Struggles in the Age of Globalization*. New Haven: Yale University Press, 2006.

Goldsby, Jacqueline. *A Spectacular Secret: Lynching in American Life and Literature*. Chicago: University of Chicago Press, 2006.

Gómez-Barris, Macarena. *Where Memory Dwells: Culture and State Violence in Chile*. Berkeley: University of California Press, 2009.

Gonzales-Day, Ken. *Lynching in the West, 1850–1953*. Durham, NC: Duke University Press, 2006.

González, Gilbert G. *Labor and Community: Mexican Citrus Worker Villages in a Southern California County*. Urbana: University of Illinois Press, 1994.

González, Marcial. *La Europa y la América; o, La emigración europea en sus relaciones con el engrandecimiento de las repúblicas americanas*. Santiago: Imprenta del Progreso, 1848.

González Miranda, Sergio. *Hombres y mujeres de la Pampa: Tarapacá en el ciclo del salitre*. 2nd ed. Santiago: LOM Ediciones, 2002.

Goode, Jamie. "Never the Same Since? Grafted v Ungrafted Vines." *World of Fine Wines*, no. 13 (2006): 73–77.

———. *The Science of Wine: From Vine to Glass*. Berkeley: University of California Press, 2005.

Goode, Jamie, and Sam Harrop. *Authentic Wine: Toward Natural and Sustainable Winemaking* Berkeley: University of California Press, 2011.

Goodman, David. *Gold Seeking: Victoria and California in the 1850s*. Stanford, CA: Stanford University Press, 1994.

Goodman, John Bartlett, III. *The Key to the Goodman Encyclopedia of the California Gold Rush Fleet*. Edited by Daniel Woodward. Los Angeles: Zamorano Club, 1992.

Goodwin, Paul B., Jr. "The Central Argentine Railway and the Economic Development of Argentina, 1854–1881." *Hispanic American Historical Review* 57, no. 4 (1977): 613–32.

Gootenberg, Paul. *Imagining Development: Economic Ideas in Peru's "Fictitious Prosperity" of Guano, 1840–1880*. Berkeley: University of California Press, 1993.

Gordon, T. R., A. J. Storer, and D. L. Wood. "The Pitch Canker Epidemic in California." *Plant Disease* 85, no. 11 (2001): 1128–39.

Grandin, Greg. *The Empire of Necessity: Slavery, Freedom, and Deception in the New World*. New York: Metropolitan Books, 2014.

———. *Empire's Workshop: Latin America, the United States, and the Rise of the New Imperialism*. 2nd ed. New York: Owl Books, 2007.

Greenberg, Amy S. *A Wicked War: Polk, Clay, Lincoln, and the 1846 U.S Invasion of Mexico*. New York: Alfred A. Knopf, 2012.

Greenhill, Robert G., and Rory M. Miller. "The Peruvian Government and the Nitrate Trade, 1873–1879." *Journal of Latin American Studies* 5, no. 1 (1973): 107–31.

Gregory, Tom. *History of Yolo County, California, with Biographical Sketches of the Leading Men and Women of the County Who Have Been Identified with Its Growth and Development from the Early Days to the Present*. Los Angeles: Historic Record Company, 1913.

Griffin, Charles C. "Francisco Encina and Revisionism in Chilean History." *Hispanic American Historical Review* 37, no. 1 (1957): 1–28.

Grivas, Theodore. *Military Governments in California, 1846–1850*. Glendale, CA: Arthur H. Clark, 1963.

Groves, R. H., and F. di Castri, eds. *Biogeography of Mediterranean Invasions*. New York: Cambridge University Press, 1991.

Grut, Mikael. *Pinus Radiata: Growth and Economics*. Capetown, South Africa: A. A. Balkema, 1970.

Gudde, Erwin G., and William Bright. *California Place Names: The Origin and Etymology of Current Geographical Names*. Berkeley: University of California Press, 2004.

Gunn, Lewis C., and Elizabeth Le Breton Gunn. *Records of a California Family: Journals and Letters of Lewis C. Gunn and Elizabeth Le Breton Gunn*. Edited by Anna Lee Marston. San Diego: A. L. Marston, 1928.

Gustafson, Axel Ferdinand. *Soils and Soil Management*. New York: McGraw-Hill, 1941.

Gutiérrez, Ramón, and Richard J. Orsi, eds. *Contested Eden: California before the Gold Rush*. Berkeley: University of California Press, 1998.

Gwynne, Robert N., and Cristóbal Kay. "Agrarian Change and the Democratic Transition in Chile: An Introduction." *Bulletin of Latin American Research* 16, no. 1 (1997): 3–10.

H. Iglesias, Julio. *José Santos Ossa: Perfiles de un conquistador, biografía.* Santiago: Editorial Cultura, 1945.

Haas, Lisbeth. *Conquests and Historical Identities in California, 1769–1936.* Berkeley: University of California Press, 1995.

Habel, Jan Christian, and Thorsten Assmann, eds. *Relict Species: Phylogeography and Conservation Biology.* New York: Springer, 2010.

Haber, Stephen. *Industry and Development: The Industrialization of Mexico, 1890–1940.* Stanford, CA: Stanford University Press, 1989.

Hackel, Steven W. *Children of Coyote, Missionaries of Saint Francis: Indian-Spanish Relations in Colonial California, 1769–1850.* Chapel Hill: University of North Carolina Press, 2005.

Hagen, Joel B. *An Entangled Bank: The Origins of Ecosystem Ecology.* New Brunswick, NJ: Rutgers University Press, 1992.

Haggard, Stephen, and Steven B. Webb. *Voting for Reform: Democracy, Political Liberalization, and Economic Adjustment.* New York: Oxford University Press for the World Bank, 1994.

Haine, E. A. *Railways across the Andes.* Boulder, CO: Pruett, 1981.

Hall, Linville J. *Around the Horn in '49: Journal of the Hartford Union Mining and Trading Company.* Wethersfield, CT: L. J. Hall, 1898.

Halsey, Frederic Magie. *Railway Expansion in Latin America.* New York: J. H. Oliphant, 1916.

Halttunen, Karen. *Confidence Men and Painted Women: A Study of Middle-Class Culture in America, 1830–1870.* New Haven: Yale University Press, 1982.

Hanke, Lewis, ed. *History of Latin American Civilization: Sources and Interpretations.* 2 vols. Boston: Little, Brown, 1967.

Hansen, A. A., D. K. Barnes, and R. R. Hill, Jr., eds. *Alfalfa and Alfalfa Improvement.* Madison, WI: American Society of Agronomy, 1988.

Harberger, Arnold C., and Richard Just. "A Conversation with Arnold Harberger." *Annual Review of Resource Economics* 4, no. 1 (2012): 1–26.

Harker, Mary Margaret. "'Honest Harry' Meiggs: Who Left San Francisco Discredited, Later to Become South America's Builder of Railroads." *California Historical Society Quarterly* 17, no. 3 (1938): 195–207.

Harlow, Neal. *California Conquered: War and Peace on the Pacific, 1846–1850.* Berkeley: University of California Press, 1982.

Harmon, Albert, Harlan Soeten, and Karl Kortum. *Notes on the Gold Rush Ships.* San Francisco: San Francisco Maritime Museum, 1963.

Harris Bucher, Gilberto. *Emigración y políticas gubernamentales en Chile durante el siglo diecinueve.* Valparaíso: Ediciones Universitarias de Valparaiso de la Universidad Católica de Valparaiso, 1996.

———. *Emigrantes e inmigrantes en Chile, 1810–1915: Nuevos aportes y notas revisionistas.* Valparaíso: Universidad de Playa Ancha Editorial, 2001.

———. *Tres estudios sobre marineria nacional y extranjera en el Chile del siglo XIX.* Valparaíso: Universidad de Playa Ancha Editorial, 2002.

Hart, James D. *New Englanders in Nova Albion: Some 19th Century Views of California.* Boston: Trustees of the Public Library of the City of Boston, 1976.

Harte, Bret. *Bret Harte's California: Letters to the Springfield Republican and Christian Register, 1866–67.* Edited by Gary Scharnhorst. Albuquerque: University of New Mexico Press, 1990.

Hartog, Hendrik. *Public Property and Private Power: The Corporation of the City of New York in American Law, 1730–1870.* Chapel Hill: University of North Carolina Press, 1983.

Hartwig, Fernando. *Federico Albert, pionero del desarrollo forestal de Chile.* Santiago: Editorial Universidad de Talca, 1999.

Harvey, David. *The Condition of Postmodernity: An Enquiry into the Origins of Cultural Change.* Cambridge, MA: Blackwell, 1990.

———. "What Kind of Geography for What Kind of Public Policy?" *Transactions of the Institute of British Geographers,* no. 63 (1974): 18–24.

Haskell, Sidney B. "Fertilizer Use in the United States." *Annals of the American Academy of Political and Social Science* 117 (1925): 265–70.

Haughney, Diane. "Neoliberal Policies, Logging Companies, and Mapuche Struggle for Autonomy in Chile." *Latin American and Caribbean Ethnic Studies* 2, no. 2 (2007): 141–60.

Hawkes, John G. "A Chilean Wild Potato Species and the Publication of Its Name, *Solanum maglia* (Solanaceae)." *Taxon* 42, no. 3 (1993): 671–73.

Hayes, Benjamin I. *Pioneer Notes from the Diaries of Judge Benjamin Hayes, 1849–1875.* Los Angeles: Privately printed, 1929.

Hayes-Bautista, David E., et al. "Empowerment, Expansion, and Engagement: *Las Juntas Patrióticas* in California, 1848–1869." *California History* 85, no. 1 (2007): 4–23.

Heffer, Jean. *The United States and the Pacific: History of a Frontier.* Translated by W. Donald Wilson. Notre Dame, IN: University Notre Dame Press, 2002.

Heizer, Robert F., ed. *Handbook of North American Indians.* 20 vols. Washington, DC: Smithsonian Institution, 1978–2008.

Held Winkler, Emilio. *Colonización alemana del sur de Chile: Documentación de su origén.* Valparaíso: Talleres de Alba, 1996.

Helper, Hinton Rowan. *The Land of Gold: Reality versus Fiction.* Baltimore: Henry Taylor–Sherwood, 1855.

"Henry Meiggs: The Famous Railroad Builder." *Phrenological Journal and Science of Health* 66, no. 1 (1878): 15–18.

Hernández Cornejo, Roberto. *Los chilenos en San Francisco de California.* 2 vols. Valparaíso: Imprenta San Rafael, 1930.

———. *El roto chileno: Bosquejo histórico de actualidad.* Valparaíso: Imprenta San Rafael, 1929.

Hersh, Seymour M. *The Price of Power: Kissinger in the Nixon White House.* New York: Summit Books, 1983.

Heyene, Roberto. *El bandido chileno Joaquín Murieta en California.* Translated by Carlos Morla Vicuña. Santiago: Imprenta de la República, 1879.

Heyman, Max L., Jr. *Prudent Soldier: A Biography of Major General E.R.S. Canby, 1817–1873.* Glendale, CA: Arthur H. Clark, 1959.

Hillman, Joseph. *The Cultivation of Citrus Fruits: A Short Treatise with Special Reference to Fertilization*. New York: W. S. Meyers, 1907.

Hirata, Lucie Cheng. "Free, Indentured, Enslaved: Chinese Prostitutes in Nineteenth-Century America." *Signs* 5, no. 1 (1979): 3–29.

Hitchman, James H. *A Maritime History of the Pacific Coast, 1540–1980*. Lanham, MD: University Press of America, 1990.

Hittell, John Shertzer. *All about California and the Inducements to Settle There*. San Francisco: California Immigrant Union, 1870.

———. *A History of the City of San Francisco and Incidentally the State of California*. San Francisco: A. L. Bancroft, 1878.

———. *Mining in the Pacific States of North America*. San Francisco: H. H. Bancroft, 1861.

———. *Resources of California, Comprising Agriculture, Mining, Geography, Climate, Commerce, etc. and the Past and Future Development of the State*. San Francisco: A. Roman, 1863.

Hobhouse, Henry. *Seeds of Change: Six Plants That Transformed Mankind*. 5th ed. Emeryville, CA: Shoemaker and Hoard, 2005.

Holdich, Thomas Hungerford. *The Countries of the King's Award*. London: Hurst and Blackett, 1904.

Holinski, Alexandre. *La Californie et les routes interocéaniques*. 2nd ed. Brussels: A. Labroue, 1853.

Hoover, Mildred Brooke, et al. *Historic Spots in California*. Edited by Douglas E. Kyle. 5th ed. Stanford, CA: Stanford University Press, 2002.

Hoover Institution Fellows Profile. "Milton Friedman." Available at http://www.hoover.org/fellows/10630.

Hopkins, Caspar T. "The California Recollections of Caspar T. Hopkins (*Continued*)." *California Historical Society Quarterly* 25, no. 4 (1946): 325–46.

Horan, Elizabeth. "California Dreaming: Gabriela Mistral's Lucid Cold War Paranoia." *White Rabbit: English Studies in Latin America*, no. 3 (August 2012): 1–33.

Horden, Peregrine, and Nicholas Purcell. *The Corrupting Sea: A Study of Mediterranean History*. Malden, MA: Blackwell, 2000.

Hornborg, Alf. "Zero-Sum World: Challenges in Conceptualizing Environmental Load Displacement and Ecologically Unequal Exchange in the World-System." *International Journal of Comparative Sociology* 50, nos. 3–4 (2009): 237–62.

Hornborg, Alf, and Carole L. Crumley, eds. *The World System and the Earth System: Global Socioenvironmental Change and Sustainability since the Neolithic*. Walnut Creek, CA: Left Coast, 2007.

Hornborg, Alf, Brett Clark, and Kenneth Hermele, eds. *Ecology and Power: Struggles over Land and Material Resources in the Past, Present, and Future*. New York: Routledge, 2012.

House, S. "The Man Who Made Pines: David Douglas and His Conifer Introductions from the Pacific Northwest." *Acta Horticulturae*, no. 615 (September 2003): 281–88.

Hu-DeHart, Evelyn. "Coolies, Shopkeepers, Pioneers: The Chinese of Mexico and Peru (1849–1930)." *Amerasia* 15, no. 2 (1989): 91–116.

Hughes, J. Donald. *An Environmental History of the World: Humankind's Changing Role in the Community of Life*. 2nd ed. New York: Routledge, 2009.

Hugo, Victor. *Napoléon le petit*. Amsterdam: I. Stemvers, 1853.

Human Rights Watch and Observatorio de Derechos de los Pueblos Indígenas. "Undue Process: Terrorism Trials, Military Courts, and the Mapuche in Southern Chile." *Human Rights Watch* 16, no. 5 (B) (2004): 1–63.

Humboldt, Alexander von. *Political Essay on the Kingdom of New Spain*. Translated by John Black. 2 vols. New York: I. Riley, 1811.

Hunsinger, George, ed. *Torture Is a Moral Issue: Christians, Jews, Muslims, and People of Conscience Speak Out*. Cambridge, UK: Wm. B. Eerdmans, 2008.

Hunt, Rockwell D. *California Firsts*. San Francisco: Fearon, 1957.

Huntley, Henry Veel. *California, Its Gold and Its Inhabitants*. London: T. C. Newby, 1856.

Hurtado, Albert L. "'Hardly a Farm House—A Kitchen without Them': Indian and White Households on the California Borderland Frontier in 1860." *Western Historical Quarterly* 13 (July 1982): 245–70.

———. *Intimate Frontiers: Sex, Gender, and Culture in Old California*. Albuquerque: University New Mexico Press, 1999.

———. *John Sutter: A Life on the North American Frontier*. Norman: University of Oklahoma Press, 2006.

Hutchinson, Thomas Joseph. *Two Years in Peru, with Exploration of Its Antiquities*. 2 vols. London: Sampson Low, Marston, Low, and Searle, 1873.

Hutchison, Elizabeth Quay. *Labors Appropriate to Their Sex: Gender, Labor, and Politics in Urban Chile, 1900–1930*. Durham, NC: Duke University Press, 2001.

Hutton, William R. *Glances at California, 1847–1853: The Diary and Letters of William Rich Hutton*. Edited by Willard O. Waters. San Marino, CA: Huntington Library, 1942.

Idris-Soven, Ahamed, Elizabeth Idris-Soven, and Mary K. Vaughan, eds. *The World as a Company Town: Multinational Corporations and Social Change*. The Hague: Mouton, 1978.

Igler, David. *The Great Ocean: Pacific Worlds from Captain Cook to the Gold Rush*. New York: Oxford University Press, 2013.

———. *Industrial Cowboys: Miller and Lux and the Transformation of the Far West, 1850–1920*. Berkeley: University of California Press, 2001.

Ignatiev, Noel, and John Garvey, eds. *Race Traitor*. New York: Routledge, 1996.

Isenberg, Andrew C. *Mining California: An Ecological History*. New York: Hill and Wang, 2005.

Ivanov, A. I. *Alfalfa [Lyutserna]*. Edited by D. D. Brezhnev and translated by A. K. Dhote. New Delhi: Amerind, 1988.

Jackson, Alfred T. *The Diary of a Forty-Niner*. Edited by Chauncey L. Canfield. 2nd ed. New York: Houghton Mifflin, 1920.

Jackson, Robert Howard, and Edward Castillo. *Indians, Franciscans, and Spanish Colonization: The Impact of the Mission System on California Indians*. Albuquerque: University of New Mexico Press, 1995.

Jacobsen, Nils. *Mirages of Transition: The Peruvian Altiplano, 1780–1930*. Berkeley: University of California Press, 1993.

Janick, Jules. "Plant Exploration: From Queen Hatshepsut to Sir Joseph Banks." *HortScience* 42, no. 2 (2007): 191–96.

Jansen, Sarah. "An American Insect in Imperial Germany: Visibility and Control in Making the Phylloxera in Germany, 1870–1914." *Science in Context* 13, no. 1 (2000): 31–70.

Jarvis, Lovell S. *Chilean Agriculture under Military Rule.* Berkeley, CA: Institute of International Studies, 1985.

Jelinek, Lawrence J. *Harvest Empire: A History of California Agriculture.* San Francisco: Boyd and Fraser, 1979.

Jiménez, Alejandra, et al. "Do Climatically Similar Regions Contain Similar Alien Floras? A Comparison between the Mediterranean Areas of Central Chile and California." *Journal of Biogeography* 35, no. 4 (2008): 614–24.

Johnson, Chalmers A. *Blowback: The Costs and Consequences of American Empire.* New York: Metropolitan Books, 2000.

——. *Nemesis: The Last Days of the American Republic.* New York: Metropolitan Books, 2006.

——. *The Sorrows of Empire: Militarism, Secrecy, and the End of the Republic.* New York: Metropolitan Books, 2004.

Johnson, David A. "Vigilance and the Law: The Moral Authority of Popular Justice in the Far West." *American Quarterly* 33, no. 5 (1981): 558–86.

Johnson, John J. "Early Relations of the United States with Chile." *Pacific Historical Review* 13 (1944): 260–70.

——. *Pioneer Telegraphy in Chile, 1852–1876.* Stanford, CA: Stanford University Press, 1948.

Johnson, Susan Lee. *Roaring Camp: The Social World of the California Gold Rush.* New York: W. W. Norton, 2000.

Johnston, Robert D. "Beyond 'The West': Regionalism, Liberalism and the Evasion of Politics in the New Western History." *Rethinking History* 2 (1998): 239–77.

Jolly, Michelle E. "Inventing the City: Gender and the Politics of Everyday Life in Gold-Rush San Francisco, 1848–1869." PhD diss., University of California, San Diego, 1998.

Jones, Dave. "Reporter's Notebook from the Chilean President's Visit to UC Davis." June 27, 2008. Available at http://dateline.ucdavis.edu/dl_detail.lasso?id=10480.

Kahn, Judd. *Imperial San Francisco: Politics and Planning in an American City, 1897–1906.* Lincoln: University of Nebraska Press, 1979.

Kamat, Sangeeta. "The Privatization of Public Interest: Theorizing NGO Discourse in a Neoliberal Era." *Review of International Political Economy* 11, no. 1 (2004): 155–76.

Kaplan, Wendy. *California Design, 1930–1965: Living a Modern Way.* Cambridge, MA: MIT Press, 2011.

Kapur, Devesh, John P. Lewis, and Richard Webb. *The World Bank: Its First Half Century.* 2 vols. Washington, DC: Brookings Institution, 1997.

Keeley, Jon E. "Native American Impacts on Fire Regimes of the California Coastal Ranges." *Journal of Biogeography* 29, no. 3 (2002): 303–20.

Kelly, Mike, Ellie Wagner, and Peter Warner, eds. *California Exotic Pest Plant Council—1997 Symposium Proceedings.* Vol. 3. Berkeley: California Exotic Pest Plant Council, 1997.

Kelly, William. *An Excursion to California over the Prairie, Rocky Mountains and Ranches of That Country.* 2 vols. London: Chapman and Hall, 1851.

———. *A Stroll through the Diggings of California.* London: Simms and M'Intyre, 1852.

Kenny, William Robert, Jr. "History of the Sonora Mining Region of California, 1848–1860." PhD diss., University of California, Berkeley, 1955.

Kiernan, Victor G. "Chile from War to Revolution, 1879–1891." *History Workshop Journal* 34, no. 1 (1992): 72–91.

———. "Foreign Interests in the War of the Pacific." *Hispanic American Historical Review* 35 (February 1955): 1–36.

Kimball, Nell. *Nell Kimball: Her Life as an American Madam, by Herself.* Edited by Stephen Longstreet. New York: Macmillan, 1970.

Kindell, Alexandra. "Settling the Sunset Land: California and Its Family Farmers, 1850s–1890s." PhD diss., Iowa State University, 2006.

Kip, Leonard. *California Sketches: With Recollections of the Gold Mines.* Reprint ed. Los Angeles: N. A. Kovach, 1946.

Kirkendall, Andrew J. "Kennedy Men and the Alliance for Progress in LBJ Era Brazil and Chile." *Diplomacy and Statecraft* 18, no. 4 (2007): 745–72.

Kirker, Harold. "El Dorado Gothic." *California Historical Society Quarterly* 38, no. 1 (1959): 35.

Klaiber, Jeffrey L. "Los 'cholos' y los 'rotos': Actitudes raciales durante la Guerra del Pacífico." *Histórica* 2, no. 1 (1978): 27–37.

Klein, Naomi. *The Shock Doctrine: The Rise of Disaster Capitalism.* New York: Metropolitan Books/Henry Holt, 2007.

Klubock, Thomas Miller. *Contested Communities: Class, Gender and Politics in Chile's El Teniente Copper Mine, 1904–1951.* Durham, NC: Duke University Press, 1998.

———. *La Frontera: Forests and Ecological Conflict in Chile's Frontier Territory.* Durham, NC: Duke University Press, 2014.

———. "The Politics of Forests and Forestry on Chile's Southern Frontier, 1880s–1940s." *Hispanic American Historical Review* 86, no. 3 (2006): 535–70.

Knight, Alan. "Peasants into Patriots: Thoughts on the Making of the Mexican Nation." *Mexican Studies/Estudios Mexicanos* 10, no. 1 (1994): 135–61.

Knight, H. G. "Research in the Bureau of Chemistry and Soils." *Scientific Monthly* 36 (April 1933): 308–17.

Knower, Daniel. *Adventures of a Forty-Niner.* Albany, NY: Weed-Parsons, 1894.

Knowles, Tim, and Liz Sharples. "The History and Development of Chilean Wines." *International Journal of Wine Marketing* 14, no. 2 (2002): 7–16.

Knudsen, Jan Sverre. "Dancing Cueca 'with Your Coat On': The Role of Traditional Chilean Dance in an Immigrant Community." *British Journal of Ethnomusicology* 10, no. 2 (2001): 61–83.

Komareck, E. V. *Proceedings, California Tall Timbers Fire Ecology Conference.* Tallahassee, FL: Tall Timbers Research Station, 1968.

Kornbluh, Peter. *The Pinochet File: A Declassified Dossier on Atrocity and Accountability.* New York: New Press, 2003.

Korhonen, Pekka. "The Pacific Age in World History." *Journal of World History* 7, no. 1 (1996): 41–70.

Körner, Emilio, and J. Boonen Rivera. *Estudios sobre historia militar*. Santiago: Imprenta Cervantes, 1887.

Kotler, Neil G., ed. *Sharing Innovation: Global Perspectives on Food, Agriculture, and Rural Development*. Washington, DC: Smithsonian Institution Press, 1990.

Krebs, John Stuart. "Monterey Pine: An Introduced Species in Chile." PhD diss., University of Colorado, 1973.

Kropp, Phoebe S. *California Vieja: Culture and Memory in a Modern American Place*. Berkeley: University of California Press, 2006.

Kuhlmann, Charles Byron. *The Development of the Flour-Milling Industry in the United States with Special Reference to the Industry in Minneapolis*. Boston: Houghton Mifflin, 1929.

Kurtz, Marcus J. "Chile's Neo-Liberal Revolution: Incremental Decisions and Structural Transformation, 1973–89." *Journal of Latin American Studies* 31, no. 2 (1999): 399–427.

Ladurie, Emmanuel Le Roy, and Micheline Baulant. "Grape Harvests from the Fifteenth through the Nineteenth Centuries." *Journal of Interdisciplinary History* 10, no. 4 (1980): 839–49.

Lai, Walton Look. "Chinese Indentured Labor: Migrations to the British West Indies in the Nineteenth Century." *Amerasia* 15, no. 2 (1989): 117–38.

Laite, Julian. *Industrial Development and Migrant Labor in Latin America*. Austin: University of Texas Press, 1981.

Lamar, Howard, ed. *The New Encyclopedia of the American West*. New Haven: Yale University Press, 1998.

Lang, M. F. "New Spain's Mining Depression and the Supply of Quicksilver from Peru, 1600–1700." *Hispanic American Historical Review* 48, no. 4 (1968): 632–41.

Langley, Henry G., ed. *San Francisco Directory for the Year Commencing October 1864*. San Francisco: H. S. Crocker, 1864.

Lansing, Marion Florence. *Against All Odds: Pioneers of South America*. Freeport, NY: Books for Libraries, 1969.

La Pérouse, Jean-François de Galaup de. *The Journal of Jean-François de Galaup de La Pérouse, 1785–1788*. Edited and translated by John Dunmore. 2 vols. London: Hakluyt Society, 1994–95.

Lapp, Rudolph M. *Blacks in Gold Rush California*. New Haven: Yale University Press, 1977.

Larkin, Thomas. *The Larkin Papers*. Edited by George P. Hammond. 11 vols. Berkeley: University of California Press, 1962.

Larraín, Jorge. "Changes in Chilean Identity: Thirty Years after the Military Coup." *Nations and Nationalism* 12, no. 2 (2006): 321–38.

Larson, Brooke. *Trials of Nation Making: Liberalism, Race, and Ethnicity in the Andes, 1810–1910*. New York: Cambridge University Press, 2004.

Latta, Alex, and Beatriz E. Cid Aguayo. "Testing the Limits: Neoliberal Ecologies from Pinochet to Bachelet." *Latin American Perspectives* 39, no. 4 (2012): 163–80.

Latta, Alex, and Hannah Wittman, eds. *Environment and Citizenship in Latin America: Natures, Subjects and Struggles.* New York: Berghan, 2012.

Lausent-Herrera, Isabelle. "The Chinatown in Peru and the Changing Peruvian Chinese Community(ies)." *Journal of Chinese Overseas* 7, no. 1 (2011): 69–113.

Lavín, Joaquín. *Chile, a Quiet Revolution.* Santiago: Zig-Zag, 1988.

LaWall, Charles H. *Four Thousand Years of Pharmacy: An Outline History of Pharmacy and the Allied Sciences.* Philadelphia: J. B. Lippincott, 1927.

Lawrence, Vera Brodsky. "Henry Meiggs: Maverick Entrepreneur." *19th-Century Music* 9, no. 1 (1985): 26–41.

Lawton, Harry W., Philip J. Wilke, Mary DeDecker, and William M. Mason. "Agriculture among the Paiute of Owens Valley." *Journal of California Anthropology* 3, no. 1 (1976): 13–49.

Leadbeater, Charles. *Britain: The California of Europe?* London: Demos, 1999.

Lee, Erika. "The 'Yellow Peril' and Asian Exclusion in the Americas." *Pacific Historical Review* 76, no. 4 (2007): 537–62.

Leger, Elizabeth Anne. "Local Adaptation, Increased Colonization Ability, and Resistance to Natural Enemies: The Invasion of the California Poppy (*Eschscholzia californica*) in Chile." PhD diss., University of California, Davis, 2004.

Leggett, Herbert B. *Early History of Wine Production in California.* San Francisco: Wine Institute, 1941.

Letelier, Orlando, Joan E. Garcés, and Saul Landau. *Orlando Letelier: Testimonio y vindicación.* Madrid: Siglo Veintiuno Editores, 1995.

———. "The 'Chicago Boys' in Chile: Economic 'Freedom's' Awful Toll." *Nation*, August 28, 1976, 137–42.

Letts, John S. *California Illustrated: Including a Description of the Panama and Nicaragua Routes; By a Returned Californian.* New York: W. Holdredge, 1852.

Lévesque, Rodrigue. *Railways of Peru.* 3 vols. Gatineau, QC: Lévesque, 2008.

Levinson, Jerome, and Juan de Onís. *The Alliance That Lost Its Way: A Critical Report on the Alliance for Progress.* Chicago: Quadrangle Books, 1970.

Lewis, N. B., and I. S. Ferguson. *Management of Radiata Pine.* Stoneham, MA: Butterworth-Heinemann, 1993.

Lewis, Ronald L. *Transforming the Appalachian Countryside: Railroads, Deforestation, and Social Change in West Virginia, 1880–1920.* Chapel Hill: University of North Carolina Press, 1998.

Limerick, Patricia Nelson. *The Legacy of Conquest: The Unbroken Past of the American West.* New York: W. W. Norton, 1987.

———. *Something in the Soil: Field-Testing the New Western History.* New York: W. W. Norton, 2000.

Limerick, Patricia Nelson, Clyde A. Milner II, and Charles E. Rankin, eds. *Trails: Toward a New Western History.* Lawrence: University Press of Kansas, 1991.

Lincoln, Margarette, ed. *Science and Exploration in the Pacific: European Voyages to the Southern Oceans in the Eighteenth Century.* Rochester, NY: Boydell and Brewer, 1998.

Linder, Staffan Burenstam. *The Pacific Century: Economic and Political Consequences of Asian-Pacific Dynamism.* Stanford, CA: Stanford University Press, 1986.

Bibliography

283

Linebaugh, Peter, and Marcus Rediker. *The Many-Headed Hydra: Sailors, Slaves, Commoners, and the Hidden History of the Revolutionary Atlantic.* Boston: Beacon, 2000.

Lipsitz, George. "The Struggle for Hegemony." *Journal of American History* 75, no. 1 (1988): 146–50.

Lohmann Villena, Guillermo. *Las minas de Huancavelica en los siglos XVI y XVII.* Seville: Escuela de Estudios Hispano-Americanos, 1949.

Lomas, Charles W. "Dennis Kearney: Case Study in Demagoguery." *Quarterly Journal of Speech* 41, no. 3 (1955): 234–42.

López Urrutia, Carlos. *Breve historia naval de Chile.* Buenos Aires: Editorial Francisco de Aguirre, 1976.

———. *Chilenos in California: A Study of the 1850, 1852 and 1860 Censuses.* San Francisco: R and E Research Associates, 1973.

———. *Episodios Chilenos en California: 1849–1860.* Valparaíso: Ediciones Universitarias de Valparaíso, 1975.

———. *Los Atherton.* Atherton, CA: Talleres de Menlo College, 1973.

Lorenzo S., Santiago, Gilberto Harris B., and Nelson Vásquez L. *Vida, costumbres y espíritu empresarial de los porteños: Valparaíso en el siglo XIX.* Viña del Mar: Instituto de Historia, Universidad Católica de Valparaíso, 2000.

Lotchin, Roger W. *San Francisco, 1846–1856: From Hamlet to City.* New York: Oxford University Press, 1974.

Lövei, Gábor L. "Biodiversity: Global Change through Invasion." *Nature* 388, no. 6643 (1997): 627–28.

Loveman, Brian. *Chile: The Legacy of Hispanic Capitalism.* 3rd ed. New York: Oxford University Press, 2001.

———. "Critique of Arnold J. Bauer's 'Rural Workers in Spanish America: Problems of Peonage and Oppression.'" *Hispanic American Historical Review* 59, no. 3 (1979): 478–85.

———. "Military Dictatorship and Political Opposition in Chile, 1973–1986." *Journal of Interamerican Studies and World Affairs* 28, no. 4 (1986–87): 1–38.

Lucett, Edward. *Rovings in the Pacific, from 1837 to 1849; with a Glance at California, by a Merchant Long Resident in Tahiti.* 2 vols. London: Longman, Brown, Green, and Longmans, 1851.

Lynch, John. *The Spanish American Revolutions, 1808–1826.* London: Weidenfeld and Nicolson, 1973.

MacCurdy, Rahno Mabel. *The History of the California Fruit Growers Exchange.* Los Angeles: G. Rice and Sons, 1925.

Mackay, David. *In the Wake of Cook: Exploration, Science, and Empire, 1780–1801.* New York: St. Martin's, 1985.

MacNeil, Karen. *The Wine Bible.* New York: Workman, 2001.

Madden, Jerome. *The Lands of the Southern Pacific Railroad Company of California; with General Information on the Resources of Southern California.* San Francisco: Jerome Madden and S.P.R.R., 1880.

Madley, Benjamin L. "American Genocide: The California Indian Catastrophe, 1846–1873." PhD diss., Yale University, 2009.

———."'Unholy Traffic in Human Blood and Souls': Systems of California Indian Servitude under United States Rule." *Pacific Historical Review* 83, no. 4 (2015):626–67.

Magliari, Michael. "Cave Johnson Couts and the Binding of Indian Workers in California, 1850–1867." *Pacific Historical Review* 73, no. 3 (2004): 349–90.

Malinowski, Ernesto. *Ferro-carril central transandino: Informe del ingeniero en jefe, seccion del Callao y Lima a la Oroya y presupuesto de la obra.* Lima: Imprenta de "El Nacional," 1869.

Mallon, Florencia. *Courage Tastes of Blood: The Mapuche Community of Nicolás Ailío and the Chilean State, 1906–2001.* Durham, NC: Duke University Press, 2005.

Mamalakis, Markos J. *Historical Statistics of Chile.* 6 vols. Westport, CT: Greenwood, 1978–89.

———. "Historical Statistics of Chile: An Introduction." *Latin American Research Review* 13, no. 2 (1978): 127–37.

Mann, Charles. *1493: Uncovering the World Columbus Created.* New York: Alfred A. Knopf, 2011.

Margolin, Malcolm, ed. *Monterey in 1786: The Journals of Jean-François de La Pérouse.* Berkeley, CA: Heyday Books, 1989.

Marín Vicuña, Santiago. *Los Ferrocarriles de Chile.* 4th ed. Santiago: Imprenta Cervantes, 1916.

Marks, Paula Mitchell. *Precious Dust: The Saga of the American Gold Rush Era, 1848–1900.* 2nd ed. Lincoln: University of Nebraska Press, 1998.

Marsh, George Perkins. *Man and Nature: or, Physical Geography as Modified by Human Action.* New York: C. Scribner, 1864.

Marten, Effie ElFreda. "The Development of Wheat Culture in the San Joaquin Valley, 1846–1900." MA thesis, University of California, Berkeley, 1922.

Marter, J. Gilbert van. "The New England of South America." *Outlook* 86, no. 8 (1907): 410–21.

Martí, José. *En las entrañas del monstruo.* Havana: El Centro de Estudios Marianos, 1984.

Martínez Caraza, Leopoldo. *La intervención norteamericana en México, 1846–1848: Historia político-militar de la pérdida de gran parte del territorio mexicano.* México: Panorama Editorial, 1981.

Martínez Estrada, Ezequiel. *X-Ray of the Pampa.* 2nd ed. Translated by Alain Swietlicki. Austin: University of Texas Press, 1971.

Marx, Karl. *Capital: Critique of Political Economy.* Translated by Ben Fowkes. 3 vols. London: Penguin Books, 1990.

———. *Grundrisse: Foundations of the Critique of Political Economy.* Translated by Martin Nicolaus. London: Penguin, 1973.

Marx, Karl, and Friedrich Engels. *The Collected Works of Marx and Engels.* 2nd ed. 50 vols. New York: International Publishers, 2001.

Massey, Doreen. "Negotiating Disciplinary Boundaries." *Current Sociology* 47, no. 4 (1999): 5–12.

Mathes, W. Michael. "The Mythological Geography of California: Origins, Development, Confirmation and Disappearance." *Americas* 45, no. 3 (1989): 315–41.

Matilla Tascón, Antonio. *Historia de las minas de Almadén*. Madrid: Sucesores de Rivadeneyra, 1987.

Matsuda, Matt K. "AHR Forum: The Pacific." *American Historical Review* 111 (2006): 758–80.

———. *Pacific Worlds: A History of Seas, Peoples, and Cultures*. New York: Cambridge University Press, 2012.

Matte, Eliodoro. "Commencement Speech by Mr. Eliodoro Matte, MBA 1972." Convocation Ceremony for the University of Chicago Graduate School of Business, June 15, 2008, p. 4. Available at http://www.chicagobooth.edu/news/2008–06–17_matte.aspx.

Mattoon, Robert H., Jr. "Railroads, Coffee, and the Growth of Big Business in Sao Paulo, Brazil." *Hispanic American Historical Review* 57, no. 2 (1977): 273–95.

Maurice, Jacques, and Marie-Claire Zimmerman, eds. *París y el mundo ibérico e iberoamericano: Actas del XXVIIIo Congreso de la Sociedad de hispanistas franceses, París, 21, 22 y 23 de marzo de 1997*. Paris: Université Paris X-Nanterre, 1998.

Maybury-Lewis, David, Theodore Macdonald, and Biorn Maybury-Lewis, eds. *Manifest Destinies and Indigenous Peoples*. Cambridge, MA: Harvard University Press, 2009.

McCarthy, Dennis Michael Patrick. *International Business History: A Contextual Approach*. Westport, CT: Greenwood, 1994.

McClain, Charles J., Jr. "The Chinese Struggle for Civil Rights in Nineteenth Century America: The First Phase, 1850–1870." *California Law Review* 72, no. 4 (1984): 529–68.

McClellan, Rolander Guy. *The Golden State: A History of the Region West of the Rocky Mountains. . . .* Philadelphia: W. Flint, 1872.

McCollum, William. *California as I Saw It*. Edited by Dale L. Morgan. Los Gatos, CA: Talisman, 1960.

———. *California as I Saw It: Its New Cities and Villages; Its Rapid Accession of Population; Its Soil, Climate, and Productions; Pencillings by the Way of Its Gold and Gold Diggers! And Incidents of Travel by Land and Water*. Buffalo, NY: George H. Derby, 1850.

McEvoy, Arthur F. *The Fisherman's Problem: Ecology and Law in the California Fisheries, 1850–1980*. New York: Cambridge University Press, 1986.

McGinty, Brian. *Strong Wine: The Life and Legend of Agoston Haraszthy*. Stanford, CA: Stanford University Press, 1998.

McGirr, Lisa. *Suburban Warriors: The Origins of the New American Right*. Princeton, NJ: Princeton University Press, 2001.

McGrath, Roger D. "A Violent Birth: Disorder, Crime and Law Enforcement, 1849–1890." *California History* 81, no. 3/4 (2003): 27–73.

McGuinness, Aims. *Path of Empire: Panama and the California Gold Rush*. Ithaca, NY: Cornell University Press, 2008.

McKinstry, Byron Nathan. *The California Gold Rush Overland Diary of Byron N. McKinstry, 1850–1852*. Glendale, CA: Arthur H. Clark, 1975.

McMichael, Philip. *Development and Social Change: A Global Perspective*. 5th ed. Los Angeles: SAGE, 2012.

McNairn, Jack, and Jerry MacMullen. *Ships of the Redwood Coast*. Stanford, CA: Stanford University Press, 1945.

McNeill, John R., ed. *Environmental History in the Pacific World*. Burlington, VT: Ashgate, 2001.

——. "Of Rats and Men: A Synoptic Environmental History of the Island Pacific." *Journal of World History* 5, no. 2 (1994): 299–349.

——. *Something New under the Sun: An Environmental History of the Twentieth Century*. New York: W. W. Norton, 2000.

——. "Woods and Warfare in World History." *Environmental History* 9, no. 3 (2004): 388–410.

McNeill, John R., and William H. McNeill. *The Human Web: A Bird's Eye View of World History*. New York: W. W. Norton, 2003,

McNeill, William H. "History Upside Down." *New York Review of Books*, May 15, 1997, 305–11.

McSherry, J. Patrice. *Predatory States: Operation Condor and Covert War in Latin America*. Lanham, MD: Rowman and Littlefield, 2005.

McWilliams, Carey. *California: The Great Exception*. Berkeley: University of California Press, 1949.

——. "Cultural Arts in California." In *The Cultural Arts: Conference Number 2, University of California, Los Angeles, April 5–7 [1963]*. Berkeley: University of California Press, 1964.

——. *Factories in the Field: The Story of Migratory Farm Labor in California*. Reprint ed. Berkeley: University of California Press, 1999.

Meagher, Arnold J. *The Coolie Trade: The Traffic in Chinese Laborers to Latin America, 1847–1874*. Philadelphia: Xlibris, 2008.

Meagher, J. T. "Quicksilver, and Its Home." *Overland Monthly and Out West Magazine* 3 (December 1869): 501–8.

Meers, John R. "The California Wine and Grape Industry and Prohibition." *California Historical Society Quarterly* 46, no. 1 (1967): 19–32.

Megquier, Mary Jane. *Apron of Gold: The Letters of Mary Jane Megquier from San Francisco, 1849–1856*. Edited by Robert Glass Cleland. San Marino, CA: Huntington Library, 1949.

Meiggs, Henry. *Los ferrocarriles del Perú: Colección de leyes, decretos, contratos y demás documentos relativos a los ferrocarriles del Perú*. Lima: Imprenta del Estado, 1876.

Meiselas, Susan, ed. *Chile from Within: 1973–1988*. New York: W. W. Norton, 1990.

Melillo, Edward D. "The First Green Revolution: Debt Peonage and the Making of the Nitrogen Fertilizer Trade, 1840–1930." *American Historical Review* 117 (2012): 1028–60.

——. "Global Entomologies: Insects, Empires, and the 'Synthetic Age' in World History." *Past and Present* 223 (2014): 233–70.

——. "Spectral Frequencies: Neoliberal Enclosures of the Electromagnetic Commons." *Radical History Review*, no. 112 (Winter 2012): 147–61.

Meller, Patricio. "Review of the Chilean Trade Liberalization and Export Expansion Process (1974–90)." *Bangladesh Development Studies* 20 (1992): 155–84.

Meller, Patricio, and Raul E. Sáez, eds. *Auge exportador chileno: Lecciones y desafíos futuros*. Santiago: CIEPLAN/Dolmen Ediciones, 1995.

Méndez, J. C., ed. *Chilean Economic Policy*. Translated by Ann M. Gain de González. Santiago: Imprenta Calderón, 1979.

Mercier, Stephanie. "The Evolution of World Grain Trade." *Review of Agricultural Economics* 21, no. 1 (1999): 225–36.

Meyers, William S. *Food for Plants*. Nassau, NY: Nitrate of Soda Propaganda, 1907.

Michaels, Albert L. "The Alliance for Progress and Chile's 'Revolution in Liberty,' 1964–1970." *Journal of Interamerican Studies and World Affairs* 18, no. 1 (1976): 74–99.

Milkman, Ruth. *L.A. Story: Immigrant Workers and the Future of the U.S. Labor Movement*. New York: Russell Sage Foundation, 2006.

Millard, Bailey. *History of the San Francisco Bay Region: History and Biography*. 3 vols. Chicago: American Historical Society, 1924.

Miller, Constance I. "The Californian Closed Pines (Subsection Oocarpae Little and Critchfield): A Taxonomic History and Review." *Taxon* 35, no. 4 (1986): 657–70.

Mills, Herb. "Dockers Stop Arms to Pinochet: The West Coast Longshore Union's 1978 Refusal to Load US Military Aid to Chile's Dictator, Augusto Pinochet." *Social Policy* 35, no. 4 (2005): 24–28.

Milner II, Clyde A., Carol A. O'Connor, and Martha A. Sandweiss, eds. *The Oxford History of the American West*. New York: Oxford University Press, 1994.

Ministerio de Relaciones Exteriores. *Colección de los tratados del Perú*. Lima: Imprenta del Estado, 1876.

Mitchell, Daniel J. B. " 'They Want to Destroy Me': How California's Fiscal Crisis Became a War on 'Big Government Unions.' " *Working USA: The Journal of Labor and Society* 9, no. 1 (2006): 99–121.

Moerenhout, Jacques Antoine. *The Inside Story of the Gold Rush*. Edited and translated by Abraham P. Nasatir. San Francisco: California Historical Society, 1935.

Monaghan, Jay. *Chile, Peru, and the California Gold Rush of 1849*. Berkeley: University of California Press, 1973.

Monero, José M., and Walter C. Oechel, eds. *Global Change and Mediterranean-Type Ecosystems*. New York: Springer, 1995.

Montalba Navarro, René, and Noelia Carrasco Henríquez. "¿Desarrollo sostenible o eco-etnocidio? El proceso de expansion forestall en territorio mapuch-nalche de Chile." *Revista de Estudios sobre Despoblación y Desarrollo Rural*, no. 4 (2005): 101–33.

Monteón, Michael. "The British in the Atacama Desert: The Cultural Bases of Economic Imperialism." *Journal of Economic History* 35, no. 1 (1975): 117–37.

——. "The *Enganche* in the Chilean Nitrate Sector, 1880–1930." *Latin American Perspectives* 6, no. 3 (1979): 66–79.

Montgomery, J. Eglinton. "A Railroad in the Clouds." *Scribner's Monthly* 14, no. 4 (1877): 449–65.

Mooney, Harold A. "On the Road to Global Ecology." *Annual Review of Energy and the Environment* 24, no. 1 (1999): 1–31.

——, ed. *Convergent Evolution in Chile and California: Mediterranean Climate Ecosystems*. Stroudsburg, PA: Dowden, Hutchinson and Ross, 1977.

Mooney, Harold A., and James A. Drake, eds. *Ecology of Biological Invasions of North America and Hawaii*. New York: Springer, 1986.

Mooney, Harold A., and Richard J. Hobbs, eds. *Invasive Species in a Changing World.* Washington, DC: Island Press, 2000.

Moran, Warren. "The Wine Appellation as Territory in France and California." *Annals of the Association of American Geographers* 83, no. 4 (1993): 694–717.

Morel, Domingo. *Ensayo sobre el desarollo de la riqueza de Chile.* Santiago: Imprenta de la Libertad, 1870.

Moreton, Bethany E. "The Soul of Neoliberalism." *Social Text* 25, no. 392 (2007): 103–23.

Morison, James. *By Sea to San Francisco, 1849–50: The Journal of Dr. James Morison.* Edited Lonnie J. White and William R. Gillaspie. Memphis: Memphis State University Press, 1977.

Morley, Christopher. "The Bowling Green: XVI. Up the Hill." *Saturday Review of Literature,* February 9, 1935, 474.

Morrell, W. P. *The Gold Rushes.* London: Adam and Charles Black, 1940.

Morse, Edwin F. "The Story of a Gold Miner: Reminiscences of Edwin Franklin Morse." *California Historical Society Quarterly* 6, no. 3 (1927): 205–37.

Mosier, Arvin R., J. Keith Syers, and John R. Freney, eds. *Agriculture and the Nitrogen Cycle: Assessing the Impacts of Fertilizer Use on Food Production and the Environment—SCOPE 65.* Washington, DC: Island Press, 2004.

Moulián, Tomás. *Chile actual: Anatomía de un mito.* Santiago: LOM Ediciones, 2002.

Moulián, Tomás, and Pilar Vergara. "Estado, ideología y políticas económicas en Chile, 1973–1978." *Revista Mexicana de Sociología* 43, no. 2 (1981): 845–903.

Moyano Bazzani, Eduardo L. *La nueva frontera del azúcar: El ferrocarril y la economía cubana del siglo XIX.* Madrid: Consejo Superior de Investigaciones Científicas, 1991.

Moyers, Bill D. *The Secret Government: The Constitution in Crisis.* 2nd ed. Cabin John, MD: Seven Locks, 1990.

Mulford, Prentice. *Life by Land and Sea.* New York: F. J. Needham, 1889.

Mullen, Kevin J. *Let Justice Be Done: Crime and Politics in Early San Francisco.* Reno: University of Nevada Press, 1989.

Mullins, Martin. *In the Shadow of the Generals: Foreign Policy Making in Argentina, Brazil, and Chile.* Burlington, VT: Ashgate, 2006.

Muñoz, Heraldo. *The Dictator's Shadow: Life under Augusto Pinochet.* New York: Basic Books, 2008.

Muñoz Villegas, Hernan. "Chile's Distinguished Immigrant Takes Root." *Americas (English Edition)* 42, no. 2 (1990): 24–29.

Munslow, B., and H. Finch, eds. *Proletarianisation in the Third World: Studies in the Creation of a Labour Force under Dependent Capitalism.* New York: Routledge, 1984.

Murray, J. M. "David Douglas." *Forestry* 5, no. 2 (1931): 154–58.

Murray, Keith A. *The Modocs and Their War.* Norman: University of Oklahoma Press, 1959.

Murray, Warwick E. "Local Responses to Global Restructuring in the Chilean Fruit Complex." *European Review of Latin American and Caribbean Studies* no. 66 (1999): 19–38.

Nahuelhual, Laura, et al. "Land-Cover Change to Forest Plantations: Proximate Causes and Implications for the Landscape in South-Central Chile." *Landscape and Urban Planning* 107, no. 1 (2012): 12–20.

Naranjo, Pedro, Mauricio Ahumada, Mario Garcés, and Julio Pinto. *Miguel Enríquez y el proyecto revolucionario en Chile: Discursos y documentos del Movimiento de Izquierda Revolucionaria*. Santiago: LOM Ediciones, 2004.

Nasatir, Abraham P. "Chileans in California during the Gold Rush Period and the Establishment of the Chilean Consulate." *California Historical Quarterly* 53, no. 1 (1974): 52–70.

Nash, Linda. *Inescapable Ecologies: A History of Environment, Disease, and Knowledge*. Berkeley: University of California Press, 2006.

Navarro de Andrade, Edmundo, Octavio Yecchi, and E. B. Correa Montt. *El eucalipto: Su cultivo y explotación*. Santiago: Imprenta Gutenburg, 1920.

Nef, Jorge. "Chile: Myths, Realities and Misconstructions." *Journal of Iberian and Latin American Research* 2, no. 1 (1996): 3–40.

Neira, Eduardo, Hernán Verscheure, and Carmen Revenga. *Chile's Frontier Forests: Conserving a Global Treasure*. Washington, DC: World Resources Institute / Comité Nacional Pro Defensa de la Fauna y Flora / University Austral of Chile, 2002.

Nelson, E. Charles, and Alan Probert. *A Man Who Can Speak of Plants: Dr. Thomas Coulter (1793–1843) of Dundalk in Ireland, Mexico and Alta California*. Dublin: E. Charles Nelson, 1994.

Nelson-Pallmeyer, Jack. *School of Assassins: The Case for Closing the School of the Americas and for Fundamentally Changing U.S. Foreign Policy*. Rev. ed. Maryknoll, NY: Orbis Books, 1997.

Neruda, Pablo. *Canto General*. Mexico City: Talleres Gráficos de la Nación, 1950.

———. *Confieso que he vivido: Memorias*. 1974; Santiago: Pehuén Editores, 2005.

———. *Incitación al Nixonicidio y alabanza de la Revolución Chilena*. Mexico City: Editorial Grijalbo, 1973.

Newhall, Beaumont. *The Daguerreotype in America*. New York: Duell, Sloan and Pearce, 1961.

Newmark, Harris. *Sixty Years in Southern California, 1853–1913, Containing the Reminiscences of Harris Newmark*. Edited by Maurice H. Newmark and Marco R. Newmark. 4th ed. Los Angeles: Zeitlin and Ver Brugge, 1970.

Nolan, James. *Poet-Chief: The Native American Poetics of Walt Whitman and Pablo Neruda*. Albuquerque: University of New Mexico Press, 1994.

Nolte, Carl. "Experts Dig up Nautical Past of Long-Buried 1818 Whaler." *San Francisco Chronicle*, January 28, 2006.

Nordhoff, Charles. *California: For Health, Pleasure and Residence; A Book for Travellers and Settlers*. New York: Harper and Brothers, 1873.

Norton, Lewis Adelbert. *Life and Adventures of Col. L. A. Norton*. Oakland, CA: Pacific Press, 1887.

Núñez, Daisy, Laura Nahuelhual, and Carlos Oyarzún. "Forests and Water: The Value of Native Temperate Forests in Supplying Water for Human Consumption." *Ecological Economics* 58, no. 3 (2006): 606–16.

Nye, Joseph S., and John D. Donahue, eds. *Governance in a Globalizing World*. Washington, DC: Brookings Institution Press, 2000.

O'Brien, Thomas F. *The Century of U.S. Capitalism in Latin America*. Albuquerque: University of New Mexico Press, 1999.

———. "'Rich beyond the Dreams of Avarice': The Guggenheims in Chile." *Business History Review* 63, no. 1 (1989): 122–59.

O'Connor, Alice. *Social Science for What? Philanthropy and the Social Question in a World Turned Rightside Up.* New York: Russell Sage Foundation, 2007.

Oehler, Helen Irving. "Nantucket to the Golden Gate in 1849: From Letters in the Winslow Collection, Contd." *California Historical Society Quarterly* 29, no. 2 (1950): 167–72.

Oficina Central de Estadísticas. *Censo general de la República de Chile levantado en abril de 1854.* Santiago: Imprenta del Ferrocaril, 1858.

Ogden, Adele, and Engel Sluiter, eds. *Greater America: Essays in Honor of Herbert Eugene Bolton.* Berkeley: University of California Press, 1945.

Olmstead, Alan L., and Paul W. Rhode. "The Red Queen and the Hard Reds: Productivity Growth in American Wheat, 1800–1940." *Journal of Economic History* 62 (December 2002): 926–66.

Olmsted, Roger J., ed. *Scenes of Wonder and Curiosity from Hutchings' California Magazine, 1856–1861.* Berkeley, CA: Howell-North Books, 1962.

Oppenheim, Lois Hecht. *Politics in Chile: Socialism, Authoritarianism and Market Democracy.* 3rd ed. Boulder, CO: Westview, 2007.

Oppenheimer, Robert. "National Capital and National Development: Financing Chile's Central Valley Railroads." *Business History Review* 56, no. 1 (1982): 54–75.

Ordish, George. *The Great Wine Blight.* New York: Scribner, 1972.

Orsi, Richard J. *Sunset Limited: The Southern Pacific Railroad and the Development of the American West, 1850–1930.* Berkeley: University of California Press, 2005.

Ortega, Luis. "The First Four Decades of the Chilean Coal Mining Industry, 1840–1879." *Journal of Latin American Studies* 14, no. 1 (1982): 1–32.

Ortega y Medina, Juan A., ed. *Conciencia y autenticidad históricas.* Mexico City: Universidad Autónoma de México, 1968.

Orton, James. *The Andes and the Amazon; or, Across the Continent of South America.* New York: Harper and Brothers, 1875.

O'Shaughnessy, Hugh. *Pinochet: The Politics of Torture.* New York: New York University Press, 2000.

Osorio Gonnet, Cecilia. "Chilenos, Peruanos y Bolivianos en la pampa, 1860–1880: ¿Un conflicto entre nacionalidades?" *Historia* (Santiago) 34 (2001): 117–66.

Ossandón B., Carlos, ed. *Ensayismo y modernidad en América Latina.* Santiago: LOM Ediciones, 1996.

Otero Durán, Luis. *La huella del fuego: Historia de los bosques nativos; Poblamiento y cambios en el paisaje del sur de Chile.* Santiago: Pehuén Editores, 2006.

Overton, John, and Warwick E. Murray. "Playing the Scales: Regional Transformations and the Differentiation of Rural Space in the Chilean Wine Industry." *Journal of Rural Studies* 27, no. 1 (2011): 63–72.

Pablo Figueroa, Pedro. *Diccionario biográfico de extranjeros en Chile.* Santiago: Imprenta Moderna, 1900.

———. *Historia de la fundación de la industria del carbón de piedra en Chile.* Santiago: Imprenta del Comercio-Moneda, 1897.

Páez, Adriano. *La Guerra del Pacífico y deberes de la America*. Colón, Panama: Oficina del Canal, 1881.

Paine, Lincoln P. *Ships of the World: An Historical Encyclopedia*. Boston: Houghton Mifflin, 1997.

Palacios, Nicolás. *La raza chilena*. Valparaíso: Imprenta y Litografía Alemana, 1904.

Palacios Moreyra, Carlos. *La deuda anglo-peruana, 1822–1890*. Lima: Studium, 1983.

Palmer, John Williamson. *The New and the Old; or, California and India in Romantic Aspects*. New York, 1859.

———. "Pioneer Days in San Francisco." *Century Magazine*, February 1892, 541–60.

Palo, Matti, ed. *Forest Transitions and Carbon Fluxes, Global Scenarios and Policies (World Development Studies 15)*. Helsinki: United Nations University/World Institute for Development Economy Research, 1999.

Pamo, O. G. "Daniel Carrion's Experiment: The Use of Self-Infection in the Advance of Medicine." *Journal of the Royal College of Physicians of Edinburgh* 42, no. 1 (2012): 81–86.

Parry, John T., ed. *Evil, Law and the State: Perspectives on State Power and Violence*. Amsterdam: Editions Rodopi, 2006.

Paul, Harry W. *Science, Vine and Wine in Modern France*. New York: Cambridge University Press, 1996.

Paul, Rodman W. *California Gold: The Beginning of Mining in the Far West*. Lincoln: University Nebraska Press, 1947.

———. *Mining Frontiers in the Far West, 1848–1880*. New York: Holt, Rinehart and Winston, 1963.

Paull, John. "Attending the First Organic Agriculture Course: Rudolf Steiner's Agriculture Course at Koberwitz, 1924." *European Journal of Social Sciences* 21, no. 1 (2011): 64–70.

Pavilack, Jody. *Mining for the Nation: The Politics of Chile's Coal Communities from the Popular Front to the Cold War*. University Park: Pennsylvania State University Press, 2011.

Paz Brownrigg, Coya. "Linchocracia: Performing 'America' in *El Clamor Público*." *California History* 84, no. 2 (Winter 2006–2007): 40–51.

Pearson, Michael N. "Littoral Society: The Concept and the Problems." *Journal of World History* 17, no. 4 (2006): 353–73.

Peck, Gunther. *Reinventing Free Labor: Padrones and Immigrant Workers in the North American West, 1880–1930*. New York: Cambridge University Press, 2000.

Pelaéz y Tapia, José. *Historia de El Mercurio: Un siglo de periodismo chileno*. Santiago: Talleres de El Mercurio, 1927.

Penna, Anthony N. *The Human Footprint: A Global Environmental History*. Malden, MA: Wiley-Blackwell, 2010.

Pereira Poza, Sergio. "Joaquín Murieta: ¿Héroe o bandido?" *Revista de Occidente— Santiago Universitaria*, no. 369 (January–February 1999): 35–39.

Pereira Salas, Eugenio. "Algo más sobre Joaquín Murieta." *El Bibliófilo Chileno*, no. 10 (December 1964): 137–41.

———. "Bibliografía Chilena sobre el 'Gold Rush' en California." *L.E.A. (Pan American Union)* no. 9 (November 1949): 1–4.

Pérez Rosales, Vicente. *Memoria sobre la colonización de Valdivia*. Valparaíso: Imprenta del Diario, 1852.

———. *Times Gone By: Memoirs of a Man of Action*. Translated by John H. R. Polt. New York: Oxford University Press, 2003.

Pérez Yañez, Ramón. *Forjadores de Chile*. Santiago: Zig-Zag, 1953.

Perkins, William. *Three Years in California: William Perkins' Journal of Life at Sonora, 1849–1852*. Edited by Dale L. Morgan and James R. Scobie. Berkeley: University of California Press, 1964.

Peters, Charles. *The Autobiography of Charles Peters*. Sacramento, CA: LaGrave, 1915.

Peters, Erica J. *San Francisco: A Food Biography*. Lanham, MD: Rowman and Littlefield, 2013.

Peterson, Arthur G. "Agriculture in the United States, 1839 and 1939." *Journal of Farm Economics* 22, no. 1 (1940): 98–110.

Peterson, Richard H. "Anti-Mexican Nativism in California, 1848–1853: A Study of Cultural Conflict." *Southern California Quarterly* 62, no. 4 (1980): 309–27.

Phillips, Charles, and Alan Axelrod, eds. *Encyclopedia of the American West*. New York: Simon and Schuster Macmillan, 1996.

Phillips, Ralph W., ed. *Recent Developments Affecting Livestock Production in the Americas*. Rome: Food and Agriculture Organization of the United Nations, 1956.

Pickens, William H. "'A Marvel of Nature; The Harbor of Harbors': Public Policy and the Development of the San Francisco Bay, 1846–1926." PhD diss., University of California, Davis, 1976.

Pietrobelli, Carlo. *Industry, Competitiveness and Technological Capabilities in Chile: A New Tiger from Latin America?* New York: St. Martin's, 1998.

Pike, Frederick B. "Aspects of Class Relations in Chile, 1850–1960." *Hispanic American Historical Review* 43, no. 1 (1963): 14–33.

———. *The Modern History of Peru*. London: Weidenfeld and Nicolson, 1967.

———. *The United States and Latin America: Myths and Stereotypes of Civilization and Nature*. Austin: University of Texas Press, 1992.

Pillors, Brenda Elaine. "The Criminalization of Prostitution in the United States: The Case of San Francisco, 1854–19190." PhD diss., University of California, Berkeley, 1982.

Pimentel, David, and Marcia Pimentel. "Comment: Adverse Environmental Consequences of the Green Revolution." *Population and Development Review* 16 (1990): 329–32.

Pineo, Ronn, and James A. Baer, eds. *Cities of Hope: People, Protests, and Progress in Urbanizing Latin America, 1870–1930*. Boulder, CO: Westview, 1998.

Pinney, Thomas. *A History of Wine in America: From Prohibition to the Present*. Berkeley: University of California Press, 2005.

Pinochet de la Barra, Óscar. *La Antártica chilena*. Santiago: Editorial Andrés Bello, 1976.

———, ed. *Obras escogidos (período 1931–1982)*. Santiago: Centro de Estudios Políticos Latinoamericanos Simón Bolívar and Fundación Eduardo Frei Montalva, 1993.

Pinto Rodríguez, Jorge. *Las minas de azogue de Punitaqui: Estudio de una faena minera de fines del siglo XVIII*. Coquimbo: Universidad del Norte, 1981.

Pinto Vallejos, Julio, ed. *Cuando hicimos historia: La experiencia de la Unidad Popular.* Santiago: LOM Ediciones, 2005.

——. *Trabajos y rebeldías en la pampa salitrera: El ciclo del salitre y la reconfiguración de las identidades populares (1850–1900).* Santiago: Universidad de Santiago, 1998.

Pinto Vallejos, Julio, Verónica Valdivia O., and Hernán Venegas V. "Peones chilenos en las tierras del salitre, 1850–1879: Historia de una emigración temprana." *Contribuciones Científicas y Tecnológicas,* no. 109 (1995): 47–51.

Pisani, Donald J. *From the Family Farm to Agribusiness: The Irrigation Crusade in California and the West, 1850–1931.* Berkeley: University of California Press, 1984.

Pitt, Leonard. *The Decline of the Californios: A Social History of the Spanish-Speaking Californians, 1846–1890.* Berkeley: University of California Press, 1970.

Pitti, Stephen J. *The Devil in Silicon Valley: Northern California, Race, and Mexican Americans.* Princeton, NJ: Princeton University Press, 2003.

Plank, John N. "The Alliance for Progress: Problems and Prospects." *Daedalus* 91, no. 4 (1962): 800–811.

Player-Frowd, J. G. *Six Months in California.* London: Longmans, Green, 1872.

Pletcher, David M. *The Diplomacy of Trade and Investment: American Economic Expansion in the Hemisphere, 1865–1900.* Columbia: University of Missouri Press, 1998.

Polk, Dora Beale. *The Island of California: A History of the Myth.* Spokane, WA: Arthur H. Clark, 1991.

Polk, James. *Message from the President of the United States to the Two Houses of Congress, at the Commencement of the Second Session, December 5, 1848.* Washington, DC: Wendell and Van Benthuysen, 1848.

Pomareda Benal, Carlos, and Jorge A. Torres Zorrilla, eds. *Modernización de la agricultura en América Latin y el Caribe.* San José, Costa Rica: El Instituto Interamericano de Cooperación para la Agricultura, 1990.

Pomeranz, Kenneth. *The Great Divergence: China, Europe, and the Making of the Modern World Economy.* Princeton, NJ: Princeton University Press, 2000.

Pomeranz, Kenneth, and Steven Topik. *The World That Trade Created: Society, Culture, and the World Economy 1400 to the Present.* Armonk, NY: M. E. Sharpe, 1999.

Pouget, Roger. *Histoire de la lutte contre le Phylloxera de la vigne en France.* Versailles: Institut National de la Recherche Agronomique, 1990.

Powell, Lawrence N. *The Accidental City: Improvising New Orleans.* Cambridge, MA: Harvard University Press, 2012.

Pratt, Julius W. "John L. O'Sullivan and Manifest Destiny." *New York History* 14, no. 3 (1933): 213–34.

Pratt, Mary Louise. *Imperial Eyes: Travel Writing and Transculturation.* New York: Routledge, 1992.

Priestley, Herbert I. *José de Gálvez, Visitor-General of New Spain, 1765–1771.* Berkeley: University of California Press, 1916.

Prieto, Carlos. *El Océano pacífico: Navegantes españoles del siglo XVI.* Barcelona: Alianza, 1975.

Prudham, W. Scott. *Knock on Wood: Nature as Commodity in Douglas-Fir Country.* New York: Routledge, 2005.

Przeworski, Joanne Fox. *The Decline of the Copper Industry in Chile and the Entrance of North American Capital.* New York: Arno, 1980.

Pszczółkowski T., Philippo. "La invención del cv. Carménère (*Vitis vinifera* L.) en Chile, desde la mirada de uno de sus actors." *Universum* (Talca) 19, no. 2 (2004): 150–65.

Puryear, Jeffery M. *Thinking Politics, Intellectuals and Democracy in Chile, 1973–1988.* Baltimore: Johns Hopkins University Press, 1994.

Putnam, Dan. "History, Importance, and Production Dynamics of Alfalfa in California." In *Proceedings, 27th National Alfalfa Symposium and 26th Annual California Alfalfa Symposium.* Davis: University of California, Davis, 1996.

Querejazu Calvo, Roberto. *Guano, salitre, sangre: Historia de la Guerra del Pacífico.* La Paz: Editorial Los Amigos del Libro, 1979.

"The Quicksilver Mines of Old and New Almaden." *American Journal of Pharmacy* (July 1855): 338.

Quiroga, Mauricio Morales. "La primera mujer presidenta de Chile: ¿Qué explicó el triunfo de Michelle Bachelet en las elecciones de 2005–2006?" *Latin American Research Review* 43, no. 1 (2008): 7–32.

Quiroga Martínez, Rayén, and Saar Van Hauwermeiren. *The Tiger without a Jungle: Environmental Consequences of the Economic Transformation of Chile.* Santiago: Institute of Political Ecology, 1996.

Quiroz, Alfonso W. *Corrupt Circles: A History of Unbound Graft in Peru.* Baltimore: Johns Hopkins University Press, 2008.

Qureshi, Lubna Z. *Nixon, Kissinger, and Allende: U.S. Involvement in the 1973 Coup in Chile.* Lanham, MD: Lexington Books, 2009.

Raban, Jonathan. *Bad Land: An American Romance.* New York: Pantheon Books, 1996.

Rabe, Stephen G. *The Most Dangerous Area in the World: John F. Kennedy Confronts Communist Revolution in Latin America.* Chapel Hill: University of North Carolina Press, 1999.

Radding, Cynthia. *Wandering Peoples: Colonialism, Ethnic Spaces, and Ecological Frontiers in Northwestern Mexico, 1700–1850.* Durham, NC: Duke University Press, 1997.

Radetzki, Marian. "Seven Thousand Years in the Service of Humanity: The History of Copper, the Red Metal." *Resources Policy* 34, no. 4 (2009): 176–84.

Radkau, Joachim. *Nature and Power: A Global History of the Environment.* Translated by Thomas Dunlap. New York: Cambridge University Press, 2008.

Rand, Charles S. *The Railroads of Peru.* Lima: "Opinion Nacional," 1873.

Rankin, Monica A. *The History of Costa Rica.* Santa Barbara, CA: Greenwood, 2012.

Raper, Kellie Curry, Suzanne Thornsbury, and Cristobal Aguilar. "Regional Wholesale Price Relationships in the Presence of Counter-Seasonal Imports." *Journal of Agricultural and Applied Economics* 41, no. 1 (2009): 271–90.

Rasmussen, Louis J. *San Francisco Ship Passenger Lists.* 4 vols. Baltimore: Deford, 1965.

Rasmussen, Wayne D. "Diplomats and Plant Collectors: The South American Commission, 1817–1818." *Agricultural History* 29, no. 1 (1955): 22–31.

Raven, Peter H. "Amphitropical Relationships in the Floras of North and South America." *Quarterly Review of Biology* 38, no. 2 (1963): 151–77.

Raven, Ralph [George Payson]. *Golden Dreams and Leaden Realities*. New York: G. P. Putnam, 1853.

Rawls, James J., and Richard J. Orsi, eds. *A Golden State: Mining and Economic Development in Gold Rush California*. Berkeley: University of California Press, 1999.

Reagan, Ronald. *Reagan: A Life in Letters*. Edited by Kiron K. Skinner, Annelise Anderson, and Martin Anderson. New York: Free Press, 2003.

Rector, John Lawrence. *The History of Chile*. Westport, CT: Greenwood, 2003.

Reddick, Lawrence D. "The New Race-Relations Frontier." *Journal of Educational Sociology* 19, no. 3 (1945): 129–45.

Reed, Charles A., ed. *Origins of Agriculture*. The Hague: Mouton, 1978.

Reeve, Jennifer R., et al. "Soil and Winegrape Quality in Biodynamically and Organically Managed Vineyards." *American Journal of Enology and Viticulture* 56, no. 4 (2005): 367–76.

Regmi, Anita, ed. *Changing Structure of Global Food Consumption and Trade*. Washington, DC: Economic Research Service/USDA, 2001.

Reid, Thomas. "Diary of a Voyage to California in the Bark Velasco." BANC.

Reid, William A. *Nitrate Fields of Chile*. 4th ed. Baltimore: Sun Book and Job Printing Office, 1935.

Rejmanck, Marcel, and David M. Richardson. "What Attributes Make Some Plant Species More Invasive?" *Ecology* 77, no. 6 (1996): 1655–61.

Report of the Consul General of Chile, at San Francisco. . . . San Francisco: Bonnard and Daly, 1875.

Republica de Chile. *Decreto upremo 4.363: Ley de bosques*. Santiago: Diario Oficial, 1931.

Retamales, Jorge B., and Juan Carlos Sepúlveda. "Fruit Production in Chile: Bright Past, Uncertain Future." *Revista Brasileira de Fruticultura* 33, no. 1 (2011): 173–78.

Revere, Joseph Warren. *Keel and Saddle: A Retrospect of Forty Years of Military and Naval Service*. Boston: James R. Osgood, 1872.

Rey Tristán, Eduardo. *Memorias de la violencia en Uruguay y Argentina: Golpes, dictaduras, exilos (1973–2006)*. Santiago de Compostela, Spain: Centro Interdisciplinario de Estudios Americanistas "Gumersindo Busto," Universidad de Santiago de Compostela, 2007.

Rhea, James J. *The Turlock District, Stanislaus County, California*. San Francisco: Sunset Magazine Homeseekers Bureau, 1912.

Ricardo Couyoumdjian, Juan. "Vinos en Chile desde la Independencia hasta el fin de la Belle Époque." *Historia* 1, no. 39 (2006): 23–64.

Rice, Prudence M. "The Archaeology of Wine: The Wine and Brandy Haciendas of Moquegua, Peru." *Journal of Field Archaeology* 23, no. 2 (1996): 187–204.

Rice, Richard B., William A. Bullough, and Richard J. Orsi. *The Elusive Eden: A New History of California*. 3rd ed. Boston: McGraw-Hill, 2002.

Rich, Adrienne. *Blood, Bread, and Poetry: Selected Prose, 1979–1985*. New York: W. W. Norton, 1986.

Richard, Nelly. *Cultural Residues: Chile in Transition*. Translated by Alan West-Durán and Theodore Quester. Minneapolis: University of Minnesota Press, 2004.

Richards, John F. *The Unending Frontier: An Environmental History of the Early Modern World*. Berkeley: University of California Press, 2003.

Richardson, David M., ed. *Ecology and Biogeography of Pinus*. New York: Cambridge University Press, 1998.

Richardson, David M., P. A. Williams, and R. J. Hobbs. "Pine Invasions in the Southern Hemisphere: Determinants of Spread and Invadability." *Journal of Biogeography* 21, no. 5 (1994): 511–27.

Rickard, Thomas Arthur. *Journeys of Observation*. San Francisco: Dewey, 1907.

Ridge, John Rollin. *The Life and Times of Joaquín Murieta, the Celebrated California Bandit*. San Francisco: W. B. Cooke, 1854.

Ridley, Henry Nicholas. *The Dispersal of Plants throughout the World*. Ashford, UK: Kent, L. Reeve, 1930.

Rindge, Frederick Hastings. *Happy Days in Southern California*. Cambridge, MA: F. H. Rindge, 1898.

Rivera, Rigoberto. "Institutional Conditions of Chilean Fruit Export Expansion." Working Paper no. 17 of the Workshop on the Globalization of the Fresh Fruit and Vegetable System, University of California at Santa Cruz, December 6–9, 1991.

Rivera Jofre, Ramón. *Reseña histórica del ferrocarril entre Santiago i Valparaíso*. Santiago: Imprenta del Ferrocarril, 1863.

Roach, Joseph. *Cities of the Dead: Circum-Atlantic Performance*. New York: Columbia University Press, 1996.

Robbins, William G. "The 'Plundered Province' Thesis and the Recent Historiography of the American West." *Pacific Historical Review* 55, no. 4 (1986): 577–97.

Robins, Nicholas A. *Mercury, Mining, and Empire: The Human and Ecological Cost of Colonial Silver Mining in the Andes*. Bloomington: Indiana University Press, 2011.

Robinson, Forrest G., ed. *The New Western History: The Territory Ahead*. Tucson: University Arizona Press, 1998.

Robles-Ortiz, Claudio. "Agrarian Capitalism and Rural Labour: The Hacienda System in Central Chile, 1870–1920." *Journal of Latin American Studies* 41, no. 3 (2009): 493–526.

Rockefeller, Nelson. *The Rockefeller Report on the Americas: The Official Report of a United States Presidential Mission for the Western Hemisphere*. Chicago: Quadrangle Books, 1969.

Rockman, Marcy, and James Steele, eds. *Colonization of Unfamiliar Landscapes: The Archaeology of Adaptation*. New York: Routledge, 2003.

Rodgers, Daniel T. *Atlantic Crossings: Social Politics in a Progressive Age*. Cambridge, MA: Harvard University Press, 1998.

Rodriguez, Richard. *Days of Obligation: An Argument with My Mexican Father*. New York: Penguin Books, 1992.

———. "True West: Relocating the Horizon of the American Frontier." *Harper's Monthly*, September 1996, 37–46.

Rodríguez Pastor, Humberto. *Herederos del dragón: Historia de la comunidad china en el Perú*. Lima: Fondo Editorial del Congreso del Perú, 2000.

Roeding, Frederick W. *Irrigation in California*. Washington, DC: Government Printing Office, 1911.

Rohrbough, Malcolm J. *Days of Gold: The California Gold Rush and the American Nation.* Berkeley: University of California Press, 1997.

———. *Rush to Gold: The French and the California Gold Rush, 1848–1854.* New Haven: Yale University Press, 2013.

Rojas Mix, Miguel. "Bilbao y el hallazgo de América Latina: Unión continental, socialista y libertarian." *Cahiers du Monde Hispanique et Luso-Brasilien—Caravelle,* no. 46 (1986): 35–47.

Rolle, Andrew F. *An American in California: The Biography of William Heath Davis, 1822–1909.* San Marino, CA: Huntington Library, 1956.

Roniger, Luis, and Tamar Herzog, eds. *The Collective and the Public in Latin America.* Portland, OR: Sussex Academic, 2000.

Rosaldo, Renato. "Imperialist Nostalgia." *Representations,* no. 26 (Spring 1989): 107–22.

Rosenfeld, Stephanie, and Juan Luis Marré. "How Chile's Rich Got Richer." *NACLA Report on the Americas* 30, no. 6 (1997): 20–44.

Roth, David M. *Louisiana Hurricane History.* Camp Springs, MD: National Weather Service, 2010.

Rousseau, Peter L. "Jacksonian Monetary Policy, Specie Flows, and the Panic of 1837." *Journal of Economic History* 62, no. 2 (2002): 457–88.

Royce, Josiah. *California, from the Conquest in 1846 to the Second Vigilance Committee in San Francisco: A Study of American Character.* Santa Barbara, CA: Peregrine, 1970.

Ruiz Aldea, Pedro. *Los aruacanos y sus costumbres.* 1868; Santiago: Guillermo Miranda, 1902.

Ruiz Esquide, Andrea. "Migration, Colonization and Land Policy in the Former Mapuche Frontier: Malleco, 1850–1900." PhD diss., Columbia University, 2000.

Rundel, Philip W., and Gloria Montenegro, eds. *Landscape Disturbance and Biodiversity in Mediterranean-type Ecosystems.* New York: Springer, 1998.

Rundel, Philip W., and Robert Gustafson. *Introduction to the Plant Life of Southern California: Coast to Foothills.* Berkeley: University of California Press, 2005.

Russailh, Albert Bernard de. *Last Adventure: San Francisco in 1851.* Translated by Clarkson Crane. San Francisco: Westgate, 1931.

Ryan, William Redmond. *Personal Adventures in Upper and Lower California in 1848–9; with the Author's Experience at the Mines.* 2 vols. London: William Shoberl, 1850.

S. Tornero, Recaredo. *Chile ilustrado: Guía descriptivo del territorio de Chile.* Valparaíso: Librería y Agencias del Mercurio, 1872.

Saavedra, Cornelio. *Documentos relativos a la ocupación de Arauco: Que contienen los trabajos practicados desde 1861 hasta la fecha. . . .* Santiago: Imprenta de la Libertad, 1870.

Sackman, Douglas Cazaux. *Orange Empire: California and the Fruits of Eden.* Berkeley: University of California Press, 2005.

Saelzer Balde, Federico. *La evolución de la legislación forestal chilena.* Valdivia: Universidad Austral de Chile, 1973.

Said, Edward. *Orientalism.* Reprint ed. New York: Vintage Books, 1994.

Salaman, Redcliffe N. *The History and Social Influence of the Potato.* 2nd ed. New York: Cambridge University Press, 1985.

Salazar Sparks, Juan. *Chile y la comunidad del Pacífico*. Santiago: Editorial Universitaria, 1999.

Salazar Vergara, Gabriel. *Historia de la acumulación capitalista en Chile: Apuntes de clase*. Santiago: LOM Ediciones, 2003.

——. *Labradores, peones, y proletarios: Formación y crisis de la sociedad popular chilena del siglo XIX*. Santiago: Ediciones SUR, 1985.

Salinas Sánchez, Alejandro, ed. *Estudio socio-histórico del Epistolario Meiggs: (1866–1885)*. Lima: Seminario de Historia Rural Andina, Universidad Nacional Mayor de San Marcos, 2007.

Salo, Lucinda F. "Red brome (*Bromus rubens* subsp. *Madritensis*) in North America: Possible Modes for Early Introductions, Subsequent Spread." *Biological Invasions* 7, no. 2 (2005): 165–80.

Salvator, Ludwig Louis. *Los Angeles in the Sunny Seventies: A Flower from the Golden Land*. Translated by Marguerite Eyer Wilbur. Reprint ed. Los Angeles: B. McCallister, J. Zeitlin, 1929.

Sánchez, Rosaura. *Telling Identities: The Californio Testimonios*. Minneapolis: University Minnesota Press, 1995.

Sánchez G., Walter, and Teresa Pereira L., eds. *150 años de política exterior chilena*. Santiago: Instituto de Estudios Internacionales de la Universidad de Chile, 1977.

Sandler, Merton, and Roger Pinder, eds. *Wine: A Scientific Exploration*. New York: Taylor and Francis, 2003.

Sando, James A. "'Because He Is a Liar and a Thief': Conquering the Residents of 'Old' California, 1850–1880." *California History* 79, no. 2 (2000): 86–112.

Sands, Roger. *Forestry in a Global Context*. Cambridge, MA: CABI, 2005.

Sanz Fernández, Jesús. *Historia de los ferrocarriles de Iberoamérica (1837–1995)*. Madrid: CEDES, CEHOPU, and Fundación de los Ferrocarriles Españoles, 1998.

Sasnett, William J. "The United States—Her Past and Her Future." *DeBow's Review* 12, no. 6 (1852): 614–31.

Sater, William F. *Chile and the United States: Empires in Conflict*. Athens: University of Georgia Press, 1990.

——. "Chile and the World Depression of the 1870s." *Journal of Latin American Studies* 11 (May 1979): 67–99.

Sater, William F., and Holger H. Herwig. *The Grand Illusion: The Prussianization of the Chilean Army*. Lincoln: University of Nebraska Press, 1999.

Saxton, Alexander. *The Rise and Fall of the White Republic: Class Politics and Mass Culture in Nineteenth-Century America*. London: Verso, 1990.

Schama, Simon. *Landscape and Memory*. New York: Vintage Books, 1995.

Schivelbusch, Wolfgang. *The Railway Journey: The Industrialization of Time and Space in the 19th Century*. Translated by Anselm Hollo. New York: Urizen Books, 1979.

Schlatter, Juan. "La fertilidad del suelo y el desarrollo de *Pinus radiata* D. Don." *Bosque* 8, no. 1 (1987): 13–19.

Schmidtmeyer, Peter. *Travels into Chile, over the Andes, in the Years 1820 and 1821*. London: Longman, Hurst, Rees, Orme, Brown, and Green, 1824.

Schneider, Teodoro. *La agricultura en Chile en los últimos cincuenta años*. Santiago: Imprenta Barcelona, 1904.

Schoenherr, Allan A. *A Natural History of California*. Berkeley: University of California Press, 1992.

Schurman, Rachel. "Uncertain Gains: Labor in Chile's New Export Sectors." *Latin American Research Review* 36, no. 2 (2001): 3–29.

Scott, Allen J., and Edward W. Soja, eds. *The City: Los Angeles and Urban Theory at the End of the Twentieth Century*. Berkeley: University of California Press, 1996.

Scott, James C. *Seeing Like a State: How Certain Schemes to Improve the Human Condition Have Failed*. New Haven: Yale University Press, 1998.

Sears, Alfred F. "The Republic of Peru." *New England Magazine* 7, no. 4 (1892): 449.

Sears, Clare. "All That Glitters: Trans-ing California's Gold Rush Migrations." *GLQ: A Journal of Lesbian and Gay Studies* 4, nos. 2–3 (2008): 383–402.

Seasholes, Nancy S. *Gaining Ground: A History of Landmaking in Boston*. Cambridge: MIT Press, 2003.

Seaver, Joel. *Historical Sketches of Franklin County and Its Several Towns: With Many Short Biographies*. Albany, NY: J. B. Lyon, 1918.

Sehnbruch, Kirsten. "A Record Number of Conflicts? Michelle Bachelet's Inheritance of Unresolved Employment Issues." *CLAS Working Papers, Center for Latin American Studies, UC Berkeley* no. 27 (July 2009): 1–24.

Seigel, Micol. "Beyond Compare: Comparative Method after the Transnational Turn." *Radical History Review*, no. 91 (Winter 2005): 62–90.

Seligson, Mitchell A. "The Rise of Populism and the Left in Latin America." *Journal of Democracy* 18, no. 3 (2007): 81–95.

Semper, Erwin. *La industria del salitre en Chile*. Santiago: Impr. Barcelona, 1908.

Sepúlveda G., Sergio. *El Trigo chileno en el mercado mundial: Ensayo de geografía histórica*. Santiago: Editorial Universitaria, 1959.

Seyd, Ernest. *California and Its Resources: A Work for the Merchant, the Capitalist, and the Emigrant*. London: Trübner, 1858.

Shaler, William. *Journal of a Voyage between China and the Northwestern Coast of America, Made in 1804*. Philadelphia: American Register, 1808.

Shapiro, Fred R., ed. *The Yale Book of Quotations*. New Haven: Yale University Press, 2006.

Shaw, William. *Golden Dreams and Waking Realities: Being the Adventures of a Gold-Seeker in California and the Pacific Islands*. London: Smith, Elder, 1851.

Sherman, William Tecumseh. *Memoirs of General W. T. Sherman*. Edited by Michael Fellman. New York: Penguin, 2000.

———. *Recollections of California, 1846–1861*. Oakland, CA: Biobooks, 1945.

Shinn, Charles Howard. *Mining Camps: A Study in American Frontier Government*. Edited by Rodman W. Paul. Gloucester, MA: Peter Smith, 1970.

Shumsky, Neil Larry, and Larry M. Springer. "San Francisco's Zone of Prostitution, 1880–1934." *Journal of Historical Geography* 7, no. 1 (1981): 71–89.

Sigmund, Paul E. "The Chilean Military: Legalism Undermined, Manipulated, and Restored." *Revista de Ciencia Política* 23, no. 2 (2003): 241–50.

——. "The Rise and Fall of the Chicago Boys in Chile." *SAIS Review* 3, no. 2 (1983): 41–58.

Silgado F., Enrique. "Historia de los sismos mas notables ocurridos en el Perú (1513–1970)." *Geofísica Panamericana* 2, no. 1 (1973): 179–243.

Silva, Eduardo. "The Import-Substitution Model: Chile in Comparative Perspective." *Latin American Perspectives* 34, no. 3 (2007): 67–90.

Simmons, I. G. *Global Environmental History: 10,000 BC to AD 2000.* Edinburgh: Edinburgh University Press, 2008.

Simmons, Roger. *Lumber Markets of the West and North Coasts of South America.* Washington, DC: US Government Printing Office, 1916.

Simpson, E. "A Chapter on Peru: Leaves from a Captain's Letter-Book." *United Service: A Quarterly Review of Military and Naval Affairs* 2, no. 1 (1880): 28–39.

Sisson, Kelly J. "Bound for California: Chilean Contract Laborers and *Patrones* in the California Gold Rush, 1848–1852." *Southern California Quarterly* 90, no. 3 (2008): 259–305.

Skidmore, Thomas, and Peter Smith. *Modern Latin America.* 2nd ed. New York: Oxford University Press, 1989.

Skinner, John E. *An Historical Review of the Fish and Wildlife Resources of the San Francisco Bay Area.* Sacramento: California Department of Fish and Game, 1962.

Slotkin, Richard. *The Fatal Environment: The Myth of the Frontier in the Age of Industrialization, 1800–1890.* New York: Atheneum, 1985.

Slout, William L. *Olympians of the Sawdust Circle: A Biographical Dictionary of the Nineteenth-Century American Circus.* San Bernadino, CA: Borgo, 1998.

Smil, Vaclav. "Detonator of the Population Explosion." *Nature* 400 (July 1999): 415.

——. *Enriching the Earth: Fritz Haber, Carl Bosch, and the Transformation of World Food Production.* Cambridge, MA: MIT Press, 2004.

——. "Population Growth and Nitrogen: An Exploration of a Critical Existential Link." *Population and Development Review* 17 (December 1991): 569–601.

Smith, Barry C., ed. *Questions of Taste: The Philosophy of Wine.* New York: Oxford University Press, 2007.

Smith, C. Michael. *Plant Resistance to Arthropods: Molecular and Conventional Approaches.* Dordrecht, Netherlands: Springer, 2005.

Smith, Justin Harvey. *The War with Mexico.* 2 vols. New York: Macmillan, 1919.

Smith, Michael L. *Pacific Visions: California Scientists and the Environment, 1850–1915.* New Haven: Yale University Press, 1987.

Smith, Philip Chadwick Foster. *The Empress of China.* Philadelphia: Philadelphia Maritime Museum, 1984.

Smith, Roger C. "Upsetting the Balance of Nature, with Special Reference to Kansas and the Great Plains." *Science* 75 (1932): 649–54.

Smith, Stacey L. *Freedom's Frontier: California and the Struggle over Unfree Labor, Emancipation, and Reconstruction.* Chapel Hill: University of North Carolina Press, 2013.

Smythe, William E. *The Greatest Irrigated Farm in the World: A California Enterprise That Stands as a Type of Modern Irrigation Development.* San Francisco: H. S. Crocker, 189–.

Solberg, Carl. "Immigration and Urban Social Problems in Argentina and Chile, 1890–1914." *Hispanic American Historical Review* 49, no. 2 (1969): 215–32.

Solimano, Andrés. *Chile and the Neoliberal Trap: The Post-Pinochet Era*. New York: Cambridge University Press, 2012.

Soluri, John. "Something Fishy: Chile's Blue Revolution, Commodity Diseases, and the Problem of Sustainability." *Latin American Research Review* 46, no. 4 (2011): 55–81.

Sorrenson, Richard. "The Ship as a Scientific Instrument in the Eighteenth Century." *Osiris*, 2nd ser., 11 (1996): 221–36.

Soulé, Frank, John H. Gihon, and James Nisbet. *The Annals of San Francisco*. Reprint ed., Berkeley, CA: Berkeley Hills Books, 1998.

Spate, O. H. K. *The Pacific since Magellan*. 3 vols. Minneapolis: University of Minnesota Press, 1979–88.

Spooner, David M., et al. "A Single Domestication for Potato Based on Multilocus Amplified Fragment Length Polymorphism Genotyping." *Proceedings of the National Academy of Sciences* 102, no. 41 (2005): 14694–99.

Sprague, G. F., D. E. Alexander, and J. W. Dudley. "Plant Breeding and Genetic Engineering: A Perspective." *BioScience* 30, no. 1 (1980): 17–21.

Spykman, Nicholas J. *America's Strategy in World Politics: The United States and the Balance of Power*. 2nd ed. New Brunswick, NJ: Transaction, 2007.

Staab, Silke, and Kristen Hill Maher. "The Dual Discourse about Peruvian Domestic Workers in Santiago de Chile." *Latin American Politics and Society* 48, no. 1 (2006): 87–116.

Stagno, Horacio H., and Mario Allegri. *Organización y administración de la generación y transferencia de tecnología agropecuaria*. Montevideo, Uruguay: IICA, 1985.

Stahl, Jason Michael. "Selling Conservatism: Think Tanks, Conservative Ideology, and the Undermining of Liberalism." PhD diss., University of Minnesota, 2008.

Starr, Kevin, and Richard Orsi, eds. *Rooted in Barbarous Soil: People, Culture, and Community in Gold Rush California*. Berkeley: University of California Press, 2000.

St. Clair, David J. "New Almaden and California Quicksilver in the Pacific Rim Economy." *California History* 73, no. 4 (1994–95): 278–95.

Steen, Herman. *Cooperative Marketing: The Golden Rule in Agriculture*. Garden City, NY: Doubleday, Page, 1923.

Stefancic, Jean, and Richard Delgado. *No Mercy: How Conservative Think Tanks and Foundations Changed America's Social Agenda*. Philadelphia: Temple University Press, 1996.

Stefoni Espinoza, Carolina. *Inmigración peruana en Chile: Una oportunidad a la integración*. Santiago: Flacso-Chile/Editorial Universitaria, 2003.

Stegner, Wallace. *Where the Bluebird Sings to the Lemonade Springs: Living and Writing in the West*. 2nd ed. New York: Penguin, 1993.

Steinberg, Philip E. "Lines of Division, Lines of Connection: Stewardship in the World Ocean." *Geographical Review* 89 (1999): 254–64.

Stephens, Scott L., and William J. Libby. "Anthropogenic Fire and Bark Thickness in Coastal and Island Pine Populations from Alta and Baja California." *Journal of Biogeography* 33, no. 4 (2006): 648–52.

Stern, Steve J. *Battling for Hearts and Minds: Memory Struggles in Pinochet's Chile, 1973–1988.* Durham, NC: Duke University Press, 2006.

Stevenson, Tom. *Sotheby's World Wine Encyclopedia: A Comprehensive Reference Guide to Wines of the World.* London: Dorling Kindersley, 1988.

Stewart, Watt. *Chinese Bondage in Peru: A History of the Chinese Coolie, 1849–1874.* Durham, NC: Duke University Press, 1951.

———. *Henry Meiggs: Un Pizarro yanqui.* Translated by Luis Alberto Sánchez. Santiago: Ediciones de la Universidad de Chile, 1954.

———. *Henry Meiggs: Yankee Pizarro.* Durham, NC: Duke University Press, 1940.

———. "Notes on an Early Attempt to Establish Cable Communication between North and South America." *Hispanic American Historical Review* 26, no. 1 (1946): 118–24.

———. "El trabajador chileno y los ferrocarriles del Perú." *Revista Chilena de Historia y Geografía* 93 (1938): 128–73.

Stoddard, Charles Warren. *In the Footprints of the Padres.* San Francisco: A. M. Robertson, 1902.

Stoll, Steven. *The Fruits of Natural Advantage: Making the Industrial Countryside in California.* Berkeley: University of California Press, 1998.

Storti, Craig. *Incident at Bitter Creek: The Story of the Rock Springs Chinese Massacre.* Ames: Iowa State University Press, 1991.

Strain, Isaac G. *Cordillera and Pampa: Sketches of a Journey in Chili and the Argentine Provinces, in 1949.* New York: Horace H. Moore, 1853.

Strasser, Susan. *Waste and Want: A Social History of Trash.* New York: Henry Holt, 1999.

Street, Richard Steven. *Beasts of the Field: A Narrative History of California Farmworkers, 1769–1913.* Stanford, CA: Stanford University Press, 2004.

Subercaseaux, Bernardo. *Chile: ¿Un país moderno?* Santiago: Ediciones B., 1996.

Sullivan, Charles L. *A Companion to California Wine: An Encyclopedia of Wine and Winemaking from the Mission Period to the Present.* Berkeley: University of California Press, 1998.

Sullivan, G. W. *Early Days in California: The Growth of the Commonwealth under American Rule, with Biographical Sketches of the Pioneers.* San Francisco: Enterprise, 1888.

Sumner, Daniel A., and Frank H. Buck. *Exotic Pests and Diseases: Biology and Economics for Environmental Security.* Ames: Iowa State University Press, 2003.

Sutton, William R. J. "The Need for Planted Forests and the Example of Radiata Pine." *New Forests* 17, no. 1/3 (1999): 95–109.

Svenson, Elwin V., and James S. Coleman. "The U.C.L.A. Experience with Foreign Programs." *Human Rights Quarterly* 6, no. 1 (1984): 56–67.

Swatland, H. J. "Meat Products and Consumption Culture in the West." *Meat Science* 86, no. 1 (2010): 80–85.

Syers, J. K., et al. "Managing Soils for Long-Term Productivity [and Discussion]." *Philosophical Transactions: Biological Sciences* 352, no. 1356 (1997): 1011–21.

Taffet, Jeffrey F. *Foreign Aid as Foreign Policy: The Alliance for Progress in Latin America.* New York: Routledge, 2007.

Taylor, Bayard. *Eldorado: Adventures in the Path of Empire.* 1850; Berkeley: Heyday Books, 2000.

Taylor, Marcus. *From Pinochet to the "Third Way": Neoliberalism and Social Transformation in Chile.* Ann Arbor, MI: Pluto Press, 2006.

———. "Labor Reform and the Contradictions of 'Growth with Equity' in Postdictatorship Chile." *Latin American Perspectives* 31, no. 4 (2004): 76–93.

Tchen, John Kuo Wei. *New York before Chinatown: Orientalism and the Shaping of American Culture, 1776–1882.* Baltimore: Johns Hopkins University Press, 1999.

Thomas, William G., II. *The Iron Way: Railroads, the Civil War, and the Making of Modern America.* New Haven: Yale University Press, 2011.

Thompson, F. M. L. "The Second Agricultural Revolution, 1815–1880." *Economic History Review* 21, no. 1 (1968): 62–77.

Thompson, Warren. *Growth and Changes in California's Population.* Los Angeles: Haynes Foundation, 1955.

Thorne, Marco G., ed. "Bound for the Land of Cannan, Ho! — The Diary of Levi Stowell, 1849 (Continued)." *California Historical Society Quarterly* 27, no. 3 (1948): 259–66.

Thornton, John. *Africa and Africans in the Making of the Atlantic World, 1400–1680.* New York: Cambridge University Press, 1992.

Tinkham, George H. *California Men and Events.* Stockton, CA: Records Publishing, 1915.

———. *History of San Joaquin County, California with Biographical Sketches.* Los Angeles: Historic Record, 1923.

Tinsman, Heidi. *Buying into the Regime: Grapes and Consumption in Cold War Chile and the United States.* Durham, NC: Duke University Press, 2014.

———. "Reviving Feminist Materialism: Gender and Neoliberalism in Pinochet's Chile." *Signs* 26, no. 1 (2000): 145–88.

Tong, Benson. *Unsubmissive Women: Chinese Prostitutes in Nineteenth-Century San Francisco.* Norman: University of Oklahoma Press, 1994.

Topik, Steven C., and Allen Wells. *The Second Conquest of Latin America: Coffee, Henequen, and Oil during the Export Boom, 1850–1930.* Austin: University of Texas Press, 1998.

Toro, J., and S. P. Gessel. "Radiata Pine Plantations in Chile." *New Forests* 18, no. 1 (1999): 33–44.

Toussaint, Éric, and Damien Millet. *Debt, the IMF, and the World Bank: Sixty Questions, Sixty Answers.* Translated by Judith Abdel Gadir et al. New York: Monthly Review, 2010.

Towne, Charles W., and Edward N. Wentworth. *Shepherd's Empire.* Norman: University of Oklahoma Press, 1945.

Trouillot, Michel-Rolph. *Silencing the Past: Power and the Production of History.* Boston: Beacon, 1995.

Trumper, Ricardo, and Lynne Phillips. "Give Me Discipline and Give Me Death: Neoliberalism and Health in Chile." *Race and Class* 37, no. 3 (1996): 19–34.

Tullis, F. LaMond. "California and Chile in 1851 as Experienced by the Mormon Apostle Parley P. Pratt." *Southern California Quarterly* 67, no. 3 (1985): 291–307.

Turner II, B. L., et al., eds. *Global Land Use Change: A Perspective from the Columbian Encounter.* Madrid: Consejo Superior de Investigaciones Científicas, 1995.

Turrill, Charles B. *California Notes*. San Francisco: E. Bosqui, 1876.
Twain, Mark. *Mark Twain's Notebooks and Journals*. Edited by Frederick Anderson, Michael B. Frank, and Kenneth M. Sanderson. 3 vols. Berkeley: University of California Press, 1975.
———. *Roughing It*. Hartford, CT: Americana, 1891.
Twomey, Michael J., and Ann Helwage. *Modernization and Stagnation: Latin American Agriculture into the 1990s*. New York: Greenwood, 1991.
Tyler, Ronnie C. "Fugitive Slaves in Mexico." *Journal of Negro History* 57 (January 1972): 1–12.
Tyrell, Ian. *True Gardens of the Gods: Californian-Australian Environmental Reform, 1860–1930*. Berkeley: University of California Press, 1999.
Tyson, Dr. James L. *Diary of a Physician in California: Being the Results of Actual Experience, Including Notes of the Journey by Land and Water and Observations on the Climate, Soil, Resources of the Country, etc.* 2nd ed. Oakland, CA: Biobooks, 1955.
Ulloa Valenzuela, Francisco. "El *Pinus radiata* D. Don en algunos suelos de los alrededores de Valdivia y en otros lugares en el sur de Chile." PhD diss., Universidad Austral de Chile (Valdivia), 1964.
Ulmer, Melville J. "Friedman's Currency." *New Republic*, November 6, 1976, 8–9.
United Nations Children's Fund. *Informe annual de actividades, 2004—Chile*. Las Condes, Chile: Fondo de Naciones Unidas para la Infancia, 2004.
United States Congress. *Covert Action in Chile, 1963–1973: Staff Report of the Select Committee to Study Governmental Operations with Respect to Intelligence Activities, United States Senate*. Washington, DC: US Government Printing Office, 1975.
United States Department of State. *Papers Relating to the Foreign Relations of the United States*. Washington, DC: US Government Printing Office, 1870.
United States House Committee on Foreign Affairs. *Regional and Other Documents Concerning United States Relations with Latin America*. Washington, DC: US Government Printing Office, 1966.
United States Office of the Inspector General, Department of Defense. "Evaluation Report on Training of Foreign Military Personnel—Phase 2: School of the Americas" (November 14, 1997). In *Policy and Oversight Report No. PO 98–601*. Washington, DC: Government Printing Office, 1997.
Universidad Alberto Hurtado–Centro de Ética. "¿Es *Chile* una sociedad *racista?*" *Informe Ethos* no. 20 (2002). Available at http://etica.uahurtado.cl/html/informe_ethos_20.html.
Universidad Austral de Chile, Pontificia Universidad Católica de Chile, y Universidad Católica de Temuco. *Catastro y evaluación de recursos vegetacionales nativos de Chile: informe nacional con variables ambientales*. Santiago: Corporación Nacional Forestal y Comisión Nacional del Medio Ambiente, 1999.
Unruh, John David. *The Plains Across: The Overland Emigrants and the Trans-Mississippi West, 1840–60*. Urbana: University of Illinois Press, 1979.
Upham, Samuel G. *Notes of a Voyage to California via Cape Horn*. Philadelphia: Published by the author, 1878.
Uribe Orrego, Luis. *Nuestra marina mercante, 1810–1904: Reseña histórica*. Valparaíso: Talleres Tipográficos de la Armada, 1904.

Valdés, Juan Gabriel. *Pinochet's Economists: The Chicago School in Chile.* New York: Cambridge University Press, 1995.

Valdés, Ximena. *Condiciones de vida y trabajo de las temporeras en Chile.* Santiago: S. ed., 1992.

Valdivia Ortiz de Zárate, Verónica. *Nacionales y gremialistas: El "parto" de la nueva derecha política Chilena, 1964–1973.* Santiago: LOM Ediciones, 2008.

Valencia, Francisco. "New Almaden and the Mexican." MA thesis, San José State University, 1977.

Vandercook, W. A. *California Nitrates.* Los Angeles: W. A. Vandercook, n.d.

Van Dyke, Theodore Strong, T. T. Leberthon, and A. Taylor. *The City and County of San Diego.* San Diego, CA: Leberthon and Taylor, 1888.

Van Hoy, Teresa Miriam. *A Social History of Mexico's Railroads: Peons, Prisoners, and Priests.* Lanham, MD: Rowman and Littlefield, 2008.

Van Klaveren, Alberto, ed. *América Latina en el mundo: Anuario de políticas externas latinoamericanas y del Caribe, 1993–1996.* Santiago: Editorial Los Andes, 1997.

Van Veen, Johan. *Dredge, Drain, Reclaim: The Art of a Nation.* 5th ed. The Hague: Martinus Nijhoff, 1962.

Vaught, David. *Cultivating California: Growers, Specialty Crops, and Labor, 1875–1920.* Baltimore: Johns Hopkins University Press, 1999.

Veblen, Thomas T., Kenneth R. Young, and A. R. Orme. *The Physical Geography of South America.* New York: Oxford University Press, 2007.

Vega, Alicia. *Itinerario del cine documental Chileno, 1900–1990.* Santiago: Centro EAC, Universidad Alberto Hurtado, 2006.

Vega, Garcilasso de la. *First Part of the Royal Commentaries of the Yncas.* Translated by Clements R. Markham, 2 vols. London: Hakluyt Society, 1871.

Ver Steeg, Clarence L. "Financing and Outfitting the First United States Ship to China." *Pacific Historical Review* 22, no. 1 (1953): 1–12.

Victor, David G., and Jesse H. Ausubel. "Restoring the Forests." *Foreign Affairs* 79, no. 6 (2000): 127–44.

Vicuña Mackenna, Benjamín. *Obras Completas de Vicuña Mackenna.* 7 vols. Santiago: Universidad de Chile, 1937.

Villalobos Rivera, Sergio, and Jorge Pinto Rodríguez, eds. *Auracania: Temas de historia fronteriza.* Temuco, Chile: Ediciones Universidad de La Frontera, 1985.

Viotti da Costa, Emilia. *Crowns of Glory, Tears of Blood: The Demerara Slave Rebellion of 1823.* New York: Oxford University Press, 1994.

Vitousek, Peter M., Carla M. D'Antonio, Lloyd L. Loope, and Randy Westbrook. "Biological Invasions as Global Environmental Change." *American Scientist* 84 (1996): 468–78.

Waldin, Monty. *Biodynamic Wines.* London: Mitchell Beazley, 2004.

Walker, Ignacio. *Chile and Latin America in a Globalized World.* Singapore: Institute of Southeast Asian Studies, 2006.

Wallerstein, Immanuel. *The Modern World System.* 3 vols. New York: Academic Press, 1974–89.

——. "The Time of Space and the Space of Time: The Future of Social Science." *Political Geography* 17 (1998): 71–82.

Ward, Samuel. *Sam Ward in the Gold Rush*. Edited by Carvel Collins. Stanford, CA: Stanford University Press, 1949.

Warner, Charles Dudley. *Our Italy*. New York: Harper and Brothers, 1891.

Warner, Sam Bass, Jr. *Streetcar Suburbs: The Process of Growth in Boston, 1870–1900*. Cambridge, MA: Harvard University Press, 1978.

Watson, Douglas S. "The Great Express Extra of the *California Star* of April 1, 1848." *California Historical Society Quarterly* 11, no. 2 (1932): 129–37.

Watson, James L., and Melissa L. Caldwell, eds. *The Cultural Politics of Food and Eating: A Reader*. Malden, MA: Blackwell, 2005.

Weber, David. *The Mexican Frontier, 1821–1846: The American Southwest under Mexico*. Albuquerque: University New Mexico Press, 1982.

Webster, Kimball. *The Gold Seekers of '49: A Personal Narrative of the Overland Trail and Adventures in California and Oregon from 1849 to 1854*. Manchester, NH: Standard Book, 1917.

Wells, Allen. "All in the Family: Railroads and Henequen Monoculture in Porfirian Yucatan." *Hispanic American Historical Review* 72, no. 2 (1992): 159–209.

Wells, William V. "A Visit to the Quicksilver Mines of New Almaden, California." *Harper's Monthly Magazine*, June 1863, 25–41.

Wetmore, Charles A. "Harry Meiggs in Peru." *Overland Monthly and Out West Magazine* 7 (August 1871): 175–82.

Whitbeck, R. H. "Chilean Nitrate and the Nitrogen Revolution." *Economic Geography* 7, no. 3 (1931): 273–83.

White, John H. *A History of the American Locomotive: Its Development, 1830–1880*. New York: Dover, 1980.

White, Richard. *"It's Your Misfortune and None of My Own": A New History of the American West*. Norman: University Oklahoma Press, 1991.

———. *The Organic Machine: The Remaking of the Columbia River*. New York: Hill and Wang, 1995.

———. *Railroaded: The Transcontinentals and the Making of Modern America*. New York: W. W. Norton, 2011.

White, William Francis [pseud. William Grey]. *A Picture of Pioneer Times in California, Illustrated with Anecdotes and Stories Taken from Real Life*. San Francisco: W. M. Hinton, 1881.

Whitman, Walt. *Democratic Vistas*. Washington, DC: J. S. Redfield, 1871.

———. *Leaves of Grass*. New York: Wm. E. Chapin, 1867.

Wickson, Edward J. *Rural California*. New York: Macmillan, 1923.

Wierzbicki, Felix Paul. *California as It Is and as It May Be; or, A Guide to the Gold Regions*. New York: Burt Franklin, 1970.

Wik, Reynold M. *Steam Power on the American Farm*. Philadelphia: University of Pennsylvania Press, 1953.

Wilde, Oscar. *The Picture of Dorian Gray*. 1891; London: Penguin, 1982.

Williams, Albert. *A Pioneer Pastorate and Times, Embodying Contemporary Local Transactions and Events*. San Francisco: Wallace and Hassett, 1879.

Williams, Gerald W. *The Forest Service: Fighting for Public Lands.* Westport, CT: Greenwood, 2007.

Williams, Jacqueline. "Much Depends on Dinner: Pacific Northwest Foodways, 1843–1900." *Pacific Northwest Quarterly* 90, no. 2 (1999): 68–76.

Williams, Michael. *Deforesting the Earth: From Prehistory to Global Crisis.* Chicago: University of Chicago Press, 2003.

Williams, Raymond. *Culture and Society: 1780–1950.* New York: Columbia University Press, 1958.

Williamson, John, ed. *Latin American Adjustment: How Much Has Happened?* Washington, DC: Institute for International Economics, 1990.

Wills, Garry. *Reagan's America: Innocents at Home.* Garden City, NY: Doubleday, 1987.

Wilson, Christina. "Where Art Means Politics: La Peña's 25th Anniversary." *Colorlines*, April 30, 2001, 40.

Wilson, Curtis M. "Port of Monterey and Vicinity." *Economic Geography* 23, no. 3 (1947): 199–219.

Wines, Richard A. *Fertilizer in America: From Waste Recycling to Resource Exploitation.* Philadelphia: Temple University Press, 1985.

Wing, Joseph E. *Alfalfa Farming in America.* 2nd ed. Chicago: Sanders, 1916.

Winn, Peter, ed. *Americas: The Changing Face of Latin America and the Caribbean.* 2nd ed. Berkeley: University of California Press, 1999.

———. *Victims of the Chilean Miracle: Workers and Neoliberalism in the Pinochet Era, 1973–2002.* Durham, NC: Duke University Press, 2004.

Wirth, John D., ed. *The Oil Business in Latin America: The Early Years.* Washington, DC: Beard Books, 2001.

Wolf, Ronald S. "Using Theoretical Models to Examine the Internationalization of Company Viña Concha y Toro." *Revista de Negocios Internacionales* 5, no. 1 (2012): 7–19.

Wolmar, Christian. *Blood, Iron and Gold: How the Railroads Transformed the World.* New York: Public Affairs, 2010.

Wood, Raymund F. *California's Agua Fría: The Early History of Mariposa County.* Fresno: California Academy Library, 1954.

Woods, Daniel Bates. *Sixteen Months at the Gold Diggings.* New York: Harper and Brothers, 1852.

Worster, Donald. *Rivers of Empire: Water, Aridity, and the Growth of the American West.* New York: Oxford University Press, 1985.

Wright, Marie Robinson. *Republic of Chile: The Growth, Resources, and Industrial Conditions of a Great Nation.* Philadelphia: George Barrie and Sons, 1904.

Wyman, Walker D. "California Emigrant Letters, Concluded." *California Historical Society Quarterly* 24, no. 4 (1945): 343–64.

Yoacham, Cristián Guerrero. "Notas criticas para una bibliografía Chilena sobre las relaciones entre Chile y Los Estados Unidos, versión preliminar." Typescript, UCh, 2003.

Young, George F. W. *The Germans in Chile: Immigration and Colonization, 1849–1914.* New York: Center for Migration Studies, 1974.

Young, Gordon. *Days of '49*. New York: George H. Doran, 1925.

Yung, Judy, Gordon H. Chang, and Him Mark Lai, eds. *Chinese American Voices: From the Gold Rush to the Present*. Berkeley: University of California Press, 2006.

Zaret, Kyla Sara. "Distribution, Use and Cultural Meanings of Ciprés de las Guaitecas in the Vicinity of Caleta Tortel, Chile." MA thesis, University of Montana, 2011.

Zerbe, Richard O., Jr., and C. Leigh Anderson. "Culture and Fairness in the Development of Institutions in the California Gold Fields." *Journal of Economic History* 61, no. 1 (2001): 114–43.

Zierer, Clifford M. "The Citrus Fruit Industry of the Los Angeles Basin." *Economic Geography* 10, no. 1 (1934): 53–73.

Zimmerer, Karl S. "The Ecogeography of Andean Potatoes." *BioScience* 48, no. 6 (1998): 445–54.

INDEX

Page numbers in italics indicate illustrations.

Adams, David Quincy, 96

African Americans, 51, 52, 56, 69–70, 80–82, 86, 221n42. *See also* slavery

Agosín, Marjorie, 172

agriculture (California): agricultural workers, 9, 106, 193, 200; alfalfa introduced/used, 2, 67, 86, 92–97, 225n34; citrus industry, 2, 93, 97, 98, 102–5, 225n34; crop rotation, 96; dairy industry, 92–93, 95; impact of Spanish missionaries on, 8, 211n3; irrigation, 96 (*see also* irrigation); potato introduced, 1, 15, 20, 24–25, 199, 200; seasonal production, 8–9; sodium nitrate used, 6, 92–93, 97, 102, 104–6, 109; soil exhaustion, 67, 92–93, 104, 143, 224n18; viticulture and wine industry, 137–38, 148, 151–53, 238n46; wheat, 34, 43–45, 211n3. *See also* fertilizer

agriculture (Chile): agricultural workers, 9, 127, 177, 184, 200; fruits/vegetables for export, 3, 8–9, 160–61, 162, 176–77, 200; irrigation, 96, 128, 162; railroads and, 127–28, 134–35; under Spanish rule, 8; US–Chile programs and, 145–46, 157, 158, 160–63; viticulture and wine industry, 137–38, 148, 150–53, 238n46;

wheat grown/exported, 2, 33–34, 38–44, 46, 143–44, 200, 214nn30,33; wheat varieties, 44–45

Aguirre Cerda, Pedro, 145

Ah Toy (Chinese courtesan), 53

Alaska, 25

Alberdi, Juan Bautista, 135

Albert, Federico, 139, 142–43

Alegría, Domingo and Reinaldo (father and son), 60

Alegría, Fernando, 173

Alemparte, José Antonio, 83

Alessandri Rodríguez, Jorge, 165, 242n28

Alexander VI (Pope), 16, 207n3

alfalfa, 2, 67, 86, 92–97, 109, 199, 225n34

Allende, Isabel, 188, 199, 200

Allende Gossens, Salvador, 158–59, 165–67, 242n28

Alliance for Progress, 156–57, 158, 160

Alta California (newspaper). See *Daily Alta California*

Álvarez, Felice, 50, 59–60

Amador County, CA, *xvii*, 75, 89

Amanda Philippi, Rodolfo, 142

American (ship), 116

Améstica, Rosario, 54, 200

Ancón, Treaty of, 98

Anderson, Benedict, 201

Anderson, C. Leigh, 87

29, 33, 34, 35–38, 199; Chileans in, 31, 45–48, 50, 54–57, 59–62, 67 (*see also* Chilecito); commodity prices in, 41, 42–43, 114; crime and vigilantism in, 48, 51, 53–54, 56–62, 216n27, 217nn36,37; demographics, 54–55; fires in, 35, 45; labor markets, 80; lodging houses and hotels, 36, 37, 46, 54; lumber use in, 36, 114–16, 140; Meiggs and, 114, 116, 135–36; Mission Dolores Cemetery, 47, 48, 215n1; North Beach district, 116, 227n6; photographs of, 34, 34–35; promotion of, 191; prostitution in, 48–52; reconstructed in brick, 45–46; sidewalks, 42; waterfront development (landmaking), 33, 35–38, 37, 116, 117, 198, 199; Wilde on, 199; work stoppage in solidarity with Chilean workers, 172
San Francisco Bay, 26, 27, 33, 41
San Joaquin and Kings River Canal Company, 96
San Joaquin County, CA, *xvii*, 39
San Joaquín Republican (newspaper), 88
San José, CA, 62
Santa Clara Valley, CA, *xvii*, 47, 62–67. *See also* Spanishtown
Santiago, Chile, 113, 118–19, 134, 136, 150, 228n12
Sasnett, William J., 79
Sater, William, 210n50
Saturday Evening Post, 98
Saunders, William, 103
Schama, Simon, 192
Schmidtmeyer, Peter, 142
Schneider, Teodoro, 128, 230n35
School of the Americas, 166, 242n34
Schwarzenegger, Arnold, 180–81, 181
Science (journal), 106
Scott, James C., 154, 208n14
Scribner's Monthly, 113, 129. *See also* Montgomery, James Eglinton
sea otters, 15, 21, 25–26
Sears, Alfred F., 122
Seigel, Micol, 202

Serra, Junípero (Padre), 17, 53, 103. *See also* Franciscan missions (California)
settler capitalism, 189–90. *See also* California gold rush
Seward, William H., 81
Seyd, Ernest, 191
Shaler, William (Capt.), 26
Shaw, William, 72–73
Sherman, William Tecumseh, 122–23
Shew, William, 34, 34–35
Shinn, Charles H., 87
ships and shipping: and California gold rush, 2, 28–30, 33, 34, 35–38, 199; Cape Horn Route, *xvi*, 29; and Chilean wheat trade, 39, 40–42, 44; Chile-California maritime connections, 5, 10, 15–16, 28–30, 31–32; China-Peru worker transports, 130; cost of Chile-to-California passage, 82; North American trade ships in the Pacific, 18–19, 25–26; refrigerated shipping, 161; sodium nitrate trade, 104; system of exchange, 41. *See also* Pacific Ocean
Sieroty, Alan, 157–58
Sierra Nevadas, *xv*, 70, 199, 210n43. *See also* California gold rush; mining
Silbaugh, Preston N., 159
slavery, 80–82, 83, 221n42
Sloat, John (Commodore), 27
Smil, Vaclav, 108
Smith, Persifor F. (Gen.), 74–75
Smith, Silas, 43
Smythe, William Ellsworth, 95
sodium nitrate: agricultural use, 6, 67, 92–93, 97, 102, 104–6, 109, 223n1; Chilean mining and export of, 6, 67, 91, 97–102, 104, 106, 107, 108–9, 113, 129, 159, 186, 200; names for, 100, 224n19; synthesis of, 106–8; use in weapons manufacturing, 106
soil: Monterey pine and soil degradation, 142–44, 147; soil exhaustion, 67, 92–93, 143, 224n18 (*see also* fertilizer)
Solimano, Andrés, 180